"The *Master Lecture Series* should be a *must* for any counselor in training who aspires to perform well on the NCE and CPCE exams. This book is replete with critical knowledge, practical information, and tips that will allow students and future professionals to be successful in the field. Professors teaching core courses should have this book as a reference to enhance their programs as well!"

Roberto Swazo, PhD, PSL, *professor and program director of the School Counseling Program at Indiana University-Purdue University-Indianapolis and coauthor of* Narrative Therapy with Spanish Speakers: Creative Bilingual Strategies for Individual, Family, and Group Sessions

"Dr. Rosenthal's *Master Lecture Series* for the NCE, CPCE, and CECE is personally and professionally engaging. His relaxed and humorous style promotes stress-free studying. His tips and hints are easy to follow and to incorporate into short, medium, and longer study sessions. The exam takers' positive testimonials you have seen are spot on."

Therese Chavaux, PhD, LPC, *associate professor at Grand Canyon University and faculty advisor to the Epsilon Counselor Honor Society*

Master Lecture Series for

THE NCE, CPCE, CECE, AND STATE COUNSELING EXAMS

Who Else Wants to Say, "I Passed"?

The *Master Lecture Series* Boosts Exam Scores While Reducing Test Anxiety and Study Time

Say goodbye to boring study sessions. Dr. Rosenthal's *Master Lecture Series* makes learning enjoyable. Revolutionize your exam prep and have fun doing it!

This study guide will transform your comprehensive exam journey into an engaging adventure that you'll actually enjoy!

The *Master Lecture Series* is a great standalone exam prep guide and the perfect companion to the *Encyclopedia of Counseling* and the *Human Services Dictionary*.

The new edition includes updated and expanded lectures on every exam area and questions and answers on all major topics, including those frequently asked by users of Dr. Rosenthal's materials. The book includes a complete test anxiety prevention program, with hundreds of never-before published tiny test hints for effective micro-study sessions, exclusive memory devices, and the most advanced Super Review Boot Camp he has ever created.

This is the perfect study tool for every counselor wanting to take their career to the next level.

Howard Rosenthal, EdD, CCMHC, HS-BCP, LPC, MAC, NCC, an award-winning educator, is professor emeritus of human services and addiction studies at St. Louis Community College at Florissant Valley. He is the author of the best-selling *Encyclopedia of Counseling* and *Favorite Counseling and Therapy Techniques*.

Master Lecture Series for

THE NCE, CPCE, CECE, AND STATE COUNSELING EXAMS

Fourth Edition

The Updated and Expanded Vital Information and Review Questions Program

Howard Rosenthal

NEW YORK AND LONDON

Designed cover image: © Thinkstock

Fourth edition published 2024
by Routledge
605 Third Avenue, New York, NY 10158

and by Routledge
4 Park Square, Milton Park, Abingdon, Oxon, OX14 4RN

Routledge is an imprint of the Taylor & Francis Group, an informa business

First edition published by Routledge 1993
Second edition published by Routledge 2006
Third edition published by Routledge 2009

Library of Congress Cataloging-in-Publication Data
Names: Rosenthal, Howard, 1952– author.
Title: Master lecture series for the NCE, CPCE, CECE, and state counseling exams : the updated and expanded Vital information and review questions program / Howard Rosenthal.
Description: 4th edition | New York, NY : Routledge, 2024. | Revised and updated print version of the audio CD: Vital information and review questions for the NCE, CPCE, and state counseling exams, issued in 2009.
Identifiers: LCCN 2023025005 (print) | LCCN 2023025006 (ebook) | ISBN 9780367699550 (hardback) | ISBN 9780367699536 (paperback) | ISBN 9781003149712 (ebook)
Subjects: LCSH: Counseling—Examinations—Study guides. | Counseling psychology—Examinations—Study guides. | National Counselor Examination—Study guides.
Classification: LCC BF636.6 .R673 2024 (print) | LCC BF636.6 (ebook)
DDC 158.3076—dc23/eng/20230802
LC record available at https://lccn.loc.gov/2023025005
LC ebook record available at https://lccn.loc.gov/2023025006

ISBN: 978-0-367-69955-0 (hbk)
ISBN: 978-0-367-69953-6 (pbk)
ISBN: 978-1-003-14971-2 (ebk)

DOI: 10.4324/9781003149712

Typeset in New Caledonia and Friz Quadrata
by Apex CoVantage, LLC

Contents

About the Author

Howard Rosenthal, EdD, a founding Human Services-Board Certified Practitioner (HS-BCP), received his master's degree from the University of Missouri, St. Louis, and his doctorate from St. Louis University. He is a Licensed Professional Counselor (LPC) in the state of Missouri, a National Board Certified Counselor (NCC), a Master Addictions Counselor (MAC), and a Certified Clinical Mental Health Counselor (CCMHC).

He is the author of the best-selling counseling exam prep book and audio program of all time: the *Encyclopedia of Counseling, The Authentic Purple Book* and the *Special 15th Anniversary Edition of the Vital Information and Review Questions* for the NCE and CPCE. Both publications made it into the 2010 Routledge Counseling and Psychotherapy *Top Ten List* for the United States and overseas, with the *Encyclopedia* taking the number one slot. He penned the first ever *Human Services Dictionary*, now an extremely popular examination preparation resource.

His book *Favorite Counseling and Therapy Techniques* (a publisher's best seller, also available in a Chinese edition) and the companion book *Favorite Counseling and Therapy Homework Assignments* include contributions from many of the top therapists in the world.

His text *Therapy's Best, Practical Advice and Gems of Wisdom From Twenty Accomplished Counselors and Therapists* contains extremely lively interviews with some of the finest helpers who literally help shaped the destiny of our field.

Dr. Rosenthal's humorous, reader-friendly writing style landed him an interview – along with other influential authors such as Barry Sears of *Zone Diet* books and Mark Victor Hansen, co-author of the *Chicken Soup for the Soul* series – in Jeff Herman's book, *You Can Make It Big Writing Books: A Top Agent Shows You How to Develop a Million-Dollar Bestseller*.

Some of his other popular books include the *Encyclopedia of Human Services, Master Review and Tutorial for the Human Services-Board Certified Practitioner Examination (HS-BCPE), Not With My Life I Don't: Preventing Your Suicide and That of Others, Routledge Classic Mental Health Edition Before You See Your First Client: 55 Things Counselors and Mental Health Providers Need to Know*, and *Help Yourself to Positive Mental Health* (with Joseph W. Hollis). Rosenthal has now lectured to over 100,000 people, making him one of the most popular speakers in the Midwest.

He holds the national record for winning the most "teaching tips of the year" awards given by the publication *Teaching for Success*. He has been inducted into the St. Louis Community College Hall of Fame, is an Emerson Excellence in Teaching Award Recipient, received Missouri's Wayne B. McClelland Adult Achievement Award, and is a John & Suanne Roueche Excellence Award recipient. He is listed in *Who's Who in America* and Samuel T. Gladding's *The Counseling Dictionary* in the "Prominent Names in the Counseling Profession" section. He has written over 20 articles for *Counselor, The Magazine for Addictions Professionals* alone and is one of the leading bloggers for Victor Yalom's Psychotherapy Net.

He is professor emeritus of the Human Services and Addiction Studies Program for St. Louis Community College at Florissant Valley. In 2022 he won the college's highest academic award as the 47th David L. Underwood Lecture Recipient.

Dr. Rosenthal's website is www.howardrosenthal.com

Acknowledgments

Many years ago, I worked for a large organization and was going to be honored at a board meeting for my accomplishments along with several other employees. I couldn't have been more excited. After all the employees with commendable achievements had been named, the board president, without the slightest hint of emotion or eye contract with any of us quipped, "Is that it?" A board member nodded affirmatively, and the president said, without missing a beat, "Let's move on. Guests [that would be me] are free to leave."

Wait a moment. I had to be missing something. Weren't we there to be recognized? "Let's move on" . . . excuse me but what about, "Nice job"? It would have been uplifting to hear "We are lucky to have you at the organization." Even a single word, "Thanks," would have been nice. Or at the very least the proverbial, "Don't let the door hit you on the way out."

Thankfully, as the author of exam prep materials, including the audio program that spawned this very book, I have been lucky enough to be on the flip side of that coin hundreds of times. Over the years I have received an unending stream of praise. When I open my email each morning, regardless of what is going on in the world, my wonderful readers and listeners write to share their excitement over passing their comprehensive counseling exam(s). Let me tell you, it is a *great feeling*, and I never get tired of hearing these life-changing success stories. Thus, first and foremost, I want to acknowledge each one of these counselors because you (yes, you!) gave me the motivation to create my past materials, as well as this book.

Next, accolades go out to my wife Patti, associate dean of social work and director of the office of field education at the University of Missouri, St. Louis (UMSL), who is always available to share her knowledge and creative ideas.

My sincere appreciation goes out to Professor Baorong Guo, Ph.D., for her truly valuable expertise and input.

"CJ" Courtney Jones, MSW, is a true psychotherapeutic and multicultural scholar by anybody's definition and has been immensely helpful.

And team Rosenthal, a.k.a. my sons Paul and Patrick, are always ready, willing, and able to assist with the technological side of the project.

Finally, I can't say enough about my wonderful editor at Routledge Taylor & Francis, Anna Moore, who has successfully worked with me on numerous counseling, psychotherapy, and human services publications, including the *Encyclopedia of Counseling* and the *Human Services Dictionary*.

The reader should have supreme confidence knowing that my publisher Taylor & Francis has been doing business since 1852 or 1798, depending on how technical you want to get. I therefore can safely say they are clearly doing something right, and I have worked diligently to make certain this text will be another feather in their cap!

1

Experience My Popular Audio Program Updated, Expanded, and in Print

Get ready to take your career to the next level. Hi. My name is Dr. Howard Rosenthal and I want to personally thank you for purchasing what I believe is by far one of the finest preparation programs ever created to help you pass the most popular counselor comprehensive exams. This list includes the National Counselor Examination, also known as the NCE, the Counselor Preparation Comprehensive Examination or CPCE, and the Counselor Education Counseling Comprehensive Examination or CECE.

If your graduate school requires oral and written boards or comps, this book is your meal ticket to success as well.

Believe me, I'm no Johnny-come-lately to this arena. I created the first ever comprehensive audio program to pass the National Counselor Exam over 28 years ago. Back in the day, the original program consisted of a huge amount of information jam-packed into six audio cassettes. (If you are too young to remember cassettes, I'll pause while you Google it!)

On four of the cassettes, dubbed the *Vital Information* program, yours truly lectured on every area of the exam. On the two additional cassettes, titled *Review Questions*, a separate program, I included 225

DOI: 10.4324/9781003149712-1

tutorial or teaching questions and answers . . . kind of like a practice test on steroids.

In a short period of time, it was obvious counselors wanted both parts of the cassette series, and the combined set was eventually called *Vital Information and Review Questions for the NCE, CPCE, and State Counseling Exams*. Just as a sizable number of counselors had nicknamed my *Encyclopedia of Counseling*, "The Purple Book," helpers were fond of calling my audio program "The listen and learn program" or the "Rosenthal Audio Program."

But America's love affair with cassettes ended, and they became nearly extinct, as the country embraced a new audio medium, CDs or digital compact discs. (More Google search time, anybody?)

But time marches on, as they say, and CDs, which had been the rage, became antiquated technology and also went the way of the dinosaur. In recent years, finding a vehicle with a CD player has become a serious challenge. Most computers and electronic devices stopped sporting CD drives as well.

CDs presented yet another problem. I must also be brutally honest with you and tell you that we had a terrible time with cybersecurity. Translation: Folks stealing and producing illegal copies of my audio program. Since most of the fake programs lacked key material, they likely unknowingly hurt a lot of counselors' exam scores!

To be sure, all these factors were relevant, but the most powerful impetus to write this book was prompted by the fact that I received an unending string of emails, all with the same request: "May I purchase a transcript or book version of your audio program?"

Up until now, the answer was "unfortunately no." Some versions of my audio programs included a generous 12- or 15-page note-taking guide, but counselors were adamant that a mere note-taking guide could not take the place of the over 20 hours of information my program provided. Hmm, I had to concede they had a point. Counselors wanted the entire program in print, not merely a note-taking guide or a reasonable facsimile.

Another huge issue was also that the CDs were getting old. Dated, if you will. The most recent set has a publication date of 2009. But what I am about to share is remarkable, even to me. In 2023 sales were still red hot and some counselors were still using *only* the CDs to study, and many were still posting some admirable scores. You might legitimately be asking, "How in the world is that possible?"

Awesome question! First, a lot of the principles of counseling are timeless since some aspects of efficacious helping never go out of style. Second, a lot of counselors don't know this, but when I create an exam prep program I try as hard as possible to ascertain where the field is going so the materials won't be outdated. As the author I engage in intellectual time traveling. I try to anticipate which concepts, theories, and techniques will be the next big things. Based on the results I have seen from my audio program, I must pat myself on the back (something we should all do more often!) and say, "You know, I did a pretty darn good job."

But even with my propensity to make some excellent educated predictions, nobody can anticipate everything. This can only be accomplished by creating a new edition and you, my dear reader, are reading it right now.

As I prepared to write this book, I had one key rule, and here it is:

IF IT AIN'T BROKE, DON'T EVEN THINK OF TRYING TO FIX IT!

The success of the program was so admirable for such an extended time, I made up my mind I would make the *fewest possible changes to the audio transcript* (which would be the book you are now reading in print). I wanted the material to be as close as possible to what made it a raving success. I wanted you to have access to what thousands upon thousands of counselors insisted worked so well for them.

It reminds me of something we have all experienced. You've been buying a product for many years, and it is flat out your favorite. But then, the company changes it and calls it new and improved, or something like that. You try it, and suffice it to say you are not impressed. You end up saying, "I wish they would have left it alone and not changed it."

Anybody ever have that happen to the food in your favorite restaurant? Yeah, me too.

Now because over ten years have passed since the last audio program was released, I was forced to make *some* changes. Dated information and terminology were deleted and lots and lots of information was added. Many current counseling concepts and experts didn't even exist when the last version of this program was created.

Add to this the fact that we know a lot more about a host of topics. We have a name for that: we call it "progress." In essence, you now have the fabled audio program updated, expanded, and brought up to speed in print.

AT LAST: THE SECRET SAUCE IN THE ROSENTHAL MATERIALS REVEALED

You are now going to be reading to the best version of this amazing study guide ever produced.

When I first created this program, I never in my wildest dreams imagined that counselors from coast to coast would be writing me, calling me, and emailing me to thank me for helping them to pass their graduate exit exam or assisting them to become a licensed professional counselor or snare the National Certified Counselor, or NCC. It also proved a highly successful tool for counselors taking the Counselor Preparation Counselor Examination and the new Counselor Education Counseling Exam. Ditto for any oral, written, comps, or boards.

Does this program really work? You bet it does. Testimonial after testimonial attest to the fact that this program delivers the results that you need . . . and it has been doing so for a very long time.

Some counseling students, counselors, and counselor educators insist my audio program, as well as my book, the *Encyclopedia of Counseling*, and my *Human Services Dictionary*, have achieved cult-like status in the field. Other experts have referred to my materials as the gold standard, the benchmark, by which all other programs are judged.

A legitimate question you might be asking is what makes your materials different? Sure, when I first released my programs there were very few competitors in this field. Not today. If anything, the exact opposite is true! You almost can't open a web page nowadays without being visually accosted by a company trying to sell you a counseling exam prep package. In fact, on those few occasions when this did not occur, I contacted the IT department or user support to make sure my computer was working correctly! Okay, I'll admit, I'm exaggerating a little, but not *that* much.

The difference, my dear reader, is what I have come to refer to as the secret sauce in the Rosenthal materials, and it has existed from day one.

As I am writing this chapter, I have a vintage copy of my 2002 *Encyclopedia* on my desk. Let me take a trip down memory lane, dust it off, and please indulge me while I quote from a brief excerpt on the back cover which reads, "The *Encyclopedia of Counseling New and Revised Edition* is written in Dr. Rosenthal's popular reader-friendly style, which reads like a novel but imparts knowledge like a post-graduate seminar."

There it is. That *is* the secret sauce. No ketchup, mustard, or exotic spices from a faraway land. The secret sauce is merely the fact that I have always believed that education need not be dry, dull, or boring and I believe it even more today. My materials are upbeat and dare I say it: actually make studying enjoyable (and yes, I will use the F word) and fun! Humorous? Yes, at times when it is appropriate.

I always admired the superb teachers and professors who made classroom and seminar material engaging, I became a lecturer and a professor myself to keep up the fine work and to follow in their footsteps.

I will share a funny little story to illustrate my point. A year or so after I got into the exam prep business, I heard about a competitor's program. Counselors had told me it was quite good but extremely expensive and boring. I was curious how my program would fare against the competition. I knew I would not be an impartial judge, so I sought the help of a friend who was one of the most accomplished counselors I knew personally. This was a counselor who was a key player in the counselor licensing movement and was later the head of a state counselor licensing committee and even the president of a major counseling organization. Nice credentials, very nice.

This counselor eagerly agreed to do the comparison for me and would get right back to me. I often heard professionals say this counselor was the straightest shooter in the business, meaning if something was good, this individual would say so, and if something was bad, this counselor could be brutally honest, forthright, and not pull any punches.

But something just didn't seem right. About a month passed, and I had heard nothing, I contacted this individual who said, "Howard, I apologize. I know I said I would get right back to you, but the materials in the competitor's program are so boring I kept falling asleep. I can't imagine how anybody could use them."

Now, to be sure, individuals differ when rating books and audio programs. Just look up almost any item on Amazon. But when you are talking comprehensive counseling exams, these instruments cover so much, it would be sheer torture to spend hundreds of hours studying materials that could double as sleep therapy.

Now you might ask: Does everybody really like your material? I will be 100% honest and say that if you look online there are a very small number of people who are not enamored with my reader-friendly, user-friendly style. But my honest response is that for every person you can show me who says my presentation style is not their cup of tea, I have emails and reviews from thousands of others who say they loved it! Some have invited me to dinner if I ever visit their town, although I haven't taken anybody up on it . . . yet. The comments I find the most powerful, touching, and amazing are those folks – and there have been lots of them – who have told me they felt like I was a good, trusted friend and they grieved when they finished my materials. Some insisted it was like I was part of their family. They didn't want the exam prep process to end. Is that crazy in a good way, or what?

But let's forget about these people that I've helped in the past. Now let's focus on you. Yes, you. You're the person I'm going to help now. Since I don't like wasting your valuable time, let me swing into action and tell you what the exam is really like. But the first question we must tackle is which exam (or exams) are you going to take?

THE NCE: THE EXAM THAT LAUNCHED THE MODERN-DAY COMPREHENSIVE EXAM COUNSELING MOVEMENT

Let's begin with the National Counselor Examination created by the National Board for Certified Counselors (NBCC), also called the National Counselor Examination for Licensing and Certification. Keep in mind that when I use the abbreviations NBCC and NCE, these abbreviations are both registered with the United States Patent and Trade Office.

By the way, and I mean this seriously, the field of counselor licensing and certification is inundated with abbreviations and acronyms, so get used to it! Just in this chapter alone I will introduce you to enough alphabet soup terminology, as we sometimes call it in the field, to capsize a cruise ship!

The National Counselor Examination consists of 200 items. Since 40 of the items are being field or pilot tested (a.k.a. experimental items) to determine their suitability on future exams, a perfect score on the test would be 160. Again, 40 items are unscored items. **When you are taking the exam, always remember it would be theoretically possible to miss 40 items and still receive a perfect score**.

How will you know which items are being field tested? Quite frankly, you won't. Therefore, you must do your best on every single item. Again, and remember this, I cannot emphasize this strongly enough. Say you're taking the test and you think to yourself, "Gosh. I bet I missed at least 45 or 50 questions on the test."

Instead of castigating yourself or reaching for a hit of your favorite psychiatric medication to control your self-induced panic attack, you should answer yourself back with, "If I really missed just 45 or 50 questions, there's an excellent possibility I made one of the highest scores ever posted on the exam." Hey, how's that for cognitive therapy? You've got to love it.

Each item on the NCE is a multiple choice, or multipoint, format. Sometimes you will encounter the abbreviation MCQs or multiple-choice questions in counseling literature. You will read the question, and then pick A, B, C, or D as an answer choice. Remember, there is never more than one correct answer. Therefore, if you mark more than one correct answer, say, two choices, then your answer will be marked incorrect.

Also, here's a great hint. There is no penalty for guessing. Thus, if a sane individual doesn't know the answer, then guess.

What are the questions like on the exam?

According to NBCC, the questions have several basic formats. The first type is what is called a direct question. A direct question is something like, "Who is the father of psychoanalysis?"

A variation of this would be the reverse or negative question, for example, "Who is the only theorist who is not a psychoanalyst."

The second most common format type of question is an incomplete sentence question. For example, "The father of psychoanalysis is ____." One of the answer stem responses, A, B, C, or D, would give you the correct answer to the blank.

The final type of question is what is known as a calculation item. A calculation item would read something like, "There were three separate studies of psychoanalysis. In one study there were 50 clients, in another study there were 100 clients, and in the final study there were 150 clients. What is the mean or average number of clients used in these psychoanalytic studies?"

A quick test hint is that when you spy a computation question there is a good chance it will relate to the normal curve, but more on that later.

NBCC asserts that the questions require three types of cognitive skills. Some questions will require you to recall, or in plain everyday English memorize, key material. Other questions are intended to test your knowledge of application, while still others test your ability to do an analysis or problem solve.

Listen up, this is very important. Unlike my questions in this text, questions on the real exam are not worded so that one question on one item will help you solve another item. The difference is that my questions and answers are tutorial in nature. I discovered, without a doubt, that tutorial questions are far better in terms of helping you master the material than just taking practice tests. In fact, many counselors I have worked with who were taking traditional practice tests discovered these exams only served to lower their confidence and self-esteem, which is something I don't want any part of.

What's really on the exam you will be taking? According to NBCC, it's unethical to reveal precisely what is on the exam. Moreover, the exam questions change from one administration of the test to the next. Thus, if you take the test in October, the questions will be different than if you take it in the spring. There are several versions of the exam.

We do know this about the exam, though. First, you will have 3 hours and 45 minutes to complete the exam. **Do not rush! Take your time**. Even I am amazed that in all the years I have been involved in counselor exam prep, I have almost never heard a counselor say they didn't have enough time. Seriously, this number is so small you could count the number of these folks on one hand.

All right, now for some specifics. The NCE has eight content areas said to be aligned with the eight Council for Accreditation of Counseling and Related Educational Program (CACREP) content areas. Thus, professors, counselors themselves, and yours truly often merely refer to these as the CACREP areas on the exam. You will notice that this book follows these content areas, which I have listed in the following:

1. Professional Counseling Orientation and Ethical Practice.
2. Social and Cultural Diversity.
3. Human Growth and Development.
4. Career Development.
5. Counseling and Helping Relationships.
6. Group Counseling and Group Work.
7. Assessment and Testing.
8. Research and Program Evaluation.

The names of the content areas remain static and have changed only imperceptibly over the years. **Since exam updates were made in 2020, NBCC no longer shares the precise number of questions from each CACREP area. A possible hint, however, is that when NBCC did post numbers, the "Counseling and Helping Relationships" section had the most questions, followed by the "Professional Counseling Orientation and Ethical Practice Section." "Social and Cultural Diversity" had the least questions, checking in as the smallest CACREP content area**.

Now stay with me here. NBCC tells us that each of the eight content domains I just mentioned will contain questions with information from one of six field work domains, or so-called work behavior analysis domains, listed in the following.

1. Professional Practice and Ethics: 19 scored items (12% of items)
2. Intake, Assessment, Diagnosis: 19 scored items (12% of items)
3. Areas of Clinical Focus: 47 scored items (29% of items)
4. Treatment Planning: 14 scored items (9% of items)
5. Counseling Skills and Interventions: 48 scored items (30% of items)
6. Core Counseling Attributes: 13 scored items (8% of items)

Note the total number of items graded adds up to 160.

Now in case you are scratching your head wondering where these mystical domains came from, here is the *Cliff Notes* version. A job analysis conducted by the Center for Credentialing & Education (CCE) over the course of the calendar year (May 2016–July 2017) with 16,000 credentialed counselors yielded the six work behavior analysis domains. The decision about what to include was completed in June 2019.

So just to make certain you understand this, let us take a simple example. A question on the NCE asks about running a group, so the content area would be Group Counseling and Group Work; however, the question is asking something about ethical behavior, so the field work domain would come from Professional Practice and Ethics. **Don't overload your brain trying to ascertain which content area and work domain the question is derived from . . . if you know the material, it won't matter!**

In terms of your final score, you will receive a score for each of these six areas, and you will receive an overall exam score. Thus, with eight content scores, six behavior area scores, and an overall score, you will be receiving 15 scores. **At this point in time, only the overall exam score counts toward your licensing and certification**.

Translation, and this is great news, folks, you could have some seriously weak areas and still pass the exam. But wait, I have more comforting news I think you are going to like! Again, and I know I said this before, but I can't emphasize this too strongly: The exam setup seems rather complex, but when you are taking the actual exam, I recommend you don't waste a single precious second worrying about which content area and domain the questions are addressing! Seriously, what difference does it make? If you know the material (and you will after spending a little quality time with this text and ideally my *Encyclopedia of Counseling* and my *Human Services Dictionary*), it won't matter what content area and domain the exam is addressing.

Just what is the cutoff or so-called passing score? Well, don't hold my feet to the fire on the answer since a passing score varies with different administrations of the exam. A score of 90 to 110 out of 160 questions being scored is generally enough to pass. The passing score can change from one version of the test to another. This clearly explains why one person in your counseling agency insists they passed the exam, while another, who snared the identical score, did not. NBCC reminds test-takers that one version is not harder than another, just different. In plain, everyday English, NBCC has shared that 83% of counselors taking the exam for certification are currently passing it based on 9,905 test-takers. Of those taking the exam for licensing, 71% are passing the exam based on the results of 12,393 test-takers.

A common question I receive is, "Hey Dr. Rosenthal, I've studied all your materials. Do you think I will get a perfect score on the exam? I would love to say, "Absolutely," but that would be a bald-faced lie. My response is generally something like, "Sure, when the moon turns to green cheese!"

In all the years I've been doing this and have communicated with an endless string of counselors, I have never come across a single individual who snared a perfect score on the NCE. Add to that the fact that I have also perused a few statistics released pertaining to exam scores, and here again, no perfect scores emerged.

I must be fair, however, and say that if you are the one person who has achieved perfection in this regard, hats off to you and I apologize in advance.

I have intentionally brought this topic up to ensure you have realistic expectations about the exam. The object is to pass, and OMG, a very high score would be nice, but as Albert Ellis often mentioned in his Rational Emotive Behavior Therapy books and lectures (and yes, I shall cover his groundbreaking approach in this book), demanding perfection is irrational and can result in an unhappy and anxious state of mind.

Also, keep in mind that your state can require a higher or lower score on the NCE than NBCC's passing score if you are taking the exam to secure state licensure. In today's world of technology, you will be taking the NCE on a computer. That's right, a computer.

In the past I went into great detail about the facilities where you would take the exam, but since so much has changed – and continues to change – over the years, I will just stick with the basics!

MAY I TAKE THE NCE AT HOME? NO WAY! WAY!

The death of the paper and pencil exams was announced way back in April 2017 when NBCC announced all exams would be administered electronically at Pearson VUE test centers or on school campuses. Translation: Paper and pencil versions were being eliminated. Now, fast forward to the present.

Currently, counselors can take the NCE the old-fashioned way in person at a Pearson VUE Testing Center or using Pearson OnVUE, which means you may take the exam from home.

If you decide to take the exam from home, there are lots of stipulations, such as no pets or children in the room. Your computer system must also have the proper specifications. Let me share what might be the most important factor first: **If you need special accommodations, then home testing is not for you! Special accommodations can only be met using the in-person testing format at a Pearson VUE test center**.

Whether you test at home or in a Pearson VUE testing site, there are numerous regulations about IDs, signatures, palm-prints, whether you might need a passport as an ID, photos of the room you are taking the exam in if you are at home, and when and how long breaks can be. I insist you carefully review the materials provided by NCC and Pearson VUE to make your choice.

Look, this is a very important decision, and nobody can make it for you. True, when I first heard about in-home testing, I thought it was the greatest thing since sliced bread, but after you peruse all the rules and regulations you might conclude that taking the exam at a testing center will better meet your needs. In my opinion, no study guide, including mine, can adequately make this pick for you.

In the following I have provided the NBCC link that allows you to sign up for the exam and provides two YouTube videos: one for counselors taking the exam at a testing center and yet another for those who want to take the exam using their home computer.

Click here and punch this NBCC information into your browser: www.nbcc.org/exams/onvue

WHAT YOU NEED TO KNOW ABOUT THE COUNSELOR PREPARATION COMPREHENSIVE EXAMINATION

I have had tremendous success helping counselors pass the CPCE. This is the exam researched, developed, and distributed via the Research and Assessment Corporation for Counseling (RAAC) and Center for Credentialing & Education (both are corporate affiliates of the National Board for Certified Counselors).

WHAT EXACTLY IS THE CPCE?

The CPCE was first introduced in 1997 and is now used by over 400 programs to assess a student's knowledge of counseling. The exam – created to standardize the measurement of students in counseling programs – is often dubbed an "exit exam," and in some instances the exam may be used as a graduation requirement in place of writing a thesis or scholarly paper. In other programs, all students must take the CPCE prior to graduation. Always check with your graduate advisor for specifics pertaining to your institution of higher learning.

Since the CPCE is based on the exact same eight content areas as the National Counselor Examination, my preparation materials are ideal!

HOW DOES THE CPCE DIFFER FROM THE NCE?

Unlike the NCE, which contains 200 questions, the CPCE has just 160 questions, and you have four hours to complete the test. Simply put, it is a shorter exam, but you have more time to complete it. Moreover, on the NCE, the number of questions in any given exam area will vary. For example, there are more questions on helping relationships than there are on human growth and development. Not so on the CPCE. All eight content areas contain 20 questions. In each of the eight areas, three questions are being field-tested. Once again, the test-taker, that would be you, is not told which questions are not going to be scored. Hence, you will be graded on 17 questions, which constitutes 12.5% per area. To put it a different way: a perfect score on the CPCE would be 136 (17 × 8 = 136). On the NCE you answer 200 questions and 160 are graded. On the CPCE you answer 160 questions and 136 are graded. The Center for Credentialing & Education reports the instrument has excellent validity.

Theoretically the NCE should have more of a clinical, mental health, or practical application slant than the CPCE, but not every counselor who has taken them both notices this while taking the exam.

THE NEW KID ON THE BLOCK: THE COUNSELOR EDUCATION COMPREHENSIVE EXAMINATION

Some graduate schools are using the CECE to replace the CPCE. The development of the exam was spearheaded and coordinated by Dr. Richard Halstead at the University of St. Joseph in West Hartford,

Connecticut (USJ) as an alternative to the CPCE. Counselor educators around the nation have contributed by writing and evaluating questions. The questions are evaluated on an ongoing basis.

The CECE uses the *exact* same CACREP eight content areas as the CPCE. The exam has 15 items per content area (15 × 8), or 120 items total. Unlike the NCE or the CPCE, there are **no** pilot or field-tested questions. One terrific feature is that the CECE – often dubbed an exit exam – is currently being administered without a fee to the student! Nice. The time limit for the exam is set at three and a half hours (i.e., 210 minutes). **Preparation should be identical to the CPCE**. The student often takes the exam on Blackboard (an online teaching platform) and may be monitored on Zoom. The passing score is set by your graduate school, so please speak with your graduate program for specifics.

In September 2021, 127 counseling programs were using the exam. Most of those institutions began using it during the COVID-19 pandemic.

At this point in time, students who need more information about taking the CPCE or the CECE and want to discover what constitutes a passing score should speak with your graduate advisor rather than contacting the organizations or institutions who create the exams or disseminate them.

Policies may vary from university to university, and your institution will set the minimum criterion score: translation, what you really need to pass. Finally, some universities add an extra assignment to the exam, which is not created by the experts who create the exam, such as an essay question. Here again, address all inquiries about this to your graduate advisor.

THE ANATOMY OF THIS BOOK ON THE HEAD OF A PIN

All right, I don't like wasting anybody's time so let's get right to the point and delineate precisely what you will find in the pages.

One overall factor is that since I can't use vocal inflections, I will use **bold,** ***italics*****,** or <u>underlining</u> or whatever it takes to get your full attention regarding must-know key points. It would be your English professor's worst style nightmare, but you're going to love it!

One other deviation from the original audio lectures is that if a person has achieved very high notoriety in counseling, and accurate data are available, I will share the year they were born and, if applicable, deceased. For example, Sigmund Freud (1856–1939).

Let me be crystal clear that the idea is not to memorize these dates! This information is included just to give you a ballpark idea in what era the person's work was conducted. Also, since it is not uncommon for two people to have the same name, knowing these dates can often make certain you are researching the right person when conducting a Google or literary search!!!

THE MAIN COURSE: VITAL INFORMATION

First, I will provide you with lively spirited lectures on each of the eight key areas on the exam while adding vital information from the six fieldwork domains. I have also added some brief information on marriage and family/couples counseling since students have found this to be helpful.

Now while this might not sound like a lot of information, a little math might surprise you. These lectures filled ten audio CDs even without the numerous updates you will find in this book. Or, to put it another way, if you sat down to listen to the presentations, it would take you well over ten hours to listen to them even if you never took a break to get a glass of water.

NEXT: THE TUTORIAL QUESTIONS WITH ANSWERS

Here I have included hundreds of short questions and answers to teach you the material. These so-called tutorial questions were included on another six audio CDs, or approximately 60 additional hours of material; however, this text has 75 more questions and answers than the CD version.

In all the sections, but most notably this one, I have lots of repetition, something most exam prep guides do not use. I will often explain the concept in a different way, so if you didn't understand it the first time, you might just "get it" the second or third time.

NEVER BEFORE PUBLISHED TINY TEST HINTS CAN RAISE YOUR SCORE IN A BIG WAY!

For the first time ever (drum roll please), I have included hundreds of tiny test hints. Truth be told, although I am excited about this entire book, this might just be the section that I am most enthused about! This is the first edition ever to include a brand new hot off the presses chapter where I share these never before published bite-sized test hints. Just by reading these small hints, and most are just a simple sentence or two and literally take just seconds to read, you can study at warp speed and likely dramatically raise your score. These vest pocket hints are perfect for powerful micro-study sessions while you are waiting for your microwave dinner to finish cooking!

I've been sharing some hints that are very similar to the ones in this book with buyers from my website and the feedback has been blow-away fantastic. In my opinion these amazing tiny test hints can literally impart information faster than flash cards or anything else you can name! Counselors have been amazed how much information they can assimilate in such a short period of time.

TEST ANXIETY: RELAX, I'VE GOT YOU COVERED

Some readers may not know that when an author comes up with an idea for a book, the publisher sends the concept out to several accomplished professional counselors, some of whom are book authors themselves, to help provide guidance and feedback. I wondered if maybe I could shorten the book a tad by eliminating the test anxiety section of my audio program. NOT!

Much to my chagrin, every reader championed the idea of keeping the test anxiety information (replete with an entire guided imagery the reader can perform from the comfort of their home) in the book. Every professional reader found it extremely helpful.

FINAL OVERVIEW AND SUPER REVIEW BOOTCAMP

A signature part of my *Encyclopedia of Counseling* and my audio program was the "Final Overview and Super Review Bootcamp." This book will carry the torch for this wonderful resource and includes the latest 4.0 version. When you read this section of the book you will discover I give you a terrific comprehensive review and update you on new material in the field, and perhaps you will learn some new information you never learned in graduate school.

The bootcamp provides a super review that you can use several days prior to the exam. Heck, this review can even be used on the day of the exam to review major concepts.

If you have been out of school for 20 or 30 years, don't sweat it. Hundreds of folks who have used my programs have been in the same situation, and yes, they have passed their licensing, certification, or comprehensive written and oral boards.

Again, this new version has more information and scores of tutorial questions and answers that have never appeared before, to make it the finest program I've ever created.

THE SHEER MAGIC OF MEMORY DEVICES

Me: (To my Google Assistant.)	What day of the week is it?
Google Assistant:	Wednesday.
Me: (To my brother.)	Hey Wayne, what was the weather on the day I received my doctorate in counseling?
My brother:	Let's see, that was a Tuesday. The high was 85 degrees and the low was 69 degrees. We had roast beef for dinner.

As you can see, some people need memory devices (that would be me) and some people don't (that would be my brother, who possesses the best memory of anybody I have ever met).

I began using memory devices to pump up my own anemic GPA as an undergraduate college student, and when I did my GPA shot up like a rocket. They also helped me tackle one exam after another in graduate school right up to my oral and written comprehensive exams.

In this program, I will also include my exclusive mnemonic or memory devices. A simple memory device would be something like, "spring forward, and fall back" to remind you which way to set the clock when the time changes.

Using this same principle, you can remember that, in classical forward conditioning created by Ivan Pavlov, the "meat" in his research is the "US" by repeating over and over, "In the US, we eat a lot of meat." Experiment with my memory devices.

I also urge you to make up your own. You will discover that these strategies only need to make sense to you, and that often the silliest, craziest ones work the best.

This book can be used as a superb standalone study guide, or, for the ultimate exam preparation, combine it with my legendary *Encyclopedia of Counseling* and my *Human Services Dictionary*.

I'm really excited for you, so let's get started.

2

Master Lecture 1: Research and Program Evaluation

I'm going to begin with the section you have probably been dreading the most so we can get it out of the way, and that is research and program evaluation. Now be truthful. Are you shaking, cringing, running for shelter, or calling your physician for the latest antianxiety medicine? I can sympathize with you. I have been through programs where it was hinted at, or more blatantly stated, that research and evaluation courses were well . . . the flunk-out courses!

I remember taking a statistics and research class. I came to class the first day and a student was sitting behind me. He tapped me on the shoulder and asked, "How many times have you taken this course?" I said, "What?" He repeated, "How many times have you taken this course?" I said, "What in the world are you talking about? This is my first day of class." He said, "Oh well, I'm taking it for the fifth time."

People who have used previous versions of this program have praised this section because they felt that *I kept the information and the definitions very simple and easy to understand.* In fact, this section was so powerful that some listeners began to feel a tad guilty because they began to enjoy the topic of research.

On several occasions I consulted the finest former behavioral science statistics professor and college administrator I've ever met,

DOI: 10.4324/9781003149712-2

Dr. Stan Kary. Stan has a lively presentation style that reminds me of my own style. We work well together.

Let's begin. Keep in mind that even if you loved research and statistics and have been out of grad school for a few years, you'll hear some current terms and concepts that I'm betting will be new to you.

According to the ACA Ethical Code Section G Research and Publication:

> Counselors who conduct research are encouraged to contribute to the knowledge base of the profession and promote a clearer understanding of the conditions that lead to a healthy and more just society. Counselors support the efforts of researchers by participating fully and willingly whenever possible. Counselors minimize bias and respect diversity in designing and implementing research.

So, what exactly is the object of scientific research?

The type that you see in the counseling journals is intended to produce findings that can be replicated by others using the same methods. Basic research is said to contribute to a theory, while applied research helps answer the question of whether the theory helps solve real-world problems. If an experiment can be replicated, it is said to be reliable. Remember the old adage KISS, which stands for, "Keep it simple, stupid." I have used it many times in my teaching and writing and I'm using it again because it is once again relevant.

The emphasis in psychoeducational research agrees with the KISS philosophy. Experiments emphasize parsimony, which means that the findings should be explained and interpreted in the simplest and most economical way. On some tests, the concept of **parsimony** is known as **Occam's razor** (named after William of Occam). In terms of research, the ideal format is known as the experiment, or the so-called **true experiment**. Occasionally the term genuine comparative experiment will be substituted.

National counselor exam test expert and a former professor at the University of Florida at Gainesville Larry Loesch one time pointed out that in a true experiment, the researcher has control over, "All relevant variables. Thus, research of this nature is usually conducted in laboratories or related high controlled settings."

Here's an old philosophical problem. If you conduct your research in a lab you certainly control all the variables, but it's sterile.

In a lab, subjects rarely behave the way they do in real life. On the other hand, if the research is done in a real-life setting, few variables are under the control of the researcher. The wise social scientist, knowing these shortcomings, looks at all the data to piece together the dynamic mystery of human behavior.

Now in an experiment, you keep out variables that are undesirable so the experiment will not be confounded. Confounding is really a simple concept. A **confounding variable** impacts both the independent and dependent variables (IVs and DVs). If you forgot what the IV and DV are about, hold on for a moment and I'll dust off your memory. Let's assume that you want to do an experiment to see if a new prescription antidepressant is effective.

Unbeknownst to you, the researcher, in addition to ingesting the medicine, the folks in your study were also ingesting natural remedies for depression such as St. John's Wort, an herbal remedy, or 5HTP. We would say that the experiment was confounded or not accurate because the natural remedies might have influenced the subject's depression. The natural remedies would constitute an **extraneous variable**, but I'll talk a lot more about that in a few minutes.

When conducting an experiment, the researcher looks at variables. For your exit, licensing, and certification exam, you will probably need to distinguish **independent variables** from **dependent variables**. Relax; it's a piece of cake. **The IV is the variable that the experimenter manipulates, while the DV is the result**. The outcome, in plain everyday English, is the **outcome data or the DV**.

IV = Independent variable, also known as the experimental variable

DV = Dependent variable or the outcome data you are measuring in the experiment such as weight, IQ, number of alcoholic drinks, time, or amount of money spent on gambling

A good, no make that great, memory device, is that the D in DV stands for data. An easy way to remember the DV is to remember that it is always some form of human response and that human responses can come in many ways and forms. How well can you see or how well can you hear? How much weight have you gained or lost? Has your IQ score gone up or down?

How high or low is your blood pressure? How big or small is your tumor? Did your score on the depression inventory go up or down? Now, if a relationship exists, then the DV is dependent on some level of the IV, which, of course, is the independent variable that the researcher is free to manipulate.

How can you remember what an IV is? One great memory device is to think of a person in the hospital who has an IV in their arm. An individual with an IV looks like they are receiving some experimental treatment or variable. Again, the IV is the experimental variable. The IV is in the experimental variable and we want to know if it will affect the DV.

Another memory device I personally rely on is to think of myself as the researcher/experimenter and say to myself, "I administer the IV." In fact, say it out loud right now, "I'm the researcher and I administer the IV." Let's try to make this easy.

Here again, use what works for you. Maybe you can come up with something that is easier or more meaningful to you based on your background. If it works for you, I say go for it.

In a true experiment, we have a group of subjects who are not being manipulated or experimented on, if you will. These people who do not get the IV, or the so-called experimental variable, are known as the **control group**. The other group who *does* receive the IV, or the experimental variable, is known as the **experimental group**. Now that makes sense, doesn't it? Since we are experimenting with these people, they are logically the experimental group.

A lot of experts relate the IV/DV distinction to their students using the two-blank method. You merely fill in the two blanks. For example, what is the impact of blank on blank? The first blank is always the IV, while the second blank contains the DV. If you fill the blanks in wrong, then they won't make sense. Try it. It sounds complex, but it is really very simple.

IV ____________ DV____________ (fill in the blanks and see if it makes sense).

If you say, what is the impact of cognitive behavior therapy (CBT) on clients with alcohol use disorder, it makes sense. Cognitive behavior therapy is the IV – the first blank – and the number of alcoholic beverages consumed – the second blank – is the DV. But if you say, what impact does alcohol use disorder have on CBT, it seems nonsensical, or at the very least it doesn't flow as well. So, to answer the question (maybe on your real exam!) the IV would be the cognitive behavior therapy and the DV would be the number of alcoholic drinks.

Let's create a hypothetical experiment, right here, right now, to clarify this information. Let's assume that we want to discover whether REBT, rational emotive behavior therapy, created by Albert Ellis, formerly known as RET, really helps gamblers who are spending too much money at the casino.

One group of gamblers receives no treatment. We will call this the control group. Now say this out loud. Come on, the person next to you won't think you're crazy. Maybe that person will, but frankly who cares. "THE GROUP MADE UP OF INDIVIDUALS WHO RECEIVE NO TREATMENT IS THE CONTROL GROUP."

Now come on, he's just going to think you're on a cell phone. Say it out loud, "The control group never gets the IV, or the experimental variable." Again, say it louder, "The control group never gets the IV, or the experimental variable." OK, you lived through it.

Control group = Receives no experimental treatment (the IV). Often these subjects are merely placed on a waiting list.

Experimental group = Receives the IV or experimental variable, say, counseling sessions.

Now, another group of gamblers receives 16 sessions of REBT. The 16 sessions of REBT will be our IV or experimental variable. Our **experimental hypothesis** is that problem gamblers who undergo 16 sessions of REBT will spend less money at the casino than those who do not receive this treatment. At the end of the experiment, we will compute the DV, our outcome data, which will depict how much money those in the control group are dropping at the casino each day and how much money, if any, those in the experimental group are dropping at the casino daily.

Researchers point out that all experiments have at least two levels for the IV. In our example, one group, the control group, receives no therapy. That's one level, since therapy is the IV. The other level is 16 sessions of REBT. If we had another experimental group that only received eight sessions of the IV, then that would be another so-called level of the IV.

The number of groups can clue you in on the number of IV levels. Since an experimenter could bias a sample, the concept of random sampling is often used to assign subjects to the control group and the experimental group.

Let me explain. Would this experiment now really be fair if I pick super-motivated clients for my experimental group and I pack the control group with folks who have no desire to quit gambling? I think you would agree the answer is an unequivocal no.

On the other hand, would this experiment really be accurate if I packed the experimental group with people who totally hated therapy and were angry because they really wanted to attend Gamblers Anonymous, or GA? I don't think so.

To avoid this problem, technically known as sample bias, the researcher often uses the concept of random sampling. Random sampling keeps the researcher honest.

Let me give you a simple analogy of how random sampling works. We've all been to some function where there was a drawing and something was being given away. Everybody puts their name in a big bag or maybe a fishbowl. Then the master of ceremonies closes their eyes and picks a name. Random sampling is very similar to this.

In random sampling, every member of the population has an equal chance or probability of being selected for the study. The selection of one member has no effect on the selection of another member. Again, random sampling keeps the research honest.

Now let's get real here. Some big hotshot researcher probably isn't going to go around sticking their hand in a waterless fishbowl.

In yesteryears researchers would secure their random numbers from a random number table, often found in statistics textbooks, or they would resort to using computer programs that generate random numbers for a given sample size. Currently, random number generators can easily be found on the Internet.

Test hint. Even though the researcher has randomly selected their sample, a further step is necessary.

The researcher must *also* randomly assign the subjects to the experimental and the control groups. Then and only then do you have true randomness. You need random sampling and random assignment.

What's that you say? You went to school many years ago. Here's some new terminology for you.

NCE authority Larry Loesch noted many years ago that the true experiment is rare in counseling and development studies. He used the term quasi-experimental research (actually coined by Donald Campbell and Julian Stanley) to describe a study in which subjects or clients cannot randomly be assigned to groups.

Thus, on your exam, here's a mega test hint: Any research that fails to use random assignments or lacks a control group will be considered a quasi-experiment. If a question describes a study using intact groups, then the research is quasi-experimental. **Again, say it out loud or at least very loud in your mind, "All intact group studies aimed at showing cause and effect are quasi-experimental. If the groups for your study were not chosen randomly, the research is quasi-experimental."**

Dr. R's summary on the head of a pin: In the true experiment the participants in the study are randomly assigned to the treatment group (or groups) and the control group.

In quasi-experiments the participants are NOT randomly assigned to the treatment group (or groups) and the control group.

It doesn't mean that there isn't something to be learned from quasi-experiments. We do have to be careful, however, with how we interpret the research results.

Moving right along, some researchers use what is called a stratified sample, in which persons from subgroups, or so-called strata, are selected. An even more precise method is proportional stratified sampling, in which the sample mimics the general population.

Hence, if one third of the population were Native American, one third Asian American, and one third African American, the sample would support the same one third, one third, one third ratios. You would randomly select one third Native Americans, one third Asian Americans, and one third African Americans.

Another probability sampling type is what is known as cluster sampling. Here you use a naturally existing group, such as a group of people in the neighborhood, students in a counseling class, or perhaps the clients in an addiction treatment center. You as the researcher would then randomly select from the existing cluster.

As of late, a probability technique called *N*th sampling or **systematic sampling** is being employed. Your test might even refer it to *K*th sampling. The first person in your sample is often picked randomly. However, from that point on you would pick individuals at regular intervals, such as every 10th person or, say, every 15th person from your population. Keep in mind this technique violates the random sampling definition that every member of the population has an equal chance of being picked. Statisticians have recently been debating the merits of systematic or simple random sampling (SRS) versus systematic sampling. Again, the systematic approach is simple and often easier to utilize than relying on a random sample. One drawback, to put it bluntly, is the systematic approach is less random than traditional random sampling.

From an empirical standpoint, the results in most experiments seem to be similar no matter which of the two methods you use. Some researchers are turning to the **systematic sampling method**, especially when researching homogeneous populations (such as all counselors enrolled in a master's program in counseling) since it's easier.

Now listen closely because this is very important. The representativeness of the sample is, without a doubt, more crucial and more important than the procedure that is used to pick or acquire the subjects. Just for the record, all the samples I have mentioned thus far are called probability samples.

A sample can also be a **nonprobability sample**, in which the subjects are selected by methods not based on probability theory. For example, a procedure called judgment sampling relies on the judgment of the researcher to choose subjects that are thought to be representative of the population.

Another nonprobability method is called **convenience sampling**. With convenience sampling, an intact existing group is used with no random sampling.

The final type of nonprobability sample is the **quota sample**. In a quota sample, the subjects have prespecified characteristics so that your sample will mimic the same type of characteristics that you assume exist in the general population being studied.

When a researcher begins to think about conducting an experiment, the researcher begins with an idea or a hunch that is formally known as a **hypothesis**. A British biostatistician, Sir Ronald Fisher, or **R.A. Fisher** (1890–1962), has been dubbed the father of statistics and experimental design and first conceived hypothesis testing. Each experiment has at least two hypotheses, the **null hypothesis** and the **experimental hypothesis**. The hunch is the experimental hypothesis.

In the experiment I proposed earlier, my experimental hypothesis is that clients with a gambling problem who attend 16 sessions of REBT will spend less money at the casino than individuals in the study who have the same diagnosis who do not receive the treatment. **The experimental hypothesis is written with a capital H with a small 1 to the right of it**.

If we had a second hypothesis to test, say, 8 sessions of REBT, or perhaps 16 sessions of reality therapy, we might designate these hypotheses using H2 or H3.

Since some textbooks and exams refer to the experimental hypothesis as the alternative hypothesis, don't be surprised if you occasionally see the hypothesis designated by an uppercase H, with a tiny A (i.e., a sub-A) that stands for the alternative hypothesis just to the right of the H.

The **null hypothesis** asserts that there is no difference in gambling in those who attended the 16 individual sessions of REBT and those who did not attend. Null means nothing, zero, no significant difference between the control group and the experimental group.

On some exams, the null hypothesis is designated with an uppercase H with a very tiny zero, often referred to as a subzero, written to the right of the letter H. Time for another test hint.

As of late, a new term is popping up called the modern form of describing a hypothesis. In the so-called modern form, the hypothesis is written in the present tense without the word significant and without any mention of measurement. Hence, you might say there is no difference in people with a gambling issue who received REBT and those that did not. You might also have sub-hypotheses, such as there is no difference between female subjects who gamble too much and receive REBT and those that don't. In this new terminology, a null hypothesis might include interaction hypotheses, such as there is no difference between gamblers in the study with a graduate degree and age who receive REBT.

To determine if a difference is relevant between the control group, the people who did not receive the REBT, and the experimental group, the people who received the 16 sessions of REBT, the researcher uses what is known in the trade as a **test of significance**.

Now, you might ask, why do we need a test of significance? I'm being a little simplistic, but let's make up this example. Say we run the experiment. The average subject who received REBT spends $500 per day at the end of the study, while the average subject who received no treatment spent just $50 at the casino per day. Is REBT helpful?

Some people reading this book will say, "If we run the experiment again and get the same results, then yeah, sure it helped." Other readers might quip, "No way, Rosenthal. The results could be the result of chance factors. Unless you can duplicate the results for five experimental trials, then I'm not buying it."

A third person believes that we need to get the same results for ten trials to call this significant. The point, we have three educated people who can't seem to agree on what a significant difference really is.

What is a significant difference? Social scientists needed to have a standard, and that standard is based on probability. Tests of significance operate on the principle of probability, which is abbreviated with a lowercase p.

In the social sciences, the difference between groups is considered significant, where p is equal to or less than .05, or what researchers refer to as p at the 0.05 level. On your exam, this could be written as p with the letter v on its side, pointing toward the letter p. In other words, the mathematical < sign, and then the number .05.

Now, when p is 0.05, there is only a 5% chance that the difference in the two groups occurred via chance. Simply put, there is a 95% chance that the IV, in this case the REBT, really produced a difference in the drinking as measured at the end of the study.

If p has the < sign, it means that the probability is less than 5% that the differences occurred by chance. Some researchers demand that p be quite a bit lower than .05. These researchers will use the 0.01 or 0.001 level to rule out chance factors more effectively.

If we go all the way down to the 0.001 level, you could run the experiment a thousand times, and you would only get a different answer about one time. **The smaller the p , the more convincing the experiment.** OK, time for another pointer for your comprehensive test. Some exams call the level of significance, which is most likely set at .05, again, occasionally at .01 on our field, the confidence level, or the **alpha level**.

The likelihood a statistical hypothesis test will find a real/true effect if it exists is defined as *statistical power*. The greater the statistical power, the more confidence you can have regarding the validity of the research.

Now listen closely; this is very important. No matter how precise a statistical test is, there is still a chance, or a probability, that the results were caused by chance factors. We call this error. Researchers speak of two types of errors. We have type I or alpha errors, and we have type II or beta errors.

In the **type I error**, we reject null when it is true. For example, we conclude that the REBT helps lower the amount spent on gambling when it did not. In a **type II error**, we accept null when it is false. Here, we conclude that REBT didn't help the persons who are gambling too much money at all when indeed it was helpful.

When one of the error factors goes up, the other goes down. Just imagine a seesaw in your mind. Time for another must-know test hint.

The probability of making a type I error is equal to the level of significance. Thus, if your *p* value is .05, then .05 is the probability of making a type I error. If your *p* value exceeds .05, then we accept the null hypothesis. Remember how I said I'd come back to talking about extraneous variables that confounded an experiment? Well, here it is.

Extraneous variables, also known as errors, have been emphasized a lot on comprehensive exams in this field in the last few years. Specifically, I'm referring to the concepts of **internal and external validity** popularized by David T. Campbell and Julian C. Stanley.

Internal validity attempts to answer the question, "Does the experiment really, truly demonstrate that the DV changes or lack of them were caused by the IV? Does the experimental condition or treatment make a difference?"

Then, there's external validity that attempts to answer the question, "Can the findings of this study really, truly be generalized to other groups of people, other programs, or other settings?" When we speak of validity, what we're asking is, "Is our experiment valid? Does the experiment really do what we say it is going to do?"

As you might suspect, there are things inside the actual experiment and things happening outside of the actual experiment that may render the experiment invalid. Let's briefly discuss threats to internal validity.

One threat to internal validity occurs when the researcher cannot control procedures that impact the experiment. For example, say you had an REBT therapist who had countertransference toward unemployed clients in the study and was not performing the therapy properly with them.

Here's another example. This one involves instrumentation. Say you were conducting a biofeedback/neurofeedback study, and the meter was giving inaccurate readings. When instrumentation or measurement methods or observer's judgment changes impact the experiment, we call it an **instrumentation threat**.

Another threat to internal validity is called **maturation**. The concept of maturation simply implies that time, rather than the IV, impacts the results. Issues such as a person maturing or becoming older in the study would be an example. This is especially true in the developmental studies of young children.

Subjects and clients becoming too fatigued to benefit from the treatment would be examples of maturation threats to internal validity. Sometimes a pretest can cause internal validity problems since a person sometimes improves on a test merely by taking the test a second time.

Some experts believe that a single group time-series design helps control maturation threats. Comprehensive exams often mention the concept of statistical regression as a threat to internal validity.

Statistical regression to the mean occurs when extreme scores regress towards the mean or the arithmetic average when a task or a test is readministered. Usually very high initial scores fall, while unusually low scores move up. This would have little or nothing to do with the all-important IV/DV relationship. Selections of groups are also a threat to internal validity.

Here is a humorous, but true, little story from my childhood to illustrate the point quite well. My dad had heard golf was a tough game and he went with a friend of his to play their first ever round. His friend used a putter, rather than a driver, to tee off for the first shot (the worst possible club, I might add, since a putter is for very short distances). The ball went flying off the course onto the parking lot, but it hit the surface of the parking lot and bounced a long distance back onto the green and it landed just inches from the hole. His friend tapped the ball in for a birdie, or a score of two.

His friend shrugged his shoulders and said to my dad, "I don't know, this game really doesn't seem that difficult." (!!!!) But, true to the concept of regression to the mean or average, he wasn't much of a golfer, and legend has it, he never was able to snare another single birdie ever again in his golfing career.

An experiment where the groups are not really the same at the beginning of the study creates a problem. Intact groups also pose a threat, and random sampling is your best defense against selection problems.

In a **longitudinal study** that goes on for a long time, the issue of **attrition or experimental mortality** enters the internal validity picture. Why? The study can be invalidated if one group loses more people than another, or perhaps the final group is not like the original group because so many people dropped out.

When subjects are **demoralized or experiencing rivalry**, internal validity is also threatened. I know I've spent a lot of time on this topic, but that's because I fully expect that you will see a set of questions on this topic. Now, your exam could also use the term external threat to validity. This term implies that the experimental findings will not generalize to the real world.

When a person performs better because the individual is being observed, such as in the famous Hawthorne effect, we refer to this as a **reactive** effect. A reactive effect is a threat to external validity.

Maybe the subjects in our study are not drinking when alcohol is available to them during the study at the treatment center but just wait till they get out and hit the bars. Translation, according to the notion of external invalidity: the laboratory, as mentioned earlier, is not always the same as the real world.

Key test hint. A study *cannot* have good external validity unless it has good internal validity. However, good internal validity will *not guarantee* good external validity.

Although you probably won't be asked on your comprehensive exam to mathematically calculate a test of significance, you should be familiar with the names and purposes of the more popular statistical tests.

A very popular test is the ***t*-test or Student's *t*-test**, which tests a hypothesis between two normally distributed samples, such as in our REBT experiment. The test is appropriate for studies using 30 subjects or more.

If the same group is measured on two occasions, say, for example, using a pre- and a post-test, we refer to it as a **dependent or correlated *t*-test**. When this is not the case, we refer to the test as an **independent sample or uncorrelated *t*-test**.

Now, if you want to compare more than two groups, you'll need an **ANOVA**. No, not a constellation of stars, but the analysis of variance, especially when different levels of the IV are used such as 8 sessions of therapy in one group, 16 sessions in another, a placebo in another, and a medication in yet another.

The results of an ANOVA are expressed using R.A. Fisher's statistic known, as an ***F* value**.

What do you do if you have more than one DV? You must use a MANOVA, or multivariate analysis of variance. In our study, perhaps we would measure the amount of money spent at the casino, as well as say the subject's level of depression using a depression inventory.

Finally, we have the **ANCOVA**, or analysis of covariance. The analysis of covariance can be used to adjust the groups so that a variable that might correlate with the DV will not throw off the study.

For example, we might discover that one of the groups has read one of Albert Ellis's books on REBT and that they gamble less money at the casino than the other groups to begin with. This technique would allow us to statistically remove the difference caused by this so-called extraneous variable.

Now, catch your breath. In fact, take a break. Come on, you deserve it. This is heavy-duty stuff.

Okay, did you take that break? Great.

Back to action; you can handle it. In addition to experimental research, we have **correlational research**, which asks the question, "Does a relationship between two variables exist? If so, what's the magnitude and direction of the relationship?"

The **Pearson product moment correlation**, expressed by a lowercase *r*, is the correlation of choice in most counseling studies. A correlation coefficient can go from –1.00 to 0 to +1.00. A perfect correlation such as weight in pounds correlated with weight in ounces would be 1.00 or +1.00.

–1 correlations and +1 correlations are called **perfect correlations**. Of course, perfect correlations are very rare in the real world except in physical measures. Most positive correlations aren't that strong. Take height and weight.

The correlation, or association, if you will, between these two variables is positive because as height goes up, generally weight goes up a little bit too, but it's not going to be 1.00. A **negative correlation** is indicated when one variable goes up while another goes down. Aerobic exercise and pulse rate might be an example.

The more you exercise, the lower your pulse. Negative correlations are often referred to as **inverse correlations** or relationships. A **zero correlation** signifies no relationship. The number of cans of hairspray sold in New York City and the price of tea in Chicago,

Illinois, would probably be a zero correlation or nearly zero. This is mega important so repeat after me.

"Correlation does not imply cause and effect." Come on, I'm very serious about this. Say it again. **"Correlation does not imply causation."** Even though most experts believe that this is the most common type of research in our field. Again, purportedly first stated by Karl Pearson (1857–1936). "correlation does not imply causation"

Indulge me as I share my famous Martian example I made up so my college students could better understand the concept.

The head Martian demands to know what causes it to rain on Earth. He sends a spaceship with a top scientist to Earth to investigate. The Martian scientist looks around on earth, and everywhere he looks, by golly, he sees umbrellas. He gets into a spaceship, zips back to Mars, and tells the head guy, "Hey, next time give me a difficult problem. This was too easy. Umbrellas cause it to rain."

The head Martian scratches his head and says, "That's strange. I accidentally put another Martian scientist on the case. He too thought the problem was very simple to solve. However, said that rain is caused by something called windshield wipers on cars, trucks, and other vehicles."

The point is that correlation indicates the strength or lack of strength of an association, or relationship, not causation. Test hint, the higher the number, the stronger the correlation. It doesn't matter whether the number is positive or negative. Hence, if your test asks which is a stronger association, 0.70 or –.90, the answer is –90. Please, pretty please with sugar on top: read the previous sentence again! Why? Because even though .70 is a positive correlation and –.90 is a negative correlation, the –.90 is indicative of a stronger relationship.

Now let's talk about the **normal bell-shaped or Gaussian curve**, named after the German Mathematician Carl Friedrich Gauss (1777–1855). **A normal curve, a.k.a. normal distribution, is a curve where the mean, median, and mode all fall in the middle of the curve**. When you draw it or represent it graphically, it looks like a bell; hence its nickname: the bell curve.

The theory is that most physical and psychological characteristics are spread out or distributed throughout the population in this approximate curve. In other words, if you were to survey enough people on *any* given trait – you name it, height, weight, IQ – and you plot a curve, it would look like the bell.

The so-called **mean, median, and mode are measures of central tendency**. They are called measures of central tendency because even in a skewed distribution, they tend to be in the "center" of the curve. **In fact, in a true normal or bell-shaped curve, one of the definitions is that the mean, the median, and the mode are the same value**.

The **mode** is the most frequently occurring score or category. Now listen carefully. **The mode is always going to be at the top or the high point of the graph for the distribution**. This fact comes in very handy when an exam asks where the mode is on a graph. A curve with two high points is called a **bimodal curve**. A bimodal curve has two maximum areas of concentration. In fact, if you take a piece of paper and you draw a bimodal curve, it's going to look like a camel's back.

Some distributions have more than two modes, and they are logically called **multimodal curves**.

I want to continue my discussion by talking about the **median**. That's right. Just like the center of the highway, the median cuts the distribution in half if you rank order the scores from the highest to the lowest.

Thus, the median is the exact middle of the distribution or the 50th percentile. I repeat, in statistics, the median is the middle score or hypothetical middle score when the data are rank ordered.

Let's say you gave an exam to five people and the scores were 15, 15, 20, 95, and 99. The median would be 20, as two scores fall above it and two scores fall below it.

The mode is 15 since it's the most frequently occurring score. **The mean is the most useful measure of central tendency**. You simply add up the scores and divide the total by the number of scores.

For example, if your electric bill is $144 a year. . . . Yeah, dream on. I really wish mine was that low too. Remember, this is just an example. Then you would compute the mean or arithmetic average by dividing 144 by 12 months, which gives you a $12 per month as your average or mean electric bill.

If you're in a bowling league and you bowl a 450 series for three games, then your average would be 150 because you're going to divide 450 by three games. Now, although the mean is the most powerful measure of central tendency, it is not the best statistic for evaluating a **skewed distribution**.

A skewed population has extreme values, and the curve appears to lean to one side or the other if you draw it. When you have extreme scores, such as family size, income, or height and weight, the median is the statistic of choice because it is not impacted by extremes.

When the curve tail goes to the left, the distribution is said to be negatively skewed. When the curve tail goes to the right, the distribution is said to be positively skewed.

A counselor emailed me recently and suggested this humorous memory device. If we all use the Rosenthal materials and score high on our exams, the distribution would be negatively skewed. You've got to love it.

When we draw a curve of scores, we call it a frequency polygon. To represent this frequency polygon more accurately, we draw a vertical line to the left of the curve. This is called the **y-axis**, or the ordinant. The DVs are placed on the y-axis or the ordinant. A very elementary memory device I use is that the y-axis goes up and down just like the letter y. As I said earlier, I like to keep it simple, folks!

Next, we graphically place a line underneath the curve. We call this line the **x-axis**, or the abscissa. We place the IVs in the experiment on the abscissa.

Another neat way to display a distribution, especially if we have intervals, is to use a **bar graph**, or what statisticians call a **histogram**.

When explaining data, we speak of variation or variability. Measures of variation explain how individuals vary among themselves. **The range is a measure of variability**. Now to compute the range, you merely take the difference between the highest and the lowest score.

Hence, if the top score on an exam was 100, and the lowest score was 50, then the range would be 50. Unfortunately, the range is affected by sample size, and the range usually increases as sample size increases.

Next, we have the variance, which is a measure of dispersion of scores. Finally, we have the **SD** or the **standard deviation**, which you've no doubt heard so much about.

The SD is the square root of the variance. The SD concept is very useful when we discuss the spread of scores. Why? Well, because one positive, negative standard deviation contains 68.25% of the cases.

95.4% of the cases fall between plus minus two standard deviations and 99.74 fall between three plus minus SDs of the mean. Take this IQ score example.

The SD for IQ scores is 15. Therefore, if 100 is the mean IQ on an IQ test, then 85 to 115 would be the range for IQ scores in the plus/minus one SD range.

Nowadays, many exams and texts just use: 68%, 95%, and 99.7% for the sake of brevity, or even 68–95–99.

Again, assuming the mean is 100, if you have an IQ of 115, you are roughly at the 85th percentile of all IQ scores. If you have an IQ score of 130, you're roughly at the 97th percentile. That's awesome.

Another way to analyze the formal, normal distribution is via **Z scores**. **A Z score is the same as a standard deviation**. Z of 2.5 merely means 2.5 standard deviations above the mean.

A Z score of negative 2.5 conveys that you are 2.5 standard deviations below the mean. We can also use a concept called a ***T* score**. In a *T* score the mean is 50 with each 10 points, landing at a standard deviation above or below the mean. Sounds complicated, but it's not.

Let's say they ask you on your comprehensive exam, "What *T* score is one SD above the mean?" The answer would be 60. If they asked you, "What *T* score is one SD below the mean?" The answer would be 40. Some medical tests use the *T* score to report your health status.

***T* scores simplify things by eliminating negative numbers that can appear when you use Z scores**.

Finally, we have a concept that's called stanines.

Stanines scores, originally called standard nine scores, true to their name, divide the distribution into nine equal intervals with a mean of five and a standard deviation of two.

The stanine goes from the lowest ninth of the distribution to the highest. Time for another surefire test reminder.

Averages, including the mean, the median, and the mode, also called measures of central tendency; the range; the variance; standard deviation; and any other statistical device that merely describes a group are called descriptive statistics.

Descriptive statistics are not experimental since we do not manipulate variables. Now, there is an excellent chance that any comprehensive licensing or certification exam could ask a question or two about scales of measurement proposed by the American psychologist Stanley Smith Stevens (1906–1973) way back in 1946.

The **nominal scale** uses numbers to identify or classify. This is easy enough to remember since nominal and number both begin with

n. Your cell phone number, a diagnostic category number (i.e., code) from the ICD or the DSM, a type of therapy, a political party, a number on a baseball player's uniform, marital status, eye color, and blood type all indicate a nominal scale of measurement.

Nominal scales are qualitative but not quantitative. For example, baseball player number eight is not twice as good as baseball player number four, at least we hope.

Next comes the **ordinal scale**, which is used to describe variables that can be rank ordered.

For example, high income, average income, and low income would be an example. How about this one: sprinters who finished first, second, and third in a track and field event. High, medium, and low would also fit this category. Educational level such as high school, bachelor's, master's, master's plus 30, or PhD/EdD. Occasionally a measurement can be controversial. Likert scales, discussed elsewhere in the book, have been categorized as ordinal and interval (e.g., strongly agree, agree, neutral, disagree, strongly disagree) by various experts.

The **interval scale** comes next. Numbers are scaled at equal distances, but there's no real zero point. Most tests given in school are interval scale tests. You could receive a zero on a history test. Nevertheless, this does not mean you have zero knowledge of history. A client with an IQ score of 120 is not twice as smart as somebody with an IQ score of 60. Fahrenheit and Celsius temperature fit into this category.

The final scale, the highest form of measurement, is called the **ratio scale**. On the ratio scale, there is a true absolute zero point, such as on the Kelvin temperature scale.

Each number is at a distance measured from zero. Height, weight, age, and volume fall into this category. You can very easily compare on this scale two different people because a person who is 6 feet tall really is twice as tall as someone who is 3 feet tall. A person who weighs 200 pounds truly weighs double what somebody who tips the scales at 100 pounds. A parent who is 50 years old is twice as old has their 25-year-old child.

This is a great scale but nearly impossible to use for counseling research. Why? Well, think about it. How do you know that one person is twice as depressed or, say, twice as phobic as somebody else?

I want to provide you with a kind of a mini dictionary of popular research terms that you might see on your exam. I promise to keep the explanations brief and simple, so you can go back and read them again and again until you know them by heart.

Term number one is **survey**. This is the simplest approach to research. It's conducted by giving a questionnaire or a so-called opinion poll to a sample population. A return rate of 30 to 50% is typical.

The problem is that when you get a return rate under 75%, that's too low to generalize about your data. Other experts feel that you need at least 100 responses to use a survey. For all practical purposes, an interview may be a better method.

Term number two, **ethnographic research**. This is an old anthropological approach. The researcher looks at overall dynamics in the culture or the situation, such as a counseling session, rather than focusing on a single factor to study. Ethnographic research is holistic and inductive. Observational research and case studies are considered ethnographic.

The ethnographic approach is said to be qualitative rather than quantitative or statistical. This approach is based on what we call inductive reasoning or logic. **Inductive reasoning** is a process where you generalize based on specific observations. My counseling seminar I professor accepts late assignments; therefore, my seminar II professor will also accept late assignments.

Deductive reasoning is top down or the opposite. It occurs when a specific hypothesis or hypotheses are derived from general principles. For example, you say all statistics professors are mean. Thus, I'm sure my statistics professor, Mr. Smith, won't let me take the final over. That's deductive.

Term number three, the **halo effect coined by Edward Thorndike**. The halo effect occurs when you rate an individual on one characteristic (usually looks), but you're really influenced by another. Say you were rating counselors on the effectiveness of their counseling technique, but you're giving the best ratings to those you find physically attractive. This would constitute a prime example of the halo effect. The **horn effect/bias** or negative halo effect is the direct opposite. For example, you don't like facial hair; thus you are less likely to hire job candidates with beards since you feel they will be less competent. Keep in mind that although your bias might be unconscious, the halo and horn effect often come into play in job interviews and career counseling settings.

Term number four, the **Hawthorne effect**, is the notion that people who are getting special attention or know they are being monitored in a study may perform differently than they normally would.

The principle, as I'm sure you are aware, received its name from the old Western Electric Hawthorne works plant study that included George Elton Mayo (1880–1949) and took place from 1924 to 1932, in which workers' output did not go down even when the lighting conditions were purposely made horrendous for workers.

The findings indicated that the experimenter's presence or attention had an impact on the workers being studied. Thus, the mere fact that someone is part of an experiment would change their behavior even in cases where the independent variable was not responsible for that particular change. (Recent findings do not necessarily support the Hawthorne effect.)

Term number five, the **Rosenthal effect**, also known as the **Pygmalion effect**. The Rosenthal effect suggests that the *experimenter's expectations* may inadvertently influence the subjects in a study. Remember the old 1966 study when psychologist Robert Rosenthal (1933–) and Lenore Jacobson basically lied to teachers and told them that certain kids were bloomers and would improve during the year.

The kids themselves were told nothing. Nevertheless, the teacher's expectations of the kids unconsciously influenced their behavior toward the children. Not only did these kids excel, but in many cases, their IQs even shot up.

Experimenter effects such as this and the halo effect can be overcome by using blind experimenters or blind judges who do not know which subjects are experimental and which subjects are control subjects. When the subjects *and* the experimenter do not know who is receiving the IV, then we refer to the study as a **double-blind study**.

Studies for prescription medicines are conducted in this manner. Just for the record, the effect is named after the famous psychologist Robert Rosenthal, and not yours truly. He's much more famous than I am.

Term number six, **norms**. When referring to testing or experimentation, the term norms refers to the normal, typical, or average person who took the test. It's that simple.

Term number seven. In research, the letter ***N*** always indicates the number of subjects in a study. Thus, we have what is termed the ***N* equals 1**, or so-called **single-subject design**. It can also be called an intensive experimental intrasubject design. This type of research focusing on the behavior of *one person* is used primarily for behavior therapy or behavior modification/applied behavior analysis.

You will also hear researchers refer to this paradigm as a **case study**, and it was first used in a big way in our field by none other than Sigmund Freud, the founding father of psychoanalysis. In the last several years it seems to be making a comeback.

But let's go back to using $N = 1$ for behavioristic purposes first. First, you will take a measure or a baseline. **The baseline is really a measure of behavior where there's no treatment, no intervention**. This is signified with an **upper-case A**, or simply the capital A. Then you apply the intervention or treatment. This is signified by an **upper-case B**, and you return to the baseline to see if the behavior is different.

Some exams call this an AB design, or an ABC design if two treatment interventions are used. If you return to the baseline, we call it an ABA design. Finally, the ABAB design lets you see if the treatment really works the same on two occasions, and it ends the experiment in the desirable treatment phase.

An AB design that tracks more than one behavior is referred to as a multiple baseline design. Hence, you might want to track drinking and smoking, for example, as your baselines.

Now I threw a lot of As and Bs at you. You need to read the last two paragraphs back. Go ahead and do it right now. All right, you read it once again. Smart move.

Term number eight, the **concept of counterbalancing**. You'll see your old friends the uppercase letters A and B on questions of this ilk. Researchers have discovered that the presentation of stimuli can bias an experiment. Hence, a good researcher may counterbalance an experiment by giving some subjects stimuli A and then B, while other subjects receive stimuli B prior to A.

Term number nine, the concept of **percentile rank**. A client's percentile rank tells you how many people scored equal to or lower than the client. A percentile rank of 80 indicates that the client scored higher than 79% of the population who took the test and lower than 19%.

Now, listen closely. It does not indicate that the client got 80% of the test items correct, although it could mean that. That's percentage, not percentile.

Do yourself a favor and read those last two paragraphs again. You can almost guarantee yourself you'll see a question about the topic of percentile versus percentage on the test.

Term number ten, the concept of the **raw score**. Raw meat is unchanged, uncooked. Raw scores, the same thing. Raw scores are unaltered, untransformed. You have done absolutely nothing to the score.

Backtracking a bit, if you took the GRE, an IQ test, and an SAT, we could take the raw scores and convert them to Z scores, then easily compare how you did on all three in terms of your percentile rank.

Term number 11, **longitudinal research**, or what we call developmental research. You follow the same group of people over a period of time. Sometimes we call these **trend studies**.

Term number 12, **directional hypothesis and nondirectional hypothesis**. A direction asserts how things will be different. For example, "Problem gamblers who receive therapy will gamble less": that's a directional hypothesis. A nondirectional hypothesis says, "Problem gamblers who receive therapy will be statistically different than those who do not receive therapy." It does not say or show how they will be different.

Term number 13, **meta-analysis/meta-research**, occurs when you combine numerous research studies on a given topic (such as all studies on motivational interviewing or all studies on systematic desensitization).

Before I close, I would like to introduce you to the concept of **parametric versus nonparametric tests**. As you might suspect, statisticians have been looking at numbers for a long time. As I mentioned earlier, numbers can be classified in terms of four categories, ranging from nominal to ratio numbers.

I like to look at these four scales as being strong or weak in terms of the amount of information they can give you. For example, the nominal scale is relatively weak. As a result, you wouldn't ask a weak person or a weak number to lift a heavy load or give you a lot of information.

A license plate number or number on a sports jersey (both nominal) are only used for identification. It can't tell you much more. The same is true for an ordinal number. It can tell you which one is greater, but not how much greater.

A sergeant is greater than a private, but how much? Again, a relatively weak number. Such numbers do not lie on a continuum. They are either one thing or another. You are an 8th-grade history teacher or a 9th-grade family and consumer sciences teacher. A schizophrenic or not a schizophrenic.

Numbers that do not lie on a continuum are said to be **nonparametric**. In other words, you can't draw a line, or at least not a straight line, with these numbers.

With this type of number, you can't draw a line from one number to the next because you don't know anything about the space between the numbers. When you go from 1 inch to 2 inches, you have one fourth of an inch, one half of an inch, and so on.

How would you do this with the 8th-grade history teacher and the 9th-grade family and consumer sciences teacher? Simply put, you can't. On the other hand, numbers that can tell you about the space between the whole integers are on a continuum. These numbers are said to be **parametric**.

As I mentioned before, in one case, you have an arbitrary zero the interval scale, and in another, the ratio scale, you have a set zero. What does all this mean?

Well, one of the first things a statistician asks is: what kind of numbers make up the data?

If the numbers are **categorical,** then, here, the researcher knows immediately that a **nonparametric** test like the **chi-square** will be used to test your hypothesis. If the data are on a continuum, then some type of parametric test like a *t*-test or an ANOVA will be used.

Since the chi-square is a likely nonparametric candidate to pop up on your exam, let's take a moment to examine this robust test of significance. It is a test that is used whenever you are working with categorical data, and it's used a lot in social science research.

An example would be trying to determine the effectiveness of therapy between two groups when you only have the number that is in the groups and another score.

Another example: how many Democrats voted for Republicans, or was there a significant difference between the way Republicans and Democrats voted on an issue? Here, your data would only include the number of Democrats or Republicans. You would not be able to tell if the difference in voting patterns was significant or not.

How many college graduates versus those who did not attend college are no longer diagnosed as having a major depressive disorder after receiving therapy? Again, you don't have any type of performance data, so you can get an average. You only have distinct categories. **Whenever you have data that are categorical, you would use the chi-square**.

There is no such thing as a 1.5 schizophrenic or a 0.75 Democrat. These numbers represent a category and not a continuum.

For example, if we were to examine individuals who took the national counselor examination and ask: Did significantly more individuals reading this book pass than those who didn't read this text? Or, to put it another way, how many people are in each group? We would use a chi-square to examine this issue.

If we ask which group obtained a significantly higher score, these data are on a continuum, and thus, we will use a *t*-test.

Before leaving this area let me share nine key research trends in counseling:

1. More research seems to have multiple authors and female authors.
2. Increased attention is being paid to multicultural issues, LGBT issues, and neurocounseling.
3. Field-based practitioners and professionals are submitting *fewer* contributions.
4. Meta-research is increasingly used to examine a given topic or theme.
5. Cohen's *d* is being used to determine effect size (ES) to express how strong a finding is, going beyond merely stating that a finding is significant or not (0.2 is small, 0.5 is medium, and 0.80 is considered large).
6. Most studies use graduate students or adults, and a lot of researchers would like to see us move away from this.
7. Big data from the Internet is being used to generate huge sample sizes.

8. *N*-1 case studies, first popularized by Freud and Piaget, are making a comeback. These are often qualitative rather than quantitative.
9. Counselors and graduate students feel they need more training in APA publication guidelines to amass the skills to submit research.

All right. We made it through research and you're still kicking. That's great. Let's go on to another topic. Have a great day.

3

Master Lecture 2: Human Growth and Development

Now, I want to talk about human growth and development, another area of the NCE, the CPCE, and the CECE. Noted textbook author Ed Neukrug believes developmental models are transtheoretical in the sense that human growth and development theories can be used with most counseling approaches. Let's explore some of the more popular theories.

One of the key names in cognitive development and child psychology is **Jean Piaget**. Piaget was born in 1896 and he died in 1980. Piaget was a precocious child. He published his first scientific paper at age 11, and he wrote over 30 volumes without formal training or a degree in psychology.

In fact, he was trained in biology, specifically zoology, and he worked with Alfred Binet on parts of the first intelligence test. He wanted to learn how children solve problems. Piaget has been criticized because he did most of his research on his own children. Some people say that he was a bit informal in terms of relying on this method.

Piaget has been categorized as what we call a structuralist. That is to say that he believed that there are universal stages of psychological

DOI: 10.4324/9781003149712-3

development and that each stage represents a qualitative difference in the way a person thinks or solves a conflict. He has also been called a universal constructivist. Here's why.

Simply put, the stages of development are universal, and the child literally **constructs** their cognitive development. Therefore, Piaget has been dubbed one of the pioneers in constructivist educational theory. Heredity is responsible for programming the unfolding of the stages.

The way a person acquires knowledge about the world is what Piaget called a **scheme**. Patterns of organized thought or behavior are called a schema or schemata in Piagetian theory.

At first, a child may put things in their mouth or grasp at them, but eventually a physical scheme becomes psychological. The child develops a viewpoint or a mental structure to learn about the world. This is called an internalized or interiorized scheme. An infantile scheme thus changes to a mental or internal scheme. Later schemes grow out of earlier ones.

Piaget says thinking and cognitive processes develop via **assimilation** and **accommodation**. These are two very important terms. Assimilation is when you learn from an existing scheme or take knowledge by using a cognitive structure that already exists.

For example, an infant learns that a rubber doll is soft and pliable by sucking on it, in contrast to accommodation, where you modify a scheme to incorporate new information. In accommodation, the child creates a new cognitive structure to deal with new information and situations. For example, an infant who is bottle fed must use accommodation to learn to drink from a cup.

Piaget stated that assimilation and accommodation are complementary. They occur simultaneously. Humans strive for equilibrium between the two, or what Piaget called **equilibration**. Simply put, equilibration is the balance of assimilation and accommodation in a new situation.

To review. When a child uses their existing understanding of the world to make sense out of the environment, that's assimilation. When the child changes their previous ways of knowing the world to make sense out of the new information, that's accommodation. **The bedrock of Piaget's theory rests on his four orderly stages of development**.

One, the sensorimotor stage; two, the preoperational stage; three, the concrete operational stage; and four, the formal operational stage. Let's dissect these stages one by one, remembering that Piaget relied on case studies, often using his own children, to verify his theory.

As I talk about these stages in Piaget's theory, remember that Piaget considered himself the founder of a new discipline that he called genetic epistemology. Epistemology is just a big, fancy-schmancy that means the philosophy of the nature of knowledge.

Stage number one, the sensorimotor intelligence stage, from birth until approximately two years. This stage is categorized by lots of reflexive behavior, such as sucking or grasping. Piaget called it sensorimotor, since the emphasis is on the senses, especially touch, vision, and motor, because there is an emphasis on motor activities such as sucking or grasping, as I mentioned earlier.

An important concept in this first sensorimotor stage is what is known as **object permanence**. It occurs between the 9th and 12th month. Here, the child discovers object permanence, which is the ability to recognize that an object still exists even when it is out of reach and out of sight.

Before the child masters object permanence, which would occur, of course, before the ninth month, if you place a toy behind the child, the child no longer reaches for it. This is what some would call out of sight, out of mind.

To review, a child who has mastered object permanence knows that something exists even when it is out of sight. For test purposes, remember that object permanence could also be called symbolic or representational thought.

With object permanence come the concepts of **causality** and **space**. For example, a child learns that a hand causes a toy to move from one space to another.

Last, the child learns **time**. That is to say, one thing occurs before another.

Forging on, **stage two. The preoperational stage or the preoperational period, ages two to seven, in which the child develops language**. In Piaget's theory, an operation is simply a thought or a cognitive skill, so don't let that throw you. An important factor in this stage is that the child lacks the ability to see another person's point of view.

Piaget called this **egocentrism**. He didn't really mean that the child was selfish or self-centered. Instead, what he meant was that the child could only see their own point of view. Again, egocentrism implies that the child cannot see another person's point of view.

A child might say something like, "The rain is following me." If you stand across from a five-year-old, point to your own left hand, and tell the child point to your left hand, the child will point to your hand on their own left, which of course is your right hand.

Piaget and the Swiss psychologist Barbel Elizabeth Inhelder (1913–1997) even did experiments where they had the child look at a model of a mountain. They would say to the child, "What would the mountain look like from another person's point of view, in other words, a person sitting on the other side of the mountain?" Of course, the child is not able to tell you.

The second stage is also characterized by what we call **centration,** which is focusing on one key part of an object and forgetting about the rest. The child in the second stage develops what we call **schema**. This is sometimes called symbolic play. It's the ability to use symbols and language.

For example, a mass of Play-Doh modeling compound can become a cake, a pie, or even a mountain. A soda bottle could become a spaceship. Piaget warns us not to put too much stock in language at this age. Why? It's what is known as **nominal realism**.

For example, if you tell a child that his doll's name can be changed from Joe to Mickey Mouse, the child cannot comprehend this. A name is seen as a property like a shape or a color. Language develops during this stage. **A child in the preoperational stage cannot comprehend the reversal of actions**.

Now, stage number three, concrete operations, ages 7 to 11, in which the child can comprehend conversations. In this period, a child can mentally manipulate objects for the first time. Piaget tells us that counting begins in this period.

Before this time, a child, for example, can't really count without matching up something to the objects such as a pencil, fingers, a toothpick, or something of that nature. **The key concept in the concrete operations stage is conservation**.

Here's a great memory device. Conservation starts with a C, so does concrete operations, and so does counting. They all occur in the Piagetian stage with a C, concrete operations.

Now, let's look at the concept of conservation. You have water glasses and one is short and squatty and the other is tall and thin. Now you pour the water from the short glass into tall, skinny glass and you ask the child, "Which has more water?" The child who has not mastered conservation will tell you that the tall, skinny water glass has more.

You cannot fool a child who has mastered conservation. The child who has mastered conservation will know that the amount of water has not changed.

Here's another great example. Let's say you have a cake. You have two identical cakes, but you cut each cake into a different number of pieces. We take the first cake and we cut it into three pieces. We take the other cake that's the same size, and we cut it into eight pieces. The child is going to say that the cake with eight pieces has more cake in it unless this child has mastered conservation.

Conservation helps the child understand the concept of volume and reversibility. Now the child understands units, volumes, and, again, the concept of reversibility and what it's like to be in somebody else's shoes and understand their viewpoint.

Stage number four. Formal operations, from ages 11 to 12 to about 15.

A great memory device here is that you can remember that, as people get older, they often become more formal; hence the formal operations stage, or operational stage, would be the last stage.

The formal operations stage is the beginning of abstract, hypothetical, and deductive reasoning. The child learns the concept of experimentation with problems and begins to understand metaphors.

Formal operations allow some adolescents to tackle subjects like algebra. I say some because Piaget and some other researchers believed that only 50% of all adults ever make it to Piaget's final stage. Even Piaget admitted that bright adults could sometimes only use formal operations in their own field.

For example, some physics majors who are experts in internal combustion engines might be incapable of changing an air filter or cabin filter in their own vehicles. Some research revealed that only 15 to 25% of college students ever use formal operational thinking.

Most experts agree that Piaget did little to discuss the application of his ideas to the counseling session. Some have suggested that the child's cognitive level, rather than their chronological age, should be used to determine what grade the child is placed in in school.

Finally, abstract counseling approaches rarely, if ever, are appropriate for children below the age of 12. Why? Well, the answer is easy. Because younger children often have not mastered abstract thinking skills.

What do Piaget's critics say about his four-stage model of cognitive development?

First stage theories can be incorrect. As an example, research shows object permanence can occur earlier than Piaget mentions. Also, stage theories such as Piaget's don't generally lend themselves to operational definitions that can be replicated in research settings. His stages don't truly display the qualitative differences he discusses. Not every child will have an identical learning path.

In fact, development may not be linear or predictable. Moreover, the theory seems to ignore emotions and social relationships in the process of cognitive development.

Again, keep in mind many of his observations came from watching his own children.

Another point of contention is that a child who is paralyzed or has other physical disabilities could not manipulate the environment as Piagetian theory requires – sometimes referred to as an action-oriented approach to experience cognitive development – and obviously this is not true since according to this theory these children could not display cognitive development!

Although his theory has been immensely valuable, few experts consider themselves strict adherents to his teachings.

Finally, Piaget's theory is based (some might say biased) on Western culture and ignores the influence of other cultural, environmental, and even educational factors.

If Piaget is *the* name in cognitive development, then the American psychologist **Lawrence Kohlberg (1927–1987)** is *the* name in **moral development**. Lawrence Kohlberg was a graduate student in the 1950s at the University of Chicago, where he studied Piaget.

Piaget had set forth a two-stage theory of morality, and in 1958 Kohlberg wrote a dissertation on this, and he went on to say that he felt Piaget's theory just didn't have enough depth, so he created his own theory.

Piaget's theory of moral development talked about **heteronomous morality or moral realism**, which is where you do the right thing due to parents, teachers, and so on. The word hetero means "other." Piaget also had a stage two, **autonomous morality or moral independence**. In this stage, beginning at approximately age 8, rules and regulations are relative and can be changed. Actions are judged partially on intent.

In this second stage, you understand that rules are made by people, and thus, they can be altered or adjusted. Kohlberg believed after he researched these Piagetian moral stages that there are three levels of morality, and each has two stages. **Remember this: for Kohlberg, morality is a decision and not a trait**.

The first level of morality, approximately ages two to seven, is called preconventional morality. At this level, consequences dictate feelings. Again, in preconventional morality, behavior is guided by punishment and rewards.

Stage one is what is known as obedience and reward orientation. Here, the fear of punishment is strong. **Stage two is what is known as instrumental relativist orientation, where the child is motivated by reward**.

Level two is known as conventional morality. Here, you try to meet the standards of the family, your nation, and your culture. You identify with people in power. You try to live up to a socially defined role.

Stage three occurs in level two, and it's what we call the good boy/good girl orientation. Here, you do the right thing to please others and get recognition.

There is also stage four in this level, or what is called law and order or social authority order orientation.

Then there's level three, the highest level, which is what is known as postconventional or self-imposed morality. Here, the person acts on principles rather than rules, and thus, it is sometimes called a prior-to-society viewpoint. The person has a self-accepted standard of behavior.

Stage five is called the social morality of contract, and here the person wants to maintain respect with equals in the community.

Stage six is what we call the universal ethical principle of conscience. In this highest stage, there is concern over self-condemnation over violating one's principles, and, of course, some never reach stages five and six. In stage six, you are concerned with equal rights of all people.

OK, now I know that Kohlberg seemed a little complex, but there's plenty of review in my materials. Before leaving the subject of

Kohlberg, I want you to know that not everybody thinks his theory is the be all, end all.

Carol Gilligan (1936–), an American psychologist and feminist, penned a book in 1982 titled *In a Different Voice*. She contends that Kohlberg's theory focuses too heavily on morality and justice and ignores moral issues like compassion, caring, and responsibility to others that are significant to women and girls.

As a colleague of Kohlberg's, Gilligan was critical of the fact that Kohlberg did his research on a small group of boys and hence his findings might not be applicable to women. She feels that perhaps this theory is even a tad sexist, because, again, it relies on research based on males and male-focused stories.

Bottom line, Kohlberg's theory may be more accurate when applied to males than females.

The next expert I want to talk about is **Erik Erikson (1902–1994)**, who is another heavy hitter in developmental psychology. He is famous for coming up with the term **"identity crisis."**

Please don't confuse Erik Erikson with **Milton H. Erickson (1901–1980)**, the latter a famous hypnotist and brief therapist whom Jay Haley studied under.

One way that I distinguish the two is by the spelling of their names since you might only see the last name on an exam. Erik Erikson does not use a C in his name, and Milton Erickson spells his name with a C. One memory device that works for me is to remember that Erik Erikson was famous a little earlier, so he didn't need a C in his name.

Erik Erikson has been classified as a **maturationist**, as was Freud. Maturationism suggests that developmental stages are **genetically determined**. Maturational counselors try to free positive instincts and give the person self-control over negative ones.

The environment provides the external demands; thus, the **maturational counselor** allows clients to relive earlier conflicts with the goal being freedom of choice. I think it's interesting that Erikson, who considers himself a disciple of Freud, met Freud by painting portraits of Freud's children.

Now listen up; this is critical. Although **Freud's model of development is psychosexual**, remember that **Erik Erikson's model is psychosocial**, as he emphasized the importance of social factors.

Although the strict Freudians say, "It's all over at about age five," meaning that the personality is roughly set in stone by age five or six, **Erikson's stages cover the entire life span**. Freud's last stage, on the other hand, occurs in puberty and theoretically lasts for the remainder of one's life.

Erikson's theory is guided by the epigenetic principle or what we call epigenetic development. Epigenetic is a term you may remember from your biological studies of embryology. It means the development proceeds according to predetermined steps or stages. (Note: Recently epigenetic, or above the genes, refers to how lifestyle impacts your life. Thus, a person who smokes has a greater chance of getting lung cancer than somebody who does not even if they both possess identical genes.)

Erikson describes eight stages, and each has traditionally been characterized by polarity. That is to say, there is a **positive pole and a negative pole for each stage**. The positive is supposedly indicative of successful development. The negative pole is indicative of unsuccessful development. **Each stage, therefore, sets up a conflict or a crisis, a turning point, if you will**.

I must say, however, that Erikson feels that he has been misunderstood, because his interpretation is the person does not merely choose one pole or the other. There are various shades of grey in this continuum from the positive to the negative side of the pole. Moreover, the individual who fails to work successfully through a conflict at one stage may do so later.

Erikson discussed the notion that a person would try to become what a parent or significant other wants.

Erikson doesn't really believe this leads to ideal mental health. On the contrary, he believes that we need to strive to become unique and autonomous. **He called the unique self "the ego identity."** In some of the early literature his psychosocial stages are called ego psychology, or eight stages of ego identity. Let's take a look at **Erikson's famous eight stages**.

Stage one, Trust versus Mistrust, from birth to approximately one year of age. If physical infancy needs are not met, a child will not feel trust. If they are met, then the person will feel trust. If the needs are not met, there is a fear or a mistrust of others in the environment.

It is theorized that talking, playing, and cuddling with the child will help. This first stage coincides with Freud's first stage, "the oral stage."

Stage two, Autonomy versus Shame and Doubt, one year to three years, the so-called toddler years. In this stage the child learns to experiment and explore.

However, if parents or caretakers are overprotective or inconsistent, the child develops doubt and may be ashamed of their own behavior. The child develops mobility and control over bodily functions. This stage coincides with Freud's anal stage.

Stage three, Initiative versus Guilt, from ages three to six. Incidentally, the ages may vary by a year or two if you research these stages in various textbooks over the years. In this stage, the child is encouraged by the parent to meet new people and explore the environment. If this happens, the child will achieve initiative or feelings of competence.

If the parents stifle this, well, the child feels guilty for taking initiative or trying to be independent. This is similar to Freud's phallic stage.

Stage four, Industry versus Inferiority, ages 6 to 11 or 12, the so-called elementary school years. The child learns to get along with authority figures like teachers and to get along with peers.

The child learns to manipulate objects and events by themself, thus learning to solve problems to complete a task. The term industry refers to setting and attaining personal goals. The child who is unsuccessful may feel inferior. The Freudians call this "the latency period."

Stage five, Identity versus Role Confusion, from ages 12 to 18, the adolescent years. The major task is to go from childhood to adulthood and clarify life goals and establish a new identity. This is the stage in which someone finds themselves, so to speak.

We've all heard somebody, especially a teen, say, "I'm trying to find myself." If they don't, the result is what Erickson called "Role confusion." Exam hint, some tests will use Erickson's term psychosocial moratorium to describe an adolescent who experiments with roles in the quest to understand their true identity.

Adolescents go through an **Egocentrism stage**, like the one described by Piaget. Here the adolescent is overly concerned about themself and may exhibit excessive self-introspection. The adolescent can also feel invincible. In general, adolescents have more emotional difficulties than preschool and preadolescent children.

Stage six, Intimacy versus Isolation, from ages 18 to 35, young adult years. Intimacy and love become the major issues.

When the individual can't achieve this, the person feels that there is no one else to rely on or depend on. This generates feelings of alienation and isolation.

Stage seven, Generativity versus Stagnation, from ages 30 to about 35 to approximately 60; these are the middle adult years. Here is where the person experiences the **midlife crisis**. Generativity means caring about others, for example, your immediate family or even future generations.

The individual who cannot achieve this stagnates and becomes self-centered. In older textbooks, this stage may be referred to as "Generativity versus Self-absorption."

Stage eight, Integrity versus Despair from the ages 60 and beyond the late adult years. This is the final stage. If the person can't look back on their life without major regret then despair or resentment would manifest itself.

Remember, to successfully complete this stage, the person would need to have successfully completed all the previous stages. By the way, Erickson did landmark work in a field that we call psychohistory.

In other words, he used psychoanalysis to analyze great figures such as **Martin Luther** (a seminal figure in the Protestant Reformation) and **Mahatma Gandhi** (an Indian lawyer who advocated non-violent protest methods to create political and social change). Erikson was a well-rounded scholar, and he spent a lot of time discussing the American Indians' (now called Native Americans) child-rearing practices.

Criticisms of Erik Erikson's Eight-Stage Theory of Psychosocial Development

1. The theory puts more emphasis on infancy and childhood than adulthood.
2. Seems to put more emphasis on boys/men than on girls/women.
3. Some experts reject the notion a person must complete one stage/crisis before going on to another, although Erikson claimed he was misunderstood in this respect. Life is not necessarily like a prerequisite for a course in an educational institution! Also, an individual can often tackle several conflicts simultaneously.
4. Supports the Freudian notion that the sexes differ because of biology.

5. Hard to know if findings of his regarding Ghandhi or Martin Luther would apply to everybody else.
6. Theory is not necessarily applicable to other cultures. Little emphasis is placed on social and cultural factors.
7. Did not emphasize biological influences and genetics in regard to development.

Another name to know in cognitive development is **William G. Perry (1913–1998)**. In his 1970 book (updated in 1998), *Forms of Intellectual and Ethical Development in the College Years: A Scheme*, he asserts that young adults, particularly college students, think differently than adolescents.

Perry's theory takes off and continues where Piaget's stops. Perry's latest research delineates **four levels with nine positions**.

The first level is known as **dualism**. Authorities are either right or wrong. This is absolutist thinking: "an expert will know the answer."

The next stage is **multiplicity**. The person acknowledges multiple viewpoints but lacks the ability to really evaluate these viewpoints, especially if they're contradictory.

The next stage is **relativism**. The individual understands that all knowledge is relative and there are many ways to perceive reality.

In the final stage, dubbed **commitment to relativism**, the person decides how to view the world while realizing that new information may cause them to modify their choices. Perry incidentally did not set age brackets for the levels and stages.

I must also mention the work of the US psychologist **Daniel J. Levinson (1920–1994)** from his book, *The Seasons of a Man's Life*, first written in 1985. Levinson, as you may recall, postulated the **midlife transition** (similar to Erickson's midlife crisis) that occurs in the midlife transition period at ages 40 to 45.

Here, the man seriously questions his life in general and his career path. Many experts feel that Levinson has misled us since a lot of men do not experience this crisis. **Levinson postulates four eras of a man's life**.

One, childhood and adolescence; two, early adult transition; three, the midlife transition; and four, late adulthood. Levinson mentions that the eras apply to different cultures, and thus, they are seemingly universal.

He suggests that the transitions are caused by social and biological factors. Gail Sheehy's well-known 1976 book *Passages* drew heavily on Levinson's work. Finally, you might find it interesting that in 1996, Levinson wrote *The Seasons of a Woman's Life*, but counselors never embraced it the way they did his earlier book about men.

All right, you knew **Sigmund Freud's (1856–1939)** name would pop up sooner or later. Here it is. I'll keep the discussion short because Freud's name will come up again and again in the section on counseling theories since, whether you like him or not, he is the number one figure in the entire history of psychology.

His contribution to developmental psychology, well, it's his psychosexual stages, of course. **Now, remember, Erikson's eight-stage theory is psychosocial. Freud's five stages are psychosexual**.

Freud's dynamic psychosexual stages are the oral stage, birth to one year; the anal stage, approximately ages one to three; the phallic stage, ages three to six years; the latency period, approximately ages 6 to 12; and the genital stage, age 12 and beyond.

Exam hint, unlike Erikson, Freud's stages do not truly cover the entire life span. Moreover, the stages focus on the libido, our sex energy from the id, as it relates to a different part of the body. When the person does not overcome a conflict at any stage, the person becomes **fixated** at a given stage.

Let's start with **the oral stage, from birth to one year**. The child is occupied with sucking in the mouth because hunger cessation is the child's number one source of pleasure. The mouth is the erogenous zone. Oral fixations like smoking, overeating, and even drinking excessively are said to have their roots in this stage.

The oral personality is said to be clinging and passive dependent. For example, a person who is addicted to television is said to be an oral character. The oral stage sets the brand or prototype for future love relationships. Remember that deprivation of oral gratification leads to fixation.

The second stage is the anal stage, from age one to three. This is the period of toilet training and sphincter control. The anus is the erogenous zone. If the parents are too punitive or too indulgent not punitive enough, then conflicts will be manifested.

Anal-retentive characters are said to be compulsive; unusually neat; frugal, or what most of us would call stingy, if you want to be direct about it; and obstinate. They hoard things, they're very orderly, and they're condescending toward others. Perhaps you know somebody like this.

On the opposite side of the coin, we have the anal-expulsive character who has a messy desk at work and unclean house and is not well organized. Some people may see this person as scatterbrained and impulsive, and oh, yes, such persons are usually very generous and have poor handwriting.

The next stage is the phallic stage, from ages three to six. This is a stage where the child has an interest in his or her own genitalia and that of others. This is a stage where the famous Oedipus complex occurs. Now, let me give you a wonderful hint.

If you want to remember that **the Oedipus complex occurs in the phallic stage**, just remember that Oedipus has a P and phallic stage is the only Freudian stage with a P.

Freud borrowed the term Oedipus from the Greek tragedy in which Oedipus unknowingly kills his father and marries his mother. In this stage, unconscious incestuous desires toward the parent of the opposite sex are characteristic.

The little boy wants all his mom's attention and would like to see dad out of the picture. He wonders how babies are made and he wants hugs from his mom. He may try to sleep with her. He does whatever he can to get to her attention.

Again, this is done unconsciously. He's not aware of any of these motivating factors. The male child fears that his dad will castrate him. This is what we call a castration complex. He may even notice that girls have no penis. This creates castration anxiety.

To resolve this anxiety, he represses his desire for his mom and identifies with his dad. In women, Freud speaks of the **Electra complex**, which is analogous to the Oedipus complex. The girl supposedly develops negative feelings toward her mom when she discovers she lacks a penis, or what Freud termed **penis envy**.

This, of course, is analogous or parallel to the little boy's castration anxiety. The little girl wants to beat mom for dad's attention, but when she realizes she can't, she identifies with the aggressor (mom) to resolve the conflict.

If your exam asks: What is the most controversial part of Freud's theory? You probably already guessed it. The answer is the Oedipus/Electra complex.

Now, we move on to the **latency stage, from ages 6 to 12**. In this stage, sexual urges are repressed. **This is the only stage which is truly nonsexual**. Children will turn their attention to school, hobbies, or sports. There's a heavy emphasis on developing friends of the same sex.

The latency stage is asexual and is said to be social, again unlike the other stages. **The final stage is the genital stage, from ages 12 to adulthood.** The last stage begins with puberty, and you remain in it for life. Boys now feel it's OK and not icky to notice girls, and both sexes become interested in the opposite sex. As you may have guessed, Freud has been criticized for having a theory that assumes everybody should be heterosexual and does not include other sexual orientations.

The individual becomes less narcissistic, less self-centered, and more interested in others. For the record, many scholars find it very difficult to agree with Freud's position that the last stage takes place in adolescence.

Some final Freudian terminology and then we'll move on. When you read about Freud, you'll run into the word **libido**, which is the psychic energy behind the biological drives, primarily sexual. You will also see the word **Eros**. This is the god of love from Greek mythology, and to Freud, Eros signified self-preservation.

He also spoke of a weaker power, **Thanatos**, the self-destructive or death wish. Simply put, Eros is the life instinct, Thanatos the death instinct.

Criticisms of Freud's five-stage psychosexual developmental theory:

I once had a statistics professor who summed it up nicely. "If you want to create a theory which stands the test of time, create one like Freud's which is scientifically untestable." Try creating a study to verify libidinal urges in very young children. The theory is slanted toward sexuality and not social influences.

He did not take cultural background into consideration, and therefore the theory may not be applicable to various cultures.

The noted analyst **Karen Horney (1885–1952)** felt Freud's theory was degrading to women, and lots of experts have suggested his theory puts too much emphasis on males.

Scholars also assert his focus was on heterosexual outcomes as being the norm, with no discussion of other sexual orientations.

Some more important material in this area of the exam: you should be familiar with studies on maternal stimulation.

The name that is often mentioned with mother–child interaction would be the famous Harlow studies, which relate to infant monkeys that were separated from their mothers at birth.

Harry Harlow (1905–1981), a well-known American psychologist, provided young monkeys with two substitute or surrogate mothers. One was created using bare wire. The other was a very soft terrycloth-covered surrogate mother. The research conclusively demonstrated that when infant monkeys had a choice of the wire mother or the terrycloth mother, they preferred the cloth mother.

Over a 25-day period, the infant spent an average of over 12 hours a day with the terrycloth mother, yet, they spent almost no time with the wire substitutes. By attaching a milk bottle to the two models, he found that feeding or food giving is not enough to create a successful mother child bond.

In fact, outside of feeding time, the infant monkeys chose the terrycloth surrogates. The bottom line is that tactile stimulation such as touching and hugging are very important in the mother–child bond.

In fact, other studies of monkeys where monkeys were deprived of a real mother or a surrogate for the first eight months or so revealed that monkeys were unable to bond with the mother figure at all after that.

Moreover, the monkeys that were not able to have a mother in the first eight months tended to isolate themselves from other monkeys. In humans, you may see the term **anaclitic depression**, coined by analyst **René Spitz (1887–1974)**, which refers to infants who were separated from their mothers for an extended period.

Such children are initially very sad and weepy, but after about three months, the pattern changes and they begin to have frozen, emotionless faces and kind of a faraway stare. Spitz even discovered that institutionalized children who received less caretaker interaction than normal often experienced retarded physical growth as well as mental growth.

On this section of the exam, you may also be confronted with the word **instinct**, which simply means an inborn behavior. Instincts can also be called **species-specific behavior**.

There is also a fine chance you will come across the term **fixed action pattern, or FAP**. Fixed action patterns are ritualistic behaviors that are characteristic of the species, and they are elicited by what is known as a **sign stimulus, also known as a releaser**. Although FAPs are more common in the lower species, some researchers would say that humans have FAPs that are elicited by sign stimulus . . . although the examples in humans are not perfect.

It has been said that half the battle in doing well on advanced counseling exams is just knowing the terminology! So true.

For example, when an infant sucks with their lips, the lips are pressed together, and this could be an example of a FAP elicited by a sign stimulus such as a baby bottle with a nipple. Most infants will grab an object such as a rope or even somebody else's hair if given the chance. People often yawn when they see others yawn and routinely face the door when standing in an elevator. Scientists and developmental researchers are split on whether the examples I have given are pure FAPs in response to a sign stimulus.

Another big name that comes up in this area is that of a European naturalist or ethologist – and ethology means the study of animals in their natural setting – and that name is **Konrad Lorenz (1903–1989)**.

It is difficult to open a child development book without seeing a picture of young ducklings following Konrad Lorenz around. He is known for making us aware of a concept that is known as **imprinting** in small ducklings.

The ducklings will follow or attach themselves to the first moving object they see. This could be a mother or a substitute for a mother such as a light bulb, or you'll see them following Konrad Lorenz around.

What's important about imprinting that applies to human beings?

Lorenz put us in touch with a concept we call a **critical period**. A critical period is kind of a now-or-never time. **Imprinting must take place in a certain time or doesn't take place at all. Many people, though, would say in child development, we have the same thing**.

There are biological critical periods in a child's life. The child bonds in these periods or learns certain things, and it can never again be learned in life if it doesn't happen within the critical period.

Another name that you could come across on this part of the test is the British psychologist **John Bowlby (1907–1990)**. John Bowlby did a lot of work on attachment and bonding. You can remember that Bowlby starts with a B, and so does bonding. Bowlby felt that bonding with the maternal figure is imperative for good mental health and that poor bonding leads to psychopathology.

Another thing you might want to keep in mind for this part of the exam is that birth order questions often pop up on comprehensive exams. According to most of the research, these findings are not set in stone. Some people don't agree with the concepts of birth order, but what I'm about to say, for the most part, most experts do agree with.

Firstborn children excel the most. They're the most likely to attend college and engage in scholarly behaviors, though they are usually not as sociable as later children. Firstborn children are very conservative, but overall, they are thought to have an advantage over their peers and over their siblings.

Middle-born children are sociable yet not as family oriented as their siblings. May feel overshadowed and have a negative view of their childhood.

Only children, like firstborn children, also have problems feeling close to their peers. In terms of self-esteem, it is highest in the only child. Generally, the firstborn child has a higher IQ, and the second child has a little lower, the third a little lower, and so on and so forth.

Of course, if you're number five or six in the family, I've got this uncanny suspicion that *you* are the exception to the rule!

Another name that comes to mind in this area is American psychiatrist **Harry Stack Sullivan (1892–1949)**. Sullivan, unlike Freud, although he was analytic, based his theory on observable human interactions, or the so-called interpersonal theory of psychiatry.

According to Sullivan's interpersonal theory, a child preserves euphoria by following parental sanctions and standards. This is personified as what he termed **"Good me."** Parental punishment becomes personified as **"The bad me."** Sometimes this is characterized by the anxiety-ridden, or repressed, **"Not me."**

Sullivan says children initially have **prototaxic thinking**. That is to say, the child does not see themself as separate from the environment. Next, the child's thinking becomes **parataxic or serial thinking**. For example, the dog barks and it begins raining. The child believes that the barking caused the rain. In **parataxic distortion, a defense mechanism**, feelings may be tied to negative events or people. A typical scenario would be a client who is afraid of his mother.

Later the client acquires a supervisor who has similar physical traits and now feels a sense of fear.

Sullivan calls the last stage of thinking **syntaxic, which is logical or rational thinking.** Sullivan feels that remnants of prototaxic and parataxic thinking get in the way of everybody's ability to think rationally. This, of course, causes some behavioral difficulties.

In Sullivan's theory, interpersonal relationships are said to be more important than infantile sexuality. The strict Freudians don't agree with this. Let me give you a hint here. Sullivan is the major figure in what your exam may refer to as the **Dynamic Cultural School of Analysis**.

OK, get up and stretch. You deserve it, you know it. Did you stretch? Great. Let me give you a brief review of other important points that you could come across on an exam regarding human growth and development.

Here's some key factors. Number one, developmental psychology is basically the study of psychic or mental changes, which take place over the life span. Theorists ultimately wish to describe development, explain it, and predict how the person will develop.

Number two, a key issue in this area of the exam, will probably always be the **nature versus nurture debate**. In other words, is it heredity and nature that determine development, or is it the environment, which is nurture?

Number three, theories and theorists are often known as empirical theories, and researchers who believe in empirical theories are what we call **empiricists**. Again, we call these people who believe in empirical theory empiricists. **Empiricists insist that changes can be measured** quantitatively. We can look at the quantity of behavior. That's the empiricist theory.

Then we have organismic theorists, who believe that changes are qualitative. The organismic viewpoint is more theoretical. Piaget, for example, has been categorized as the major proponent of the organismic approach.

Number four, there are three basic approaches to human development. First, the behaviorists, which I'll cover in detail in another section of this book. This is an empiricist view. There is also the **maturational view**, where the behavior is age related and the mind is seen like a growing tree or bush. The maturing of the mind is viewed as somewhat genetic and predetermined.

Then there is structuralism, or the structuralist viewpoint. Structuralists believe heavily in interaction with the environment. Maturationism and structuralism are organismic approaches, while the behaviorists' approach is an empiricist view. You may also run across the word **nativism,** which means knowledge is innate. **Innate implies that the behavior is inborn and present at birth**.

Number five, be familiar with the term **heritability or heritability estimate**. This is simply a fancy 25-cent term that refers to how much genetic factors influence mental or physical characteristics, or how much of a condition can be attributed to heredity.

Finally, number six. Be familiar with **Lev Vygotsky (1896–1934)**. Vygotsky was born in Belarus and created a social development theory of learning in which he postulated that social interactions greatly influence development. He was also convinced that thought and language cannot exist without each other.

Nevertheless, when most counselors and educators think of Vygotsky, they usually think of his concept dubbed **the zone of proximal development, or ZPD. The ZPD refers to the differences or difference between what a child can do on their own versus what they can accomplish with help or assistance. The concept of scaffolding, coined by the US psychologist Jerome Bruner (1915–2016), is often used in conjunction with Vygotsky's work and refers to what a child can achieve with the assistance of others.** This analogy makes sense, since in engineering a scaffold refers to a temporary structure used to elevate a cleaning or construction crew.

For example, what the child can do with assistance from a parent, a teacher, or a more advanced student, and what the child can do on their own. To repeat: What the child can do with help versus what the individual can do on their own without help. Vygotsky insisted that learning occurs in this zone.

Although it is less apt to be on your exam **Vygotsky posited three stages of speech**. 1. **External, also known as social speech, occurs from birth to three years of age**. This includes crying, laughing, or even shouting to convey feelings and needs. "I want my toy" would also be an example. The focus is on emotions and uncomplicated thoughts. 2. **Egocentric, from three to seven**. The talk is about the self and often occurs even if nobody is listening. 3. **Inner speech, ages seven and beyond, or "silent talk," without talking aloud such as counting in one's head**.

Another likely candidate for exam questions in this area or the theories portion of the exam is **Information Processing theory, also known as the Information Processing model**. This paradigm, derived from cognitive psychology, views the mind like a computer processing system. Unlike behaviorism, the individual is not seen as a passive learner. Learning is constructed by the learner and people are selective about what they learn. Learning is active either in the cognitive or the physical sense, and prior beliefs impact the process.

We all have selective attention and tune out unimportant information such as when you are at a sporting event or a play and not listening carefully to the folks attending the event.

The senses amass information in **the sensory memory (approximately four seconds or less!**). When memories are created from visual stimuli, we call them visual, and when they are the result of **auditory input or based on hearing, we call them echoic**. Next, we have the short-term working memory, or STM (about 15 to 30 seconds). This material is then encoded into **long-term memory, or LTM, which can hold memories forever**. To retrieve learning, it must be transferred back from the LTM to the STM. When something cannot be recalled it is designated as **retrieval failure**.

In this theory your STM is like a computer processor – and will hold about seven digits; think a phone number without an needing to memorize an area code – and your LTM is similar to a hard drive.

A Critique of Information Processing theory on the head of a pin

The key issue is that the computer metaphor may not be valid, hence invalidating much of the model. As behaviorists point out: since we can't directly observe every action of the human mind, a computer or computer processor may *not* work like the human mind! If this is the case, then stages in the theory, the terminology (say LTM, STM, etc.), flow-charts, and so on are not realistic.

Childhood Milestones

I also want to mention some landmarks or milestones of development that are sometimes mentioned on exams. First, there is the **smile response at six weeks**, then the **stranger response or stranger anxiety that occurs at about seven months. At approximately 15 months of age, the child learns to walk alone**.

Then there is the child's notion of their own **gender identity that occurs at approximately the age of three or four**. Then **at**

ages six to nine, the child learns to see death as an irreversible process.

I want to leave you with one last concept. Before, we talked about psychoanalytic development, and we talked about Freud's model. There's been an update of that theory, proposed by **Margaret Mahler** (1897–1985), an Austrian American psychiatrist and psychoanalyst. This particular conceptualization concerns the infant and their mother.

In the first few weeks of life, it is said that babies are driven by primitive needs like eating and sleeping. This stage is called **normal autism**, since the child is unaware that anyone else exists. Then the child enters a period of **symbiosis,** at approximately two months. Here, the opposite is true. That is to say, the child feels like they are part of the mother, kind of a fusion, if you will.

This fusion is the foundation that will later result in independence. Strictly speaking, the word **symbiosis implies that two individuals cannot exist without each other**.

From five months until about age three, according to Mahler's theory, the child is in the **separation individuation period**. Here, the child develops their own unique self, which is separate from the caretaker. **Your exam could refer to this separate identity as the differentiation process**.

Mahler refers to this process as the psychological birth, where the baby breaks out of the protective membrane. In this stage, the baby will crawl away from the mother, yet look back frequently. There is ambivalence for this child regarding separation and independence.

Strictly speaking, the alternating feelings of closeness combined with the need for distance are known as rapprochement. Again, alternating feelings of closeness combined with the need for distance are termed rapprochement.

The perfect or ideal mother will allow comfort and reassurance, which allow the child some independence. According to this theory, the first six months can serve as a breeding ground for later psychopathology.

All right, now we are going to move on to another topic. Take a break and have a super day.

4

Master Lecture 3: Social and Cultural Diversity

> ***Key reminder before we get started!*** *Terminology and politically correct language in this area of study changes at warp speed. What is appropriate as I am writing this could be obsolete by the time you read these words. I thus suggest you check the latest counseling publications such as ACA's Counseling Today and relevant journals prior to the exam.*

Hi, this is Dr. Howard Rosenthal right back at you. We're going to unpack social and cultural diversity. But first, I want to say something. Perhaps you're sitting there saying, "I didn't understand this explanation" or "I didn't understand that explanation."

You will find that in different parts of my materials there is repetition and review. If you didn't understand it at one point, you'll get it the next time around, maybe when I explain it in a totally different manner. Also, in my *Encyclopedia of Counseling* text I often intentionally explain various principles, terms, concepts, and theories in a way that's a little bit different than I have done in this book. I may additionally describe a concept in yet another way in my *Human Services Dictionary*. Hence you may discover that the alternative explanation will make more sense to you. It also means that if you see a

DOI: 10.4324/9781003149712-4

concept or a theory on the actual exam illuminated in a different way, it won't throw you for a loop. Therefore, it should come as no surprise that I always recommend combining this book with the *Encyclopedia* and my *Dictionary* for the ultimate prep package.

Often, I get a chuckle out of my reader's response to my alternative explanations. The other day I received an email from a counselor in training who quoted me from two different works of mine where I described a statistical concept. The reader said and I quote, "Okay, Dr. Rosenthal, your definitions were different in each book. Which is it?"

Imagine this counselor's surprise when I wrote back and began by writing, "Both of them."

With that little gem of wisdom let's take a deep dive, as the saying goes, and swing into action!

Now I'd like to talk about social and cultural diversity, originally referred to as social and cultural foundations, which is one of the major areas that you'll find on virtually all comprehensive counseling and certification exams. The major topic in this area is multicultural counseling, which many experts believe grew out of the civil rights movement and the minority movements for equality in the '60s and '70s.

Perhaps, the first famous counselor to deal with multicultural counseling issues was **Frank Parsons (1854–1908)**, who is billed as the father of guidance. Parsons, way back in 1908, began looking at cultural forces and their impact on adolescents who would be entering the workforce.

Multiculturalism (often considered the fourth force in psychology) describes a society in which people from many different cultures live together. **Multicultural counseling refers to the way we do psychotherapy in a multicultural society**. Unlike other models and approaches to counseling, multicultural counseling, or cross-cultural counseling as it is called in earlier literature, is not a type of counseling used for one type of client or presenting problem. Our world is becoming increasingly global and increasingly diverse – did you know that estimates suggest that the **United States will become a "white minority" nation by 2045** – which means we as counseling professionals are almost always engaging in multicultural counseling.

Multicultural counseling (you may also hear counselors call the process intercultural counseling) is simply counseling

or therapy conducted where the counselor and client have different cultures. Therefore, I suggest that almost every encounter a counselor has will be a multicultural experience. The chances of you working with only clients who have the exact same sociocultural background as you are at the tail end of a bell curve (you'll remember that the "tails" of the bell curve contain the least statistically likely occurrences).

Sometimes when we think of sociocultural identity or diversity, we gravitate towards the assumption that we are talking about race. However, identity encompasses much more than one's race. Identity can include one's age, race, ability status, ethnicity, language spoken, religion or spirituality, geographic location, gender, sexual orientation, social status, **socioeconomic status** (also "SES," which refers to a person's income and economic mobility), and so much more. **Pamela A. Hays offers the acronym ADDRESSING as a way to capture cultural "influences." The acronym stands for age and generational influences, developmental or other disabilities (both "Ds"), religion and spiritual orientation, ethnic and racial identity, socioeconomic status, sexual orientation, indigenous heritage, national origin, and gender**.

Identity includes personal aspects (self-defined characteristics) and social aspects (those characteristics which are shaped by relationships and the environment). To complicate things a bit further, aspects of our identity may be more salient (noticeable or important) in specific contexts. In addition, identity is considered more dynamic (changing, fluid) than static.

All this is to say, even if you were to try to work with only people who share a similar sociocultural identity, it would likely be impossible.

Let's do a few more definitions while we are at it. **Diversity is a state of difference and variety**. People are diverse in a variety of aspects, including age, race, ethnicity, religious beliefs, and even opinions. **Minority is at its base definition the smaller part or number**. In terms of culture, when we talk about a minority group, we are often talking about the group with less social privilege. Even groups with a great number may have less social privilege. Social privilege, or more simply privilege, describes the advantages and benefits a person has. These advantages are often unearned and based on the group a person belongs to, which is symbolized in **Peggy McIntosh's "invisible knapsack."**

In the case of white privilege, McIntosh suggests an invisible knapsack might include times such as: when seeking medical or legal assistance, my race won't be a disadvantage. Or it is relatively easy to find neighborhoods where I will be accepted and my neighbors won't be adversarial. If a law enforcement officer pulls me over I can be reasonably sure it was not because of my race.

Culture encompasses the shared values, behaviors, customs, arts, symbols, language, achievements, and so on of a group of people. Often culture is passed down between generations. Like identity, we work from an understanding that culture is also dynamic and evolving over time. **Subculture is a section of a group of people within a larger culture**. A very simple example would be the subgroup of rock and roll fans among the group of all music lovers. **Some describe culture in terms of regional, national, ecological, and universal culture**.

Regional and national culture is likely pretty obvious to you. One example is how you cheer for your local sports team or feel pride when athletes from your country succeed in the Olympics. Another example is how people sometimes describe cultures as **collectivistic**. In collectivistic cultures, group harmony is prioritized over autonomy. People from collectivistic cultures may also be described as allocentric (roughly the opposite of egocentric) or interdependent. In contrast, people from individualistic cultures may prioritize the needs of the individual over those of the group. People from individualistic cultures may be described as **idiocentric** (i.e., interest in the self over others) or **independent**.

What about **ecological culture**? Does our physical environment really help define our culture?

Absolutely. Appropriate clothing and housing would look very different for someone living near the equator, for example, than for somebody living in a community at the North Pole. Where we live certainly does have an impact on our behavior. When I think of ecological culture, I always think of my acquaintances who live up north, telling me that people from the Midwest (um that would be me!) and the South don't know how to drive when it snows or how to prepare.

This concept is called **personalism**. Personalism states that we must all adjust to the natural environment, and therefore, culture is indeed molded by geological and geographic factors.

How do people develop a culture? Albert Bandura's (1921–2021) social learning theory (SLT) provides one explanation. Social learning theory posits that people learn by watching and mimicking the behaviors of other people. **The behaviors which are expected by the group can be called norms**. In the case of culture, this would look like some people in a counseling group modeling a desirable action, except on a much larger scale. **Culture is passed down through observational learning and reinforcement of successive desirable action**.

In my culture, adults often modeled the desirable behavior that I should call people in authority "ma'am" or "sir." I was often scolded when I would forget to use "ma'am" or "sir." Additionally, this behavior was reinforced when others would comment how polite I was when using these honorifics. As you can imagine, as "ma'am" and "sir" have fallen out of common use, I had to adapt. Some multicultural experts insist these labels assume you know the gender of others. But this is also a great example of how cultures change over time.

Sometimes social learning theory supports the transmission of positive aspects of culture. Unfortunately, negative and harmful behaviors can be modeled too. Someone can likewise be reinforced in their use of slurs and discriminatory behavior. Fortunately, just as I adapted to changing ways, others can similarly adapt to engage in more prosocial behavior.

There are also different proposed models of identity development. Let's look at two of these models as they relate to racial identity development.

The Racial/Cultural Identity Development model describes identity development in five stages. In **the first stage, conformity**, a person prefers the **dominant (sometimes called microculture)** culture. For people who are not part of the dominant culture, they may experience dislike or devaluing of their own culture (more likely for people in the **microculture**).

In **the second stage, dissonance**, a person may gain an awareness of and begin to question beliefs about their own identity. They may start to question previous views of the dominant culture as the ideal.

In **the third stage, resistance and immersion**, the person may begin to reject the dominant culture and develop a stronger preference for their own culture. At this point, a person may experience significant and challenging feelings, including disillusionment.

In **the fourth stage, introspection**, the person may be more open to exploring the consequences of holding strong feelings against the dominant culture. They may begin to focus more internally on their own culture and take a more balanced approach to understanding that no culture is all bad or all good.

In **integrative the fifth stage awareness**, the person is more confident and secure in their own identity and works to move beyond their own identity towards multiculturalism. The individual has pride in their own cultural and racial heritage. Racism is viewed as an illness.

A similar model exists specifically for white people. The **White Racial Identity Development** model begins with **naivete**. In this stage, a white person may have little awareness of race or little contact with people from different racial groups.

In **the conformity stage**, the white person may not view themselves as having a racial identity. They may believe in a more universal culture or believe that white culture is justifiably superior.

The dissonance stage occurs when an experience allows for greater awareness of culture and oppression (unjust treatment). The white person may begin to question their views and feel painful emotions related to past views or behaviors.

During **resistance and immersion**, the white person examines racism and oppression. This increased awareness can lead to additional feelings of anger and guilt.

In **introspection,** the white person may begin to redefine their view of whiteness and feel disconnected from other definitions of whiteness. Appreciation of diversity and personal racial identity is increased during integrative awareness. Finally, the white person moves to a place of dedication to antiracist action.

There are additional models for both minority and majority people as well as biracial/multiracial people. Identity development occurs for other aspects of culture as well. For example, there is a model for the identity development of gay and lesbian people.

Moving right along, **acculturation, enculturation**, and **encapsulation** sound incredibly similar, so let's have a glance at these three terms. **Acculturation is the process of learning the customs and expectations of a culture**. It is often used to describe the process by which a person adapts, or assimilates, within a new culture.

Assimilation is often viewed as people of a different culture being absorbed into the majority culture while giving up the norms of their own culture. **Enculturation** is similar and can be defined as the acquisition of cultural norms of one's own culture. When someone is first navigating a new culture, it can lead to a feeling of culture shock. When a culture keeps its own cultural practices while incorporating elements of the dominant culture, we refer to this phenomenon as **cultural pluralism**.

Cultural encapsulation is the lack of awareness and understanding of another's culture and its significance. **Gilbert Wrenn's (1902–2001)** classic *Counselor in a Changing World*, first released in 1962, helped popularize the notion of the culturally encapsulated counselor. This is precisely what we *don't* want to see in a helper!

Although you likely already understand the importance of multicultural counseling, the codes of ethics highlight it. **Cultural competence** isn't always clearly defined but, in general, describes the ways (behaviors, skills, practices) in which we effectively work with people from a culture different than our own. I've heard experts refer to cultural competence as the opposite of cultural encapsulation. Thus, becoming a counselor with cultural competence requires us to not only learn about the cultures of others but also to explore our own culture.

Some in the field have suggested a shift towards **cultural humility**, which places a greater focus on self-evaluation, learning from others, and a commitment to lifelong learning, would prove superior to cultural competence. One argument is that cultural competence suggests a focus on mastery and completion, whereas cultural humility focuses on interpersonal aspects and learning. Others argue further that a focus on cultural competence is actually antithetical and constitutes a "new racism." To address these concerns, **Josepha Campinha-Bacote** has suggested a blending of the two, or what is called **cultural competimility (a word formed by cultural competence and cultural humility)**, which focuses on "the synergistic process . . . in which cultural humility permeates . . . components of cultural competence." And yes, that one doesn't quite roll off the tongue like some other concepts in this book!

So, what happens when we practice in a **culturally incompetent** manner? Besides failing our ethical obligations, we risk alienating and, at worst, discriminating against our clients. Which, as you might have guessed, is not therapeutic. And, on a larger scale, we end up with some groups who unjustly bear the brunt of the burden of mental illness. For example, although rates of mental illness among African Americans is similar to the general population, disparities in care exist in terms of access to care, access to appropriate care, appropriate diagnosis, and engagement with providers who communicate in patient-centered ways.

Discrimination, in terms of social behavior, is evident when people are treated differently because of one or more of their identities. Discrimination is often rooted in biases and stereotypes and leads to prejudiced behavior. Bias, or biases, describes attitudes we hold based on stereotypes or generalizations. Bias and stereotyping, in the context of human nature, can be explained.

For some of the same reasons most of us care what people think of us, we often develop a preference for our reference group. **A reference group** is a term used in sociology to describe the collection of people to which we belong (or aspire to belong) against which we compare ourselves. While we often compare and contrast on an **intergroup level**, that is, among groups as a whole, there are also differences at the **intragroup level** (within a single group).

Intragroup differences can be explained by intersectionality. Intersectionality describes the way that social categorizations intersect and interact to create nuanced experiences. This term was considered first coined by civil rights advocate **Kimberlé Crenshaw (1959–)**. Intersectionality also helps describe the complexity of systems of oppression. For example, among all Black people, a wealthy Black man may have a uniquely different experience than a poor Black woman who has a disability.

Our family, culture, and society also shape our worldview. **Worldview can be defined as one's conceptualization of life**. For example, we sometimes hear how people view the "glass as half full" while others view the "glass as half empty." When our worldview includes harmful beliefs about people different than us, we may externalize that harm in the forms of discrimination or **microaggressions**.

What are microaggressions, you ask? **Microaggressions are subtle, everyday messages that insult someone. Microaggressions may even be subconscious or not easily identified as**

harmful. For example, a white person suddenly crossing the street or holding a bag more tightly and closer to their body when a person of color is near exemplifies a type of microaggression. This isn't only related to race. Another example cited in various sources is assuming that a nurse is female and a doctor is male. Hence a patient sees a female in a health care setting and says, "Nurse, can you help me?" **Microaggressions could be described as a form of covert discrimination, discrimination that is subtle or disguised**. Covert discrimination can be just as insidious as overt, public, or obvious, forms of discrimination.

On a larger scale, this harm may show up in the form of institutional (sometimes systemic or structural) **isms**. Ism (and its plural form, isms) is now a word with a definition. Specifically, when we are talking about isms, we are talking about distinct practices, ideologies, and so on. In discussions of multicultural counseling, isms more specifically talk about harmful ideologies held against "minority" groups. Some examples would be ageism, heterosexism, racism, ableism, sizeism, colorism. When the ideology, the ism if you will, is built into the laws of a society or organization, we have the **institutionalized isms**.

One potential impact of institutionalized isms and covert discrimination is **internalization. Internalized oppression happens when, over a period of time of being stereotyped and oppressed, people who are in the oppressed group start to use this framework internally**. This can look like people of color holding and perpetuating stereotypes and discrimination against other people of color. One example is when Black people view "whiteness" as the ideal and encourage others to approximate whiteness. When bias and discrimination are accepted as the norm or fact, people harmed by this ideology can take on that view of themselves and their group. Let's look at another example of this.

One commonly held stereotype in the United States is that girls are bad at math. In one study, researchers gave both men and women a group of difficult math questions. One group of participants was asked to predict how women would do on the task. This question was viewed as a way to prime, or bring to mind, the stereotype that women are bad at math. The result was women performing worse and having increased anxiety when the stereotype was primed. This is referred to as a **stereotype threat**. So, before you take the test, remember, people of all genders can and do perform well on a variety of tasks and tests (including math). **Internalized oppression can lead to many negative consequences including poor self-concept, mental distress, and depression**.

Of note, we must consider the impact of **a self-fulfilling prophecy perpetuated by the environment**. When we live in a society that doubts the ability of women in math, are we more likely to encourage women to pursue math or are we more likely to accept that math just isn't the field for women? **This systemic level of embedded stereotypes and discrimination can be called institutionalization**.

One good example of this as it relates to **institutionalized racism is redlining**. You may have heard about redlining, but let's look at why this is an example of institutionalized racism. Redlining is a process where a group divides a map based on "risk," where "high risk" areas are lined in red. In "red" areas, people typically have lower access to tools for successful homeownership, such as mortgage refinancing. Unfortunately, this practice often led to communities of color, especially Black communities, to have fewer pathways to homeownership. This built-in form of inequality has led to ripples of inequality in areas even outside of homeownership, such as higher rates of stroke and preterm labor (resulting in early or premature child birth) to this day.

Stereotyping, discrimination, oppression. These aren't things that support us living our best lives, so why do they still exist? There are many explanations. One explanation is **in-group bias. In-group bias is a tendency to prefer people of one's own group over people outside of the group or other groups in general. Another related term is ethnocentrism, which describes a tendency to view one's cultural group as correct and the best**.

Biologically and socially, our tendency to prefer people in our own group makes sense. Historically, people have relied on their groups for things like nourishment, protection, healing, and support. Family is a smaller scale version of an in-group. Additionally, we still see animal groups who live in packs, herds, and flocks for survival. Some research even suggests that this can be explained on an evolutionary and genetic basis. In that way, we are wired to prefer our groups. However, these preferences can lead to prejudices towards other groups. **Prejudice is a preconceived notion (often negative) held about another group, sometimes without even interacting with the group**.

But research also tells us that many of these groupings are actually arbitrary. In other words, some of our groups are socially constructed. We, as a society, create dividing lines where there isn't really a significant difference. This includes things like concepts of gender and gender roles, though you've mostly likely heard this in conversations about race. Historically, people attempted to find scientific proof of differences among races, often called scientific racism. When people say "race is a social construct," they are explaining how, even though we divide people based on the color of their skin, there isn't any scientific reasoning (or significant differences other than the actual pigmentation) behind the divisions.

These arbitrary groupings can have very real consequences. Therefore **being "color blind" (also, culture blind) or "not seeing color" can also be harmful**. Until a time when the color of a person's skin doesn't also carry social consequences, taking a colorblind approach is dangerous. For example, for a white counselor working with a client of color, overlooking race may limit the counselor's ability to identify microaggressions or discrimination that client faces.

Our tendency to want to create groups and categories is natural. It makes things easier and allows us to make decisions more quickly. Imagine life without categories for a moment. Children spend a good part of early life categorizing. They find out a side table, a kitchen table, and a bedside table are all "tables" and things can be put on them. What if you had to decide whether the T-shirt, long-sleeved shirt, and blouse were all shirts that can be worn? We'd never get through the day. We often use it to simplify decisions about safety so we can respond quickly. Post-traumatic stress disorder or PTSD is an example of when our brains may overgeneralize a "danger" signal. But that's for another section.

Categorization is natural. It is what we do with it that can be harmful. What turns a natural tendency into a pathway to harm? Let's look at some explanations, keeping in mind that questions related to social psychology, even if they seem a little off topic, can indeed pop up on the multicultural and diversity portion of the exam.

Obedience is one explanation. Obedience is compliance with an order, often made by someone in authority. One of the commonly referenced studies on obedience is the Milgram experiment. Starting in the 1960s, **Stanley Milgram (1933–1984)** a noted US social psychology professor at Yale, ran experiments to test the power of authority on obedience. In his studies, participants were told to give an electrical shock to other participants (who were confederates, secretly working with Milgram, and not getting shocked) by a person who seemed to hold authority as the experimenter. The intensity of the shocks and the false signs of distress of the confederates increased. Unexpectedly, many participants continued sending shocks! These studies have often been used to explain how instances of genocide have been perpetrated by seemingly normal, moral people.

Just for the record, Milgram's study has been replicated even in settings outside of the college, and indeed later research indicated there really is **obedience to authority**.

Jonathon Freedman (1927–) and Scott C. Frasier (1943–) in 1966 mention another important phenomenon related to obedience. This is known as the famous **foot in the door technique**. It says that if you ask for a small request that is somewhat negative, and that request is granted, then you can go back to the person, ask for a larger request, even if it's somewhat negative.

Now, this is certainly something to keep in mind if you are doing, say, in-home child abuse investigations or something similar. If you ask, "May I come in your home?" the client is much more likely to cooperate when you tell the client you need to conduct your initial assessment.

Another study that is commonly described is the Polish American psychologist **Solomon Asch**'s **(1907–1996)** 1951 experiment on **conformity**. In this experiment, one participant was put in a room with confederates (who again, worked for Asch) and asked to identify the line that matched a sample line. Confederates indicated an incorrect answer. The results showed that when feeling pressure from the group, the participants commonly conformed at least once and chose an incorrect answer *even when they clearly knew the answer was wrong!* The research was so powerful texts and exams often refer to similar situations as an **Asch situation**. Have you ever experienced this when comparing answers for homework?

It can be extremely uncomfortable to feel outside of the group. So, when people who might not otherwise discriminate are in an environment where they feel pressure to behave in a certain way, they may just choose to conform. Interestingly, two other experimenters, **Stanley Schachter (1922–1997) and Jerome E. Singer (1934–2010),**

showed that some subjects will also mimic the emotional state of a confederate in the room.

Another explanation comes from **cognitive dissonance theory, which was created by Leon Festinger (1919–1989)**. Cognitive dissonance is the discomfort we feel when two beliefs, attitudes, or values are at odds or conflicting. Sometimes cognitive dissonance leads to positive change. When someone learns that discrimination is harmful and they view themself as a caring person, the discomfort of this conflict may lead them to stop discriminating. They adapt their existing schema to accommodate the new information.

Unfortunately, cognitive dissonance can also have negative consequences. **The forced or induced compliance effect is one path to reducing cognitive dissonance. A bully may conclude their behavior is justified for various reasons**.

So, how does culture come into play in psychotherapy? It does in many ways across the intervention process. Before a client even comes to your office, culture may come into play. Stigma and mistrust may mean a person who could benefit from therapy doesn't even show up in your office.

If they do seek services, they may experience microaggressions from staff, other clients, or even in forms or the office environment. The **transgender client** who is misgendered by front desk staff may choose not to come back. The **polyamorous client** (i.e., one who is involved in several consensual romantic or sexual relationships) may feel uncomfortable only being able to list one of their partners on intake forms. Even the term **"couples counseling"** assumes a partnership of two. Will grandma and second cousin be welcomed in a family therapy setting?

Culture is also present in assessment. Some people may view discussing certain topics with a stranger or someone in authority as inappropriate. Or, for some people, a client and counselor of different genders may not be able to work together. People from different cultures vary in terms of tone, expression of emotion, concept of time, and directness. Discussed a bit later, but even the screening and assessment tools counselors use may not be appropriate for clients from different cultures. One tool that a counselor might use to explore culture is the **culturagram, a graphic assessment tool of how culture impacts the client and the family created in 1994 by noted social worker Elaine Congress**. A culturagram is like a **genogram**, another popular pictorial tool, but the culturagram emphasizes culture in order to increase the counselor's understanding of the client and the family.

Diagnosis can also be impacted by culture. Our most-used diagnostic manuals in the United States (the DSM and the ICD) may not accurately capture symptomology as it varies across cultures. **The DSM is based primarily on research from North American and European clients**. For example, in some cultures, mental distress can present as physical symptoms (headaches, stomach pain, lethargy).

There are also some conditions that are thought to be specific to certain cultural groups. In DSM-IV these were called "culture-bound syndromes." In the DSM-IV, this was a list of disorders that had symptoms that seemed to occur in only certain areas of regions. An example is "susto," a Spanish term that describes somatic symptoms someone might experience as a result of trauma. Some conceptualize susto as relating to the soul or spirit. The DSM-5 has some changes that reflect an attempt to move towards better understanding of culture. The DSM-5 contains both a chapter on "cultural formulation" and **"cultural concepts of distress."**

Cultural concepts of distress provides more specificity than the culture bound syndrome's listing, and the DSM-5 also provides a clinical interview assessment tool for cross-cultural counseling.

Beyond this, lack of understanding of a client's culture can also lead to misdiagnosis. For example, displays of emotion may be labeled as poor affect tolerance when these displays may be very appropriate culturally. Lack of understanding or biases can also lead counselors to incorrectly diagnose a client. One such example is the misdiagnosis of schizophrenia among Black people. For example, were you aware that over **50 studies show that Black Americans are over twice as likely to be diagnosed as schizophrenic when compared to White Americans? This can have huge consequences, including the fact that an incorrect diagnosis can lead to erroneous treatment planning and intervention**.

The treatments themselves may also be inappropriate for clients from different cultures. Just as a good counselor wouldn't use **cognitive processing therapy (CPT), an evidence-based therapy often used to treat PTSD,** with a three-year-old, they should also be considering what evidence supports the use of types of therapy based on the client's culture. Often this is referred to as **culturally sensitive or culturally responsive care. Some researchers and clinicians have even proposed the need for culturally adapted treatments. This takes place when a type of therapy is changed in some way to be more culturally relevant**. On the exam, you may be more likely to hear the terms "cultural humility" and "cultural competence," as these are more often commonly used in the code of ethics and other literature than terms like "culturally responsive."

Counselors run the risk of potentially doing harm if they aren't considering the influence of culture in their work. For example, it might be inappropriate to treat a belief about discrimination as a cognitive distortion when a client reports thoughts about others treating them poorly. Challenging this thought could lead the client towards self-blame for discrimination being perpetrated by others.

Before moving on, let me introduce some fancy terminology used by multicultural or cross-cultural counseling experts. The first term is **etic**, and the second term is **emic**. These terms were first coined by **Kenneth Lee Pike (1912–2000)**, a linguist and anthropologist, but have been modified and adapted by multicultural scholars and the counseling community. The terms illuminate two different approaches to understanding and counseling diverse clients. Experts refer to these concepts as the etic/emic viewpoint, or the etic–emic continuum.

More specifically: There are two broad schools of thought related to how counselors should engage in multicultural counseling. One approach is the **emic approach**, which contends that counselors should target counseling toward the cultural background of the client. An emic counselor likely works from the perspective of **cultural relativity. Cultural relativity simply states that the personality can only be understood within the context of the culture that the person was raised in**.

In contrast, the **etic approach** asserts that clients should receive counseling in the same basic manner. **The etic approach works primarily from the perspective of universal culture**. The idea of universal culture highlights the similarities among people. For example, someone working from the perspective of universal culture might point to **Maslow's hierarchy of needs** as an example of all humans sharing similar basic needs.

A great memory device that I use here is that when you practice etiquette, you treat all people the same. The etic viewpoint sounds like etiquette, doesn't it? **You can use this memory device to trigger the thought that when you use the etic viewpoint, you treat the subculture or the particular person just like you would any other client**.

The etic–emic distinction is a concept you should remember for the test. Some textbook authors assert that theoretical stances favor one viewpoint over the other. Hence, Freud's dynamic, psychoanalytic approach and Albert Ellis's REBT seemingly favor the etic pole. Why?

According to some authors, these theories use the same interventions for virtually everybody. Roger's person-centered counseling, on the other hand, would be slanted toward the emic viewpoint, according to some experts. To this point, we've focused on the impact of the client's culture. We must not forget the impact of our own culture as counselors. The cultural identity development models outlined previously are also relevant to the counselor. Consider the impact of a white counselor in the naivete stage (which would hopefully never happen if the person has been in a good educational program) working with a Black client in the resistance stage. What might happen if the Black client expresses anger about the oppression coming from white people? Counselors must consider their position both within society and within the stages of identity development.

Multicultural counselors also talk about the so-called autoplastic/alloplastic dilemma. Autoplastic means the person changes themself to cope with the environment. When using REBT or Beck's cognitive therapy to change one's thoughts, this clearly falls into the autoplastic realm. Alloplastic means the client tries to change the world or the environment.

Here again, when you get a distinction like this, why not use a memory device? One that I've found very easy to use is if you think of auto, such as driving your car, you must make changes in yourself such as turning the steering or pushing the start button to drive the car. If you learn autohypnosis or self-hypnosis, you learn to change yourself. That's what you do in the autoplastic approach. You have the client change themselves.

Not so when implementing an alloplastic strategy. The counselor attempts to change (or has the client try to change) the environment. Advocating for a wheelchair ramp at an agency, helping the client find a job or housing, or even providing individual or family therapy to help change other family members would constitute an alloplastic intervention. **The autoplastic/alloplastic dilemma for the counselor is whether to change the client's response, which is autoplastic, or to eliminate the cause, which is alloplastic. Of course, the autoplastic/alloplastic concepts can be used in terms of counseling virtually any client, but most experts point out its relevance in multicultural counseling.**

Counselors can also use their understanding of their own culture to understand challenges a client may have with therapeutic surrender. Some counselors believe the most difficult part of multicultural counseling is **therapeutic surrender**. **By therapeutic surrender, we mean that the client must build an allegiance and rapport with someone, namely the counselor or therapist, who is from a different culture and must trust the helper**.

Considerations of culture don't only impact psychotherapeutic work. It also influences testing and research.

In psychoeducational and personality testing, we often talk about the importance of reliability and validity. We must also consider how cultural differences might impact the outcome of these psychometric properties. For example, if a test is written in a language that the test-taker doesn't know, what's the best thing to do? If you have someone interpret, that might change how the person answers. A translation may be inaccurate or not ask quite what the original was asking. Often, for these reasons and more, tests are translated multiple times between the original and target language.

Additionally, as we've discussed before, stereotypes can be primed, or cued. What if a question primes a stereotype that causes the test taker to perform poorly? Likewise, certain concepts or ideas may not hold true across cultures. In this case, the test may not be valid or reliable for people with a different culture.

One way to identify how to appropriately score a test (or perhaps even whether to use the test) for someone of a specific culture is to look at the normative, or norm, group. **The norm group is a reference group that sets benchmark scores**. It gives us a way to meaningfully compare scores based on certain test taker characteristics. For example, you wouldn't compare a child's score on an intelligence test to an adult's score. Similarly, you may want to understand the group of people for which test scores were created.

To overcome these concerns, some have worked to develop **culture-free** or **culture-fair tests**. As you can imagine, this can be incredibly challenging. It requires that the test questions include information that is available to different types of people. But reducing bias in testing is also very important. Testing, including psychological testing, has very real outcomes for people. Intelligence testing can have a lifelong impact. Additionally, testing can be used in malicious ways. An example of this was the use of literacy tests to prohibit access to voting ("poll tests"). This practice was later outlawed by the Voting Rights Act.

Culture is also related to research, in terms of both research about culture and the ethics of culture. Historically, people from minority groups have been either underrepresented in research or not treated appropriately in research. One commonly cited example of this is the **Tuskegee Syphilis Study**.

The Tuskegee Syphilis Study, which ran from 1932 to 1972, is a good example and has been billed as one of the most unethical studies in American history. Promoted as a government healthcare program to treat "bad blood," the men were misled, and the study's intent was actually examining the effects of untreated syphilis in 600 Black men. For one, the participants were not provided with appropriate informed consent. Even after penicillin was deemed an effective treatment way back in 1947, and yes it was widely available, participants were not offered the treatment. Or, to put it a different way, the experiment was nontherapeutic.

As the result of a court settlement in 1974, 10 million dollars was awarded to infected men, their families, and genuine treatment services.

Additionally, when we talk about **evidence-based treatment (EBT)**, we are often referring to research that supports the effectiveness of a specific type of therapy. For example, we might say that **trauma-focused cognitive-behavioral therapy (or TF-CBT) is effective for people with PTSD**. However, similar to exploring the norm groups in testing, it is important for counselors to know the types of people who were involved in treatment studies. Researchers would also want to understand norm groups when using psychological tests in their studies.

I hope you are coming to see that multiculturalism exists in various important ways in the counseling field. Many examples were provided about how racial differences can impact the work of a counselor. Let's look at a few other special populations that may come up on your exam.

First, let's take the issue of counseling people who belong to the **LGBTQ+ (lesbian, gay, bisexual, transgender, queer)** community. And where else would we start but definitions?

Sexual orientation describes the attraction a person has to other people. The famous **Kinsey studies suggest that sexual orientation should be considered on a continuum of only same-sex attraction to only opposite-sex attraction**. Additionally, some people may experience no sexual attraction and use the term **"asexual."** Some people say the Kinsey scale is limiting based on a **binary understanding of sex and gender**.

Gender identity is one's felt sense of their gender. This differs from biological sex. Sex includes things like sex chromosomes, secondary sex characteristics, reproductive systems, and hormones. We historically considered to sex to be male or female, but some people are born with ambiguous characteristics. The current term commonly used to describe this is intersex (a combination of male and female traits).

Studies show that the LGBTQ+ population is growing. According to a Gallup poll, 7.1% of US adults identified as LGBT in 2021 (more than double the percent as 2012) compared to 5.6% in 2020. In addition, about 20%, or one in five, people in Generation Z identify as LGBT.

People are also becoming more aware and accepting of LGBTQ+ people, though **homophobia (so-called fear of homosexual people) does still exist**. This increasing acceptance has led to systemic change, including the legalization of same-sex marriage as well as the use of gender-neutral markers on identification and the availability of gender-neutral restrooms.

Historically, this group has faced discrimination including within the field of counseling. Not until between 1973 and 1974 did the American Psychiatric Association (APA) remove homosexuality as a diagnosis from the DSM, the Diagnostic and Statistical Manual of the American Psychiatric Association. Counselors must be aware of myths and stereotypes about LGBTQ+ people.

Let's turn our attention to another special population, **older adults**. Unfortunately, counselors are often prejudiced regarding older adults. **When we discriminate or show prejudice toward persons because of their age, it is an example of agism (also spelled ageism)**.

"Older adult" is defined as someone who is 65 years old (traditional retirement age) or older. (Note: Some government bodies and agencies will use 60.) As people live longer. this group is quickly increasing and is expected to account for more than 20% of the population by 2040. Similar to the rest of the United States, the population of older adults is becoming more diverse in terms of race and ethnicity.

The impact of the COVID-19 pandemic was high among older adults, who accounted for significantly more deaths due to COVID-19 than other age categories. COVID-19 also led to increased mental distress (symptoms of anxiety and depression) among older adults. COVID-19 generated feelings of loneliness and decreased social connection for older adults. Related to mental health in general, counselors must also understand the high rates of substance misuse and suicide among older adults.

Additionally, the **divorce/separation rate** among older adults is increasing and was about 15% in 2020. In 2019 nearly 10% of older adults lived in poverty despite 20% of older adults working or actively seeking work and education levels among older adults rising. The poverty rate was disproportionately high among minority older adults. Older adults are also providing care for younger family members, with a little over 1 million grandparents who provided care for grandchildren under age 18 who also lived with them.

In previous editions, I have included information about "How to do therapy with various groups such as Blacks, Asians, Native Americans, etc." As the field has changed and adapted its perspective, I have tried to include the most up-to-date information for you. Therefore, in this version, we *won't* cover "How to do therapy with ______." You may be asking yourself, "Does this mean I should treat all clients the same?" You might also not be asking yourself that after reading the previous text in this chapter. However, it is worth it to dig a little deeper here.

We are becoming a more global society. With this, we are learning that it is difficult to put people into categories in any organized way. Our previous ways of grouping people were often based on stereotypes and a lack of understanding of intersectionality. For example, the experiences of first-generation and second-generation immigrants in the same family may be incredibly different. **Experiences differ based on a variety of social categories, and therefore it is difficult to prescribe one way to work with certain groups of clients**.

What we are really experiencing is a shifting away from trying to figure out one way to work with all or certain groups of clients. Historically, we may have approached this by saying we should ignore client differences and treat them the same way. Now, we are learning that grouping people in order to treat them based on specific characteristics (in essence, another form of treating them the same way) is not the way to go either. In fact, what we are likely moving towards is an understanding that we cannot pick a specific way to treat people because of these differences.

The newest version of the DSM (DSM-5-TR) was released with a focus on integrating cultural competence in ways the field has been moving towards for years. Cultural changes to the DSM-5-TR include:

1. The term **"racialized"** has replaced the traditional **"race/racial"** to emphasize that race is a social construct (i.e., notions created by the society).
2. "**Ethnoracacial**" now used in the DSM 5TR and the US census (and US society more generally) has historically conflated race (i.e., socially constructed categories based on physical characteristics such as skin color) and ethnicity (i.e., social divisions based on cultural similarities within certain regions such as religious practices) with terms such as "Hispanic." Ethnoracial is a term used to acknowledge the overlap of these terms in the categories we use.
3. "Experienced gender" is a term used to add some depth to our understanding of gender. One's "assigned gender" is typically defined at birth based on outward sex characteristics (i.e., genitalia), whereas we know that people can have a different internal sense of their gender that does not (or does) align with the gender they were assigned.
4. The terms **"minority"** and **"non-white"** have been eliminated on the premise that these describe racial groups in relation to White people with **pan-European** ethnicity origins (i.e., related to or identifying with people in Europe).

Exam questions go through a lengthy process of creation, review, testing, and implementation. So, how do we deal with this?

I would recommend developing a broad understanding of some of the historical context that might be showing up in the room with your clients. With this understanding, you can develop a sense of the impact of culture and, more specifically, cross-cultural therapy. For example, you'd want to be cognizant of the history of slavery, systemic oppression, economic disadvantage, and violence perpetrated by the medical (and mental health) field on Black people in the United States. Knowing this would allow you to understand some of the *potential* barriers to care and building rapport. Additionally, you'd want to educate yourself on the experiences and stereotypes (e.g., the so-called "model minority") that people from Asian cultures have experienced and the *possible* impact on help-seeking behavior and the therapeutic relationship.

5

Master Lecture 4: Counseling and Helping Relationships

All right, let's start on yet another section of the exam, counseling and helping relationships. In this chapter, I shall discuss theories of counseling and psychotherapy.

Ah, here's that name again, **Sigmund Freud**. **Born in 1856, and he died in 1939**. **Freud was the father of psychoanalysis**. For exam purposes, remember that **psychoanalysis is both a form of psychotherapy** as well as a school of personality. In older textbooks, you may see the word hyphenated, hence psycho-analysis.

Before Freud, clinical psychology was dominated by phrenology and mesmerism. The German physiologist **Franz Joseph Gall (1758–1828) was the originator of phrenology**. According to phrenology, mental faculties correspond to protuberances on the skull, bumps on the head, if you will.

Then came mesmerism, named after its creator, Franz Anton Mesmer (1734–1815). Mesmer – a physician who had a keen interest in astronomy – believed that there was a special magnetic fluid which could be liberated via his technique of animal magnetism. Mesmer believed that animal magnetism had healing properties.

DOI: 10.4324/9781003149712-5

He would often place patients in a bathtub structure shaped like a large jar. He would pass magnets over their bodies to heal them. At times, he would even put broken glass into the structure to try to increase the intensity of the healing process. Later, he relied on his hands.

A French Royal Commission said that he was a phony, and thus he retired to Switzerland, where he died in poverty. Some start for clinical psychology, huh? His students, however, carried on his work using a trancelike state termed **hypnosis after the Greek word hypnos, meaning sleep**.

Freud was trained as a doctor and did neuropsychological research in Vienna. Then he became interested in emotional disorders, so it was off to Paris to study hypnosis under the great neurologist and hypnotist, **Jean-Martin Charcot (1925–1893)**.

According to all reports, Freud was not a good hypnotist. Luckily, for the history of mental health treatment, he hooked up with a Viennese neurologist, **Josef Breuer (1842–1925)**, who used hypnosis. **Breuer also relied on catharsis or the so-called talking cure**.

Catharsis and the word abreaction are often used synonymously. **Both refer to the curative effect of talking about your problems and emotions to purge them**. Freud became impressed with this method when he and Breuer treated the **famous Anna O. case. We now know that Anna O.'s real name was Bertha Pappenheim.** Ironically, some scholars believe it was actually Breuer and not Freud who provided the treatment, with Breuer relaying his experiences to Freud after treatment was completed!

Freud began using catharsis and something he called **free association, which is simply a technique where the patient is told to say whatever comes to mind**. Later, he called this method **psychoanalysis**. Of course, he gave Breuer credit for helping to discover this treatment modality.

Then, in 1900, he wrote his most influential work, *The Interpretation of Dreams*, which included his famous **self-analysis**. Analytic scholars have called this book the bible of psychoanalysis, meaning that it was the most important work in the history of psychoanalysis.

Freud called the dream the royal road to the unconscious mind, and hence, dream interpretation became a critical factor in the analytic process. You see, Freud felt that dreams have two parts – manifest content and latent content.

The manifest content is the dream itself. The process by which latent dream thoughts are derived or deciphered from manifest content is called dream interpretation. Making the latent content conscious or manifest is known as dream work. Let's clarify this. In other words, if you dream of a house, that's the manifest content, but if the house is really a symbol of something else in your unconscious mind, then the unconscious symbol is the latent content.

One thing to remember when studying Freud is that great strides were being made at the time in physics. Some of his techniques and theories seem a bit physics-like, if you will.

For starters, **Freud's theory is often called a dynamic theory**. From a physics standpoint, dynamic means the study of motion and the forces that impact motion.

In therapy, dynamic refers to the energy, or mental forces in the mind. Now you know why textbooks **very often refer to Freud's theory as psychodynamic in nature**.

For comprehensive exam purposes, however, be aware, psychodynamic therapy is performed face to face. It is generally briefer than classical Freudian analysis. I say face to face, as classical Freudian psychoanalysis, just like you've seen in the movies, relies on the couch to help the patient free associate.

The client or patient, also known as an analysand, is lying on the couch and cannot see the analyst. Possibly the fact that Freud said he could not stand to be stared at for eight or ten hours a day might have had something to do with this unusual technique. **Analysis is long and drawn out, and it's slow, and unless you are receiving it pro bono (i.e., for free) or on a sliding scale, it is expensive**.

You lie on that couch three to five, or even six, times a week, for three to five years. And I'm telling you, psychoanalysis can be expensive. Many people have spent over $100,000 to complete an analysis. Currently there is not an insurance company or a managed care firm in the world that would foot the bill for a complete Freudian analysis.

Psychoanalysis works best with motivated individuals who are *not* making major life changes. It is decidedly not the treatment of choice for crisis situations.

The bedrock of Freud's conceptualization of the human mind is his so-called **structural theory,** which states that **the mind, or psychic apparatus, consists of three parts – the id, the ego, and the superego**.

These are psychological constructs, not physiological entities. In other words, you can't put an id under the microscope and see it, and you can't take it to the biology lab and dissect it.

Let's look at these entities. First, we have the **id**. It's dominated by what we call the **pleasure principle**. The id, or the it, includes all the instincts inherited at birth. It has no morals, no organization, and no sense of time. It houses biological drives.

Id processes are unconscious, but they come out in dreams, slips of the tongue called parapraxis, neurotic or what we would call emotional symptoms, and free association. The id seeks satisfaction of instinctual needs. The id is said to be chaotic.

Next, we have the ego. The ego attempts to balance the forces of the id and the superego. Often, you'll see the fulcrum analogy or the seesaw analogy, where the fulcrum is the balance point. That balance point is said to be the ego. The ego is attempting to balance personality components we call the superego and the id.

The ego is dominated by the reality principle. The ego is reasonable and logical. It uses judgment to suspend the pleasure principle. The ego is driven by survival. The ego mediates between the person and reality. It has often been called **the executive administrator of the personality**.

Then, there's the superego. It contains the ego ideal, which is a set of moral standards that the person tries to reach or, to put it another way, the perfect person in terms of what the person's parents' want, if you will. The superego acts as the conscience.

The superego is said to evolve as a result of a child successfully passing through the Oedipus complex. It contains a person's moral code of right and wrong; hence, it is molded by parental messages about what one should and should not do.

The balance of the id, the ego, and the superego can be viewed as an intrapsychic energy conflict. I told you Freud's theory had a grain of physics, didn't I? He spoke a lot about the **libido, which is the energy of all life instincts**.

Some would say that Freud's major contribution to the behavioral sciences was not his id, ego, superego structural theory but his earlier topographical hypothesis or topographic notion, which asserts that the personality is like an iceberg.

Let me explain. Freud believed that the psyche – and the word "psyche" comes from the Greek word "soul" – is made up of three parts – **the conscious, the preconscious, and the unconscious.**

Imagine an iceberg, where the smallest part of it is above water; this is the conscious mind. Then we have the preconscious, which includes information that can be recalled if somebody tries hard enough. For example, if I asked you where you went or what you did on your last birthday, you probably wouldn't have it on the tip of your tongue, but you could think about it and recall it.

Then there is the unconscious mind, which was seen as the largest part of the mind and, true to the iceberg theory, is said to be deep below the surface of the water, or deep below awareness. It's only available through analytic techniques. Now you know why some people call this depth psychology.

Here is where the concept of **symptom substitution** comes into play. Let's say a client sees you for a given problem, say, a facial tic. Assume you deal only with the symptom: you merely try to remove the facial tic.

If you cure the client of the tic, according to psychoanalytic theory, another dysfunctional behavior, say, nail biting, will manifest itself since the symptom is merely a signal that something is wrong in the unconscious at a deeper level, and you didn't deal with that unconscious conflict. Symptom substitution is used as a rationale for why counselors should *not* merely use strategies to eliminate symptoms.

The behaviorists do not believe in the theory of symptom substitution and see the removal of symptoms as a desirable goal. The Freudians believe that dreams, slips of the tongue, free association, and projective measures validate the concept of the unconscious mind. Overall, **whether you agree with Freud or not, his theory is the most comprehensive one in history, with his collective works filling an awesome 24 volumes.**

Some scholars have referred to Freud's view of human nature as deterministic. In other words, behavior is determined by biological drives, instincts, psychosexual stages, and unconscious forces.

Perhaps one of the most popular parts of Freud's theory was his theory of ego defense mechanisms, later refined and popularized even further by his sixth child and youngest daughter, Anna Freud (1895–1982). Defense mechanisms, or ego defense mechanisms if you will, conceal or hide the real source of anxiety from the self and literally keep the ego from being overwhelmed.

A defense mechanism denies or distorts reality, and the mechanism does so unconsciously so the person is not aware of the process. Let's take a brief look at the major defense mechanisms.

The first is repression. This is the granddaddy of them all. Repression occurs when a threatening or painful thought or memory is blocked out of your memory. A traumatic or life-threatening memory, such as child sexual abuse, might be an example. The repression, nevertheless, was said to generate anxiety.

Remember repression is automatic, and it is seen as the most important defense mechanism.

Suppression is next on the list, and here's a bit of info that could save you a point or two on many exams I've seen. **Suppression is not repression. Repression is involuntary and automatic. Suppression is deliberate. It's where you say to yourself, "I'm just not going to think about that situation anymore." Some books will refer to this as denial of reality**.

Now, of course, it goes against the Freudian theory that all of these are unconscious processes, but most textbooks nowadays do list suppression, so you should know what it is even if the strict Freudians don't believe that it should have made our hit list.

Next, we have **reaction formation, in which you replace a threatening or anxiety-provoking impulse with its opposite**. An individual with an unconscious sense of aggression may want to lead a peace march, or a person who has an urge to steal may try to lead a campaign about peace and law and order.

I believe it was Shakespeare who in *Hamlet* described this principle best when he wrote, "The lady doth protest too much, methinks."

The next ego defense mechanism I want to talk about is **regression. Simply put, regression occurs when a person reverts to a behavior that they have outgrown**. For example, say a sixth grader does poorly on a test. Then, the student falls on the floor, and gets into a fetal position. Here we have a textbook example of regression. The child is striving to go back to a time when life felt secure.

Next on the list, we have **rationalization**. We all know this one. We attempt to defend our behavior or excuse it by citing a socially acceptable reason. In essence, a somewhat negative behavior or thought may be viewed or seen in a positive fashion.

Remember Aesop's fable in which the fox couldn't reach the grapes, so he decided they were probably sour anyway? That's **the sour grapes variety of rationalization**. It occurs when we underrate a reward. You say something like, "I really didn't want the high-paying job. Look at all the taxes I'd have to pay if I were making several million dollars a year." Oh yeah, sure.

The opposite is known as the sweet lemon variety. This is where you overrate the reward.

For example, say you land a job you are working in 100-plus–degree heat. The job pays a very low wage, but you tell your friends you are glad you landed this terrific job because it lets you sweat off a lot of water weight. Once again, oh yeah, right. You're really being honest, aren't you?

Then we have projection. This is where you dislike something in yourself and find it unacceptable, so you attribute it to somebody else.

An individual, for example, who wants to end a relationship may see their partner as becoming distant and wanting to terminate the affiliation. Here you cannot effectively deal with something within yourself, so you falsely attribute it to somebody else. The great behaviorist Andrew Salter once commented that projection occurs when you think you're looking out a window, but you're really looking in a mirror. What a great definition.

Next is displacement. Here the object is to find a safe target for your feelings. The person who wants to stand up to their boss but can't because they might be fired comes home, screams at their family, and kicks the family dog. Hopefully the family dog will have a sense to kick the person back.

Next is sublimation, which has nothing to do with subliminal perception. Sublimation occurs when an unacceptable, unconscious urge is channeled into a socially acceptable manner.

Let's say that unconsciously you're aggressive. You like to hit people or hurt people. Fine, then you seek out a socially acceptable job as, say, a professional boxer or wrestler, maybe a football player. Like to cut on them? Why not become a surgeon and get paid for your work? Now you can see that doctors and especially surgeons are not real crazy about Freud's theory of sublimation.

Freud viewed sublimation as a mechanism they could be healthy and a sign of maturity. We would rather see a physician performing surgery than wielding a knife to threaten or hurt somebody they are robbing! (Okay, that's an extreme example, but I think you get the point.)

The goal of Freudian therapy is to give the patient insight to be able to understand and control unconscious motivation. The tendency in which the patient tries not to deal with unconscious issues or traumatic memories is known as resistance, and analysis helps overcome it.

Before moving on, I cannot forego mentioning a concept that is central to Freudian theory and psychodynamic therapy. That, my friend, is the notion of **transference**. **In transference, the patient reacts to the therapist as if the therapist is a significant other from the past**.

When the client expresses positive feelings to an analyst or helper, we refer to this dynamic as positive transference. Negative feelings from the client are known as negative transference.

The term **ambivalent transference** can mean the client has positive and negative feelings toward the analyst. However, when the term is used in multicultural counseling, it implies that the client treats the counselor like anybody else who is in a position of authority: with ambivalence.

The final type of transference is known as countertransference. In countertransference it is the therapist who has unconscious unresolved issues about the past, not the client. Here, the counselor is reacting to the client as if the client is someone from their own past, and this gets in the way of objectivity.

Is there a client that you can hardly wait to see every week? Somebody you think about and obsess about constantly? How about a client you just dread working with? You always seem to cancel their appointment. If so, then, my dear reader, you are a victim of countertransference.

Let's move on to some other schools of thought.

We will begin with the **Swiss psychiatrist and analyst Carl Gustav Jung**, born in 1875, and he died in 1961. Once considered Freud's "crown prince," he broke away from Freud as he felt Freud overemphasized the sexual nature of the libido.

Jung thus developed his own theory known as analytic psychology. He disagreed with Freud's negative view of mankind. In addition, Jung felt that libido was more general and constituted more of a life force rather than just a sexual force. Here are Jung's key concepts.

First, he was convinced that we all possess a **collective unconscious** mind that is universal to all cultures, and it's filled with **archetypes**. Remember that collective is like collecting. The collective unconscious houses a behavioral repertoire that we have inherited over time.

Archetypes are symbols in the unconscious mind that seem to mean the same thing to anybody anywhere in the world regardless of what period of time they are living in.

Jung also said that we have a personal unconscious of repressed materials, as did Freud. He emphasized that the human psyche consists of a persona, which is a social mask that hides deep feelings. He felt that we all have a shadow, which is behind the mask, and it consists of hidden personal characteristics.

Jung also believed that we are all androgynous. We all have male and female characteristics. He talked about the anima: ANIMA, which is the feminine side of the personality in men, and the animus, ANIMUS, which is the masculine side of the woman.

In case you haven't taken Latin, or it's been a few years, just use a memory device for this, such as MA sounds like Ma, and that's the feminine side of the personality, Ma like your mother, and Animus, MUS, sounds like male, the masculine side of the personality.

Again, play around with these memory devices. See what works for you; you don't necessarily need to use mine. I'm just trying to jumpstart your creative powers here. Also, keep in mind that I cannot anticipate what concepts you will or will not need memory devices for.

Jung also speaks of the self that encompasses the entire psyche. Incidentally, Jung postulated that societal norms cause us to repress the animus or the anima. **Jung also felt that humans go through a process known as individuation, a psychological or, in later writings spiritual process in which they try to reach their full or total potential. Individuation was Jung's term for becoming a separate and unique individual from others**.

Unlike Freud, Jung saw individuation for maximum potential as the driving force in human beings. **Jung has been referred to as the father of the modern study of adult development. Why? Unlike Freud, he felt that the personality continues to change into the adult years. This is a far cry from the Freudian position that it's all over by age five or six in terms of personality development**.

Last, I must mention that you have probably heard of Jung's work for a different reason. The notions of introversion and extroversion have their roots in his theory. **In fact, the well-known Myers-Briggs Type Indicator (MBTI) self-report questionnaire is based on his work. The MBTI is used by numerous Fortune 500 companies and is available in nearly 30 languages. It has been used since 1943**.

Jung also devised the well-known word association test. This is where the client is given a word and told to say the first thing that comes to his or her mind. Carl Jung will be remembered as the father of analytical psychology.

The other famous theorist who worked with Freud was Alfred Adler. He was born in 1870, and he died in 1937, two years before Freud's own death. He rejected Freud's sexual theory of neurosis and founded the Society for Individual Psychology in 1911.

Adler's individual psychology emphasizes social factors and states that humans try to become members of a group. He felt that the "will to power," or "the striving for superiority," is the major source for motivation in humans. According to Adler, we are not sexual creatures.

Adler, who had accidents, rickets (a disease characterized by soft, weak bones from a longstanding vitamin D deficiency), and pneumonia that almost killed him before age five as a child, focused heavily on the **inferiority complex** and **organ inferiority**. **Adler said, "We use compensation to try to deal with inferiority."** A person might, for example, become very scholarly to overcome a feeling of physical inferiority. Dealing with inferiority and striving for perfection are innate qualities according to Adlerians. Therapists who utilize Adler's teachings are fond of asking clients for their earliest recollections.

Adler also stressed the importance of birth order and lifestyle. In terms of the family constellation, Adler believed that sibling interaction could have more impact on an individual than parent/child interaction.

Our lifestyle is a self-fulfilling prophecy and based on the way we think of ourselves. One of Adler's students, **Rudolph Dreikurs (1897–1972), an Austrian American psychiatrist, was a pioneer in using group therapy in private practice and taught counselors in schools how to apply individual psychology to kids with behavioral difficulties**.

A common confrontation technique Adler popularized is known as **"spitting in the soup."** Here the counselor reveals and exposes to the client the true hidden motive for their self-defeating behavior. Adler believed that if the client continues to behave in a dysfunctional pattern, it will not be as pleasurable (hence the metaphor of drinking soup after one has spit in it . . . yuck!). Adler felt focusing on discrepancies relying on confrontation in therapy was very useful. However, it is up to the client how to use the information provided via this technique.

Another analytic therapist I would like to mention is **Karen Horney (1885–1952)**.

She, along with **Erich Fromm (1900–1980)** and Erik Erikson, are often labeled **Neo-Freudians or ego psychologists. An ego psychologist stresses ego functions that are not derived from the id. The emphasis here is on the individual as a social being**.

Ego psychologists feel that the Freudians placed too little emphasis on social factors. **Horney mentions what she calls basic anxiety, which results from a lack of love in childhood that leads to insecurity**.

To overcome feelings of insecurity, Horney mentions three trends. One is moving toward others, and this would be characterized by making excessive demands for love. Two, moving against others by exaggerating your own dominance, power, and prestige. The third is moving away from others by withdrawing. All of these are dysfunctional.

Now, let's switch gears and deal with the opposing camp, a rival school of therapy, **behavior therapy**, sometimes referred to as healthy psychology. **Behavior therapy is not a single type of therapy but rather a collection of therapies to reduce dysfunctional behaviors and increase or refine productive behaviors**. There's no room for symptom substitution in this model. The emphasis is on behavior.

Behaviorists don't believe the Freudian notion of symptom substitution, which asserts that a symptom is really a substitute gratification for an unconscious impulse not expressed during a psychological stage. Simply put, behavior therapists do indeed attempt to eliminate dysfunction behaviors and symptoms.

Behavior therapy can be overt. Overt means behavior we can see. But this approach can also focus on covert issues. Covert means a process, a thought, or a feeling or mental image that we cannot see. Incidentally, before I go on, just to give you a quick example of symptom substitution.

Say that you were drinking too much alcohol, and you just dealt with the alcoholism – at least according to the Freudians – and you stopped drinking. You didn't really deal with the unconscious process of what is causing the alcoholism. Therefore, you would have another symptom, maybe a facial tic, or more likely another addiction. Maybe you would develop a cocaine addiction or gambling addiction. Or maybe just drinking way too much coffee if it is available at AA or Alcoholics Anonymous meetings you are attending. Again, the behavior therapists do not buy it. With behavior therapy, the premium is dealing with the behavior. Behavior therapy is said to follow a scientific approach.

In fact, doing behavior therapy is analogous to performing a psychology or counseling experiment. The client's difficulty is described in terms of a target behavior, and a method is set up to assess whether the client reaches the target behavior regardless of the type of behavior therapy utilized.

The first thing that the behavioristic counselor should do is take a baseline. The word baseline refers to the frequency with which the behavior occurs without any treatment being applied. It provides a comparison starting point so the helper can determine if the intervention is working. Hardcore behaviorists believe that if you can't measure it, it doesn't exist.

Hence, if a client says to a behavior therapist, "I have weak ego strength," or, " I'm codependent," that means absolutely nothing. You can't see it. You can't touch it. You can't measure it. The behavior therapist wants a behavioral description.

Not simply, "I have weak ego strength," but rather, "I shake when I have to give a speech in front of my history class," or "I'm unable to ride the elevator in my office due to extreme anxiety and fear." Not, "I'm codependent," but rather, " I call my significant other an average of 23 times a day while I'm at work to make sure they are not having an affair."

You must describe the problem using an operational definition so that virtually any counselor will know precisely what the behavior in question really is. This is also desirable when conducting research.

Some would say that behavior therapy has its roots in John Locke's (1632–1704) philosophy of associationism and the principle of tabula rasa. Tabula rasa conceptualizes the mind like a blank slate or a blank clean-scraped tablet at birth, and the environment molds it. To put it another way, the mind is empty at the time of one's birth.

Other behavioral historians point to the work of the American psychologist **Edward Thorndike (1874–1949)**, who published his famous "Some Experiments in Animal Intelligence" comparative psychology article before the age of 25, using puzzle boxes to study cats. The now-famous **law of effect postulated that responses that are accompanied by satisfaction are repeated**.

The other big name in behaviorism is that of the Russian physiologist **Ivan Pavlov (1849–1936),** who won a Nobel Prize in 1904 for his work on the dog's digestive system. Pavlov is credited with the **classical conditioning paradigm**, although many historians actually insist that a University of Pennsylvania professor, **Edwin B. Twitmyer (1873–1943)**, came up with the paradigm a year prior to Pavlov's announcement of his findings. Twitmyer worked with the human patellar knee reflex and Pavlov with salivating dogs. Why the significance of Twitmyer's work was not seen as valuable at the time is still hotly debated by scholars.

That said, 99% of the time, an exam is <u>not</u> going to mention Twitmyer, but it will mention Pavlov. **By the way, when I use the word paradigm, it just means a model or conceptualization of behavior**.

Now, here's how Pavlovian conditioning worked when Pavlov published his findings in 1897, and it still works this way today.

If you show a hungry dog meat or food, the dog will drool or salivate. This is an unconditioned reflex (UR, or on occasion abbreviated UCR) or response. You don't need to teach the dog to do it.

When you see the word conditioning on your exam, just mentally substitute the word learned. When you see the word unconditioned in relation to Pavlov, merely substitute the words not learned, meaning that the person or the animal already knows how to do it. They don't have to be taught how to do something. I guarantee you this simple device will make life a lot easier when studying behaviorism.

Let's get back to Pavlov and Pavlov's dogs and his great famous experiment. When a dog sees a piece of meat, **the meat is called a US or UCS. US or UCS means an unconditioned stimulus.**

When the dog sees the meat, or meat powder, then assuming the animal doesn't sneeze, which purportedly some of the dogs did in Pavlov's trial, the dog salivates. You show it the meat, the dog salivates.

The drooling or salivation is an unconditioned response or what we call a UR. In your mind, just substitute not learned. The dog need not attend Harvard or go to MIT to learn to salivate, OK? If this seems difficult to comprehend, imagine I put a lemon just inches from your nose. Chances are you, like Pavlov's dogs, will salivate.

Thus, a US produces a UR – pretty simple, right? Now, let's take a bell and present it just before the dog sees the food. We pair them up, if you will. After we pair them up for a number of trials, we will ring the bell, and without showing the dog the meat . . . bingo, the bell alone causes the dog to salivate. This is what we call a conditioned response, or a CR. **So, remember we call the bell the conditioned stimulus, or CS. You can mentally substitute the term learned stimulus.**

Bottom line, after training or conditioning, the CS, the bell without the meat, causes a CR, or conditioned response, and the dog salivates.

Now, this is pretty darn complicated, so let me show you a way to make it easier. One way to remember that the meat is the US, or UCS, is to remember that in the US we eat a lot of meat.

Go ahead, repeat it out loud. Come on, your family might already think you're a little strange spending all this time studying for the exam; say it out loud. "In the US, we eat a lot of meat."

I know it's corny, but it's a memory device that has worked for countless students of mine, and I'm convinced it could work for you. **The US is the meat in the study. You can also remember that the CS, the conditioned stimulus, or the bell, comes before the UCS by remembering that C comes before U in the alphabet – again, make it easy**.

On some exams, and this is a great hint, folks, the CS on some newer exams will be called the NS or neutral stimulus, which means that it has no power: a bell has no power of its own. How would you remember that the NS comes before the US or UCS? **Simple, just remember N comes before U in the alphabet**.

Read the last few paragraphs several times, if you haven't heard a discussion on Pavlov for a while, and you'll be saying in the US we eat a lot of meat in your sleep. The most efficient time between the CS, the bell, and the UCS, the meat, is about 0.5 of a second, or half of a second.

Now, here's a real point saver for the exam. Do you know what happens when we flip things around and put the US, the meat, before the bell? Generally, nothing happens. We call it backward conditioning, and it usually does not work. Or, using your memory device once more for good measure: C comes before U in the alphabet. Putting U before C (i.e., UCS before the CS) . . . no way! It just isn't going to work.

All right, bottom line on this Pavlovian stuff, when the bell alone causes the dog to salivate without the meat, then we say that a CR, a conditioned response, has taken place. This is what we call classical conditioning.

Another term you'll hear behaviorists throw around is stimulus generalization. This is where a stimulus that is similar to the CS or NS produces a CR. For example, a car horn or a piano note may elicit salivation as well as a bell. Pavlov called this irradiation.

The converse, or the opposite, is what we call stimulus discrimination. In stimulus discrimination, a human or an animal can distinguish one stimulus from another. For example, say you only give food with the bell but not when you hit a note

on a piano or car horn. When the bell, and only the bell, elicits the response, then this is stimulus discrimination.

Now if the discrimination process between the piano note and the bell is almost identical, or too similar, it becomes too difficult to discern one from the other, and the dog will bark and show emotional distress, just like a human neurotic, according to Pavlov. Researchers call this experimental neurosis. Keep in mind terminology was different years ago and today we would merely say the dog would show dysfunctional or disturbed behavior.

Just a gentle reminder that Pavlov's method can also be called respondent conditioning.

Students say to me, "Dr. Rosenthal, I can't remember whether it's Skinner or Pavlov who created the respondent model." Try this on for your size. Studies on dogs salivating use reflexes. Salivating is a reflex. Reflex begins with r, so does respondent, both refer to Pavlov.

I want to mention that there is a phenomenon called spontaneous recovery. This means that if you keep presenting the bell without the meat, eventually the salivating – or, as my students often say, slobbering, not quite as politically correct, but accurate – the salivating will no longer occur.

It's not really forgotten. It's just inhibited because it will appear again. If the dog gets to take a rest from the trials and then you present the dog with the bell, the dog will begin to salivate. This is what we call spontaneous recovery.

I want to tell you about another major figure in the behavioristic helping movement.

That is **John Broudus Watson, usually referred to as John B. Watson**, who was born in 1878 and died in 1958. He put his name in the history books by coining the term behaviorism in 1913. **He's been called the father of American behaviorism. Watson is best known for his 1920 experiment, often dubbed the Little Albert experiment, conducted with his graduate student Rosalie Rayner (1898–1935), his research assistant and later wife. (Their relationship is a juicy story, but not relevant to our current discussion, so you can research it after you pass your exam!)**

In this experiment, **a 9-month-old, Albert B**, was exposed to a loud noise, which is a UCS or a US. The loud noise was paired with a harmless rat, which is a CS. It is noteworthy that prior to the experiment, little Albert was not scared of the furry white animal.

After a few trials in which Watson and Rayner paired the rat with a very loud noise, the child not only feared the rat, but generalization set in and Albert also began to fear rabbits, cotton, and a fur coat. Watson even donned a Santa Claus mask with the big white furry beard and little Albert feared that too.

Now little Albert had a phobia of white furry objects. **Incidentally, when counselors technically or strictly speaking use the word phobia, it relates to a specific or known fear, such as the fear of a furry object or fear of an elevator. The term anxiety is substituted when the cause of the source of the fear is unknown. (Obviously this is not always true, since counselors often talk about test anxiety.)**

What was so important about the Watson and Rayner experiment? Well, think about it. This landmark research indicated you didn't need a fancy psychoanalytic explanation of the unconscious mind to explain the process of a phobia or a disorder. You simply learned the problem. It was learned, just like so many other things in life.

The tragedy of this already controversial experiment is that Watson never cured Little Albert of this experimentally induced phobia. Mary Cover Jones (1897–1987), several years later, using another child, Peter, who was nearly three years of age and conditioned with the same fear, paired the feared object up with food.

After the feared object was paired with food, she was able to eliminate the phobia in the situation. This showed that not only could a phobia be learned, but Mary Cover Jones showed the fear could be unlearned. Therefore, we can briefly state that the problem was learned and the cure was unlearning.

The experimental work of Mary Cover Jones and Watson became the basis of South African psychiatrist Joseph Wolpe's (1915–1997) systematic desensitization, in which Pavlov's classical conditioning was applied to the process of psychotherapy. Wolpe believed that you could unlearn habits. Wolpe nicknamed Jones "the mother of behavior therapy."

Thus, the unwanted reaction or behavioral repertoire was simply faulty learning. To unlearn an anxiety-producing

pattern, Wolpe suggested the principle of reciprocal inhibition, which simply means you show the anxiety-producing stimulus in the presence of relaxation or something else that serves as an anxiety-inhibiting behavior, such as sex or assertiveness.

Wolpe is best known for systematic desensitization, which is a counterconditioning form of therapy for treating phobias that has four distinctive stages after you build a rapport with the client.

In the first stage, you teach the client how to relax via relaxation training, which is about four to six sessions.

Often the Jacobson method of tensing and relaxing muscles is utilized. Though, really, you could rely on any method of relaxation.

In the second stage, you would construct an anxiety hierarchy with 10 to 15 items. The items must be evenly spaced. If they are too close together, treatment is slow.

If they are too far apart from one another on the hierarchy level, going from one level to the next is going to be difficult. It is best to have the client's rate items on a **SUDS scale**. **SUDS stands for subjective units of distress scale. Some exams use the term subjective units of disturbance**.

Let's hit you with a hypothetical example to make sure you understand this concept. Let's say that somebody has anxiety related to taking your comprehensive counseling exam. Of course, I realize this wouldn't be you. You would be the exception, but just play along with me.

The first item on your hierarchy that would produce, say, 100 points on the subjective units of distress scale would be imagining that you're actually taking the exam. The second thing on the hierarchy could be imagining that you're driving to the test or booting up your computer to take the exam. Maybe that's an 85 on the SUDS scale.

Number three would be imagining that you are staying at a hotel the night before the exam, studying in the university library, and so on and so forth. **The third stage is imagining this hierarchy**. This is called desensitization in the imagination, or the inter position phase.

There's the last stage, which we call in vivo. In vivo means in real life, and thus the counselor gives the client a homework assignment where they experience the real-life situations listed on their hierarchy. This generally begins when the client is desensitized in their imagination to about 75% of the hierarchy items.

The counselor might instruct the client to drive to the exam site and see how much anxiety they experience.

A popular behavioral technique for sexual dysfunction based on counterconditioning is the Masters and Johnson 1970 method known as sensate focus, which is well known in the behavioral sciences. The strategy is named after sex researchers William H. Masters (1915–2001) and Virginia E. Johnson (1924–2013).

Here the couple is told to engage in non-erotic touching while they are very relaxed. This model is very similar to systematic desensitization, and the couple is slowly working up to intercourse. **Sometimes we call this behavioral sex therapy**.

Although Masters and Johnson were pioneers in researching human sexual responses, the team was criticized from an ethical standpoint for eliminating participants who professed same-sex attraction, not to mention the larger issue of studying sex in a laboratory.

Behavioral therapists and behavioral therapies also favor assertiveness training in which the client learns to discriminate between nonassertive, assertive, and aggressive behavior in interpersonal relationships. This model has its roots in the work of the American psychologist, hypnotist, and Freudian critic Andrew Salter (1914–1996), who wrote a landmark 1949 book titled *Conditioned Reflex Therapy* that drew heavily on the work of Pavlov. **Some experts have dubbed Salter the "true father of behavior therapy."**

Just as an aside: if you can beg, borrow, or steal a copy of this book, do so. It's wonderful. The writing style has been praised. I'm <u>not</u> saying you'll agree with what's in the book. Salter basically felt that any problem, whether it was drinking too much alcohol, lack of creativity, or having an elevator phobia, was the same problem inhibition.

Truth be told, what Salter really did today would probably be closer to aggressive training than assertiveness training, but it is very well written. A great book to read after you finish your exam.

Assertiveness training, as it's practiced today, relies very heavily on modeling, coaching, relaxation training, and behavioral rehearsal. Assertiveness training examines behavioral responses to discern whether the behavior is nonassertive, assertive, or aggressive, with assertive responses being

the most desirable. Again, intervention is based on the client learning to behave in an assertive manner.

Keep in mind some counselors are critical of behavior therapy, stating it's too simplistic to mechanistic and fails to deal with critical issues in childhood or in the past.

Another type of behavior therapy is aversive conditioning. Here, a noxious UCS is paired with an undesirable behavior, a CS, so that avoidance results when the client is exposed to the CS alone.

Sounds complicated, but it's not. Take the drug **Antabuse (disulfiram),** which is a nausea-inducing drug. If you pair Antabuse up with alcohol – and alcohol is a CS – eventually the alcohol alone will induce nausea, and the theory is that the alcohol consumption will be curbed or eliminated. Unfortunately, disulfiram can be fatal for some people, so it hasn't worked out very well.

Some behaviorists treat clients by employing flooding. In the technique of flooding developed by **Thomas Stampfl (1923–2005)** in 1967, **also known as deliberate exposure with response prevention**, the client is exposed to a highly anxiety-provoking stimulus for an extended period of time, say for 40 to 60 minutes, with no feared consequence. A person with a fear of spiders would be placed in a room with a spider but would not be harmed in any way. **This constitutes a superb example of in vivo therapy or an in vivo approach**.

Implosive therapy, also known as implosion therapy, created by Thomas Stampfl and Donald J. Levis (1936–), is like flooding. However, it's conducted in the imagination. Images are used in treatment, and very often they're psychodynamic in nature, as Stampfl believed that avoidance behaviors are related to childhood sexual aggressive conflicts.

Looking for a great memory device? Since these two terms, implosive and flooding, are so closely related, you can remember and distinguish implosion from flooding on your exam by remembering that implosive begins with an I, like imagination. Implosive therapy is always conducted in the imagination.

In fact, to have Freudian or psychodynamic theory integrated into the approach, it would have to be done in the imagination.

There is a high-tech behavior therapy called biofeedback, in which the client is hooked to a sophisticated electronic

device that monitors bodily functions like muscle tension, hand temperature, pulse rate, or blood pressure.

Somehow, once the client can see what their own body is doing via the process of monitoring, such as looking at a screen or listening to sounds via a set of headphones, the person can actually control their own responses. Biofeedback was an incredible discovery because for years, we believed that you could not control the autonomic nervous system, or ANS.

Things like heart rate, pulse rate, or hand temperature would fall into this category. One experimental psychologist, Neil Miller, demonstrated that even rats can learn to control these autonomic processes, and thus, it was no surprise that humans could learn to do so.

If the idea of bio or biological feedback seems a little strange, consider this. A mirror in a bathroom scale are both essentially biofeedback devices, and you've been using them for years. Biofeedback, like systematic desensitization, is an excellent choice of treatment for anxiety disorders and phobias.

A great little exam hint is that in recent years the trendy term neurofeedback refers to biofeedback procedures.

Behaviorists also rely on Albert Bandura (1925–2021), who pioneered the concept of social learning theory (SLT) in 1977, also labeled observational learning in some sources. He later renamed his paradigm social cognitive theory (SCT) in 1986 to emphasize the huge impact of cognition on behavior. Bandura's contribution can be explained thusly. We all know that we learn via direct reinforcement. Nevertheless, Bandura found we can also experience **vicarious learning**, such as when we see somebody else getting a positive reward or reinforcement for a behavior. The theory asserts that observation, imitation, and modeling help mold behavior. Again, his SCT update throws cognitive functions into the mix. According to Bandura's theory, we should pick our role models with great care inasmuch as we imitate them.

The key issue here is that the reinforcement is not provided directly to the individual but to a model, somebody you see performing the behavior. The result is what we call a cognitive symbolic mediational process. Some exams just refer to this phenomenon as observational learning, which seems to be the hot term right now.

Paradoxical intention, first developed by the Austrian psychiatrist Viktor Frankl (1905–1997), the father of existential logotherapy, is another amazing behavior therapy technique (yep, you read that correctly . . . a behavioral technique within a humanistic/existential psychotherapy). In paradoxical intent, the client is instructed to exaggerate the inappropriate behavior, either covertly or overtly.

When a client says, "I have a fear that I will appear anxious when I give my speech in front of my graduate counseling class," the counselor might instruct the client to intentionally try to appear as anxious as possible. That's correct. I meant what I said.

Paradox merely implies that something seems one way, but it's really another. The paradox is that this client often can't shake or display anxious behavior when they attempt to do so.

This technique was also favored by family therapists, especially Jay Haley (1923–2007) and Milton H. Erickson (1901–1980), who have used it a lot. It should never be used with suicidal or homicidal clients.

I might mention that the American psychologist Knight Dunlap (1875–1949), who worked with John B. Watson on various occasions, spent most of his life analyzing habits and suggested something called a beta hypothesis or hypothesis b, which is similar to paradox. In Dunlap's beta hypothesis, the client engages in the unwanted behavior when they would not normally do so.

Paradoxically enough, this often eliminates or reduces the frequency of the behavior. And you thought behavior therapy was just common sense. The beta hypothesis would work well for blushing or nail biting. The practice of engaging in any undesirable behavior, when it normally would not occur very often decreases the behavior.

No discussion of behavior therapy would be complete without mentioning the **multimodal therapy approach created by Arnold Lazarus (1932–2013)**. Lazarus, who was born in South Africa and originally worked with Joseph Wolpe, created a model that uses the **acronym BASIC ID**.

In the acronym, B is behavior, A is affective responses (affective means emotional), S is sensations, I is imagery, C is cognitions, I is interpersonal Relationships, and D is drugs (prescription medicines or biological factors).

This is what we call a holistic, multifaceted, or eclectic model since it takes into consideration a myriad of factors.

Since we already covered Pavlov's respondent classical conditioning, let's turn our attention to **Burrhus Frederic Skinner's (1904–1990) model of operant conditioning, also called instrumental learning. B.F. Skinner's work has its roots in Thorndike's studies mentioned earlier. Skinner basically renamed Thorndike's law of effect reinforcement theory**.

Skinner's theory is quite simple. When an animal, and that includes humans, emits a behavior, or what Skinner termed an operant, there can be a consequence. The consequence can increase the probability that the behavior will occur. If this is the transpires, we call it a positive reinforcer or reinforcement. Or a consequence can decrease the probability that the behavior will occur. We call this punishment.

I'm only going to say this once, and it's very important, so listen up. **Negative reinforcement is not punishment. I probably just saved you a point on your exam. All reinforcers increase behavior, both positive and negative. A positive reinforcer increases a behavior when it's added following an operant. A negative reinforcer increases behavior when it's taken away after an operant often by providing relief**.

Simple example. A positive reinforcer might be giving your child their favorite food after they clean their room. A negative reinforcer might be removing noxious stimuli like a loud noise from a room or work area every time production goes up to a certain level. In other words, when you take the noise away, the behavior goes up. In both cases, the behavior goes up.

Repeat after me. All reinforcers, both positive and negative, raise behavior or strengthen it.

In recent years, exams have been using the terms positive and negative punishment. Maybe this terminology didn't exist when you were in graduate school. We didn't call it positive and negative punishment.

This could get a little tricky. If you remember what I told you, that reinforcers always increase behavior, and punishment always decreases it, you'll be in good shape. Here's how positive and negative punishment works. If you add something after the behavior, then positive punishment has taken place.

For example, if you receive a speeding ticket and it reduces your tendency to speed, then this would be positive punishment, again, if and only if it lowers behavior. If you take something away from the child, say, their favorite video game, and it lowers behavior, that's negative punishment.

You must know whether the consequence raised or lowered the behavior to figure out if we are talking about a reinforcer or punishment; it is that simple. Remember when we talk in everyday life, we don't necessarily use these terms in the proper way or literal format. Even self-help books generally do not.

Another thing I want to talk about here is **ABA, or applied behavior analysis. The old name for ABA was behavior modification**. If you get technical, in the past most therapists and theorists used the term behavior therapy to refer to classical conditioning models of therapy and behavior modification to refer to Skinnerian or instrumental models.

That said, ABA employs techniques from operant conditioning (think Skinner) and classical conditioning (think Pavlov). **On occasion ABA has been billed as behavioral engineering**.

The next must-know principle is the **Premack principle, created in 1965**. **It's based on the work of the American psychologist David Premack (1925–2015)**. The principle asserts that a good reinforcer can be based on what the person likes to do. If the person likes to watch television, they must engage in the desired behavior to watch television.

The theory purports that a high probability behavior (HPB) like watching television can reinforce a lower-probability behavior, or LPB, such as cleaning out your garage or completing your dissertation. This approach thus emphasizes that the reinforcing HPB can vary widely from person to person. As an example, some people might find watching television very boring and for them it would not serve as a viable HPB.

Patterns of reinforcement are often called schedules of reinforcement. There are two major categories, continuous and intermittent. Continuous simply means that you reinforce each desired behavior. Continuous is best for new behaviors, but it becomes ineffective in terms of maintaining the behavior.

If you give the reinforcer every single time the animal or the person does something that is desirable, the person generally satiates or habituates.

A quick example should drive home the point. I was discussing this principle in a college class I was teaching when a student in my class said he didn't believe me. He loved his wife's home-made fried chicken more than any food in the world and could eat it forever. She agreed to cook enough for every meal to see what would transpire. The first few days my student loved it as he was eating fried chicken for every meal and for snacks. However, after a few days he was begging his wife to discontinue the experiment and reluctantly agreed there might be some validity to the principles of satiation and habituation.

ABA exam hint. When a counselor or researcher goes from reinforcing every behavior, or what we call continuous reinforcement, to using intermittent reinforcement and not reinforcing each behavior, we call it thinning. Skinnerians speak of two types of intermittent schedules. We have the ratio schedule and the interval schedule.

In ratio scheduling a certain number or average number of responses are emitted before the behavior is reinforced. If a child gets a gold star after completing four math problems, that's a ratio schedule. **In an interval schedule a certain time or average amount of time elapses before a response is reinforced.**

If a child works on their math for ten minutes, regardless of how many problems the child completes, we give this student a gold star. That's an interval schedule since it is based on time. **Here's an easy way to remember interval schedules. Remember that in everyday English we use the phrase time interval to refer to time, and interval schedules are based on time, whereas ratio is the opposite. It's based on the number of behaviors.**

The variable ratio (VR) scale produces the highest rate of behavior and is very hard to extinguish. Fixed interval (FI) produces one of the lowest rates of behavior. Incidentally, your paycheck is usually based on a fixed interval scale. If you always work 40 hours and you receive a paycheck, you are on a fixed interval schedule. Fixed: because you always need to work 40 hours; it never changes to 36 or 29 or 54. The 40 hours is a static figure.

Once again, when the time or number of behaviors remain static, we say that we are using a fixed schedule. If the number of behaviors or time varies, we say that we are using a variable schedule.

For example, if your employer kept changing the amount of time needed for you to get your weekly paycheck, we would say that he or she was using a variable interval scale.

So far, I've been talking about primary reinforcers. However, you should know that behaviorists also use what is known as a secondary reinforcer. A secondary reinforcer might be referred to as a learned reinforcer or a conditioned reinforcer on your exam.

The reason for this is that a secondary reinforcer has no power of its own, but it takes on power because the person knows that it stands for or is associated with the primary reinforcer. Let me give you an example.

Say that you give a child a plastic token. The token itself is not really a reinforcer. The kid could care less about whether they receive it. It's probably not going to raise behavior. However, if you tell the child that they can turn the token in to the teacher or counselor in for a new baseball glove (assuming the child likes baseball), then the plastic token becomes a secondary reinforcer. It takes on the power of a primary reinforcer.

The smell of barbecue, talking while feeding your baby, or verbal praise would be other examples of secondary reinforcers. I personally believe that money is the most powerful secondary reinforcer in the world.

Think about it. The money in and of itself really isn't reinforcing. You can't really date a dollar bill or have an intelligent conversation with a quarter. If you believe you can, then you're much more disturbed than I thought you were and I'm not sure this book – wonderful as it is – is going to help you. Anyway, as we all know, you can trade that money for things that are really reinforcing.

If a behavior is repeatedly displayed without reinforcement, it goes away or extinguishes. This is what we call extinction. Extinction can simply be defined as withholding reinforcement, or the lack of reinforcement.

When parents ignore a child's behavior, they are practicing extinction. One thing that you need to be aware of is that

when you ignore or extinguish a behavior it usually gets worse before it gets better. The getting worse part will be referred to on your exam as an extinction burst or response bursting.

Key point: If a parent ignores a child's behavior with the goal of eliminating or lowering the behavior and it gets worse, this is often a sign the technique is working rather than failing.

The final behavioristic term you should be familiar with is shaping. In shaping, the counselor or teacher reinforces behaviors that approach the ultimate target behavior. Thus, if you were attempting to teach a student to hit a golf ball you might initially reinforce the student for just looking at the golf ball.

Next, you might reinforce the student for looking at the golf ball. Next for looking at the golf ball, gripping the club correctly, and keeping their lead arm reasonably straight on the backswing. You would add more steps until the new golfer can take a complete swing using the proper fundamentals.

On your exam this could also be called reinforcing using successive approximations or shaping, or just successive approximations.

Now you know quite a bit about classical analysis, neo-analytic theory, behavior therapy, and ABA, so let's look at some of the other schools of counseling that fall between these extremes. **I'll begin by talking about REBT, which is rational emotive behavior therapy, created by the New York clinical psychologist Albert Ellis.**

In some of the older books, you might see it written as RT or RET. Ellis added the E to let us know that he did stress emotion. More recently, he added the B after the eminent psychologist Raymond Corsini (1914–2008), a top expert in theories of counseling and psychotherapy, convinced Ellis that RET was actually slanted heavily toward behavior therapy.

Ellis was born in 1913 and died in 2007 and was originally trained as an analyst. Ellis felt that analysis was too slow, and the results were not always positive. Besides, Ellis asked, why should he have to listen to the patient babble on for years, lying on the couch, when he knew what was wrong during the first few minutes of the first session?

Ellis thus became didactic and active directive with his clients. He became a teacher, didactic, who would literally teach his clients to think their way out of an emotional disturbance.

He became active directive by talking as much, if not more than, the client and directing the nature of the counseling sessions.

Like most teachers, **Ellis believed in homework assignments**. Like what? Like trying out a new behavior, or **bibliotherapy. In bibliotherapy, the client would read books, or pamphlets, to supplement the therapy process**. Books like Albert Ellis and Robert Harper's *Guide to Rational Living*, or Ellis's book, *How to Master Your Fear of Flying*.

If his theory seems a bit well, educational, it truly is. The client is seen as a learner.

This sounds amazing, but Ellis wrote 80 books and over 1200 articles. By the way, if you were going to ask when he had time to sun and fun on the beach, Ellis often quipped that he couldn't imagine anything more boring than relaxing on the beach! (He usually added a foul word to the sentence, which I have decided as your author to forego sharing!)

The gist of Albert Ellis's theory is captured by the statement that was made by the stoic philosopher Epictetus, who in the first century AD said, "Men are disturbed not by things but the view which they take of them." Ellis's major premise is that you feel the way you think.

Forget about those stimulus response studies with animals, because Ellis points out human beings are the one animal who talks to themselves. Ellis believes that we are disturbed by irrational ideas, illogical unscientific thinking. **We think in declarations, self-talk, or what Ellis originally called internal verbalizations. Let me tell you what some of these irrational ideas are**.

Irrational idea number one is **the notion that you must receive love and approval from all significant others. Ellis calls this absolutist thinking, and he says the words such as should, ought, and must cause emotional disturbance. Ellis has termed the irrational process of thinking this way MUSTerbation**.

Ellis has a great sense of humor if you have ever heard him lecture (or seen videos of his presentations), often joking that musterbation is much more pernicious than masturbation. Ellis says you may want love, for example, but you don't need it. In fact, he calls folks who insist they need love love slobs. I guess you figured out Ellis never minces words.

Irrational idea number two: **the idea that you must be thoroughly competent and adequate at all times**. Ellis calls this an idiotic notion. Again, notice that "must" in the person's thought process. Ellis says that this is crazy because nobody is competent and perfect in every respect.

He also points out that achievement does not really make you a better individual. Ellis incidentally feels that this is the irrational idea that is behind most sexual dysfunction.

Next on the list, **irrational idea number three, which occurs when people act unfairly, and you blame them and see them as wicked or bad. Ellis suggests if you feel this way, you are the one who is acting Godlike and grandiose. "Why shouldn't another person have a right to act in a certain way?" asks Ellis**.

Irrational idea number four is the one that Ellis calls **awfulizing, catastrophizing, or terriblizing**. Unfortunately, he believes that even well-meaning counselors perpetuate this illogical belief.

Ellis says this isn't true. You have a choice about what to think to yourself; you don't have to feel this way. He points an accusing finger here at the well-known **Dollard Miller psychological hypothesis, which asserts that frustration leads to aggression**.

Not so, says Ellis. Not unless you think it leads to aggression, which he feels is irrational thinking, if you believe that frustration leads to aggression.

Irrational idea number five. This idea states that most people waste an awful lot of time doing the impossible, which is trying to control or change the behaviors of others. **This irrational position postulates that external things, or events, or people control your happiness**.

Ellis says that the bulk of the problem here is that you take other people's disapproval, criticism, or rejection too seriously. A man might say, "My partner called me stupid. That hurt my feelings." The REBT therapist would say you hurt yourself by your beliefs about your partner's remarks, because their words couldn't possibly literally hurt you.

If you say things to yourself like my partner's behavior is terrible, or how awful, or I must be stupid, or they wouldn't have said that, then you'll feel very disturbed.

Irrational idea number six is what Ellis hypothesizes is responsible for 98% of what we call anxiety. The irrational idea

here is that if something seems scary or dangerous, you must preoccupy yourself with this thing.

Ellis feels that anxiety is really generated by overconcern about what somebody else thinks about you.

Irrational idea number seven is the one that is at the root of procrastination. It consists of the idea that it's easier to avoid life's difficulties than to take responsibility and tackle them. **Ellis points out that the easy way is often the easy way out of a rewarding lifestyle. The easy way is really the hard way**.

Ellis feels that when you avoid life's difficulties, you really exaggerate their pain and discomfort.

Irrational idea number eight is the one that Ellis believes has been fostered, ironically enough, by the behaviorists and the opposing camp, the psychoanalysts. The idea can be described thusly. You tell yourself that your past is all important and that because something has a tremendous impact on your life at one time, it must continue to influence your behavior and your feelings today.

To this, Ellis is pretty direct. He says, and I quote, "Rubbish. You can dispute this irrational idea and uncondition yourself from such influences." Again, the key, or the cure, if you will, is thinking logically and rationally.

Remember how Freud used his theory to analyze himself? Ellis admits that he did likewise using REBT. He candidly admits that his mother was eligible for no prizes of mental health and that she didn't always treat him in an ideal manner. Nevertheless, he began thinking rationally at an early age. Thus, overall, he had a pretty good childhood.

Later in his life when he was shy with women, he applied REBT skills to overcome his shyness and, according to Ellis, became one of the top ladies' men in New York City. Perhaps a little sexist by today's standards, but as you may have guessed, **Ellis stubbornly refuses to feel miserable or embarrassed by anything. It's another part of his theory**.

Ellis's theory has also been dubbed a type of CBT, or cognitive behavioral therapy. Overall, Ellis recommends calm acceptance of reality. People who knew him say that he lived by his theory.

The aforementioned irrational ideas all operate in the framework of his now-famous ABC theory of personality. Here's how it works.

At A, there's an activating event, which could be virtually anything. Say, your supervisor criticizes your work.

At C, we have a consequence, which could be emotional and/or behavioral. Say that you feel worthless, sad, depressed. You start shaking. Most counselors wrongly assume that A, your supervisor's remarks, caused C. "Not so," says Ellis.

Why? **According to Ellis, it's the belief system at point B that caused the irrational thought at B, which caused the consequence at C.**

The counselor thus disputes the irrational idea, at D. D is disputing and provides rational self-talk, using REBT. Or, to put it another way, irrational thoughts at B, now disputed, are replaced with rational thinking.

Then there's E, which is where the person has a new philosophy and a new healthier emotional consequence.

In REBT, disturbance *is* irrational thinking. In fact, I remember Ellis once commented, years ago, that neurosis (back when the term was popular) can best be described as stupid behavior from a person who is not stupid.

Despite his early criticism of behavior therapy, REBT again is now considered a cognitive behavior therapy.

Let me insert a shameless plug for a lively, humorous, fast-paced, extremely informative interview I conducted with Ellis featured in my book *Therapy's Best, Practical Advice and Gems of Wisdom from Twenty Accomplished Counselors and Therapists*. The interview was titled "The REBT Story You Haven't Heard: A No Holds Barred Interview with Albert Ellis."

Ellis praised the merits of the exchange, which says a lot.

Other well-known therapists who use techniques that are like Ellis's would include **Donald Meichenbaum, who uses cognitive behavior modification or self-instructional theory.**

In addition to Albert Ellis's REBT, you should also be familiar with Aaron T. Beck's cognitive therapy. Beck lived to be 100, as he was born in 1921 and died in 2021. Beck, a

psychiatrist and a former psychoanalyst, also created the BDI, or popular Beck Depression Inventory.

Beck emphasizes rules or formulas people live by cognitively instead of irrational ideas. Beck didn't embrace the notion of irrational ideas. He felt the concept did not capture the essence of what was going on in the person.

Beck preferred the term cognitive distortions. Some of these cognitive distortions include **overgeneralization.** For example, if you go out on a date, and it doesn't go well, you might tell yourself, "I will never experience a fulfilling date."

Another distortion is **personalization** in which you blame yourself for things outside of your control. An abused child feels like a bad person when she did nothing wrong.

Beck also includes **blaming** (since it is roughly the converse of personalization) in this category. A college student who gets bad grades sees themselves as the victim of bad professors who do not grade fairly.

Or **polarized thinking**, where you view yourself as a perfect thoroughly competent counselor. Then, at other times, you see yourself as a complete flop as a helper when something goes wrong. **According to Beck, polarized thinking is all-or-none thinking**.

Yet another cognitive distortion is **magnification, or minimization**. Here you exaggerate or you put way too little stock in a situation. Noted counseling and therapy expert Gerald Corey gives the example of a counselor who makes a very minor mistake with a client but via magnification could perceive it as creating a major crisis for the client and believes it could be damaging the client's psychological health.

In minimization an individual might win a top award or snare a doctorate and lessen the significance of the event. Simply put, the person has minimized these achievements.

Beck also focuses on **selective abstraction, also known as a mental filter**. Here you focus on one detail of an event rather than the entire situation and you ignore valuable information from the environment. A host might believe an event was totally ruined because there was no lemon for the iced tea.

Another cognitive distortion is **arbitrary influences**. Here you conclude without supporting evidence and imagine the worst and you catastrophize. For example, "People at the meeting thought I looked stupid in these glasses."

Another distortion, is **labeling and mislabeling**. You label yourself based on a past event or imperfection.

If you research different sources, the number of cognitive distortions and definitions by Beck and irrational ideas proposed by Ellis (even in his own writings) can vary slightly, and there can be some overlap between the distortions and irrational beliefs. **In other words, a behavior might fit into more than one distortion or irrational belief category**.

Any way you look at it, however, Beck's cognitive therapy is at least a second cousin to REBT. Last, we have psychiatrist **Maxie Maultsby Jr. (1932–2016), who studied with Ellis and created RBT, rational behavior therapy, and rational self counseling (RSC)**.

Maultsby uses REBT principles but has the client complete **a written self-analysis**. He also uses imagery based on the theory of **rational imagery**. Maultsby felt his RBT is ideal for multicultural counseling and substance use and addiction issues, and he's well known in both of those fields.

All of the aforementioned approaches of Ellis, Beck, and Maultsby rely on cognitive restructuring, which is simply a popular term indicating that the client is taught to think in a more productive manner with regard to emotionally charged situations.

Criticisms of Ellis. Some therapists take issue with the fact that he felt that therapist attributes such as caring and personal warmth are not necessary for successful therapy. In essence there is not enough emphasis on building a relationship with the client. Psychodynamic therapists feel that Ellis underestimates the need for free association, examining the past in-depth, unconscious processes, and transference. **These criticisms would apply to all of the cognitive or cognitive behavioral therapies**.

Whether you like it or not, Ellis's theory has become one of the most popular theories around. In fact, he's one of the most well-known psychologists and sexologists in the history of psychotherapy.

In 1988, the American psychologists Patricia A. Resick, Candice Monson, and Cathleen Chard created CPT, or cognitive processing therapy, to help clients with PTSD resulting from trauma. The therapy excels in ridding the client of thinking that causes them to believe they caused the event or that

their incompetence resulted in the negative situation. Here again, like other forms of CBT, the focus is on erroneous thinking patterns. The therapy generally uses a 12-session format outlined by a treatment manual. The modality is popular with veterans, sexual assault victims, and even refugees.

Let's turn our attention from the active directive approach of Albert Ellis to the nondirective approach of Carl Ransom Rogers. If you believe in astrology, then the counselor-producing stars must have all been hitting the right keys in 1902, as both Rogers and Erik Erikson were born in that year. Rogers died in 1987.

His boyhood years were lonely and even a bit isolated, and they were filled with scholarly rather than social pursuits.

Rogers came from a strict religious background and even spent some time studying at Union Theological Seminary where he ultimately received his PhD in psychology in 1931, from the Teachers College of Columbia University.

Categorically speaking, Rogers is known as a phenomenologist. Phenomenology refers to how the individual experiences and perceives reality. The phenomenological field is the way that the individual perceives or views the world. The important point is not how the counselor views the world but how the client sees it.

This, of course, goes against the early notion of some other schools of helping that believed the counselor knows best. **In the early 1940s, Rogers began to challenge the major methods of working with clients. This was certainly controversial at the time**.

First, Rogers didn't believe that the counselor should direct the interview, nor did he believe that counselors should be teachers or advice givers. He felt suggestion; interpretation, as was done in psychoanalysis; formal diagnosis; and psychological testing should not be integral parts of the therapeutic process.

Most of all, he rejected the Freudian view of human nature. As you will recall this is the deterministic notion we talked about which suggested that a person cannot be trusted and is motivated by sex and aggression and has little control over their own behavior due to repression.

Rogers, instead, viewed his clients as basically good, trustworthy, constructive, and rational. Incidentally, Rogerian

counseling and therapy has undergone name changes on several occasions. In the 1940s, the process was initially termed nondirective counseling. Later, he named his approach client-centered counseling or therapy.

Rogers's therapy was humanistic in the sense that he no longer referred to people seeking help as patients. **He felt the very term patient conveyed illness. Thus, he preferred the term client**. In the 1970s, his theory underwent another name change.

This time, to emphasize the power and control people had over themselves and others, **what was once nondirective therapy and later client-centered therapy became known as person-centered therapy**.

Rogers postulated that during childhood, children learn to act and feel dishonest to obtain regard from others.

Therefore, and here's a very important point, children literally deny feelings to be accepted by parents, relatives, teachers, significant others, and even friends. He called this "The Principle of Conditional Regard" and said that nearly every child has been a victim of this phenomenon.

In other words, unless the child conforms to the expectations of others, praise, and more importantly love, are withheld. To resolve this dilemma, the child develops what Rogers called conditions of worth. The child begins to learn they receive regard by behaving in certain ways and by denying other feelings or distorting them.

Rogers thus makes a distinction between the organism and the self. The organism is described as a total range of one's possible experiences. The self is the accepted portion of one's experience. That is to say, the self is the part that is not denied.

In therapy, the split between the self and the organism must be healed. In fact, the split may be eliminated if the client can describe their experiences in a nonjudgmental, nonthreatening setting.

Ergo, the goal of Rogerian therapy is to create this nonjudgmental, nonthreatening setting. In Rogerian therapy, the relationship is everything. To create a therapeutic environment, the counselor provides unconditional positive regard. Unconditional positive regard occurs when the counselor supports and accepts the client regardless of their behavior.

In essence, unconditional positive regard is unconditional acceptance.

Remember that first and foremost, Rogers is considered a humanistic psychologist. Humanistic psychologists, counselors, and therapists believe that human beings, because they are different from all other animals, should be thought of using psychological concepts of a special nature. Most humanistic therapists thus do not place that much stock in animal research.

Humanists, like Rogers, also feel that behaviorism and psychoanalysis are demeaning to humans. Behaviorism because it relies on animal research (are we exactly like a mouse or a fruit fly?) and analysis because it emphasizes instincts and the destructive side of the personality. Humanists feel that people's creative abilities and potential should be major factors in the treatment process.

Abraham Maslow (1908–1970) called humanistic psychology a third force in psychology, which literally meant an alternative to psychoanalysis, the first major force in psychology, and behaviorism, which was the second major force in psychology. In the beginning of counseling, the client is in a state of **incongruence**, according to Rogers, between their awareness and experience. **For therapy to be successful, the therapist must be congruent, integrated, authentic, and genuine.**

Rogers realized that in terms of congruence and unconditional positive regard, these concepts are not expressed in an all-or-none manner. These factors exist in various shades of gray on a continuum. **Prizing the client in a non-possessive way is what Rogers calls unconditional positive regard.**

The better the counselor is able to express unconditional positive regard and the more congruent the helper is, the better the chance for successful therapy.

Another critical factor that Rogers talked about is what is known as accurate empathy. Yes, it was none other than Carl R. Rogers who put the seemingly larger-than-life term *empathy* on the helping field's map. Empathy is like walking in someone else's shoes. Empathy is sensing the client's inner world as if it's your own. After sensing it, the therapist communicates what they understand and tells this to the client. The therapist tries hard to grasp the client's experience in the here and now.

I need to mention that accurate empathy is more than just reflecting things back to the client. It's turning the client's world into your own, identifying with it personally without getting lost in it.

Just for review purposes, the three main characteristics of Rogerian therapy that facilitate change are number one, the therapist is congruent, completely themselves in the relationship. This is seen as the most important of the three characteristics. The therapist must be genuine and authentic.

Number two, the therapist provides unconditional regard and acceptance. Number three, the therapist must be able to use accurate empathy and communicate this to the client. In person-centered therapy, the relationship between the client and counselor is the most important factor. Perhaps you've heard the old Rogerian adage, "When I accept myself just as I am, I change."

The saying is a bit paradoxical, but that is what takes place in therapy, with the individual using a counselor to facilitate the process.

On the head of a pin the three core conditions of counseling are: congruence, empathy, and unconditional positive regard. Expect to see these concepts on your exam and you won't leave disappointed!

Criticisms of Rogerian person-centered therapy. Many counselors feel that person-centered therapy is excellent for the early stages of counseling, but as counseling progresses, more directive techniques such as those from TA, REBT, Gestalt, or reality therapy could enhance the sessions. Or, to put it another way, an action stage of helping is missing from Rogers' approach but would be desirable.

Finally, regarding Rogerian therapy, many, though not all, experts warn that this approach is decidedly not the treatment of choice for crisis situations such as those persons who are suicidal.

Let's switch gears now and discuss reality therapy. **Reality therapy was created by the American psychiatrist William Glasser, who was born in 1925 and lived until 2013**. Glasser, like Albert Ellis, did a lot of lecturing, and believe me, both luminaries were master presenters and worth hearing. YouTube and some counseling sites offer samples of their ideas and presentation styles.

Glasser was trained as a chemical engineer and a psychiatrist, but his training did not convince him that psychoanalysis was the most efficacious form of treatment. Glasser felt that individuals are responsible for their own actions.

Like REBT, reality therapy is cognitive, didactic, practical, and behavioral. Reality therapy also relies heavily on contracting. Because it is so pragmatic and not cloaked in complex personality theory, Glasser's approach appeals to caseworkers, teachers, juvenile workers, social workers, rehabilitation specialists, and even principals.

Simply put, since reality therapy is straightforward and easy to understand, it may appeal to interventionists who <u>don't</u> have a great deal of psychotherapeutic experience or knowledge of personality theory.

In terms of classifying reality therapy, Glasser feels that the techniques are behavioristic. He points out nonetheless that he vehemently disagrees with Skinner's operant paradigm. Reality therapy postulates behavioral change comes from internal rather than external or environmental stimuli.

Since behavior is internally controlled, it implies that the person has a choice in terms of their course of action. **Glasser describes his therapy in terms of eight concrete steps.**

Step one. Establish a relationship with the client. Glasser believes a supportive, warm, and accepting relationship is most helpful here.

Step two. Focus on the client's current behavior. Interestingly, reality therapists don't spend a lot of time focusing on the client's past. In fact, when the past is examined, it is often to discuss the successes and not the failures that occurred. Therapy, is centered on: what are you doing now?

Incidentally, forms of therapy that focus on the here and now or on the present, like reality therapy, are known as ahistoric or ahistorical forms of therapy. Logically, forms of therapy that emphasize the client's past and put emphasis on one's childhood such as psychodynamic therapies or analysis are often categorized as historic forms of counseling and therapy.

Step three. Ask the client to participate in evaluating behavior. Notice how eloquently Glasser avoids psychiatric and psychological terminology. In this stage, Glasser invites the client to look at their own behavior to ascertain whether their behavior is helpful.

The goal is that, generally, even the most resistant client can come to the realization that their course of action is inefficient and ineffective.

Step four. Develop plans for change. A good plan focuses on specifics like where, when, how, what, and how often. The emphasis is on what the client will do, not what the client won't do. The bottom line is that the client finds a practical way to turn talk into positive action.

Step number five. Get a commitment regarding changes which need to be made. Glasser believes that sticking to a plan fosters mental health. The key here is to make the commitment a reasonable one.

Step number six. The counselor never accepts excuses. Glasser feels that accepting excuses reinforces the individual's sense of inadequacy. Thus, the counselor must take a tough position in this respect. What happens, you may ask, if the plan truly doesn't work? Glasser says you go back to steps four and five and develop another plan and get a commitment to follow through with it.

Step number seven. Punishment is never utilized. You realize that this step is a bit different from some behavior and REBT therapists who may rely on punishment as a viable treatment option. When the client fails, the reality therapist remains nonjudgmental and asks the client if indeed they honestly wish to change.

The final step, number eight. **Never give up on the client**. The trademark of reality therapy is persistence. The therapist, therefore, continually conveys the message that the client can change.

Glasser believes in choice theory. He also emphasizes his concepts of **success identity** and **failure identity**. A responsible individual who develops a high degree of self-worth has a success identity. A great deal of this individual's personal strength is the result of what Glasser called "**Positive Addiction"** – also the name of a book he wrote in the '70s.

Meditation or jogging are examples that Glasser gives us of positive addiction. These are activities which are noncompetitive, and they can be performed alone. They lend themselves to self-improvement. The success identity is intended to meet the person's needs, and ironically so is the failure identity. Nevertheless, the failure identity is characterized by faulty perceptions and irresponsible behavior.

It has been said that reality therapy is geared to the three Rs – right, responsibility, and reality.

In 1981 Glasser added the element of control theory to his work. Control theory is a phenomenological concept. It emphasizes that the pictures one creates in their mind are important, and **control theory states that we behave to control the world. The world does not control us**.

Control theory is now known as choice theory. Later in his career Glasser sometimes called his approach reality therapy with choice theory. Clients choose to be disturbed or choose to live their lives in positive and productive ways. **Choice theory assumes we have the power to control ourselves, but we only have limited power to control others**. Speaking of worlds, you might say that this theory is worlds apart from radical behaviorism or strict operant learning theory.

Glasser feels that what happens outside of us is not as important as what happens inside. In other words, we try to control the world for a purpose.

Both Glasser and his wife, Carleen Glasser, compiled books on reality therapy. His basic text was his 1965 work, *Reality Therapy, a New Approach to Psychiatry*. Four years later, he wrote *Schools Without Failure*, which illuminates the merits of his approach when applied to educational settings.

He also wrote extensively about **quality education**. Therapists can also secure works compiled by his wife, which are casebooks of reality therapy and choice theory. In the year 2000, he wrote *Reality Therapy in Action*.

He co-authored *Eight Lessons for a Happier Marriage* with his wife in 2007.

Criticisms. As you may have guessed, reality therapy has been blasted on the grounds that it's too simplistic and gives little or no credence to unconscious material. Glasser does not believe that the counselor needs to deal with repressed childhood memories, dreams, or transference.

Finally, although Dr. Glasser was a psychiatrist (i.e., a medical doctor) he thoroughly disliked psychiatric medicines, which he often referred to as "brain drugs," and once told me he could never remember prescribing them.

And although this obviously won't be on your exam, I thought you might find it fascinating that Glasser, who was kind enough to contribute to several of my books, told me during a discussion around 2010 that if he were going into the field at that point in time, he would study counseling rather than psychiatry. I would imagine a lot of folks reading this text would concur with his conclusion!!!

After Dr. Glasser passed away the baton seemed to be passed on to Dr. Robert Wubbolding, an ACA Legend of Counseling who began writing reality therapy books in 1988 and created a well-known counseling concept dubbed WDEP, or the WDEP system of reality therapy.

Each letter contains a cluster of possible interventions. **W** = clients define and what they **want** from the world around them, from themselves, from the counselor, and the counseling process. These and the counselor's interventions are summarized in one letter, **W. D** = Discussions that focus on **doing,** such as actions, self-talk, feelings, and physiology. **E** = Self-**evaluation**. The most crucial component of reality therapy. Counselors ask questions such as, "Are your current actions helping or hindering your relationships?" "Is what you are doing helping or hurting?" "Are your actions against the law?" **P** = Treatment **plans** relate to the five needs proposed by reality therapy (survival, love and belonging, power, freedom, and fun).

Now, no discussion of the various types of therapies would be complete without a brief discussion of **TA or transactional analysis**.

Transactional analysis was created by psychiatrist Eric Berne (real name Eric Lennard Bernstein), who was born in 1910. He died in 1970, the same year Fritz Perls, who was the father of Gestalt therapy, died. I'll discuss Perls next.

At one point in his career, Berne studied with Erik Erikson. Strangely Berne was turned down for membership in a well-known psychoanalytic association before he decided to create his own approach. Berne became a household name in 1964 when he published a blockbuster book entitled *Games People Play*.

There is no doubt that TA helped drive the popularity of the self-help book boom in the 1960s and 1970s.

Three years later, TA was in the public eye once again as a former military psychiatrist, **Tom Harris (1910–1995)** wrote *I'm OK – You're OK*. This book literally brought TA lingo into the remote corners of the world. In 1972, there was another booster shot for the theory as Berne authored the book *What Do You Say After You Say Hello?*

In the same year therapists **Muriel James (1917–2018)** – yes, she lived to age 100 – and **Dorothy Jongeward** (1925–2021) penned the bestseller *Born to Win*, featuring TA information with Gestalt experiments. The book was a winner, embraced by the therapeutic community *and* the public alike.

TA made psychology and counseling interesting, fun, and easy to understand. At the heart of this therapy is the contract created by the client, replete with goals for the therapy process.

Some theorists saw Berne's model as a popular psychology, which took Freudian nomenclature and changed it into common everyday terms like parent, child, and adult rather than superego, id, and ego.

Because the terminology was easy to understand, the bibliotherapeutic references plentiful, and the emphasis upon interaction between individuals, TA was a natural for group therapy, and indeed became a very popular modality for group counseling.

Unlike Freudian analysis, TA is not a deterministic model. TA believes that people have choices and can reverse decisions made in the past.

Berne's early work in TA emphasized three ego states that are classifications of behavior – the parent, the adult, and the child, or the so-called PAC. Not surprisingly, many therapists insist that these entities roughly correspond to Freud's superego, ego, and id. Analysis of the ego states when performing transactional analysis is called structural analysis.

The **parent ego state, similar to Freud's super-ego,** houses attitudes and behaviors incorporated or learned from others, mostly parents and caretakers.

The **adult ego state, analogous to Freud's ego,** is said to operate independently of one's age. Its concern is current reality. It is not emotional. It is not judgmental. The adult ego state is rational and logical. The adult ego state examines the information available and then and only then decides what to do based on intellect.

The **child ego state, roughly like Freud's id,** consists of impulses that may be playful and likes to act spontaneously. It is said to be made up of old or archaic behavior from childhood. Therapists using this persuasion are reminded that only one ego state is dominant at a given moment.

Words, thoughts, metacommunication, and most notably body language are indicative of which ego state the individual is operating out of. Sometimes, TA therapists become even more technical and precise referring to different entities which reside in a given ego state.

For example, the parent ego state contains the **critical parent** that consists of the shoulds, the oughts, and the musts.

Parental messages are sometimes referred to as **parental injunctions** and produced by the **nurturing parent.** The nurturing parent is the supportive side of the parent ego state, the caretaker if you will.

In the case of **the child ego state, it is composed of the natural child, the adapted child, and the little professor**. The natural child can be impulsive and self-centered. The natural child is curious, affectionate, and uncensored.

The child ego state is what a baby would be like if there were no outside influences. The entity is like a baby in the sense that it's affectionate when needs are met but angry when they are not.

The adapted child refers to adaptations a child makes regarding natural impulses, meeting the demands of training, school, authorities, schedules, and traumatic situation influences necessitating adaptations. Adults operating out of this mode may comply at all costs, withdraw, or procrastinate.

Next, we have the little professor. **The little professor is creative and full of intuition**. Thus, the little professor is a great amateur, untrained psychologist, or counselor, who is superb at reading other's nonverbal behavior and is very good at psyching out others, according to TA.

TA believes that a creative person relying on the skills of the child ego state might write a novel, compose a song, designing an innovative office, or improve interpersonal relationships.

Using the three ego states, let's analyze a typical situation. Let's say your professor in graduate school has just given you a lengthy and tough homework assignment. The parent ego state says, "Dr. Friedhouser shouldn't be a professor. He lacks logic, and he is not realistic."

The adult ego state might respond with, "Dr. Friedhouser understands that we will need to know a lot of material if we're going to pass our comprehensive exams." The child ego state could react by saying, "Hey, nobody is going tell me to study. I'm going out clubbing tonight."

TA also recognizes strokes. Strokes are verbal and/or physical recognition. A positive stroke could be a hug, or maybe the phrase, "I love you."

A negative stroke is a form of what TA calls a discount. A negative stroke or discount implies to the person that they are not OK. Criticizing, teasing, laughing at others, ignoring them, or ridiculing them would be examples of discounting.

Another key term in TA is games. In transactional analysis, a psychological game has a concealed or ulterior motive. Games have an underlying message.

Games prevent intimacy and honesty. TA therapists admit that their clients play psychological games to win, but by winning, they're losing in life. Without therapeutic intervention, games tend to be repetitive. The TA therapist is also going to be concerned about which of four psychological positions in life define the client. They are:

The I'm OK – You're OK position that promotes mental health.

I'm OK – You're Not OK is a position that causes clients to blame others for their difficulties. In severe cases, it can abet paranoia or even homicidal and related criminal tendencies.

Then we have **the I'm Not OK – You're OK. This is the position that causes people to feel inept and inferior to others**. In extreme cases, it can cause severe depression and suicide may result.

The final **I'm Not OK – You're Not OK position is especially pernicious. Such individuals may be suicidal, homicidal, both, or schizoid (i.e., a detached individual who avoids relationships and is cold and apathetic toward life)**.

In TA, the person's life unfolds according to a life script, which is like a novel. The script is based on messages or injunctions accepted as a child. Therapy is based on creating new, healthy decisions and, in a sense, rewriting your own life script. TA therapists often rely on Dr. Stephen Karpman's drama triangle to help explain games to clients. Karpman, by the way, studied with Eric Berne.

The Karpman Drama Triangle consists of a persecutor, a rescuer, and a victim position. In a game, the person rapidly changes from one position on the triangle to the next.

TA also employs the concept of psychological trading stamps. The child ego state is said to collect trading stamps. Maybe you recall folks from the past talking about those programs where you would collect X number of stamps or books of stamps, and then you could redeem them for merchandise. In the 1950s and 1960s many folks cashed in stamps in for items they wanted for themselves or their family.

This works in the same fashion, except that these stamps are psychological in nature. **When the person manipulates somebody to reexperience childhood feelings, it's known as a racket.** When you amass many stamps, you can use them to justify a behavior such as a nervous breakdown (i.e., inability to function or perform everyday actions), a tremendous burst of anger, or perhaps a divorce.

Redemption is indicated by phrases like "I've had enough now," "I'm leaving home," "I'm at the end of my rope," or perhaps "I'm quitting school" or "That's the last straw. I'm going to exercise and get my body into shape."

Gold stamps are associated with feelings of self-appreciation. White, brown, or gray stamps are associated with inadequacy and the I'm not OK position.

One final point we need to explain, and that is the transaction in transactional analysis. Berne felt that healthy transactions are those which can be classified as complementary.

In a complementary transaction, the response is always predictable. Thus, if you diagram the ego states out and you look at a picture of two people who are communicating in a healthy fashion, you'll see that the message and the response are always parallel in a complementary transaction. Incidentally, if you'd like to see this for yourself, there's a diagram of it in my book, the *Encyclopedia of Counseling*.

A crossed transaction is not parallel and not very healthy. If you respond out of your adult, for example, and say to a colleague, "How many clients do you have today?" that's an adult to an adult exchange. If the person replies, "Three clients," that's an adult-to-adult message. It's healthy. It's complementary.

If, on the other hand, the person yells back at you, "All you care about is numbers and money," then the colleague is speaking out of their parent ego state to hook your child. That's a crossed transaction, and it's unhealthy.

Crossed transactions and ulterior transactions are used in games for a payoff. Berne called this a gimmick. TA therapists generally spend a generous amount of time analyzing the client's interactional patterns or, in TA lingo, transactions.

Based on a 2021 meta-analysis TA now checks in as a bona fide form of evidence-based practice.

Criticisms of TA – well, to use TA terminology, it's a bit gimmicky itself with all its jargon. In essence, TA may have too much jargon. Others say TA is guilty of fostering a game in its clientele, namely game calling.

Now let's forge on to **Gestalt therapy, created by Frederick Fritz Perls, who was born in 1893 and died in 1970.**

Dr. Fritz (as he was usually called) Perls attended two institutes of psychoanalysis. He was personally analyzed by Dr. **Wilhelm Reich (1897–1957)**, a physician and analyst, who was a controversial figure who died in jail after building a so-called Orgone box (also called an Orgone energy accumulator), a physical device intended to improve mental and physical and mental health, which was outlawed by the US government. Ultimately, Reich was instructed by the government to destroy all the accumulators and did not. He died in a medium-security federal prison in Lewisburg, Pennsylvania, of heart failure.

Perls was somewhat controversial himself. After studying with famous individuals like Reich, noted psychiatrist and neurologist **Kurt Goldstein (1878–1965)**, and Karen Harney, he came to the United States, where his workshops at the Esalen Institute in Big Sur, California, were extremely popular.

Gestalt is a German word with no exact English equivalent. It basically means form, figure, configuration, or the forming of an organized meaningful whole. The whole is something else than the sum of its parts. The implication is the whole is better than you might expect from the sum of the parts. Gestalt therapists altered this statement slightly and often quip, "the whole is greater than the sum of its parts." Perls saw the disturbed person as fragmented.

Hence the goal of Gestalt therapy is to help the person be aware of and reclaim fragmented parts. In other words, become whole. In this approach, the major emphasis is on awareness.

Gestalt therapy is experiential rather than simply intellectual or cognitive. The thrust is on the here and now. The therapist utilizing this paradigm literally creates experiments and frustrates the patient.

Perls was adamant in his position that awareness in and of itself is curative. Thus, via frustration, the patient realizes that they can do exactly what they expect from the therapist.

Gestalt therapists rarely ask clients why. Instead, they ask what or how. For example, "What is your right leg doing?" "How do your hands feel now?" These would be typical questions in Gestalt therapy.

Perls was fond of reminding people that nothing exists except in the here and now. Perls believed that "Why" questions do not promote awareness. Instead, they lead to obsessing about the past.

"What" and "How" questions do nevertheless boost awareness. Thinking about the future can also create problems and anxieties. Once again, Perls liked to stick with the present.

If the past is being worked on, it is worked on and treated as if the incident is being lived in the "Now." For example, a Gestalt therapist might say to a client, "Become that five-year-old who is alone and afraid to walk home all by yourself."

The technique just described helps clients deal with unfinished business. Unfinished business refers to emotional debris and turmoil, which clutters the mind and literally prohibits awareness in the "Now."

Resentment is seen as the most pernicious form of unfinished business. Especially since resentment, which is not expressed, is said to be converted to guilt. To describe the disturbed personality, Perls used his so-called onion analogy.

To reach a state of happiness, Perls felt the individual needed to peel away five distinct layers of neurosis. The phony layer, the phobic layer, the impasse layer, the implosive layer, and the explosive layer.

The phony layer. This is the game-playing level when we act like somebody we're not.

Next comes the **phobic level, or layer**. At this level, the person is scared, stiff, or phobic, to use Gestalt nomenclature.

Here we wonder, "If we really become ourselves, will people still like us? Or will we be rejected?"

The next layer is even deeper. We call it the **impasse**. A psychological impasse is a sticking point. We feel stuck, even a little dead, as if we can't mature anymore. To get past this impasse level or layer, we must not run away from it. Instead, we need to experience it.

Next, there is the **implosive level**. In the implosive level, we encounter the deadness and a lack of authenticity.

This moves us into the fifth and final level, the explosive level. In this layer, the person unleashes pent-up energy and explodes to become alive, real, and authentic.

I must absolutely mention that Gestalt relies heavily on dream work. Remember how I told you that **Freud referred to dreams as "the royal road to the unconscious mind?" Perls said, "Dreams are the royal road to integration. Dreams contain an existential message to the self."**

In dreamwork, Perls often utilized the **empty chair technique** in which the client would switch seats in order to become a person or object apart from their self that occurred in the dream, and then the client could talk or interact with that part. The empty chair technique can also be utilized for material other than dream work.

Another principle of Gestalt therapy is that the counselor asks clients to convert questions to I statements. If a client says to a Gestalt counselor, "Don't you feel it's always best to express anger?" the counselor will tell the client to express this in an I statement.

In this case, the client would say, "I feel it is always best to experience anger." Clients are further encouraged to use I language. They're asked to substitute I for the word it when discussing their body.

Gestalt also promotes techniques referred to as the exaggeration or the repetition game. Here the client has made a very important statement, but they said it in a very casual way. Hence, they have minimized the importance of the statement.

The therapist would then ask the client to repeat it over and over and over, each time directing the client to say it louder and with more emotion. This strategy is intended to make the client cognizant and aware of the statement's significance. Exaggeration techniques can also be physical, such as when the therapist might say something like, "Exaggerate the fact that your hand is shaking."

Keep in mind Gestalt requires clients to take responsibility regarding feelings and statements. Thus, the client is literally instructed to say, "I take responsibility for such and such."

Gestalt is also popularized by the popular dialogue game or what exams often call the dialogue experiment, again using the empty chair technique.

Here, **the top dog and underdog concepts** come into play. **The top dog is the critical parent with the shoulds, oughts, and musts. The top dog is moralistic, righteous, and downright mean at times, but the personality in therapy is split. There's also the underdog. The underdog is passive and victimized, but it is also defiant and fights for control**.

Thus, the client plays the top dog in one chair and the underdog in the other chair. Theoretically, the idea of this exercise is to increase awareness and foster integration of the personality. In a group situation, a Gestalt therapist will often choose one individual to work on problems for a given time period while others watch, learn, and provide feedback.

The person that the group is concentrating on is known as the person in the hot seat. Hot seat is a very popular term in Gestalt therapy. In Gestalt therapy, you'll also hear the comment, "Making the rounds." Let me assure you it has nothing to do with working in a hospital.

In Gestalt therapy, making the rounds involves speaking or experimenting with every member of your group. For example, if Jean says, "I have trouble telling people what I like about them." Then the therapist would suggest that Jean approach each member of the group with the statement, "I like you because . . . " then finish the sentence.

Perls was primarily interested in three ego defense mechanisms, which he felt blocked authenticity. These defense mechanisms are projection, introjection, and retroflection.

Projection occurs when an individual ascribes personal attributes to others or the environment.

In Gestalt therapy, however, projection is worked on directly via **a technique called playing the projection**. With this method the client plays the person that they claim to dislike or detest.

The second defense mechanism is known as **introjection**, which means you uncritically accept other people's ideas, beliefs, and notions.

Retroflection is taking something you would like to do to someone else, but out of fear, you do it to yourself.

For example, the old saying that the person who wanted to kill themself really wants to kill someone else is an example of retroflection.

Perls often used **the reversal technique** in which the client acts the opposite of the way they really are to break out of a pernicious behavior that they are engaging in.

Despite all the techniques, Gestalt warns against being technique happy or using techniques exclusively. **Gestalt therapists are urged to create an I–Thou relationship with the client.** Although Gestalt therapy was once the most popular brand of counseling in the world, it is not beyond criticism.

In fact, whenever I talk about criticisms of Gestalt, I'm reminded of the statement by Richard Bandler, one of the cofounders of neurolinguistic programming, or NLP for short. He says, "Have you heard about unfinished business? It's finished. You just didn't like the way it turned out."

As you may have guessed, cognitive therapists are turned off by the fact that **Gestalt intentionally ignores cognitive aspects of emotional disturbance**. Cognitive therapists also dislike the fact that the Gestalt helper is not placed in a teaching role.

Others do not favor combining Gestalt with TA, a very common practice, incidentally, as TA, which has been accused of having few techniques of its own, is a cognitive model, while Gestalt is not. Some people, in all fairness, do say that the two schools complement each other. However, the experts who do not believe this say, "It's a little like mixing water with oil: you really can't do it."

Other proficient helpers warn that Gestalt overemphasizes confrontation and is an aggressive form of helping despite the fact it is generally classified as a humanistic or existential form of counseling. This can lead to power abuse on the part of the counselor. Practitioners counter with the fact that Gestalt has gotten a little better in this respect. In terms of multicultural work, experts fear the Gestalt emphasis on emotional expression will not be appropriate for many cultural and ethnic groups.

Another criticism: there's not enough research to back the use of Gestalt therapy. Perhaps the most remarkable evaluation is that the early Gestalt psychologists, who were interested in figure ground perceptual phenomenon, do not believe that Gestalt therapy really has a lot to do with real or genuine Gestalt psychology.

Hmm. So, Dr. Rosenthal: "If one wanted to be extremely critical then, one could assert that Gestalt really isn't Gestalt." Yes, that is indeed what I am saying!

Very briefly, I want to mention the concept of existential therapy. Several key figures could be mentioned under the heading of the existential movement. The first, of course, is **Viktor Frankl (1905–1997)**, who holds an MD and a PhD from the University of Vienna.

Frankl spent three years from 1942 to 1945 in concentration camps such as Auschwitz and Dachau. During those years he lost his parents, wife, and brother, who were also prisoners in the camps. In the concentration camp, Frankl became convinced that even the most horrendous situations cannot take away our power to choose our own attitude.

Viktor Frankl, a psychiatrist, is the father of logotherapy and the author of the international bestseller *Man's Search for Meaning*. Logotherapy emphasizes the merits of paradox and humor in the psychotherapeutic process. Logotherapy, strictly speaking, means healing through meaning.

Most experts do not feel that existentialism is a separate school of therapy. Instead, they feel it really refers to any approach which utilizes existential philosophy. Existentialism is a system of philosophy grounded in the work of Jean-Paul Sartre, Martin Heidegger, Karl Jaspers, Nietzsche, Kierkegaard, and Martin Buber.

Buber, as you may recall, is the philosopher responsible for the I–Thou relationship, which is also stressed in the Rogerian and Gestalt schools of counseling. The I–Thou concept implies that clients are not seen as an "it" but rather as a person in the process of change. The client is not viewed as a fixed entity. Both the therapist and the client will change via the relationship.

The I–Thou concept stresses the quality of the relationship and the change for both parties involved. **The goal of existential therapy is really to restore meaning to life**.

Therapists of this persuasion speak of clients suffering from existential neurosis. Existential neurosis implies that a person could be successful, but nevertheless, the person is unhappy and unfulfilled due to a loss of meaning in life.

The existential movement, which had philosophical as well as psychological impact, as you would guess by its name, focuses on existence. Existence, it postulates, is the only reality one knows.

As a form of therapy, existentialism emphasizes the here and now. It emphasizes the uniqueness of each human being. It's a very optimistic form of therapy, in the sense that at any given time an individual can use their will to grow and to heal. **The existential therapist believes that people are responsible for their own situations**.

Thus, the existential therapists won't really allow you to blame your mean grandparents or your mother's nagging that occurred before age 12 for your unhappiness. **The existential message is that you can have freedom to choose and that your misery occurred because you allowed others to choose for you in the past**.

All in all, existential counselors have faith in their client's ability to change, and they stress autonomy.

In the United States, the existential movement was sparked by psychologist **Rollo May (1909–1994)** and later psychiatrist **Irvin D. Yalom (1931–**), who is well known for his writings on group psychotherapy, death and dying, and counseling in general.

You may be asked to identify the terms **Umwelt, Mitwelt, and Eigenwelt**. **The Umwelt refers to the biological world of self-awareness. The Mitwelt is the world of relationships or encounters with others. The Eigenwelt is the world of the identity or of the self**.

You should also remember that according to this theory, humans are free. Culture, upbringing, and external circumstances are seen as excuses. They may limit people, but they don't <u>totally</u> determine behavior.

This existential notion has been criticized. For example, interventionists using this modality often worry that poor and poverty-stricken clients will feel that they are being blamed for their predicament.

Multicultural counselors point out that external and environmental factors such as oppression, racism, and discrimination can have a huge impact and that existential theory minimizes this.

Existentialism also emphasizes death or the reality of nonbeing or nonexistence. It is said that death really gives life reality and meaning. Because of this, an individual may feel what is known as existential guilt, which refers to not utilizing present moments in a productive manner.

This predicament ensures that everybody is conscious of isolation and alienation. Existential aloneness suggests that we are unique and that we can never totally grasp the nature of someone else's experience.

One other very important point. This model emphasizes that neurotic anxiety or anxiety that would bring you to see a counselor is out of proportion for the situation. It is immobilizing until we realize that it is telling us something. It tells us that we need to change the direction of our lives. Some anxiety is normal, but anxiety that gets in the way of our creativity is not considered normal.

What do the critics charge when they talk about existentialism? They say that it's weak in terms of giving the counselor concrete techniques or strategies.

Others accuse it of being cloaked in vague and mystical language and assert that the approach is a reaction against the scientific method, for example, what you would see in behavior therapy. One thing for sure, it is decidedly not systematic, and it lacks specificity.

Time to ask you a very important question. Have you been out of grad school for a while? How about it, have you?

If your answer was yes, then it might come as a surprise to you to discover that many counseling textbooks have a chapter devoted to a classification of psychotherapeutic intervention that you most likely never studied, and that, my dear reader, is **the category of postmodern and social constructionism approaches**, most notably, **solution-focused brief therapy (SFBT) and narrative therapy**.

The postmodern view is that reality is socially constructed. In the traditional or modern view, the client often seeks therapy when they have deviated too far from what the person considers normal. For example, the therapist might administer a psychological test to the client and dispute their reality by saying, "The depression inventory indicates you're normal. You are not depressed."

In the postmodern view, however, the client's reality, for example, in this case, that the client is depressed, is accepted whether it is accurate or not. In social constructionism, the therapist does not accept the role of the all-knowing expert. Instead, the helper acts like a consultant or a partner. The counselor is said to build a collaborative relationship with the client.

Clients are seen as experts who know their lives better than anyone else. Incidentally, the term "social constructionism," came from a 1966 book by sociologists Peter L. Berger (1929–2017) and Thomas Luckmann (1927–2016) titled *The Social Construction of Reality – A Treatise in the Sociology of Knowledge*.

Social constructionist helpers, regardless of the theory they practice, are optimistic and do not blame or judge their clients. **One postmodern approach is SFBT, or solution-focused brief therapy that grew out of the strategic therapy orientation formulated at the Mental Research Institute, or MRI. SFBT, as its name implies, focuses on solutions and does not focus on the problem.**

Social worker **Steve de Shazer (1940–2005)**, although he did not work at the MRI, is often credited as a pioneer in this area. Other major contributors include **Insoo Kim Berg (1934–2007) and Bill O'Hanlon (1952–)**, who trained with psychiatrist and psychologist **Milton H. Erickson (1901–1980)**, social worker and licensed marriage and family counselor Michele Weiner-Davis, Scott Miller, and more recently counselor Bob Bertolino.

The approach is very optimistic. It assumes that the client can solve their own problems. The job of the counselor is to make the client aware of this potential or this competence.

In solution-focused therapy, the counselor looks for what *is* working. Therefore, therapists of this ilk are fond of asking exception questions.

For example, "Was there ever a time when you did get along with your father?" Or try this one, "Was there ever a period when you were not anxious?"

SFBT also makes use of a concept that Shazer and Insoo Kim Berg termed the "miracle question." **The counselor would say something like, "If a miracle occurred and your problem was solved overnight, how would you know it was solved? What exactly would be different?"**

To piggyback on this strategy, **solution-focused helpers additionally rely on scaling questions**. This is somewhat analogous to the SUDS intervention used in Wolpe's systematic desensitization.

The counselor might ask a client, "On a scale of 1 to 10, with 1 representing how you felt during the first session of therapy and 10, how you will feel when your miracle occurs, how would you rate your level of depression right this moment?" Scaling helps monitor the client's progress.

The brief therapist often relies on FFST, or the so-called formula first session task.

This merely implies that the therapist will often prescribe homework between the first and second therapy sessions.

Do brief therapies, or BTs, as they're sometimes called, really work? The jury is still out. A November 1995 survey conducted by *Consumer Reports* called "Does Therapy Help?" concluded that more sessions often yield more results.

Newer research indicates BTs can be valuable.

Now I want to mention **another postmodern school of intervention, narrative therapy, which is a viable modality for children or adults. Narrative therapy was created by the Australian social worker Michael White (1948–2008), working in Australia, and social worker David Epston (1944–), currently practicing in New Zealand. Narrative therapy suggests that we live our lives a certain way because of the stories we tell about ourselves and the stories others tell about us.**

These **stories are said to be "problem saturated."** In other words, the stories are routinely told in such a manner that change seems to be nearly impossible. Unfortunately, the stories often become self-fulfilling prophecies. **To make certain that clients do not see themselves as the problem, narrative therapists use externalizing conversations to externalize the problem. The client is not blamed for the difficulty nor is the person urged to blame others.**

This would be important if the client already has a DSM diagnosis and is labeling themselves. The therapist's questions intentionally imply that the problem is outside the person. For example. "How does the anxiety that was passed on to you from watching television shows sneak up on you and cause problems in your marriage?" The therapist, who often acts like a partner to the client, might say, "Would you join me in my fight to eliminate these episodes that keep you from having the marriage you want?"

The therapist helps the client construct and reauthor new, healthy stories. The client is often asked to tell and re-tell their story, but to highlight strengths and accomplishments rather than dwelling on problems. This is often referred to as **deconstructing the dominant narrative**. The therapist may even send the client letters, illuminating the new story. In the letters, they will point out positive, healthy changes in the client. What is fascinating is that some counselors insist that the letters have more influence on the client than the actual therapy sessions.

When conducting narrative therapy, **the counselor is not held out as an expert or an advice-giver but rather collaborates with the client, couple, or family to facilitate the healing process. The approach stresses that the client can change and that problems are not merely the result of genetics**.

Mindfulness is a concept getting mega-publicity in the counseling space recently, and it has been incorporated into a myriad of therapies, most notably **dialectical behavior therapy (DBT) by Marsha Linehan**, who was initially using the modality to help clients diagnosed with borderline personality disorder, and **Steven Hayes (1948–), who helped create acceptance and commitment therapy (ACT). Radically open DBT (RO DBT), created by psychologist Thomas Lynch, used to assist clients with perfectionistic tendencies and excessive self-control, as seen in eating disorders, also makes use of mindfulness. In a nutshell, mindfulness occurs when one has a conscious experience of what is transpiring in the present moment such as thoughts, feelings, and awareness of the body. The client makes no judgments or evaluations regarding the experience. Mindfulness can seemingly even help ward off dementia**.

Mindfulness-based cognitive therapy (MBCT) and mindfulness-based pain management (MBPM) are also popular. The current popularity of mindfulness is often traced back to **Jon Kabat-Zinn (1944–)**, a molecular biologist, who created a **mindfulness-based stress reduction (MBSR) clinic** in 1978 after he learned of meditation, yoga, and Buddhist principles. Keep in mind that MBSR and many other mindfulness techniques are secular in the sense that they are not related to Buddhism. In fact, many Buddhist scholars are often critical of the movement. **Indeed, mindfulness has been used with and without meditation**.

Although mindfulness has clearly been beneficial for numerous persons, experts are concerned that mindfulness has exploded onto the scene and has become commercialized.

For example, I just punched the word "mindfulness" into Amazon, and it lists over 40,000 book titles (not a misprint!) showcasing the term not to mention toys, gifts, journals, and so on. A silicone Mindful Buddha was the featured item at the top of the page intended to help with guided mediation and even sleep. One major worry is that many individuals promoting the technique are not trained, nor do they possess licensed mental health professional credentials. Another point of contention is that more robust research is necessary. Buddhist scholars have been critical of the movement.

That concludes my discussion of the major forms of psychotherapeutic intervention. Sure, there are lesser-known modalities of counseling.

There's psychologist **Arthur Janov's (1924–2003) primal scream, which works on the principle of abreaction, or Wilhelm Reich's (mentioned earlier) vegetotherapy in which he postulated that mental health could be achieved by repeated sexual orgasm. Certainly, either of these would be much more controversial than mindfulness! Or bioenergetics and Rolfing, which rely on body manipulation, bodywork, or massage**.

How about psychologist **George Kelly's (1905–1967) psychology of personal constructs**, where the client is often asked to write a sketch of themselves and then act it out? Although Kelly is glossed over or not mentioned at all in many, if not most, texts on counseling, he is considered **the father of clinical cognitive psychology**. (Ironically, Kelly felt his approach was not truly cognitive and needed its own category.) The sketch would illuminate who the person really wants to become. There are lots of methods, but now you know the primary principles of the major modalities used by most counselors and therapists.

One way to categorize all the helping strategies when preparing for your exam is to follow the concise model proposed by the American Psychological Association. The APA asserts all legitimate psychotherapies fall into five broad key categories: 1) analysis or psychodynamic approaches, 2) behavior therapy, 3) cognitive therapy, 4) humanistic, and 5) integrative or holistic.

There are so many modalities, there is no way I could cover all of them on this program, nor could they ask you about all of them on your test with a limited number of exam questions.

What I'm going to discuss now is very important. **Most researchers believe that the most important quality in a counselor is caring. Caring is a genuine desire to be helpful**. In addition to caring, the client and the counselor must give of themselves. This reciprocity fosters interdependence, which really means the two people are mutually dependent. Research indicates that regardless of the type of therapy used, clients become more open to their feelings and explore them more effectively. They listen to themselves and others better as the client–counselor relationship develops.

The most powerful factor for fostering change, at least according to a lot of researchers, is empathy. Empathy is simply understanding another person's frame of reference. In addition to empathy, good counselors demonstrate respect, or what is sometimes known as positive regard. Respect means the counselor is nonjudgmental. As you will recall, Carl R. Rogers emphasized these factors.

The final factor, in addition to empathy and respect, is genuineness or congruence. It has been said that good counselors practicing different schools of therapy seem to be more alike than counselors who aren't that great who practice the same school of thought.

Perhaps that's because good counselors display empathy, respect, and genuineness. These three factors are known as the human relations core.

Experts also stress the importance of the social influence core.

The first social influence factor is confidence. The counselor who feels confident will not put themself down. Instead, this counselor will set realistic goals with clients and accept mistakes.

Another social factor is intimacy. A counselor who has a problem in this area will be distant and may feel rejection in the counseling setting. Counselors with difficulty in this respect may not confront the client.

Confrontation in counseling, by the way, occurs when there's a discrepancy between different verbalizations that the client uses or when there's a discrepancy between nonverbal and verbal behavior, and the counselor points it out. Of course, if you're worried about intimacy issues, you may not confront them because you'll be worried that they will reject you.

Then there is power, which is another social influence factor. A therapist who personally feels powerless may try to coax or cajole the client to their own way of thinking. Other therapists feel powerless because of their tendency to narrowly define therapy as the act of merely listening and reflecting.

The literature indicates that the power of the therapist is determined by three factors – expertness, attractiveness, and trustworthiness. A good way to remember this is the word EAT, or the EAT formula, E for expertness, A for attractiveness, and T for trustworthiness.

Expertness is not the same as competence. Competence really refers to your own feelings of adequacy or inadequacy. Expertness occurs when the client believes that the counselor has the proper training and proper skills to help them. Even your office can be helpful here.

Psychiatrist E. Fuller Torrey (1937–) humorously refers to the **edifice complex** or office complex rather than the Oedipus complex that Freud proposed. The edifice complex would suggest that the correct decor, degrees, and wall plaques can really improve your chances of being perceived as an expert.

Attractiveness refers to how positively the client thinks and feels toward the counselor on an interpersonal level.

The final social factor is trustworthiness. In counseling, trustworthiness can increase in time if the helper seems reliable, dependable, and interested in helping. If the client feels like they are merely a check for $110.00 an hour, then I guarantee you there will be a little trust. Violating confidentiality is another great way to kill trustworthiness and pick up a malpractice suit.

A good counselor has several other important skills. **First, the counselor should be attentive, or what is known in the field as attending behavior. Attending behavior on the part of the counselor is defined as any behavior that enhances communication and builds rapport, such as open posture, active listening, and good eye contact**.

By giving the client complete attention, the client knows the counselor is listening. **Minimal encouragers, such as um-hum, yes, and go on, also helping facilitate attending. To attain excellent attending skills, the counselor cannot think about their own personal problems during a session**.

Good counselors also seem to inquire by asking mainly open-ended rather than closed-ended questions. Closed-ended questions are bad because the client can repeatedly answer them with yes and no answers. "Do you like your job?" is a closed-ended question, while "Tell me your feelings about your job" is an example of an open-ended question.

Just so you'll know, "what" questions, and "how" questions, are generally considered better than "why" questions. "Why" questions may cause anger or defensiveness on the part of the client.

And for review, or in case you've been out of school for a while, again, open-ended questions are questions where the client cannot adequately answer them with just a yes or no.

The client is much more likely to respond with some dialogue; thus generally, open-ended questions are considered better. I would like to complete this section on helping relationships by making certain that you're familiar with some intervention techniques that are literally used in many forms of counseling.

Perhaps the most popular communication skill is known as paraphrasing.

Paraphrasing occurs when the counselor restates the client's communication. One caution here, folks. Do not parrot back the client's message. Parroting back statements verbatim causes the interview to go around in circles, so you never really get anywhere.

Moreover, studies show that **clients who were the victims of parroting often felt uncomfortable, and sometimes they were even angry at the counselor**. A disgruntled client might say something to the counselor like, "I just said that, now why are you saying it?" Try to use fresh words that the client has not verbalized when you paraphrase.

Another important skill is reflecting. Reflection is really a type of paraphrasing. Technically, some scholars in the field use the term reflection when the paraphrasing deals with emotional content rather than just facts. Other experts simply refer to reflection of cognition or content, versus reflection of emotion regarding feelings, to distinguish the two types of paraphrasing.

Some of the literature in the field speaks of micro skills of attending. Here are the micro skills that facilitate helping. Number one, face the client squarely. Your body posture must indicate involvement.

Number two, adopt an open posture. Sitting with crossed arms and legs at all times is a no-no. It says to the client that my counselor is not open and is not available to me.

Number three, lean forward slightly, not like you're eating spaghetti, and not like you are preparing for a martial arts competition, but just slightly, because that says that you're interested, not bored. If the client seems threatened, then that's going to be a problem and you wouldn't want to engage in this practice. A very small office or having your chair too close to the client's seat could also cause this strategy to backfire. **Counselors must be concerned with the notion of proximity or proxemics, or how the physical distance from another person (in the instance the client or clients in a group setting) will impact communication.**

Number four, maintain good eye contact. Don't stare at the client.

Number five, finally, be relaxed. Don't spend the entire session fidgeting.

Some counselor educators tell you that you can remember these skills via the memory device SOLER. S for squarely, O for open posture, L for leaning forward, E for maintaining good eye contact, and R for being relaxed.

Again, there are scores of psychotherapy modalities, and to think it all began with Freud. Even with all those models to choose from, **most counselors still consider themselves eclectic. Eclectic counselors see clients as unique, and they are quick to point out that a good counselor should choose the best ideas from all the available therapies.**

The eclectic counselor may use a behavioral technique at one point in therapy and a nondirective one at another point in therapy. The prime mover for the approach of eclecticism was **Frederick Charles Thorne (1909–1978)**, who wrote the first edition of the text *Principles of Personality Counseling: An Eclectic Viewpoint* in 1950.

Since the 1980s, the term psychotherapy integration has been popular. The term theoretical integration focuses on combining two or more modalities, not just techniques, as you might use in eclecticism, but two or more modalities to produce results that are superior to just using a single psychotherapy modality.

Finally let me close by reminding you that I will cover some of the finer points of these methods of counseling in future chapters and even introduce a few other viable candidates as well.

6

Master Lecture 5: Group Counseling and Group Work

All right, we're ready for a brand-new section, and that is groups. Now, the various modes of counseling including the eclectic and integrative approaches can also be used in a group counseling setting. Also please remember that before starting a new group at your practice or agency (or for that matter any program), a needs assessment should be conducted.

Let's start out with the basics. **What is a group? First, a group has a definable membership. There is unity, and the members interact with a shared sense of purpose. Before the 1960s and 1970s, most help was given in a dyadic relationship. Dyad means two, the counselor and the client**.

Some historical considerations. **Jane Addams (1860–1935)**, one of the founders of modern social work, who was inducted into the Hall of Fame of Great Americans, is credited with holding moralistic group discussions focused on hygiene and nutrition. **Some experts feel Addams's work was a precursor to the modern group movement**.

Next, there's Joseph Henry Pratt, MD (1872–1956), who is often cited as another pioneer in this area. Pratt began running groups for tuberculosis (TB) patients on a weekly basis in 1905.

DOI: 10.4324/9781003149712-6

The groups, which began with a lecture, provided encouragement and allowed members to share personal stories.

The actual term group therapy was coined in 1931 by psychiatrist Jacob Levy Moreno, who was born in 1889 and passed away in 1974. Moreno, you may recall, along with his wife, Zerka T. Moreno (1917–2016), a psychotherapist, co-founded psychodrama. In 1941, Moreno created the American Society for Group Psychotherapy and Psychodrama. One year later, Samuel Richard Slavson, a teacher, often abbreviated S.R. Slavson (1890–1981), founded the American Group Psychotherapy Association. Some literature has dubbed him the father of group psychotherapy, as he began running groups in 1919.

Practitioners of individual psychology are quick to point out that Alfred Adler's group guidance in the 1920s and '30s was composed of families and this also helped to spark the group movement. **Groups are sometimes classified as primary, secondary, or tertiary in nature. These are also terms that you'll see in community mental health and community psychology and psychiatry**.

Primary groups are preventive. That's easy enough to remember because they both begin with a P. Thus, the primary group attempts to prevent or ward off a problem. Some experts claim that nearly all guidance and psychoeducational groups would fall into this category. In many cases, the group would be trying to prevent addiction or medical problems such as AIDS.

Secondary groups are preventive and remedial. The word secondary implies that some form of emotional or physical disturbance is already present. The goal of a secondary group is to shorten the length or duration of the disorder, prevent it from getting worse, if you will. A secondary group might be a group for persons who have experienced sexual assault or a group for depressed hospital patients.

The tertiary group is intended as psychotherapy for those with long-term emotional problems. Tertiary groups focus more on each individual's mental health than you would find in, say, a primary group. As you may have guessed, there is decidedly some overlapping between these categories.

In any event, **the major benefit of group work is that human behavior can often be examined best in a social context. When**

compared to individual work, the group setting offers a chance to try out new or scary behaviors in a safe setting, or what we call an in vivo or real-life setting.

Groups also have the advantage of feedback from all the people in the group, plus feedback provided by the therapist or more than one therapist in the case of a group with co-therapists. Therefore, groups help improve socialization in clients while they help counselors with a large caseload.

Let's take a moment just to **list the pros and cons of group work. First the advantages. Groups, again, allow counselors to see more clients in the same amount of time. That's the first advantage.**

Number two, groups generally cost less and are more cost effective for agencies, hospitals, and practices. I mean, just think about it. Who can see more clients and bring in more revenue in a day, a helper who only sees clients on a one-on-one basis, or one who is running groups?

Third advantage, the group gives a sense of belonging with support, which is like a microcosm of society.

Fourth advantage, groups provide vicarious learning. The client imitates appropriate behavior demonstrated by the leader or perhaps other group members . . . or maybe both. This is sometimes known as spectator therapy.

Now, let's talk about the disadvantages of groups. One, less time is focused on the client than in an individual session.

Two, the client has less interaction with the leader compared to what the person would experience in an individual counseling session with a helper.

Three, groups can be intimidating and stifle client disclosure.

Four, group sessions are often longer than individual sessions and therefore take more of the client's time. The average group is about an hour and a half long.

Five, lack of assurance of confidentiality is a major issue.

Six, misapplication: a group is used for a given problem when another intervention modality such as individual counseling or marriage and family work would be more appropriate.

Number seven, organizing the group is difficult, and groups are complex to run.

Most groups are characterized by what is known in social psychology as the risky shift phenomenon. The risky shift phenomenon postulates that group decisions are generally riskier than decisions that would be made by individual members.

A related phenomenon is known as group polarization. Here, the individual members exaggerate their initial position on a topic so that the group will have a more extreme position.

For example, if you were to put a group of therapists together who favor nondirective therapy, you would discover that by the end of the group, they would be more extreme in championing their nondirective position as the best form of helping.

For exam purposes, keep in mind that most of the time when we are talking about individual therapy, we use the words counseling and therapy synonymously. In other words, they mean roughly the same thing.

In group work, however, a distinction is usually implied. Counseling groups usually focuses on growth, prevention, and enhancement of self-awareness. Therapy groups focus more on remediation and personality reconstruction. Therapy groups usually have a longer duration, and they are much more likely to dwell on unconscious material and family of origin and social issues from the past.

Just for the record, group therapy emerged in a big way during and after World War II, due to a shortage of trained therapists, since groups allowed the professionals to work with more patients when there was a shortage of helpers.

Some counseling historians believe that Carl Rogers helped popularize this idea. **Another post–World War II impetus for the group movement was the work conducted by psychologist Kurt Lewin (1890–1947), who created field theory and formed NTL, or National Training Labs, to study group dynamics in 1947.**

Group leaders often speak of structured groups. These are groups with a central theme like anger management, shyness, securing a job, assertiveness training, or stress management. Theme groups are becoming very popular, and they are often conducted as self-help groups or support groups.

Self-help or support groups include meetings like AA, or Alcoholics Anonymous; NA, or Narcotics Anonymous; or OA, or Overeaters Anonymous. They are composed of people

with a common interest. Self-help groups and support groups, although they may use professional consultants, are not led by professional helpers. As an example, consider all your 12-step groups.

Some exams now use the term mutual-aid groups to describe groups in the category.

Exam hint. One noteworthy trend is that 50 years or so ago, counselors rarely referred clients to support groups. Today, the practice is extremely common.

Group specialists often speak of T groups. The "T" in "T groups" merely stands for "training." The T group, or sensitivity group, stresses skills that are desirable in a business or organizational setting. The thrust is on the group process and not on personal growth.

Hence, the T group deals with issues of leadership and decision making and how employees can conduct themselves in a more productive fashion.

Another type of group is the personal growth group, whose purpose is to aid healthy, normal individuals and allow them to deal a little bit better with normal life transitions.

As for the size of an effective group, in adults, some experts such as Irvin Yalom recommend 6 to 8 members, while others pump up the numbers with a recommendation of 8 to 12 members.

I've seen the number eight listed as the ideal size in several sources. In children, you might want to go as low as three or four kids to a group.

As for the length of the sessions, it varies, but most experts would agree that two hours is plenty, even for some intense group work.

If you are seeing adolescents or children, you may want to shorten the sessions to, say, 30 or 40 minutes and meet more frequently, if necessary. As of this date, one-and-a-half hours, or approximately 90 minutes, seems to be the average for most adult counseling sessions.

The American Counseling Association and the ASGW, which stands for the Association for Specialists in Group Work, recommend screening potential group members. ASGW recommends a pre-group interview or an individual interview to make sure the prospective members will have their needs met by the group.

You want to be sure that the person is appropriate and not going to impede or hinder the group's functioning. Suicidal individuals or sociopathic personalities and clients with anti-social personality traits who cannot tell right from wrong due to a weak or non-existent conscience would generally be excluded from most counseling groups, as well as persons who are very paranoid. Another poor candidate would be the highly self-centered or hostile, belligerent individual.

You could have a special group for those with anti-social personality traits (called sociopaths or psychopaths in the older literature), persons who are suicidal, or clients with anger management issues, but we're talking about most groups here.

Many leaders favor a private screening session. Although the private session is not going to be as cost effective or as time efficient as a group screening session, it is superior in terms of potential for two-way exchange. The client can tell you what they want from the group, and you can tell them what the experience is going to provide.

Ideally, you should use a group screening and an individual screening session because the group screening is also going to show you how the client will react in a group setting. Keep in mind that an individual who is appropriate for one type of group might not be appropriate for another.

Group specialist Irvin Yalom feels that cohesiveness is the primary factor to keep in mind when you are selecting participants. In terms of the person, the ability to trust is generally considered the most important trait for the group member.

The format of a group may be opened or closed. Quite frankly, there are advantages and disadvantages to both.

In an open group, you can replace members when a member leaves. New members are admitted throughout the life of the group, or most of the life of the group. This keeps the number of clients attending the open group stable, and thus, that's a positive factor.

On the negative side of the coin, the new member is unaware of what happened before they joined; hence this member has no or little knowledge of the group's history. Moreover, the change in members can be detrimental to group cohesiveness.

In the closed group, no new members are added once the group gets underway and begins. This is great for the

cohesiveness that Yalom talked about, but what if everybody quits and moves out of town? Yipes. You have nobody left in your group.

Most readers are familiar with closed groups since most college and graduate classes follow this model. Try joining a 16-week counseling class during week 15 as a new student and see if the professor and the administration allow it. I think you get my point.

Two principles of caution when forming any group. **Remember that a client's previous experience in groups is one of the least important factors**. That's right. One of the least important factors.

Another caution is that leaders may be prone to pick members who they believe are high in conformity. Although this practice may have its benefits, research demonstrates that conformists are likely to be authoritarians. Thus, this would really bring up its own dilemmas and pose its own problems.

Now I want to talk to you **about group leadership styles**. Remember how I told you to lean forward slightly when you're doing individual counseling and try to face the client squarely?

Quite frankly, this is very hard to do in a group because many, if not most groups place the clients in a circle. The advice for groups is that you will find it nearly impossible to face members squarely 100% of the time. Nevertheless, you should try in some way to turn toward the person whom you are speaking to.

One word of caution here, and I did mention this previously because it is so important. The literature pertaining to proxemics – that is, proximity, or how close you are to the person – indicates that during the initial sessions the leaning-forward behavior on the part of a counselor could be perceived as negative. Yes, some counselors insist this could backfire if the clients are of a different race than the counselor. This principle really pertains to individual as well as group sessions.

Research indicates that clients and counselors sit closer together when they are similar in social status, age, race, ethnicity, and mode of dress. The feeling of psychological closeness can often be observed in individual or group settings where the seating arrangements are flexible and the person can choose any seat they wish.

Group specialists often classify group leaders as process leaders or product leaders. The word product in this case means outcome or behavioral goal. **Most product counselors are at least somewhat slanted toward behavioral approaches**.

A statement made by a leader like "Bill will know he has accomplished his goal when his anxiety is low enough to drive over the bridge" is a product statement. The emphasis is on the product or the outcome.

The process leader, on the other hand, is concerned with interactions between members. A statement by a process leader might be something like "Bill always responds out of his critical parent when Anne speaks to him out of her natural child."

One of the desirable factors about groups is that statements by the leader, as well as other group members, promote the notion of **universality**.

This is a principle you have an excellent chance of seeing on most exams. **Universality means that as human beings, we are not the only person in the world with a given problem or difficulty**. This is evident when you hear a group member say they feel better knowing that other members in the group have similar difficulties.

Some exams may refer to universality as mutuality.

There are several very basic styles of group leadership – authoritarian, democratic, and laissez-faire.

In the authoritarian style, the leader determines the policies and gives orders to the rest of the group. Members often resent this style.

In the laissez-faire style, the leader adopts a hands-off policy and participates very little. For the most part the group runs itself.

In the democratic style, the policy is set by the group, aided by the leader, who urges group interaction, so indeed in the literal sense of the term the leadership is very democratic.

A well-known study suggested that the democratic leadership style is the most desirable in most instances, but this is not true in every case. For example, if you had to make a quick decision very rapidly in a crisis, the authoritarian mode might be the best unless the group was composed of world-renowned experts, and then the laissez-faire style might be the leadership method of choice.

Some of the literature does go beyond these three basic types. For example, some leaders are classified as **charismatic leaders. The charismatic leader uses their personal power and**

attractiveness to run a group. Clients can adore this type of leader and often become irrational because of it.

Then there is also the **confrontive leadership style.** Here, the leader reveals the impact of their own behavior on themselves as well as the impact on other group members and examines how the group members' behavior impacts them. The focus is generally the present moment.

The **speculative leadership style**, like the confrontive style, focuses on the here and now and zeroes in on the meaning of the leader's own behavior and that of the group members. Speculative leaders emphasize very heavily what is transpiring right now in the group.

Research indicates that speculative leaders are often seen as somewhat charismatic and less peer oriented than confrontive leaders. Nevertheless, overall, neither of these two approaches has demonstrated superiority in terms of the impact that the style really has on group members.

All good leaders regardless of style demonstrate empathy and caring. Some groups rely on more than one group leader. This is known as co-leadership or co-facilitation. I'd like to give you the good news and the bad news on co-leadership.

The good news is that **with co-leadership, you don't need eyes in the back of your head to see everything that is transpiring in the group. You have another pair of eyes there, yes, those of your co-leader.**

Your co-leader can be focusing on several group members' reactions while you're working with someone else. **Co-leadership is also beneficial when a leader must miss a group session due to illness or other reasons. With a co-leader, the show goes on.**

Another important factor is that **shared leadership reduces pernicious burnout**, especially when you are working with a difficult population. Co-leadership also helps leaders process their own feelings. You can meet and communicate with your co-leader between sessions or after sessions to process what has transpired and to answer the question: where to go from here?

Finally, **if one co-leader is plagued with countertransference issues, the other leader can intervene and deal with the client who is evoking the countertransference issues in the counselor.**

Co-leaders often sit across from each other rather than next to each other to minimize the us-against-them image.

For the bad news, coleaders may view this setting in such a manner that they are competing, creating co-leadership rivalry. This may cause co-leadership conflict. Furthermore, if co-leaders do not meet between sessions, they may be working at cross purposes or against each other. Hence, one co-leader may be urging a client to become more assertive, while the other wants this same client to take a passive role.

If leaders do not trust and respect each other, and they don't believe that the other leader is competent, the group will not run smoothly.

Another risk pertains to coleaders who are intimate with each other. Intimate co-leaders may inappropriately use the time to work on their own issues too much or will be gazing into each other's eyes and will be ignoring the needs of the group. Keep in mind that a therapist can have a room full of degrees, certifications, and licenses but no training in group work.

Such a person should not be running groups according to most experts. ASGW recommends that counselors who have completed a groups course supplement it with at least ten hours of supervised experience. Twenty hours is recommended by ASGW before running a group on your own.

Some counselors just don't have the personality makeup to effectively lead a group. Some experts in the field such as Gerald Corey, who has written extensively on the topic of group work, believe the group leaders should first become members of a therapeutic group themselves and then join a group for leaders and trainers.

Many experts insist that all therapists receive individual therapy themselves before going out and trying to help others. This is somewhat analogous to what psychoanalytic institutes do, for example, when they require that the analyst in training go through an analysis themselves. This is known as a training analysis.

Group leaders should always provide new clients with informed consent information. Clients should always have the information necessary to consent to the group process. Information such as where the group will meet, when it will meet, the leader's credentials, the methods used, the cost of any meeting times, and the fact that there are limitations to confidentiality.

Regarding the issue of confidentiality, you should discuss the fact that you cannot – you heard me correctly – cannot

guarantee confidentiality in a group since members may breach it. This is beyond your control as a leader.

Group leaders must keep in mind that group participants have rights. One right that patients, clients, or participants have is knowing what psychological risks will be evident by attending the group. An ethical leader discusses these risks during the initial session and often works throughout the group to reduce the risks and safeguard clients.

According to ASGW ethical guidelines, if things get too bad, a client may withdraw from a group. Yes, even if the group is closed and time limited. ASGW feels group participation is voluntary in nature, and thus, you should never force a member to stay in a group.

Two major risks for clients engaged in group work are scapegoating, which means that multiple members gang up on a certain group member, and again, breach of confidentiality.

It has been said that every group has norms. Norms are defined as parameters of acceptable behavior. Norms may be written or unwritten.

It is easier to experience norms and feel them at times than to consciously define them. **The specific guidelines that the leader sets up at the beginning of the group, such as no cursing and no smoking, are known as ground rules.**

When the ground rules become the norm or standard of behavior, then they are logically referred to as group norms. Please remember that concepts like leadership style and norms technically fall under the heading of group dynamics. **The term group dynamics refers to the study or body of knowledge pertaining to how groups operate.**

Group dynamics postulate that a group itself is indeed dynamic since it is always changing or becoming. People are interacting or reacting. Persons with an interest in group dynamics want to know what forces, both external and internal, are shaping or molding the behavior of the group and the group members.

So far, I have mentioned leadership styles and norms as group dynamics. Another factor is the presence of a shared goal or goals. **It is best if the group comes to a mutual decision, or what some experts call a mutual consensus, in terms of goal setting.**

When you study for your exam, remember that although goal setting is a very important task, most researchers have found that goal setting is still a common weakness in many groups.

Another key dynamic is structure. Earlier, I gave you examples of structured groups, such as group for assertiveness training or stress management. Nevertheless, the word structured can also be used in *another* way when examining group work. In a highly structured group, the leader has specific exercises or tasks for group members, while in a less structured group, this is not the case.

In the last sentence, I purposely used the term less structured rather than the term unstructured. Why? In the past, experts did use the terms structured and unstructured, but the term unstructured has come under fire. **All groups have some structure. Some experts even say a group cannot not have structure**.

You should also be cognizant of the fact that some research does indeed indicate that structured exercises with feedback when given in the early stage of a group result in better communication and feelings. However, **a group that just has structured exercises overall is generally not as effective**.

Another group dynamic mentioned earlier is group cohesiveness. Cohesiveness simply refers to the strength of the bonding process or the we-ness between group members. Some authors may use the word unity when describing this concept.

Cohesiveness is a double-edged sword in the sense that although it is a desirable group dynamic, it can stunt creativity and breed conformity at times.

Another group dynamic of great significance refers to group roles. In other words, what role does a group member assume? Does the member always act silly and joke about things? The joker is seen as a negative group role. Does a member invariably disagree with the group leader?

Here are some popular group participant roles. **We have the energizer who provides the group with enthusiasm. The follower who is passive and therefore goes along with everything the group wants. Any time the group slants one way or the other, the follower jumps on the bandwagon**.

Then there is the scapegoat. This is the person everybody expresses hostility toward and accuses when something goes

wrong. The scapegoat gets dumped upon, and people are constantly ganging up on the scapegoat.

We also have the peeping Tom group member, also known as the interrogator. This is the person who insists on interrogating others with a string of endless and often inappropriate questions.

Then there is the gatekeeper who believes that it is their job to make certain that everybody participates in the group. The gatekeeper, in many cases, secretly wishes they were running the group. The problem with the gatekeeper is that this person may never get around to working on their own problems.

Then, of course, we have **the storyteller who contributes irrelevant tales of woe whenever possible,**

The literature also mentions **the social isolate** who is present, but nobody even knows that this person is there. Occasionally, this member will reach out, but often their contributions go unnoticed.

Then there is the harmonizer, also known as the conciliator role. This is the member who tries to placate or make things friendly and smooth things over between group members. The conciliator will tend to soothe the anger and make the group a friendlier place to live. "Come on now, Derek, you really aren't mad at Kristina. Can we see a big hug?"

Now from a global standpoint, **members may assume basic types of roles labeled task roles or maintenance roles.**

Group experts also talk about task and maintenance roles, and these are considered positive roles, while self-serving roles hinder the group's goals.

Task roles aim to facilitate the group's ability to define goals and implement problem solving strategies. **Task roles include information providers, clarifiers, summarizers, opinion givers, elaborators, and initiators. Again, task roles are indeed positive, healthy roles.**

Maintenance roles are also seen as healthy. Maintenance roles alter, maintain, or strengthen the group. The maintenance roles offer compromises, supportive contributions, and group standards. **Popular maintenance roles that build interpersonal relationships include the observer; the compromiser; the conciliator, mentioned earlier; the follower, mentioned previously; the standard setter; and the encourager.**

Finally, we have self-serving or individual roles. Now, these are negative. They literally hold the group back, or they work against the group.

Self-serving/blocking individual roles are true to the name. They serve the individual, the self, not the group. **Members who do not participate in a constructive manner are blockers, monopolists, dominators, and critics; all would fall into this pernicious category. In essence, clients who are silent, resist, intellectualize, manipulate, withdraw, or attack are said to be playing a negative group role.**

In a healthy group, members are flexible and can move in and out of roles and change roles when necessary. It is important to note that both task and maintenance roles are necessary. If the group stays in maintenance, there will be little work on tasks. On the other hand, if the group gets stuck solely in task roles, interactions suffer. To reiterate, ideally, group roles may remain flexible.

Exam hint. Group therapists rely on the term **role conflict** to describe a situation in which there is a discrepancy between the way a member is expected to act versus the way the member naturally behaves.

Another group dynamic is known as group development. Group development is usually expressed in terms of stages.

Here's an additional wonderful exam hint, since it would be nearly impossible to remember all the models of group development, **I want to suggest that most of the models are similar enough that a basic grasp of the group stages will suffice.**

For example, most models, whether **they call the first stage forming, orientation, pre-affiliation**, **or exploratory**, deal with what is known as **the approach avoidance conflict**. In other words, clients may wish to participate, but they concurrently have a fear they won't be accepted. They may feel uneasy and suspicious. The situation presents both positive and negative aspects.

Members may try to identify with others of a similar social status. In fact, you will even see similar people trying to sit together during this stage.

The next stage, again, call it what you will; storming or transition are two of the most common names. Some people call the second stage power or control. Why? Well, the second stage marks the time of the most conflict.

Opposing subgroups may pop up, and people may try to mentally rank order themselves with others. A hierarchy or group pecking order may be evident. People will fight each other for dominance, and yes, group members may even rebel against the leader.

In the next stage, the group becomes cohesive like a family. Members are more intimate, or closer to one another, and a sense of we-ness develops. This is an action-oriented time and problem-solving phase. **Since a lot of work gets done during this period, it is logically called the working stage of the group**.

Just for a quick review:

We begin with the orientation stage, move into the rough-and-tumble transition stage, and then into the working stage, and ultimately reach the final stage, which is geared toward termination, adjourning, separation, and breaking away, often called the termination stage.

As a group leader, you may wish to construct a picture or an actual diagram of subgroups and coalitions and assess their impact on the overall group. This task is known as charting a sociogram.

The sociogram was introduced by Jacob Moreno and social psychologist Helen Hall Jennings (1905–1966) in 1950, and it graphically displays relationships of group members. It's literally a picture of what is going on in the group. A sociogram depicts attraction and repulsion by use of arrows, lines, dotted lines, and other symbols. The study of person-to-person relationships in a group setting is known as sociometry.

I want you to remember that group leaders can use all the skills used by individual counselors such as paraphrasing, attending, clarifying, empathizing, questioning, supporting, confronting, concreteness, imparting information, feedback, cultural sensitivity, and interpreting. Leaders can also utilize summarizing, blocking, and linking quite a bit.

In terms of **summarizing,** a leader might ask each member to restate what they learned during the group. The leader may wish to summarize during some of the group sessions, to model the desirable behavior for other members.

Leaders will also need to employ blocking when necessary. **Blocking is used to stop or block inappropriate behaviors like gossiping, irrelevant questioning, endless storytelling, or breaking**

confidence. For example, if somebody starts telling the group what one of the members did in another group, you will need to block it. Blocking is like blocking a punch in boxing.

Linking is used to relate what one person is saying or doing to another person's predicament. In other words, the leader illuminates points of mutual concern.

Were you aware that leaders can approach group work in various ways?

You can either focus on the group as a whole, or you can focus on one person at a time, with minimal focus on others in the group. This is a choice that can really be made regardless of what modality of counseling you are using.

Group as a whole strategies are called horizontal interventions, while focusing on an individual in the group is called a vertical intervention. Here again, why not make use of a memory device?

When you see clients, they are usually sitting vertically. Hence, when you work with one person, you're doing a vertical intervention, but if you look at the group as a whole, the group is spread out horizontally, and so that would be a horizontal intervention.

Again, jumble these memory devices around. I'm just trying to jumpstart your brain here. Try to come up with some of your own.

That's group counseling in a nutshell, folks. The group leader has one heck of a tough job inasmuch as a group leader must make more theoretical decisions than an individual counselor.

Most experts agree that group counseling is more difficult to perform than individual counseling. Moreover, there seems to be a huge researcher/practitioner split in the field that's evident if you read the journals related to group counseling.

Recently, the literature has focused a lot on gender issues, namely women's concerns in group counseling. Let's hope that more practical information continues to be made available. One prediction is that in the future group leaders will be more like life skills trainers than therapists.

One thing for sure. We know that groups work, we know they can make a difference, but research has yet to explain precisely how or why.

Final exam hint. Some group counselors do what is known in the trade as an ecological assessment to decide if a group is appropriate and, if so, what methodology will work best. The ecological assessment provides valuable information about psychological, social, cultural, and economic needs of possible group members.

Community surveys, focus groups, and a thorough demographic analysis can help you in this respect. Adept leaders often secure information from their textbooks, the Internet, and journal articles to help plan the group on a session-by-session basis.

All right. Let's forge on to another important topic.

7

Master Lecture 6: Career Development

We're zipping along through the exam areas here and trust me when I say you are learning a lot of great information.

I want to talk about lifestyle and career development. The first thing I'm going to do is to give you a smattering of historical information, which should be of help to you.

The first thing to remember is that in 1909, Frank Parsons (1854–1908), the father of guidance, had an influential book released titled *Choosing a Vocation*. Interestingly, if you look at the dates you discover he died a year before the book came out. The full impact of the work was not really felt until the 1930s.

Then in 1911, the "Vocational Guidance" newsletter was published, which was the first American periodical aimed at vocational guidance.

In 1912, there was a famous book in Germany by psychologist **Hugo Münsterberg (1863–1916) called *Psychology and Industrial Efficiency***. An American version hit the streets in 1913. **Münsterberg did studies through Harvard University, applying experimental psychology to vocational choice, and thus he has often been called the father of industrial psychology**.

DOI: 10.4324/9781003149712-7

In 1917, the army Alpha, a verbal test, and the army Beta, a performance group test, were used for assessing mental abilities in recruits for World War I.

In 1927, a very important year, the **Strong Vocational Interest Blank** was released. In the same year, Australian-born psychologist Elton Mayo (1880–1949), a name you'll want to remember, and a research team from Harvard studied the Hawthorne Works, which is in the Chicago area.

This Western Electric plant revealed new data on worker behavior known as the Hawthorne effect, discussed elsewhere in this book.

1939 proved to be a landmark year as the first DOT, or *Dictionary of Occupational Titles* , was published. It was chock full of over 18,000 US occupational definitions. Then, in 1941, the army classification test came along.

In 1942, the most influential counseling book, *Counseling and Psychotherapy* by Carl Ransom Rogers, brought career counseling a little bit closer to therapy. In 1951, psychologist Donald E. Super (1910–1994) conducted the first long-range study of career patterns, which led to the 1957 book *The Psychology of Careers*.

In 1963, psychologist Edward S. Bordin (1913–1992) and his colleagues expressed an explicit psychodynamic point of view for career counselors. Then, in 1966, a huge landmark, psychologist and noted educator John D. Krumboltz (1928–2019) hit the field with what he called a "Revolution in Counseling." Just what was this revolution in counseling? Quite simply the revolution was the application of Skinnerian principles for use in career counseling.

Then, in 1973, the prominent vocational psychologist John Orr Crites (1928–2007) came up with the "Career Maturity Inventory," which was an important measure.

What else can I tell you about this area which might just help you on the exam? I've got it. How about giving you a cook's tour of some of the major theories in career counseling? Yeah, that's a great way to begin.

I must be honest and tell you that some of the leading authorities have been extremely critical of many of the commonly accepted theories of career development. Some experts believe that traditional theories have literally inhibited the introduction of novel ideas based on updated research.

In any event, **career specialists tend to categorize theories. The first major category of career theory is what is known as the trait factor (a.k.a. trait and factor), actuarial, or matching approach. This approach attempts to match the worker and the environment**.

Everybody has different traits. A trait could be a skill, an interest in a subject, or an aptitude for a given task. Each occupation, in turn, is best filled by an individual with certain traits, including certain skills, interests, aptitudes, levels of energy, and temperament.

The key to the ultimate job, so to speak, occurs when an individual's traits match the requirements and the characteristics, or the so-called factors of the job. To make this matchup, the counselor operating out of this approach draws heavily on psychological testing, or what is sometimes known as psychometric data.

This is not a developmental approach. Career choice is construed as a one-time decision, where the right person is matched up to the right job. Trait factor theorists assume that these traits can be measured. I'd like you to remember that this approach was heavily influenced and molded by the psychological testing movement.

The bedrock of this theory rests on differential diagnosis. The diagnosis, just like a medical diagnosis, can tell you what is wrong with this person. In this case, it will tell you what's wrong with the career decision, and the diagnosis tells you what career is best for the client.

Unfortunately, studies indicated that when different judges look at diagnostic information received from trait factor counseling sessions, they have a tough time agreeing on the classification. In fact, get this, they only agree about 50% of the time, which is no better than flipping a coin.

A huge figure associated with this model is **Edmund Griffith (E.G.) Williamson (1900–1979), who lists four different categories for the diagnosis. The first category is no choice for careers, the second is uncertain choice, the third is unwise choice, and the fourth is a discrepancy between interests and attitudes**.

John Crites later saw the need and expanded on this classification system. He thought it wasn't in depth enough. Back to some of the rudiments of the theory.

With all this talk about scientific test scores, you might wrongly think that this modality is in some way some newfangled high-tech approach to vocational counseling. Well, nothing could be further from the truth.

Again, this approach was associated with a name I mentioned just a few minutes ago, Frank Parsons, the father of vocational guidance. **The origin of the trait-factor theory appears in chapter one of his 1909 book, the classic *Choosing a Vocation***.

In this book, Parsons urges the reader to, one, try to understand yourself in terms of interests, abilities, aptitudes, resources, and other qualities. And, two, know the requirements and conditions of available lines of work. Three, use reason to compare the facts related to your traits and those related to the job in question.

The other prime mover in the trait factor theory, again, Edmund Griffith Williamson. For exam purposes, remember that E.G. Williamson's approach is often referred to as the "Minnesota Viewpoint." Why? Well, Williamson was associated with the University of Minnesota for over 40 years. He began there in 1926 as a graduate student, and he retired in 1941 as a full professor.

He wrote several books. Perhaps the one that really received the most attention was his 1939 work, *How to Counsel Students – A Manual of Clinical Techniques for Clinical Counselors*. **Some scholars have asserted that the Minnesota viewpoint is the only approach to general counseling that developed from a vocational counseling base**. Of course, this modality drew heavily on Parsons's work, and in 1941, the Minnesota Occupational Rating Scales were published. The goal of this measure was to produce an actuarial, empirical, statistical tool to use in counseling to match clients with jobs. The statistical method relied on probability, the probability that a certain match would be compatible.

E.G. Williamson's strategy emphasized vocational and educational concerns. **The Minnesota viewpoint purports to be scientific and didactic. The counselor is like a tutor who gives the client information, yet the ultimate decision regarding what to do with the data is left up to the client**.

Williamson, for example, would often utilize the well-known Strong Vocational Interest Inventory as a source of information for the sessions.

Although the Minnesota approach is light years apart from Albert Ellis's REBT in terms of procedures, scholars still consider it a rational approach to helping.

Critics of the Minnesota viewpoint say that despite its heavy emphasis on objective data, it minimizes the most important data of all, the client's perception of self! The Minnesota Viewpoint has been castigated for not adequately addressing the affective (and affective just means emotional qualities) of the person.

Overall, counselors have turned away from the trait factor approach, feeling that it oversimplifies the complexities of human behavior.

Just briefly, I want to touch on a reaction to the Minnesota approach, which is **the client-centered career counseling approach**. This is rather interesting because **Rogers never really theorized, at least directly, about career counseling**.

Perhaps the most important notion was that client-centered techniques focused on the client's inner self, and this opposed the trait factor theory, which dealt mainly with the outer self. Also, while diagnosis is the main factor in the trait factor model, Rogers felt it was unnecessary, perhaps even a detriment, in the therapeutic process.

According to Rogers, the problem is always the same, lack of congruence between the self and experience. When occupational information is used in person-centered therapy, it is generally when the client asks for it. It is never volunteered by the therapist to manipulate or to persuade the client.

In recent years, we have not seen a lot about person-centered counseling being used exclusively in career counseling, but I did just want to mention it.

The next category I want to touch on is the personality approach to career development. The first name I think of when this approach pops up in my mind is the clinical psychologist Anne Roe (1904–1991). Roe believed that one's job serves as a major source of unconscious need satisfaction. Very psychoanalytic, is it not?

Roe felt that unconscious needs resulted from early life experiences in the family, especially parent–child interaction. **Basically, she felt that families are either person oriented or what she calls nonperson oriented. The parent/caretaker relationship with the child sets the stage for psychological needs ideally fulfilled by one's job and career**.

Thus, she hypothesized that counselors grew up in warm person-oriented environments. Those who grew up in nonperson-oriented families will choose occupations that do not emphasize interpersonal dynamics.

Roe also uses Abraham Maslow's hierarchy of needs to explain the career process. In doing so, she says that the individual will choose a career which gratifies their needs. Lower-order needs, like safety, would take precedence over higher-order, self-actualizing needs when choosing a job.

Thus, in addition to psychoanalytic principles, we could assert that Roe used information from humanistic self-theory.

Exam booster, Roe was the first career pioneer to create a two-dimensional classification system to categorize occupations by fields and levels. Make a mental note to yourself right now, this very moment, that when you see the phrase "fields and levels" on the exam, it is likely referring to the work of Anne Roe.

There are eight fields in this theory. One, service; two, business; three, organization; four, technology; five, outdoor; six, science (some books in recent years use the term technology); seven, general culture; and eight, arts and entertainment. The fields are categorized so they indicate the power of need gratification related to things or people.

Now for the six levels. The six levels are 1) unskilled, 2) semi-skilled, 3) skilled, 4) semi-professional, 5) professional managerial I, and 6) professional managerial II.

Now, I need to mention that in addition to the aforementioned psychological factors, Roe insists the **genetic factors, intelligence, level of education, and ability to handle responsibility enter into the picture**.

What did research say about the tenets of Roe's theory? Well, some studies using the Rorschach and the TAT – that's easy to remember because Rorschach starts with an R and so does Roe's name – supported some of her ideas, but not all of the studies have supported them.

Research dating back to 1965 agreed with one of Roe's basic tenets that people who are in person-to-person occupations would be more altruistic than people in nonperson occupations. The research did not conclude, however, that person-oriented workers recall their childhood as being warmer than the individuals from nonperson-type jobs.

Another famous theorist who believes that the choice of careers is related to unconscious processes is Edward S. Bordin, who in 1955 published the well-known textbook *Psychological Counseling*. Bordin, who worked extensively at the University of Minnesota counseling bureau, believed that a career choice serves to resolve an unconscious conflict.

Difficulty in choosing a job is viewed as a neurotic system or process from this viewpoint. Again, this is very psychoanalytic. **Bordin draws very heavily on the theories of Otto Rank (1884–1939), an Austrian psychoanalyst who was close to Freud and talked about birth trauma, and Erik Erikson,** whom we talked about elsewhere.

The psychoanalytic theory of career counseling has been criticized for emphasizing internal factors too much and not emphasizing external factors strongly enough.

Another theorist who brought Freudian theory into the career arena was psychiatrist, psychoanalyst, and first translator for Freud's works into English Abraham Arden (A.A.) Brill (1874–1948). Brill emphasized ego defense mechanisms, especially sublimation, which is mentioned elsewhere in this lecture series.

According to Brill, the job provides a socially acceptable outlet for an unconscious impulse. For example, if you harbor sadistic tendencies and you like to hurt people, you might become a boxer, a wrestler, maybe even a football player.

While we're talking about career counseling, we absolutely need to mention **the most popular personality approach to career choice. And that, my dear reader, would be the one proposed by psychologist John Holland (1919–2008). Holland spoke of a modal orientation.**

The modal orientation suggests that an individual has preferential ways or modes of dealing with tasks. A modal

orientation is really a style of behavior. He lists six types or modes. One, artistic. Two, conventional. Three, enterprising. Four, investigative. Five, realistic, and six, social.

He was quick to point out that these are not pure types. Therefore, a majority of individuals can be categorized by using a profile of three consistent, inconsistent, or dissimilar interests. For example, a profile might be RIE, which would be realistic, investigative, enterprising.

The six basic patterns are sometimes illustrated using a hexagon with similar patterns next to each other, and dissimilar patterns are placed on opposing corners of the hexagon.

One way to remember which one of the patterns would be next to another pattern is a formula called RIASEC. That's not my memory device. That's the one utilized in most textbooks. If you want to see the hexagon with your own eyes, and who wouldn't, it appears in the graphical representation section of my *Encyclopedia of Counseling*.

Now, let's talk about **the six groups. Number one, the artistic or aesthetic person**. Singers, musicians, authors, artists, and poets are often seen as fitting into this orientation. Feelings and creativity are important to such people. The artistic type values expression and is not a conformist.

The second orientation is the conventional or the conformist pattern. Bank tellers, file clerks, and most secretaries exemplify this psychological makeup. The conventional individual truly wants rules, regulations, and structure in the work setting.

Then, we have the enterprising or persuasive modality. This person likes to dominate others and therefore becomes a salesman, a politician, the owner of their own business, or perhaps a business executive.

Then, there is the investigative or intellectual orientation. This person values abstract thinking. Philosophers and mathematicians would fall into this category.

Then, there is the realistic or motoric orientation. In this orientation, working with machines and tools is preferable to working with people or working in strictly intellectual pursuits. Truck drivers, engineers, farmers, auto mechanics, and drill press operators would fit neatly into this category.

Last, we have the social or supportive type. This is the orientation you personally fit into. Social types like attention in interpersonal situations. Counselors, teachers, social workers, and other interpersonal consultants would characterize this orientation.

Let me throw in another memory device just in case the RIASEC isn't enough for you. One of memory strategies I use is AS RICE, to help recall the different modalities or modal orientations that apply to both the personality and the work setting in Holland's theory.

Again, there's the RIASEC formula. The advantage of RIASEC as a memory device, of course, over mine, is it tells you where something falls on the hexagon. The Strong Vocational Interest Inventory is based on Holland's work. **Holland's theory is probably utilized by more career counselors than any other theory**.

Another measure based on his typologies is the SDS or Self-Directed Search." (Again, typology just refers to a modal orientation.) The SDS is self-administered and self-scored. And thanks to technology, the SDS can be completed in just 20 minutes, and you can take it on a computer, tablet, or even a smart phone. The SDS website, however, states that reviewing the report is easier on a computer or tablet than a cell phone. Holland, like Roe, acknowledges levels or hierarchies in terms of skills based on one's intelligence and self-knowledge.

A person tends to be attracted toward those jobs that are commensurate with their intelligence and knowledge of self. Holland, in a sense, believes in career stereotypes, and literally maintains that people gravitate toward or seek out jobs where others who work at the job have similar values.

Workers will gravitate toward a job where others have similar beliefs about work, leisure, and even values. This, according to Holland, is precisely why a given occupation tends to attract people with similar personalities. Work reflects who we are. An adept career counselor needs to link up the personality with a matching occupation.

According to Holland, our occupation tells the world who we are. The individual's behavior is determined by their personality and the environment.

In addition to Holland's theory, another name that begins with an H in the personality career category is that of Robert Hoppock (1901–1995), a professor of counselor education, who based his theory on the work of psychologist Henry Murray (1893–1988), who, along with his colleagues at Harvard, developed a technique for an in-depth personality assessment in various dimensions. Murray termed this personology.

His research led to the formation of the projective thematic apperception test or TAT. Murray used the terms need and press to explain the function of the personality. The term needs refers to the needs of the person, while press refers to the demands of the environment. Career counselors call this the needs press hypothesis.

Hoppock contended that a career is intended to satisfy or meet one's needs, and an occupation change will sometimes occur as needs change throughout the lifespan.

The second major category of career theories entails what we call developmental theories. The bottom line on developmental theories can be explained thusly. Career choice is not a one-time decision or an act but rather a process throughout the lifespan.

The big names (also known as a "team") in developmental career theory are economist Eli Ginzberg (1911–2002), psychiatrist Sol W. Ginsburg (1899–1960), Sidney Axelrad (1913–1976), and psychologist John L. Herma (1911–1966), who in 1951 wrote the classic book, *Occupational Choice: An Approach to General Theory.*

***I want to emphasize that Ginzberg originally felt that occupational choice was an irreversible* process and a compromise. The notion suggested that an individual could not return to an earlier time in life to make the decision.**

However, in 1972, he wrote a landmark article in *Vocational Guidance Quarterly* titled "Toward a Theory of Occupational Choice A Restatement," indicating that Ginzberg began to change or refute, if you will, his own theory. He began to feel that career choice did not really end at age 20 or so. Instead, he began to see that it was a continual process throughout the lifespan.

In addition, he dropped the premise of irreversibility and noted that people can move into other fields. Finally, he replaced the theory of compromise with the notion of optimization. By optimization, he meant that the person continues to improve the match between career and the self throughout life. Or, to put it a different way, ultimately, career choice is a lifelong process over the lifespan.

To quote Ginzberg, "Occupational choice is a lifelong process of decision making for those who seek major gratification from their work. This leads them to reassess repeatedly

how they can improve the fit between their changing career goals and the realities of the world of work."

Another major name in developmental lifespan career theory is Donald Super (1910–1994). Luckily, his very name provides us with an excellent memory device. **Psychologist Donald Edwin Super is noted for his theory that states that career development allows an individual to express their self-concept.**

Of course, Super begins with S, and so does self-concept. Super's work has had more of an impact than Ginsberg's. Super derived data from the social career pattern study, which followed a group of ninth-grade boys in the early '50s all the way into adulthood.

This is what is known in the trade as a longitudinal study. Of course, it can be characterized by maturational effects since the person matures in the study. Super contends that individuals cast their self-concepts into a career that will provide the best means of self-expression.

The high point of Super's theory is his life stage structure, which is really five vocational developmental stages. Just as an aside, let me pick up on the word structure here and remind you **that some books, exams, and tests may refer to theories such as Super's as structural theories.**

Here are Super's life stages. **Stage one, growth**, birth to 14 or 15. **Stage two, exploration**. Exploration encompasses ages 15 to 24. **Stage three is establishment**, ages 25 to 44. **Stage four is maintenance**, ages 45 to 64. **Stage five is decline**, age 65 and beyond.

A good memory device I have relied on to recall Super's stages is GEE MD. Of course, since there are two Es, you could remember that exploration naturally occurs before establishment.

From a practical or pragmatic standpoint, here's what transpires in the stages. In the growth stage the person develops interests and needs related to the self-concept. Two, exploratory. The person is in a tentative phase. Career choices are narrowed and fine-tuned but not finalized.

Three, establishment. This stage is characterized by trials and stabilization. Four, maintenance. Adjusting to improve your work, position, and situation. Five, decline, working less, preretirement, and retirement.

The five stages provide a developmental framework for Super's five activities, also known as Super's developmental

tasks. One, crystallization, ages 14 to 18. Here, the individual goes through the cognitive process of picking a general vocational area of interest, planning, and using some resources in terms of the planning.

Number **two, specification**, ages 18 to 21. The move from tentative choices to a specific vocational pick occurs here. **Three, implementation**, ages 21 to 24. Securing training and securing employment.

Four, stabilization, ages 24 to 35. Actual work experience to determine if the choice is truly appropriate. **Five, consolidation**, ages 35 and beyond. Establishing yourself in a career via status, advancements, or seniority.

Toward the latter part of his career Super contended that the aforementioned ages are very flexible. The tasks do not always occur in a well-ordered sequence. A person may recycle through the various stages. Super dubbed this a mini cycle. Also, don't be surprised if you run into a question on an exam relating to career patterns, as Super suggested such patterns.

In the conventional pattern, the individual tries several jobs and then ends up with a stable one. Next, we have the multiple trial patterns in which the person hops from entry-level position to entry-level position. I often joke that this person changes jobs more often than most of us change clothes. The person never really lands a job to express their identity.

Then, there is the unstable pattern. The unstable pattern is characterized by lots and lots of jobs, more than, say, the conventional pattern, but the person finally settles down and makes a choice.

The final pattern is this stable pattern that lends itself to persons who are highly skilled, trained, and educated. In the stable pattern, the choice is permanent and may occur at a rather early age.

Research from as far back as 1961 supports the notion that one picks a vocation to implement a self-concept or self-image. I also want to mention the name **John O. Crites, who is the foremost name and career maturity research. Crites developed the "Career Maturity Inventory" used heavily by followers of Donald Super's model.**

One last point regarding Super. Super formulated the concept of the Career Rainbow. The Career Rainbow suggests

that the average person plays nine life roles: 1) child, 2) student, 3) worker, 4) partner, 5) parent, 6) citizen, 7) homemaker, 8) leisurite (a word coined by Super, by the way), and 9) pensioner.

These roles are played in four theaters: the home, the community, the school, and the workplace. The meshing of the nine roles and the four theaters tells the story of one's career. It is called a career pattern. He indicated that individuals may indeed play several roles simultaneously and that both success and failure generalize from role to role.

David V. Tiedeman (1919–2004) and Robert P. O'Hara are two other well-known developmental theorists. They postulate an anticipation stage and an induction stage in career decision making. During the anticipation, or fantasy period, exploration, crystallization of choices, and clarification occur. The person in this stage tries to imagine what it would be like to work in a specific career. During induction, there is reformation and integration, meaning that the self-concept and job expectations may be modified.

In other words, the big question is, did the occupation or career turn out to be what the person expected it to be? If not, can the person adapt to it? If the person can't, another occupation or job will need to be sought out.

Tiedeman and O'Hara are holistic and based a lot of their notions on the work of Erik Erikson's stages in respect to ego identity. Some counselors believe that Tiedeman and O' Hara merely took Super's stages and added some personality theory to the mix to create a more comprehensive theory. In recent years, **Anna Miller-Tiedeman (1934–) and Tiedeman have emphasized what they contend is an individualistic perspective in career decision.**

Trait factor, personality, and developmental theories are not the only ways of explaining career choice. There are sociological methods, which assume that the person's culture or social class can influence boundaries. We also have **the social learning behavioristic approach by Anita Mitchell, Brian Jones, and John Krumboltz, who used Albert Bandura's (1925–2021) social learning theory mentioned elsewhere in this program to explain career dynamics.**

This behavioristic approach assumes that people are reinforced for tasks they perform well, and thus, they will choose careers that they have been reinforced for in life. The behaviorists rely on actual site visits to jobs so the person can try out the job or the behavior in vivo rather than just relying on paper and pencil tests or computerized inventories or tests for feedback.

In terms of career counseling, the behaviorists believe in genetics and innate tendencies, but they tend to focus on what can be worked with, and typically this would not be altering genetics. The trick, according to the behaviorists, is to expose the person to as many job possibilities as humanly possible to see what the person best responds to in terms of a learning experience.

Another category of theories would be those which fall under the heading of decision approaches. Decision theories, believe it or not, evolve not from psychotherapy but from economics and the law of mathematical probability. Your exam might even classify Tiedeman's work as a decision theory rather than a developmental theory.

Decision theory really zeroes in on the process of decision making rather than getting involved in traits, personality factors, or job requirements. Decision theory operates under the notion that the individual who comes to you for career counseling has several viable choices or alternatives. Thus, value clarification exercises can be utilized to facilitate the process of making a choice.

Most counselors who adhere to a decision approach emphasize that personal values must be used to make a healthy decision. When you see the so-called expectancy X values in the literature, it merely refers to the likelihood or expectancy that a given act will be followed by a given outcome.

Edward E. Lawler, Krumholtz, and others have written about expectancy X values. Bandura has termed his theory a self-efficacy approach since Bandura felt that the person's belief regarding themself has a great impact on the outcome or the expectancy of an outcome.

The Gelatt decision model, named after H.B. Gelatt (1926–2021), is perhaps the model with the most notoriety. Gelatt's model calls information the fuel of the decision. Gelatt stated that three types of information are required for decisions, and the decision is dependent on which of three systems is operating.

He states that the type of information required for a decision depends on which of three systems is operating. There is **a predictive system** fueled by alternatives and the probability of outcomes. The **valuing system** about personal likes, dislikes, and preferences. The **decision system** is fueled by personal rules and information about priorities related to the two of previously mentioned systems.

Gelatt felt that mathematical game theory, which is also used in economics, will ultimately be applied to counseling in a scientific way to help aid the decision procedures that are made in counseling.

Noted counselor Bruce W. Bergland suggests that in making a sound decision, one should find the problem, brainstorm alternatives, get necessary information, process the information, make plans, set goals, implement the plans, and then evaluate their effectiveness.

It is often said that all decision dilemmas have four elements that must be assessed. One, objectives; two, choices; three, outcomes; and four, assessments.

The bottom line on expectancy theories or decision-making theories is that when one makes a choice, they assume that a given choice will yield a given outcome or consequence. As of late, more and more counselors are using the **Myers-Briggs Type theory**.

This theory was not – I repeat was not – intended to be a career counseling theory. Nevertheless, since so many counselors use it in their work, it certainly deserves honorable mention here. Catherine Cook Briggs (1875–1968) and her only daughter Isabel Myers (1897–1980), often cited as Isabel Briggs-Myers, were intrigued with the idea of classifying people using the theories of Carl Gustav Jung.

In 1956, they convinced the Educational Testing Service to publish the MBTI, or Myers-Briggs Type Indicator. The MBTI should not be used without an assessment of the client's aptitude, achievement, and interests. **Myers-Briggs uses four bipolar dimensions**.

A person who takes the MBTI receives a four-digit code, and there are 16 personality types assessed on four dimensions:

1. Where is the client's focus of attention? **Extroversion (E) or Introversion (I)**
2. How does the client take in information? **Sensing (S) or Intuition (N)**

3. How does the client make decisions? **Thinking (T) or Feeling (F)**
4. How does the client deal with the world? **Judging (J) or Perceiving (P)**.

For example, the **ENFJ** (which stands for extroverted, intuitive, feeling, and judging) pattern is typical for counselors, teachers, actors, and clergy. A person with this code is said to encourage the growth of others and will understand their emotional needs. They like to talk (really!), are warm, and inspire others to be leaders. The MBTI typology approach, again, although it is extremely popular, is not universally accepted at this time.

In recent years, counselors have been applying the postmodern constructivist approach to career counseling. The modern approach is said to be rational and scientific. The postmodern view suggests that individuals create their own view and interpretation of events, or simply what is real for them. Some historians point out that this approach has its roots in the work of psychologist and educator George Alexander Kelly, mentioned earlier, who in 1955 wrote the influential two-volume book set, *The Psychology of Personal Constructs*.

So influential was Kelly that, once again, he has been called the "father of clinical cognitive psychology."

Narrative therapy, mentioned elsewhere in this text, can also be used in career counseling. Here, the counselor uses the client's career story to assist in the career counseling process. Moreover, constructivists focus on how one's career gives meaning to life. As you can see, there is a mighty fine line between the differences of some of these theories.

Edgar Schein (pronounced shine), also mentioned in the consultation section of this book, is an organizational psychologist who promotes a theory of eight career anchors. The idea posits we all have a primary or dominant career anchor or job theme. Different people are motivated by totally different factors, and this influences what jobs or careers would be best. 1) Technical/functional competence. Examples would include engineering, computer programming, or accounting jobs. 2) Managerial competence, for individuals who prize leading/managing people, projects, and resources. Money is often the benchmark here. 3) Autonomy/independence. This anchor

focuses on having as much control as possible over your work so you can work independently. A consultant or independent contractor would fall into this category. This anchor fits a person who likes to secure recognition for accomplishing tasks on their own. 4) Security/stability. This anchor emphasizes job stability and security above all other factors. Could stay in the same position at the same organization until retirement and avoid taking risks. 5) Entrepreneurial creativity. A person who favors this anchor is creative, innovative, and likes to try things that are new and different like running their own business. 6) Service/dedication to a cause. This person wants to make a difference in the world and help others. Did anyone think the word "counselors"? 7) Pure challenge. This anchor centers on taking on tough challenges and pushing oneself to their potential. Professional athletes and those in sales positions would fit this anchor. 8) Lifestyle. This anchor values the balance between work and life. These folks may quip, "I want a job that won't affect my family, my fishing trips, vacations, and hobbies."

Research seems to indicate that people who identified their career anchors experienced better job satisfaction and stayed in their jobs longer than people who did not.

Let's look at some of the resources for career counselors. Our own federal government assists us in our work by publishing several job-related publications. The most popular and easiest one to understand is the US Department of Labor's *OOH* or *Occupational Outlook Handbook*, which can be accessed at www.bls.gov/ooh. Printed book versions are still available.

This valuable resource is updated every two years. It lists approximately 500 occupations, or double what it was when this information was in my audio CD set. Over 90% of the high schools in this country take advantage of this resource. Is it practical, you ask? You bet it is.

The US Department of Labor packs it with information about job requirements, working conditions, number of jobs available, the location of those jobs, earnings, and related occupations. It helps counselors by predicting economic trends, which can give clues about future employment opportunities.

You can select occupations via an A-to-Z index. You can also search for the highest-paying jobs. (I will save you the trouble of searching; the list is mainly medical specialty jobs held by physicians such as psychiatrists, listed as a median salary equal to or greater than $208,000.) You may also search by projection: fastest growing, most new jobs, field of degrees (e.g., a glimpse of what median salary folks make with a history or a liberal arts degree . . . how many are employed part-time . . . what percentage have graduate degrees, etc.).

Since 1938 the *DOT*, or *Dictionary of Occupational Titles*, has been a top resource for career counseling and guidance and was ideal for acquainting clients with a huge variety of jobs. Originally the *DOT* was a book (and yes, you can still purchase vintage copies of it that way) but in 1991 the government replaced it with an interactive database known as O*NET, or the Occupational Information Network. It was created in 1997 and became available to the public by 1998.

O*NET is a free online database focused on occupational information for students, job seekers, and professional helpers. The database includes information on tasks, skills, knowledge, and other facts regarding a wide range of information. http://onetonline.org.

Because O*NET is online, experts note it can be updated more easily and much faster than a book. O*NET secures information from surveys of workers and consulting occupational experts. O*NET has descriptors of skills, knowledge, tasks, occupation requirements, work abilities, interests, and values to help employers create accurate job descriptions.

At this point in time O*NET has 923 occupations classified via the Standard Occupation Classification system, or SOC. In short SOC is a federal statistical standard used by federal agencies to collect, calculate, and disseminate data on work performed for a salary or profit. SOC data help managers set salaries and labor relations experts set salaries. It can also assist students who need to explore what education is necessary for a given occupation and has information useful for job seekers.

Be aware that there are also computer-assisted career guidance systems (CAGS), many relying on online features to help with career planning and transition. CAGS provide three basic benefits: 1) Career assessment with automatic scoring features, 2) career information, and 3) a decision making

component. such as DISCOVER (used from grade 5 to adulthood since 1967, so it has some serious seniority!) or SIGI 3 – the System of Integrated Guidance and Information, with the original SIGI created by Educational Testing Service in the early 1980s. These systems are advantageous in the sense they are convenient, and you can access information and data very rapidly.

The original CAGS were slanted toward the early theoretical career counseling paradigms of matching, actuarial, or Minnesota point of view, but this is no longer the case.

I want to share several key career counseling terms before we move on. The first is spillover. Spillover implies that life satisfaction and job satisfaction are very closely related. The spillover effect asserts that the feelings of one bleed or spillover into the other.

For example, as a counselor, you may head home after work and try to analyze your adolescent's relationship difficulties. An auto mechanic might come home and start pulling the spark plugs in the family SUV.

The other term or principle is called the compensatory effect. The compensatory effect hypothesizes that we compensate for poor job satisfaction by trying to achieve high life satisfaction.

Let's say, for example, that you work in a library, and you are not allowed to talk very much or very loudly. In a case like this, the individual might just compensate by joining a debate club or Toastmasters or maybe even just yelling as loud as possible at your sporting events.

You will also hear career counselors talk about the **hidden job market. This refers to jobs not listed on job boards, company websites, or advertised. The hidden job market is often contrasted with the open or public job market in which the job opening is publicized. One of the best ways to discover openings in the hidden job market is to network.** There are currently no accurate statistics on the hidden job market, but some estimates are it could include 75–95% of all jobs!

You may ask, has career counseling really had an impact on our field? Well, the National Vocational Guidance Association was formed in 1913. In 1952, it fused with another organization to form – you guessed it – APGA, the American Personnel and Guidance Association.

Later, APGA became American Association of Counseling and Development (AACD), which is now the American Counseling Association or simply ACA. Career counseling was the predecessor to what we are doing now in the counseling movement.

That winds up career counseling. Let's get ready to zip on to another area. I'm anxious for you to get started.

8

Master Lecture 7: Assessment and Testing

Welcome back in time for a new section. Time flies when you are having fun and learning all this great information. This is Dr. Howard Rosenthal, and we are now going to talk about testing and the appraisal of the individual. **Appraisal can roughly be defined as the process of assessing or estimating the attributes of a client.** The first thing I think about when I hear the word appraisal is testing.

You already know this if you are a K-12 school counselor, as statistics indicate that testing is now 7% of your job. In fact, testing constitutes between 20 and 37% of a high school counselor's work. This is very important. **A test is simply a systematic way of measuring a sampled behavior**.

The first issue when selecting a test is to select the appropriate test format. Test format simply refers to the way the test items are presented. **The first factor you need to consider is whether the test will be an objective test or a subjective test. The NCE, the CPCE, and the CECE are examples of objective tests. In an objective measure, the scoring procedure is very specific. There is an correct answer such as answer stem a, b, c, or d**.

A short answer test or an essay test is subjective as the score is based on the scorer's judgment. **Any test based on the scorer's**

DOI: 10.4324/9781003149712-8

judgment is not an objective test. One English teacher gives an essay a C, while the other thinks it's superb and gives it an A.

Next, **you need to decide if the test will use free response items or recognition items**. A free response item allows the test taker to respond in any way they choose. **Short answer tests and projective tests are said to use free responses. Recognition items are called forced choice items.**

For example, on the NCE, CPCE, or the CECE, you must pick an answer stem from A, B, C, or D. You are not allowed to write in your own creative answer. The ABCD structure incidentally is called a multi-point item. **Thus, the comprehensive counseling exams fall into the recognition and not the free response category of tests.**

All Likert scales or multiple-choice tests are considered multipoint recognition items. A true/false or agree/disagree item is what we call a dichotomous recognition item. Dichotomous tells us the answers are opposed, contradictory, or mutually exclusive.

Another test format issue to consider is whether the test is a normative or ipsative measure. In the normative structure, each item is independent of all other test items. In a normative test, you can legitimately compare the various people who've taken the test.

A Rorschach inkblot test, Wechsler intelligence test, or Minnesota multiphasic personality inventory would be normative in nature. **The ipsative measure, however, requires the testee (another word for somebody taking a test) or examinee, again the person being tested or examined, to compare items to one another**.

The Kuder Career Assessment the Edwards Personal Preference Schedule (EPPS) would fall into the ipsative category.

Now listen closely. This is very important. **You cannot legitimately compare two or more people who have taken an ipsative measure. The ipsative measure simply tells you the strengths and weaknesses or differences within that person**.

Here's another testing term, which automotive enthusiasts who are taking in these words of wisdom can easily plug into. **Tests can be classified as speed tests versus power tests**.

Most of us, at one time or another, have taken speed tests such as a keyboarding test. How many words a minute can you type? Speed tests are timed and assess accuracy.

A power test is not timed and gives the examinee so much time that time is not an issue. An aptitude or achievement test is a power test. **Power reflects the level of difficulty mastered by the individual taking the test**.

Experts point out that if a speed test or even a power test is very well designed, the measure is intentionally designed so nobody receives a perfect score. Therefore, differences between all examinees can be measured.

Another key issue is whether the test is a maximum performance measure or a typical performance instrument. There's a lot of terminology in this section, but you're going to know it all by the end of the section. A maximum performance test assesses the best possible performance. A maximum performance measure might be an achievement test.

Running the hundred-yard dash as fast as you can is an example of an achievement test.

A typical performance measures just that: a typical or characteristic performance. Hence, an interest inventory or a personality test would fall into this typical performance category.

Tests may also be characterized as spiral versus cyclical. In a spiral test, the items get progressively more difficult. That's easy enough to remember, as a spiral staircase gets harder as you try to climb up the stairs. In a cyclical format, you have several sections, each of which is spiral in nature.

As if spiral and cyclical weren't complicated enough, **we also have very vertical versus horizontal tests. In a vertical test, there are different forms of the test for various age groups or grade levels. Most achievement tests are vertical. A horizontal test measures various factors at one time**.

An aptitude test would be horizontal, while some personality tests, for example, measure just one factor at a time. Thus, strictly speaking, they are neither horizontal nor vertical in nature.

And, oh yes, **we use the term test battery to describe the situation where we administer a group of tests to the same person. The results can be combined into a single score or profile. The assumption is that the test battery is more accurate than merely assessing the individual with a single measure**.

You should also acquaint yourself with the term parallel forms, or equivalent forms, which means that the test has various versions that all measure the same basic elements in question.

Thus, assume you take the National Counselor Exam in the fall. Your best friend decides to take the exam in the spring. Since you will both be taking different versions, many of the questions will be different. Nevertheless, the items are measuring, basically, the same counseling areas included on the exam.

Appraisal exam hint. Although all the aforementioned factors are important, the most critical issue in test selection is validity. The second most critical issue is reliability.

Validity refers to whether the test truly measures what it purports to measure. There are several types of validity. The first is what psychometricians – and the word psychometrician is just a 25-cent word for people who administer or study psychological tests and measurements – is content validity. **Content validity refers to the extent that the test samples the behavior that it is intended to measure or sample**. Next, we have what is known as **construct validity**.

Construct validity refers to the extent that a test measures an abstract trait, construct, or psychological notion. For example, measuring intelligence, motivation, self-esteem, and ego strength would be examples of this concept.

The third major type of validity is referred to as criterion-related validity. To assess criterion validity test scores, the test is correlated with an outside criterion. A criterion is simply stated as a standard. A job test might be compared to an actual score on an actual job performance. **This is sometimes called concurrent validity**.

Another type of criterion-related validity is predictive validity, which predicts future behavior. For example, GRE scores should have high predictive value for predicting graduate school performance. To make this clear, the criterion validity can be concurrent, that is to say, compared with something in the present, or it can be predictive, something in the future.

There is also a concept called **face validity**. Truthfully most experts believe it is not that important. **Face validity just asks whether the test looks like it is testing what it is supposed to test**. Most counselors have a good answer for face validity. They say, "Who the heck cares?" It doesn't matter."

Again, chances are, my friend, you will need to know this on your exam: **Validity is the most important quality or property of a test**.

The second most important factor is reliability. Reliability refers to whether a test will consistently yield the same results. In other words, does the score remain stable over repeated measurements? **Key exam hint, experts often assert that the quality of a test is determined by validity and reliability. A reliable test is not always valid. However, a valid test will always be reliable. Repeat the last two sentences out loud; yes, it is that important**.

Think about this one for a moment. It makes sense. You could have a reliable bathroom scale. Remember, reliable/reliability means consistent or stable. Assume you weigh 150 pounds, but your scale always gives you a reading that is always 2 pounds off. It always says you weigh 152. The scale is very reliable. Consistent, absolutely, but it's not valid.

Psychometricians have several ways of determining a test's reliability. The first is called test-retest reliability. Using this method, you simply test the same group of people using the same measure or the same test two times. Next, you correlate the scores to see if they are consistent or similar. Take this as a typical example. You step on the scale, and it registers a weight of 155 pounds. Now you move it a few feet on the same surface and weigh yourself again and your weight goes up to 159.5. That's quite a difference and I for one am not going to trust that scale, nor should you.

The second measure is what is termed equivalent forms reliability. In this approach, two parallel or equivalent forms of the same test are administered to the same population, and again, the scores are correlated.

Another popular reliability procedure is the split half method. When using this approach, examinees take the complete test, the whole thing. Then the researchers split the test in half.

For example, the odd-numbered questions and then the even-numbered questions. Finally, a correlation is taken between the two halves of the test because everyone takes each half of the test as if they were two different tests. Of course, you can run a correlation coefficient to see if there is internal consistency.

The last type of reliability test is useful only with subjective exams, for example, short essay tests, short answer tests, or a projective test such as the Rorschach inkblot. This technique is called interrater reliability.

In this technique, you merely take the test. Then two independent raters grade the test and you see if the scores are similar or consistent. A reliability coefficient tells you how much error or variance or unwanted noise is in the test.

A coefficient of positive 1.00 is perfect. This indicates that there is no error in the test. This occurs only in physical measurements such as correlating your weight in pounds with your weight in ounces.

A coefficient of 0.90 or plus 0.90 is considered good in a psychological test. The 0.90 means that 90% of the score is accurate, while 10% is indicative of error.

Most personality tests have a coefficient of 0.70 or above. For job selection purposes, tests with a coefficient of 0.80 or below are generally not appropriate. When you speak of the issue of testing and appraisal, many counselors think about intelligence testing.

Psychologist G. Frederic Kuder (1903–2000), who created the famed career inventory, and Marion Webster Richardson (1896–1965) are well known for creating the Kuder-Richardson Formula 20, or KR 20, a popular statistical method to computer test reliability when a test has binary or dichotomous answer choices such as true and false. When all the test items are assumed to have equal difficulty, a KR-21 is used to assess reliability. When a test has more than two answer choices such as a Likert-scale, **Cronbach's alpha** – named after psychologist and noted testing textbook author **Lee Cronbach (1916–2001)** – is utilized.

Quite frankly, counselors and therapists have traditionally done a lot of work to assess intellectual factors, but the study of intelligence is not new.

In the 1860s, the English statistician and behavioral scientist Francis Galton (1822–1911) postulated that intelligence was a unitary factor that was normally distributed like height or weight. In 1869, he chose 977 men who achieved fame. He discovered it was 300 times more likely that a famous person would have a famous relative.

Thus, Galton felt intelligence was a product of genetics. By the way, do you want to take a guess who was Galton's half cousin since they shared a grandfather? Try Charles Darwin.

The concept of intelligence being normally distributed relates to the concept of the bell-shaped distribution curve, which has haunted statistics students ever since. In 1904, Charles Spearman (1863–1945), the British psychologist, postulated a two-factor theory of intelligence. There was G, or the general factor, and S, or specific factor.

Then came the work of Louis Leon Thurstone (1887–1955), an American trailblazer in psychophysics and psychometrics, who did not believe in a single unitary intelligence and postulated a group of independent intellectual factors like memory and reasoning. He called these factors primary abilities, and he used factor analysis to isolate the abilities.

We also have psychologist J.P. Guilford (1897–1987) (the J.P. stands for Joy Paul and is rarely listed in the literature), who isolated 120 elements which add up to intelligence. Guilford is probably best remembered for his dimension of convergent and divergent thinking. Raymond Bernard Cattell (1905–1998) is another theorist who had an impact on our profession in both the United States and the United Kingdom, with his notion that there are two forms of intelligence, fluid intelligence and crystal intelligence. Fluid intelligence is dependent on the nervous system and the ability to solve complex novel problems. Crystallized intelligence is the application of fluid to education. Crystallized intelligence is the ability to use facts, but there is another Cattell in this saga.

The first psychology professor in the United States, James McKeen Cattell (1860–1944), coined the term mental test in 1890. He was the first person to use psychological tests to predict academic performance by giving tests to all freshmen at Columbia University.

The first intelligence test was developed by Alfred Binet (1857–1911), a French psychologist, and Theodore Simon (1873–1961), a French psychologist and medical doctor, in 1905. Revisions occurred in 1908 and 1911. The first test was named the Binet Simon scale.

Why was the test created in the first place? An excellent question indeed. In 1904, the French government, or more specifically the French Ministry of Public Education, wanted to discriminate normal Parisian children from those who had impaired intellectual ability. The government felt that the teachers could not be trusted to make this distinction.

These children could then be separated from the others and would be placed in a simplified curriculum. The first test, which relied on school tasks, succeeded better than anything else before it. It used the concept of age-related tasks. **An eight-year-old task, for example, would be one in which 50% of the eight-year-olds could easily answer correctly**.

Just as an aside, Binet also did seminal work on projective inkblot tests using his own daughters as subjects. **Ironically, Binet never believed that his test measured "intelligence," while Simon felt their test was "overused."**

The term IQ literally meant intelligence quotient. Quotient, you will recall, is the answer when you divide.

The IQ was computed using a formula dating back to roughly 1912 by the German psychologist William Stern (1871–1938). The formula was MA, our mental age, over CA, which was chronological age, or the actual age, times 100 equals IQ.

Howard Rosenthal, that's me, of course, came up with a memory formula that an MA or master's degree is a very high degree and should go on top of CA, you know, the numerator in the equation. **Again, the equation is MA over CA times 100 equals IQ. This is known as a ratio IQ**.

Today psychometricians prefer the deviation IQ that compares the obtained scores with the norm. In 1916 Lewis Madison Terman (1877–1955) adapted the Binet for American usage and logically called it the Stanford Binet because he was working at the Stanford graduate school of education. It has often been said that Terman Americanized the IQ test.

The Stanford Binet was updated in 1937, and then again in 1960, and then in 1986, when the formula MA over CA times 100 bit the dust; thus times change, and even the term IQ has been dropped. The new term is SAS, or Standard Age Score.

Since 2003 the Stanford Binet Intelligence Scale fifth edition, sometimes dubbed the SB5, has been used and can be administered to individuals ages 2 through 85 and beyond. Since it is based on a stratified random sample of nearly 5000 people from the 2000 census, it is based on a more accurate prediction of the American population. The current version created by the US psychologist Gale H. Roid uses ten subtests, five verbal subtests and five nonverbal subtests. They yield a full-scale IQ. Research for a SB6 version is being conducted.

The mean of the full-scale IQ is 100 and the standard deviation is 15. A small controversy remains. Some experts believe that the old Binet Form LM is still the best test for measuring the characteristics of gifted individuals.

Now, that brings us to the Wechsler scales, which most experts consider the most popular IQ tests in the world. Like the Binet, the mean score is 100. The standard deviation on the Wechsler is also 15.

David Wechsler (1896–1981), a Romanian American psychologist, published his first IQ test in 1939. It was called the Wechsler-Bellevue, as Wechsler was working as the chief psychologist at Bellevue Hospital in New York City at the time. During that era psychometricians felt that the Binet was not really the best possible test for adults, and thus the Wechsler began to grow rapidly in popularity.

Today, counselors use several Wechsler tests. The WAIS-IV, or the Wechsler Adult Intelligence Scale, is the most popular adult intelligence test in the world. A WAIS-5 could be on the horizon. **The WAIS-IV has ten core and five supplemental subtests**.

Just for the record, **the verbal and performance scales described in my earlier materials have been eliminated and replaced by what the measure calls index scores. The WAIS-IV takes about 60 to 90 minutes to administer. The WAIS-IV has a large age range and is suitable for individuals from 16 to 90 years old**.

The WISC-V or the Wechsler Intelligence Scale for children, is used for ages 6 through 16 and can be administered in 45 to 65 minutes.

Finally, we have **the WPPSI-IV, or Wechsler Preschool and Primary Scale of Intelligence, used for children aged 2 years 6 months to 7 years 6 months, which can be administered in less**

than an hour. The test is often used for assessment and admissions to schools targeted at gifted or highly talented children.

How reliable are IQ tests? Great question. Well, **IQ tests given to teens and adults are generally quite reliable, sporting a correlation of about 0.90 or higher. Are IQ tests valid? Experts note that these IQ tests work best for assessing intelligence related to school tasks, such as abstract reasoning.**

The correlation between IQ and high school grades is moderately strong, about plus 0.50. They also correlate well with everyday tasks, such as using a phone book or reading medication instructions.

Perhaps you didn't know it, but **there are infant and preschool IQ tests. These tests don't really predict future IQ scores very well. However, they are useful in terms of helping to diagnose children with an intellectual disability. When a child is under two, the predictive validity is extremely poor.**

Examples of such tests include **the Denver Developmental Screening Test II for kids one month to six years of age. The Bayley Scale of Infant Development, or BSID-4, is named after Nancy Bayley (1899–1994), an award-winning US psychologist, who developed the test. Most experts agree that this is the most widely used infant intelligence instrument. It can be used for infants from 1 to 42 months.**

Some clinicians use **the FTII, or the Fagan Test of Infant Intelligence. The Fagan is suitable for infants from 3 months to 12 months of age. IQ tests that yield a score that is obtained prior to age seven do not correlate well with IQ scores tabulated at a later age.**

We also **have group IQ tests, although group tests generally are not as accurate as individual tests. The group testing movement began in the 1970s, with its roots dating back to the army alpha, for literates, and the army beta, for illiterates or those who did not speak English, in 1917, to test the recruits during World War I. The test was created by psychologists in the army signal corps.**

In World War II, the Army General Classification Test, or AGCT, came along. Group IQ tests like the Lorge-Thorndike Intelligence Tests or Otis- Lennon School Ability Test are used frequently in schools. You should know that there are some pros and some cons to group IQ tests.

First, often listed **as a plus, you generally do not need intensive training or special courses to administer most group measures. And you can sure give the test to a lot more people in the same amount of time versus what it would take to administer an individual test to all these same people. Nevertheless, again, group IQ tests are not as accurate as your individual IQ tests**.

Many counselors insist that any IQ test should be a **culture-fair test**.

By a culture-fair test, I mean one in which bias is eliminated by using items well known to subjects, regardless of culture. The problem is that, thus far, culture-fair tests do not predict academic performance as well as conventional tests. Other experts say that the way to make IQ tests more valuable is to make them **culture free**.

On a culture-free IQ test, the solution is to take the problem-solving questions on the test and make them problems that would not depend on the knowledge of any culture.

Perhaps one of most heated debates in the social sciences has been over racial differences in IQ.

Arthur Jensen (1923–2021), an educational psychologist at UC Berkley, had the social science community arguing back and forth when he published a very lengthy 1969 article in the prestigious *Harvard Educational Review* journal. The article caused a major uproar, as it stated that blacks scored 11 to 15 points lower on IQ tests than whites, and this could be due to genetics.

One of the best responses to Jensen's argument was proposed by St. Louis psychologist, Washington University professor, and Afro-American scholar Robert Lee Williams II (1930–2020), who created the BITCH test. No, excuse me, I'm *not* cursing at you. BITCH stands for Black Intelligence Test of Cultural Homogeneity, released in 1972, which was composed of 100 questions. It can also be referred to as the BITCH-100.

At the time, Williams gave this example. Almost any black inner-city child can tell you that a deuce and a quarter means a Buick Electra 225. But let me ask you this, folks, and this is what Williams was really asking social scientists: How many high-IQ kids from middle-class neighborhoods could answer this question? "Darn few," said Dr. Williams.

Blacks scored drastically higher than whites on the test. A commonly cited example is that when the test was released based on 200 students, Black students scored 87/100 while white students snared just 51/100.

Just as an aside, one of the high points of my career was when Dr. Williams asked me to lecture to a hospital staff he was supervising. Dr. Williams also coined the term **"Ebonics" (by combining the terms "ebony" and "phonics.") He also helped found the Association of Black Psychologists**.

The point was that IQ tests are not free of cultural bias and that the victims of their results are usually poor nonwhites, often blacks and Hispanics.

One project known as **SOMPA, System of Multicultural Pluralistic Assessment**, created in 1978 by Jane Mercer June Lewis, tried to eliminate culture from tests and to create culture-free tests for 5- to 11-year-old children, but most people believe that it has failed. **Some experts say you truly cannot eliminate cultural items from an exam**.

Despite the failure of projects like SOMPA, proponents of IQ tests like Binet and the Wechsler remind us that although these tests may tell us nothing about one's genetic makeup, they are good predictors of success in life for almost any group of people. Incidentally, in recent years, **exams are often referring to IQ tests as cognitive tests**.

Finally, according to a notion dubbed the Flynn effect after James Robert Flynn (1934–2020), IQ scores worldwide are going up to the tune of approximately 3 points per decade whether we examine the Wechsler's or the Binet. Behavioral scientists are unsure whether it's because of better nutrition, early maturation among children, familiarity with testing (e.g., if you take an exam a second time your score often increases), or manual dexterity from playing, yeah, those games that you hate your kids are spending too much time on: yes, video games. Flynn contended that higher literacy rates and a cognitively challenging environment were major factors. Some researchers even point out that removing the lead from gasoline was beneficial since lead can lower IQ scores! Stay tuned; we don't have the complete answer to the riddle of the Flynn effect, but this could get very interesting, including the fact that some research points to the fact that **the Flynn effect has begun to reverse**.

Another interesting point is that the well-known **Head Start program boosts IQ, but the benefits are temporary, and they seem to fade away after just a year or two**.

Now, let's move away from intelligence tests and mention some of the most popular **personality tests. The big cheese of objective measures to diagnose disorders is a personality test known as the MMPI or Minnesota Multiphasic Personality Inventory. Today, updated and revised as the MMPI-3, it includes 335 self-report items. The MMPI-3 norms match 2020 US Census Bureau demographic projections. Also, for the first time ever, the instrument was normed using 550 Spanish speakers. and there is an MMPI-A for adolescents ages 14 through 18**.

The MMPI was first published in 1943 by Starke R. Hathaway (1903–1984), a psychologist, and J.C. McKinley (1891–1950), a neurologist, both faculty at the University of Minnesota. Today the test indicates the extent of emotional disturbance and helps counselors diagnose clients. The MMPI-3 takes 35–50 minutes to complete and even less, approximately 25–35 minutes, when taken via a computer. The MMPI-3 yields 52 scales. Examples of the scales include demoralization (DEM), general unhappiness and dissatisfaction; EAT, or eating concerns; COG, or cognitive complaints, such as memory problems or an inability to concentrate; and SHY, or feeling uncomfortable in the presence of others.

There's one test that seems to be basking in the sun lately that is a popular measure for businesses and schoolteachers. And indeed, I mentioned it earlier, and that is the Myers-Briggs Type Indicator based on Carl Jung's theory of types that tests employees for bipolar scales, which results in a four-letter type. But I had to come back to it for this possible exam booster: **The Myers-Briggs is often termed a theory-based inventory, since it is based on Carl Jung's theory, while the MMPI-3 is a criterion-based inventory. We call it criterion based because it compares the person taking it to a criterion group, say, normal individuals or people who are paranoid**.

Self-report personality inventories such as the MMPI or the Myers-Briggs are generally more accurate than projective tests. What are projective tests? Well, **projective tests are more popular with psychodynamic-oriented therapists than they are with behavioristic or brief solution-oriented practitioners. In a**

projective test, the examinee is shown a neutral stimulus that can be perceived in many ways.

Then the examinee projects their own personality by responding to the ambiguous, amorphous material. Some exams will refer to projective measures as projective expressive measures. The theory, of course, is that the client will express or reveal unconscious conflict when responding to the test. The client is asked what the test brings to mind. Then the client projects their personality.

The **Rorschach inkblot test** is the most popular projective measure, and the test is appropriate for clients ages three and up. The test was **created by the Swiss psychiatrist Hermann Rorschach (1884–1922), who died at the tender age of 37, likely from a ruptured appendix. This projective measure relies on ten inkblot cards to assess the personality**. Five of the cards are gray or black, while five of the cards are colored. **Inkblot tests such as the Rorschach or the Holtzman inkblot test (HIT), which relies on 45 cards, and 2 more practice cards created in 1961, are often categorized as association projective tests. The Holtzman was created to address deficiencies related to the Rorschach.**

Another type or category of projective test is called a construction test. The TAT, or Thematic Apperception Test, clearly falls into this category. The person being tested is asked to describe, make up, or *construct* a story about a picture on a card. The picture is ambiguous. For example, the picture might show a child playing a violin. One client might comment that the child is playing the instrument and grieving because his mother died.

Another client looking at the exact same picture could assert that the child is practicing his music because he's so excited, because he just won the school's talent show. Both clients are looking at precisely the same vague picture. The TAT was created by the psychologist Henry Murray (1892–1988) and lay analyst Christiana Morgan (1897–1967) in 1935. Originally, Murray suggested that the interpretation of the test should follow his needs press theory: internal needs, such as power, hunger, and affiliation versus the press of the environment (seeing food as a stimulus). Today, other primarily psychoanalytic systems for grading the test can be applied.

Projective tests that ask you to draw or create a picture are known as expressive projective tests. The **Draw-a-Person (DAP)** test for children and adolescents, created in 1926 **by Florence Goodenough (1886–1959),** or the **House-Tree-Person (HTP)** test fall into this category. The well-known **Bender Gestalt test (the complete name not used on some exams** is actually **Bender Visual-Motor Gestalt Test)** in which the client copies geometric figures from nine cards also belongs in this category. This instrument was created in 1938 **by Lauretta Bender (1897–1987),** a neuropsychiatrist. **The current version is the Bender-Gestalt-II or second edition**.

The Bender has been called a motoric or test of organicity, as it screens for brain damage.

Another version of the projective test is the sentence completion test, where the client is literally asked to complete a sentence.

For example, "When I think of my mother, I feel . . . " Or perhaps "The main thing I worry about is . . . " Projective tests are lauded because clients can't figure out what the perfect or best answer is. Therefore, it's difficult to fake the test or hide things while you're taking the test.

Nevertheless, projective tests, once the backbone of clinical psychology, are under fire lately. That's right. **The validity and reliability of projective tests has been seriously questioned**.

Some studies indicate that introduction to business or introduction to psychology students without advanced training can discern as much about the projective test-taker and what they're really like without even knowing the complex grading system! In some instances, the students performed as well in terms of assessing the individual who took the test as seasoned experts who give projective tests for a living.

Another type of test is the Interest Inventory. These instruments focus primarily on occupational or educational interest, and they assess preferences. Again, they are assessing preferences.

When giving an interest inventory to children or adults, be careful. Students younger than the 10th grade show instability in terms of interest, and thus, the results may not be all that valid.

Another difficulty is that it's very easy to give untruthful responses on such tests. In addition, the person may try to respond in a socially acceptable manner, though forced choice responses can often curb this tendency at least a little bit.

Some interest inventories have been criticized as focusing too heavily on professional roles and not heavily enough on blue-collar pursuits. **The most famous inventory is the Strong Interest Inventory, or SII, based on Holland's six occupational types, and it has been used since 1926.**

Now, yes, of course, I'm sure you know Holland's code themes by now, but just for review purposes, these broad areas are the realistic, investigative, artistic, social, enterprising, and conventional. **Remember RIASEC.**

The Strong is constructed by asking a large sample of men and women from various ethnicities who are successful in an occupation for at least three years what they like. When a test taker's profile matches an occupational profile, then an occupation might prove appropriate.

The Strong uses 291 items on a **Likert scale (strongly disagree to strongly agree)** and takes most folks about 30 to 45 minutes to complete. Reminder: **On the Strong there are no correct or incorrect answers.**

The second most popular interest inventory is the Kuder Career Search with person match (KCS).

Some counselors also rely on the SDS or Self-Directed Search. Yes, the SDS is administered and scored by the person taking the test. That's right. It's self-administered and self-scored. Like the Strong, the SDS relies on Holland's career types.

Despite their drawbacks, interest inventories are quite reliable. They're not as threatening to the person taking the exam as other types of tests.

Another category in psychometrics is the aptitude test. Aptitude tests predict future behavior. Such tests are usually intended to measure an inherited capability or capacity rather than what you have learned or mastered in the past. Some aptitude tests like the Seashore Measure of Musical Talents can be very specific.

A great aptitude test must have superb predictive validity. One of the most famous aptitude tests is the GATB, or General Aptitude Test Battery, which test takers have two hours

and 30 minutes to complete. It is given by state employment offices and developed by our own United States Government Employment Service. The GATB assesses 9th- through 12th-grade students as well as adults using paper and pencil, as well as manual dexterity items.

Forging right along. **We also have another category known as achievement tests. Achievement tests illuminate what you have learned or mastered, and thus, they are primarily used in academic or educational settings. The NCE, the CECE, and the CPCE** would fall into this category; so does the **GRE. The SAT and the ACT, once labeled aptitude tests, are now designed to be achievement tests. The SAT was redesigned in 2016 to test what the student has learned, and thus it evolved from an aptitude test to an achievement test. Thus, both the ACT and SAT are now achievement tests related to what the test taker learned in school.**

Some books call the GRE and tests that examine both aptitude and achievement aptitude achievement tests. The cold, hard truth is that some tests cross that fine line. They test what you've learned so far, but they *also* attempt to predict future success. **Now, that said, if an exam asks you to classify the GRE as an aptitude or an achievement test and you do NOT have the aptitude achievement option, I would select the aptitude answer stem.**

The noted American psychologist **Anne Anastasi (1908–2001)**, who wrote extensively on psychological testing, once quipped that if she had occult powers she would go back and eliminate the terms achievement and aptitude from the psychometric vocabulary, since they have led to major confusion.

Here's a good exam question. I've tried to review with you the most popular tests used in the field of counseling, but **where could you go for additional information and data on testing?** Most experts would turn to the nonprofit **Buros Center for Testing, which lists every standardized test, plus, as an added bonus, provides a critical review of each test.** Their website, http://buros.org, refers to the site as "the premier test review center." Online test reviews are available as well as **print resources such as the *Mental Measurements Yearbook* , or MMY. The MMY is updated on a regular basis and was originally written by Oscar K. Buros (1905–1978) in 1938. The current print version does not**

review every test but covers over 3500 of them and will set you back about $210.00 US. The text is considered an excellent resource for educational, business, and psychological tests written in English.

Buros was also the brainchild behind the *Tests in Print* (TIP) series. The TIP gives the test's name, acronym, time needed to administer the measure, price, publication dates, and intended population.

To sum up: The MMY and TIP are complementary with the MMY, providing full-text test reviews and the TIP listing the current test information and availability. The TIP refers you to the MMY for honest test reviews.

Professional journals are also a viable source. Then, there are the classic textbooks in the field, for example, Anne Anastasi's *Psychological Testing* or **Lee Cronbach's (1916–2001)** *Essentials of Psychological Testing*, both of which I used in my own counseling and psychology classes.

Keep in mind textbooks are short on specifics; hence, you are urged to peruse the test manual and the materials that come with the test. Many publishers now have websites that yield valuable, vital information.

A word to the wise. **Never try to rely on a single source**. Since a test must be applicable to a population, multicultural counselors feel that for testing to be appropriate, it must meet certain standards.

The adept multicultural counselor who administers or reads tests must be familiar with five key documents.

Here they are. Number one, "The Code of Fair Testing Practices in Education," by the Joint Committee on Testing Practices – which included ACA members – in 2004, which replaced the original 1988 document. The code discusses: 1) Development and selection of the appropriate tests. 2) Administration and scoring. 3) Reporting and interpreting. 4) Informing test takers.

Number two is AACD's "Responsibility of Users of Standardized Tests." Number three is the American Psychological Association's "Standards for Educational and Psychological Testing." Number four is "Multicultural Counseling Competencies and Standards – A Call to the Profession." Now, if you'd like to check this article out for yourself, it's a 1992 article from the *Journal of Counseling and Development*, volume 70, pages 477 to 486.

Number five on our hit list, ACA's own Code of Ethics. Remember that tests help counselors make decisions regarding placement, admissions, diagnosis, counseling, outcomes, licensure, and certification. I guess you probably know the most about the last one, right? They also help with self-understanding, and they're also used to save time.

Just as an aside, let me state for the record that some therapeutic modalities, such as Rogerian person-centered self-theory counseling, do not really put too much stock in testing.

In fact, as I speak, a lot of folks now are practicing brief strategic therapy, also known as solution-oriented therapy, or even possibility therapy. This approach, which was popularized by folks like Bill O'Hanlon, Insoo Kim Berg, Steve de Shazer, and Michele Weiner Davis, is intended to help the person in a very low number of sessions.

Hence, formal testing is rarely if ever used. There just isn't time. The client comes in, and the therapist focuses on the exception to the problem. Let's say the client comes in and says, "Well, I never get along with my daughter." The therapist asks what is known as the exception question, "Do you ever get along with your daughter?"

The client might say, "Well, I get along with her on holidays." The therapist and the client then try to examine what's different on holidays.

Therapists of this ilk also stress the so-called miracle question, which goes like this. "Suppose one night you were asleep, there was a miracle, and this problem was solved. How would you know? What would be different?" The idea of the question is to stimulate new problem-solving mindsets in the client.

OK, enough about solution-focused or solution-oriented brief therapy and back to appraisal.

I feel compelled to acquaint you with a very important concept known as the standard error of measurement. The SEM, or standard error of measurement, tells how accurate or inaccurate a test is.

The standard error is an estimate of the variation in a single person's score if this individual would take the test again, and again, and again, say, an infinite number of times. A smaller SEM is better since the person's scores would fall within a more narrow range.

Let's assume that an IQ test has a standard error of plus/minus three. You score 100 on the test. According to the concept of the

SEM, 68% of the time, your score would fall between plus/minus 3 points of 100, or 97 to 103.

And there's a smaller but still plausible chance that a smaller percent of the time, your score could go lower than 97 or higher than 103.

The bottom line is that it's inaccurate to say that Bob is smarter than Nancy when Bob has an IQ of 102 and Nancy has an IQ of 100. **Your exam might refer to the SEM as the confidence limits of a test.**

Overall, testing is considered a formal method of appraisal since it is based on standardized measures. Counselors also use informal measures including observations, notes, rating scales, checklists, even self-reports like a client's journal or diary, data in the case record, interviews, case conferences, and sociometric data and the sociometric approach mentioned elsewhere.

Counselors use appraisal methods to secure third-party insurance and managed care payments. To receive these payments, the counselor must be familiar with three systems.

First, we have CPT, or Current Procedural Terminology Codes. A CPT code answers the question: What service was provided to the client? Here are a few simple examples: 90837 is 60 minutes of psychotherapy. 90834 is a 45-minute session. 90847 is a 50-minute session of family therapy with the client present. **There is no reason to memorize CPT code numbers for your exam.** Medical professionals, whether it is a dentist, a physical therapist, or a physician, also **must provide CPT codes for the same reason as counselors: to get paid!!!**

Okay, so now we know what you did for the client, but *why* did you do it? Well, that's where diagnosis or putting a label on the client comes into play. It's as simple as this: No diagnosis, no third-party insurance or managed care payment.

Thus, the second resource you need to be familiar with is a global resource known as the ICD, or International Classification of Diseases, created by the World Health Organization. It is often dubbed the "bible for billing." As I am writing this chapter, ICD-11 is the newest version. The ICD is used in over 100 countries and is intended for all medical specialties. Whether you have diabetes, asthma, or headaches, you will find a code in the ICD as a diagnosis. The ICD attempts to include all known diseases – physical and mental – as well as injuries. Mental health concerns were added to the ICD 6 in 1949. In addition to clinical use, the ICD also helps medical professionals track diseases. Often you will see ICD-CM, with the CM standing for clinical modification.

Okay, so simply virtually all medical specialties and subspecialties merely use the ICD. **However, the American Psychiatric Association became somewhat of an anomaly, as in 1952 it created its own diagnostic text, the DSM, or Diagnostic and Statistical Manual of Mental Disorders, the latest of which is the DSM 5-TR, released in March 2022. The DSM is often referred to as "the bible of psychiatry**." (What's the deal with all these resources becoming bibles?)

The 5-TR refers to the fact that it is the fifth-edition text revision. Prior to DSM-5, the DSM used Roman numerals such as DSM I, DSM II, DSM III, DSM III-R, DSM IV, and DSM IV-R.

The first DSM, or DSM I, appeared on the scene in 1952 and listed approximately 60 diagnoses, while the DSM-5 raised that number to nearly 300.

Now when you assign a client a diagnosis from the DSM the text will provide a five-digit code. Thus, major depression disorder recurrent, severe would be 296.33. The ICD code is also provided, in this instance F33.2 **Insurance companies only allow billing if you submit the ICD code.** I am aware this may seem very ironic to counselors since traditionally virtually all courses and workshops in mental health focus on the DSM and often barely mention the ICD. ***Nevertheless, since midnight October 1, 2015, counselors have been required to submit ICD codes to get paid by private insurance carriers, and yes this would also include programs like Medicare or Medicaid. This is a HIPAA requirement.***

So just in case you are confused, here is the CliffsNotes version of what I am saying: The DSM provides the diagnostic criteria, while the ICD provides billing codes.

One other thing to keep in mind is when you look at a DSM diagnosis, the fifth or final digit often provides the severity of the condition. So, using our example of major depression you would use the number 1 if the depression is mild (e.g., 296.31), 2 if moderate (e.g., 296.32), 3 if severe without psychotic features, 4 if there are psychotic features evident, 5 for partial remission, and 6 if the condition is in full remission. Finally, 0 if unspecified.

The DSM also sports V codes that indicate conditions not attributed to a mental disorder, such as Academic and Educational Problems V62.3. In the ICD there will be Z, so in this instance, Z.55.9. As another quick example, Problems Related to Release from Prison, V62.5 in the DSM or Z65.2 in the ICD.

Now, listen closely. Please do not read this portion of the book for the sole purpose of memorizing DSM/ICD codes. Your exam will not ask you to memorize code numbers. There are far too many of them. The object of this section is merely to familiarize you with the basic concept of coding.

The DSM and the ICD are considered books or databases of taxonomy and more specifically nosology. **Taxonomy can be defined as the science of classification, and nosology literally means the classification of disease**. The DSM does not attempt to deal with causes. Thus, the term neurosis, which is somewhat Freudian and not always considered professional, has not been used in the DSM in over 30 years but is still used in the ICD.

So again, psychiatrists wanted a guide of nosology that was more precise regarding mental and emotional disorders; hence the birth of the "DSM."

One problem with the DSM, the ICD, or, for that matter, any diagnostic instrument is that it can create what is known as an **iatrogenic illness**. **Iatrogenic illness is an illness that is doctor induced. The term is now being actively applied to therapists and other helpers**.

Say, you tell a client they have an illness or a mental disorder. Next, the person begins to display the symptoms of the disorder, not because they really have the disorder but because you told the person that they have it. That, my friend, is an iatrogenic illness.

Another problem with the DSM is that it does not recommend a given treatment paradigm for a given problem. Hence, if you have an eight-year-old who is depressed, the DSM won't say, "Well, we recommend reality therapy and so many milligrams of an antidepressant."

Another issue that is something we need to talk about is that the DSM changes from one edition to another. The book changes what is considered a problem. For example, homosexuality is currently not considered a disorder as it was in an earlier edition. Nevertheless, overall, the DSM gets larger and seems to pick up more diagnoses with each edition.

Let me get on my soapbox and give an opinion here. **After talking with thousands of folks who are preparing for the NCE, I am convinced that most of them are spending way too much time worrying about DSM questions**.

Yes, you should read and study this section several times, and you should flip through the current edition of the DSM, but do not spend an inordinate amount of time on this topic. The chances are that there will be a limited number of questions related to this issue.

Of course, if you are taking an exam that is not generic, then that exam might stress the DSM very heavily. For example, if you were taking the National Clinical Mental Health Counselors Exam (NCMHCE) to become a Certified Clinical Mental Health Counselor or CCMHC, then that is a whole different story.

9

Master Lecture 8: Marriage and Family Counseling

OK, let's move on to a brand-new exciting section, marriage and family counseling, which includes couples counseling. Many experts have commented that one of the fastest-growing clientele for professional counselors consists of persons experiencing marriage and family problems.

Since the 1980s marriage and family specialization has become the most popular academic track in many professional counseling preparation programs. Some data suggest that counselors should be taking this area very seriously. For example, if a couple has a problem and goes for individual therapy, the chances are one in ten that the problem will get worse.

On the flip side of the coin, however, marriage counseling is said to have a success rate of over 60%, while family therapy is even higher, exceeding 70%. One issue that has complicated this area is that traditionally, marriage and family counselors have been members of the American Association for Marriage and Family Therapy, or AAMFT.

Many experts still feel that this organization is the only appropriate choice. Nevertheless, many individuals who are reading this chapter are aware that the American Counseling Association has a division known as **IAMFC, or the International Association of Marriage**

DOI: 10.4324/9781003149712-9

and Family Counselors. Philosophically, AAMFT feels that marriage and family counseling is a profession.

IAMFC, on the other hand, asserts that marriage and family counseling is a specialty you acquire after snaring generic counseling knowledge and experience.

Let me give you **a brief overview of family therapy. Our story begins in 1937, when Nathan Ackerman, MD (1908–1971), who was trained as an analytic child psychiatrist, wrote an article called "The Family as a Social and Emotional Unit" in the bulletin of the Kansas Mental Hygiene Society. Ackerman is often referred to as the grandfather of family therapy and the founder of psychoanalytic family therapy.**

His approach used Freudian, psychodynamic principles to work with families. These principles, such as dream analysis, life history, transference, and catharsis, are covered in another section of this book.

Like individual treatment using psychoanalytic theory, psychoanalytic family theory stresses that one thing causes another. This is referred to as linear causality, or the cause effect model.

Questions regarding psychoanalytic family therapy often use the term **object relations. An object is another person that the child wants to bond with to meet their needs. In plain everyday English, intrapsychic conflicts from one's family of origin continue to affect the individual's relationship with their own spouse and children.**

Analytic object relations psychologist and family therapy expert James Framo (1922–2001) suggested that this factor gets in the way of people changing because they have parental introjects. Introjection takes place when you incorporate a parent's attitude as your own. Introjects are imprints or memories from the past that are generally based on unresolved relationships with a parent.

Another possible exam term related to object relations family therapy is **splitting. Splitting occurs when a young child turns an object into either all good or all bad and then internalizes the perception. If this tendency is not resolved, this individual, as an adult, will view people as all bad or all good, or they will see the same person as being all good or all bad. Good at one time and all bad at other times.**

On your exam Framo's approach might be dubbed object-relations or family of origin therapy.

Many sources leave out the fact that psychiatrist Don Jackson (1920–1968) founded the Mental Research Institute (MRI), the first institution created to study and teach family therapy. Jackson, teaming up with Jay Haley and Nathan Ackerman, created the first-ever journal for family therapy, *Family Process*.

Another shot in the arm for marriage and family therapy came down the pike in 1965, when **social worker Virginia Satir (1916–1988) wrote the now-classic text *Conjoint Family Therapy.* The therapist joins with the family to improve family functioning. The word "conjoint" merely means that the therapist works with two or more family members.**

Most exams and textbooks mention the fact that **Satir delineated four patterns or styles of dysfunctional communication that exist when family members experience stress.**

She mentions the placater, who tries to please everybody in the family. The placater is a people pleaser. Then she mentioned the blamer, who insists that that everything is everybody else's fault. She also mentions the super reasonable analyzer, who is emotionally detached, calm, cool, and prone to intellectualization.

Finally, the detractor, who is totally removed, talks about things that are totally irrelevant.

Your exam will most likely classify Satir and another famous family psychiatrist therapist, Carl Whitaker (1922–2001), as experiential family counselors or experientialists. Since family counseling has been conducted in several formats over the years, let us talk about those for a minute.

There's a model known as **collaborative therapy, in which each family member sees a different therapist**. Occasionally, the different therapists convene to look at the situation. An offshoot of this approach is known as **concurrent family therapy. In this approach, one counselor sees everybody individually**.

This model and the collaborative model gained popularity, because initially insurance companies and managed care firms would <u>not</u> pay for couples counseling or marriage and family therapy.

Next, we have network family therapy, in which people from the outside such as neighbors, colleagues at work, or even

friends, are brought into the therapy sessions. Last, some counselors rely on the multiple family/couples therapy approach. This model resembles group therapy, and the treatment audience, if you will, is made up of several couples or families.

In most cases, however, the focus in family therapy is not on the individual client but rather on the entire family.

In counseling, the person who is asked to seek therapy is known as the **IP or identified patient**. While the identified patient may indeed have real problems, the family therapist assumes that the true cause of the behavior is the dysfunctional family. The goal is to change relationships in the family. ***The IP is the family itself.***

Key reminder: Although from a theoretical perspective counselors often view the entire family as the IP, for insurance and managed care organizations (MCOs), for billing purposes, an individual will need to be chosen and diagnosed and this should clearly be explained to the family or couple. The family or couple needs to know which person has been picked.

Family therapists are fond of a story that was popularized by psychiatrist **Murray Bowen (1913–1990)**, who observed a client that was functioning appropriately while in the hospital but would become dysfunctional and regressed when placed back in the family system.

Theoretically, according to those who believe in the family model, it works faster and more efficiently than treating a single client. Moreover, family therapy is an **excellent choice if individual therapy has not been successful.**

According to the theories of family therapy, when the relationship between family members changes, symptoms go away.

This approach is said to be interpersonal rather than intrapsychic since the counselor is trying to ascertain what is transpiring between individuals rather than merely analyzing what is going on within a single person. Instead of looking at a disturbed individual, the family therapist looks at the dysfunctional system, which *is* the family.

Just in case I haven't made myself crystal clear, let me put it as simply as possible.

In family therapy, the family is the client. The pathology, if you will, is in the family.

Family therapists are fond of the word homeostasis, which means that the family will interact in ways that keep things in balance, equilibrium, or status quo. This may sound positive, but family therapists created the term to imply that families resist change.

Proponents of family therapy often believe in the double bind hypothesis created in 1954 by anthropologist Gregory Bateson (1904–1980). The notion stipulates that "Family members are sometimes placed in a no-win, damned if you do, damned if you don't position."

The person who is the recipient of a double bind receives two mutually exclusive messages from the same person and thus cannot really respond appropriately. In extreme cases, repeated messages of this ilk can lead to schizophrenic behavior, according to this theory.

Now, in family systems theory, the family is technically an open system since elements can enter and leave the system.

Three key family therapy exam hints.

One, **the term equifinality implies that similar outcomes can occur in the family from different origins. Moreover, the term suggests that the family can achieve similar goals in vastly different ways.**

Number two, **the term equipotentiality refers to the fact that the same processes can produce markedly different results.**

Three, **focusing on the past too much when you are performing marriage and family therapy has been called the genetic fallacy.**

Another concept that you will likely see on your exam is feedback. Feedback comes from the theory of cybernetics, which asserts that a system uses feedback to stay the same or to correct itself. **In family therapy, feedback refers to a process that the family uses to adjust itself.**

Negative feedback occurs when the family goes back to the way it's always been in the past. Negative feedback, well, it remains and keeps the status quo. Positive feedback occurs when a family is forced to change, so it cannot return to its previous state.

It has been said that **most forms of family therapy rely on circular feedback, whereas traditional forms of individual therapy rely on linear feedback**.

For example, linear feedback or causality would be something like this, "You are afraid of animals because, when you were six years old, you were attacked by a pack of dogs."

Family therapists, however, generally believe in circular causality, not linear, and this deals with feedback loops. Circular causality asserts that you impact other members in a family, but their behavior also comes back in a circle to impact you.

Now, I want to talk briefly about the major schools of family therapy. The first theory I want to mention is **behavioral family therapy, as well as cognitive behavioral family therapy**.

The good news is that since I discussed behaviorism in depth in the helping relationship and therapy section of this book, we need not spend much time on it.

All the theorists I have discussed, such as B.F. Skinner, John B. Watson, Mary Cover Jones, Ivan Pavlov, Albert Ellis, Joseph Wolpe, William Masters, and Virginia Johnson remain the same. The techniques also remain the same.

Behavioral family therapists use interventions quite often that are based on **B.F. Skinner's operant conditioning. This would include things like positive reinforcement, even the use of tokens with family members. A behavioral family therapist might rely on punishment, charting, extinction, or even the Premack principle**.

A counselor might implement Wolpe's systematic desensitization based on Pavlovian theory, Albert Bandura's principle of modeling, or social learning theory. Perhaps the therapist might even use Masters and Johnson's **sensate focus for a family therapy sex problem**.

Behavioral family therapists insist that dysfunctional behavior is learned, and thus in accordance with the behaviorist theory, it can be unlearned.

A cognitive behavioral family therapist would rely on Albert Ellis's REBT or Aaron T. Beck's cognitive reframing.

Cognitive family therapists focus on thinking processes such as irrational thinking, rational thinking, or cognitive distortion. **Behavior therapists often use quid pro quo contingency contracts. This Latin phrase literally means something for something**.

A quid pro quo contract in family therapy is used to get two people to engage in comparable functional behavior.

It sounds complicated, and let me tell you, it is a tongue twister, yet in everyday life the dynamics are quite simple. Here's how you use it.

A teenager agrees to mow the lawn once a week if their father takes this teen to play billiards once a week.

Just as an aside here, and this is also a great exam word to the wise, **the Latin phrase quid pro quo is also used to discuss the issue of sexual discrimination**, which is totally unrelated to what we're talking about here but will likely make its way into the questions of many comprehensive counseling exams, so let me share an example.

If you said to an employee, "You will continue to get promotions and raises as long as you date me," that would be an example of this concept.

Psychologist **Gerald Patterson (1926–2016)** is often considered the trailblazer in terms of applying behavioral theories to families. In the 1960s, he was teaching parents to use reinforcement, modeling, and timeout with their children.

Richard B. Stuart (1933–), armed with a doctorate in social work, was trained in psychoanalytic principles (but rapidly rejected them in favor of cognitive behavioral approaches) and is considered another major pioneer in behavioral family therapy. He became convinced that good families and marriages thrived on this something for something, or once again the quid pro quo concept, if you will. His work in weight loss was also applied to marital and couples therapy.

Now, listen closely, this is very important. Out of all the systems of family therapy that I mention in this section, behavioral and cognitive behavioral family therapy would be the systems that seemingly mimic most closely what goes on in an individual counseling session using these same modalities. This approach focuses on the individual rather than the family system.

Let me be quick to say that since it violates the rule of focusing on the system, these approaches have been criticized by proponents of other schools of family therapy. Behavioristic methods have also been criticized for being too mechanistic and too simplistic, as these modalities have been for individual treatment.

The behavioral paradigm of marriage, family, and couples counseling focuses a lot on actions rather than affective or emotional responses. Last, **these approaches have been castigated for *not* stressing family dynamics**.

Let's move on to what is known as family systems theory. Just for the record, family systems theory gets its name from the Austrian biologist Ludwig von Bertalanffy (1901–1972). Aren't you glad you likely won't have to spell it for your exam?

Bertalanffy, who helped found general systems theory, or GST, postulated that all living elements are connected. Thus, you need to look at an entire system, such as the family, to understand a human or animal's behavior. System theory supports the notion of circular causality that I delineated earlier. We are all influenced by others in the family, and we, in turn, influence everybody else in the family or system.

This is in contrast to the A causes B causes C linear causality model relied upon for explanations in individual psychotherapy. Linear causality is unidirectional and thus not circular.

The major proponent and pioneer of systems theory was Murray Bowen, who was born in 1913, and he died in October of 1990. He was the first family division director of the National Institute of Mental Health (NIMH) in 1954. He also worked at the well-known Menninger Clinic where he studied schizophrenic families.

From 1959 to 1990, he was a professor of psychiatry with a training program at Georgetown Medical University. Initially, for approximately the first year that he spent at NIMH, he used separate therapists for each family member, but then, he discovered that he could use a single therapist for the entire family, and it would produce more desirable results.

Bowen's model focuses more on insight than the behavioristic approach. **Bowen generally had family members speak directly to him rather than to each other because he discovered that this could ward off arguments. His goal is to teach an individual to remain themselves within the family system**.

The notion of being yourself is called differentiation. Bowen noted that most of us have a level of differentiation that roughly matches our parents' level. He called this phenomenon the family projection process. Bowen created his theory

in the 1950s after examining what marriage and family helpers refer to as triangles.

Permit me to explain: when things are going well, people operate in dyads, or twos. However, when anxiety builds, a third party enters the picture as an ally to support one of the people. Although the idea of the triangle is to resolve the problem, it generally makes it worse. **He was convinced that individuals needed to de-triangulate**.

According to Bowen, the perfect marriage is one in which both partners have differentiation, and yet they are still capable of emotional intimacy without loss of autonomy. Differentiation is the goal of the therapist. Bowen's goal is to teach people how to respond, not merely react, to the family system.

To get in touch with your family feelings, Bowen relied upon the **Going Home Again technique** in which an individual in treatment literally returns home to their family of origin to better understand their family.

Now, listen closely. **This is very important. Since Bowen brings in people beyond the nuclear family, your exam could refer to his approach as the extended family systems theory approach**. Like psychoanalytic work with families, this approach is considered by experts an in-depth model of treatment. Bowen believes that birth order or sibling position is important.

He postulated that undesirable behavior patterns can be transmitted from one generation to the next. This is called multigenerational transmission, or transgenerational therapy.

Bowen is also well known for his use of genograms. What is a genogram? Well, I'm glad you asked. It's simply a pictorial or visual diagram. A graphic inspection, if you will, of the family that is depicted on a sheet of paper or perhaps a flip chart. To me, a genogram looks like an electronic schematic since it has these geometric figures and lines.

For example, males are represented using a square. A circle is a female, and so on. The genogram helps the therapist grasp family patterns in history. It's like a multigenerational family therapy tree assessment if you will.

Genograms can be helpful when conducting career counseling as well.

Overall, Bowen's approach seems effective, but it is difficult to research. Up until his death, he insisted that most family therapists missed the point of his work. He felt that most counselors and therapists focused too much on technique, not enough on theory.

Hence, he was not only a pioneer in this area, but he was a major critic of family therapy as well. He felt that a lack of clarity regarding family therapy theory was causing chaos in the field. Noted family therapy experts, Raphael "Ray" J. Becvar, a noted family therapy textbook author and very insightful professor of mine, and Dorothy Stroh Becvar (1941–2021), note that Bowen produced what may be the only true theory in the field.

Another popular theory is an action-oriented approach known as structural family therapy created by Salvador Minuchin (1921–2017). Every family has a structure or an organization. This model is considered an action-oriented approach for the therapist.

Minuchin received his medical training in Argentina and then came to the United States in 1950 after working as an Israeli army doctor. Minuchin had a heavy background in psychoanalysis and even studied at the famous William Alanson White Psychoanalytic Institute.

In 1960, he coauthored a book entitled *Families of the Slums* after working with inner-city kids. He has been referred to as the spokesman for family therapy in the '60s.

Although he was trained as an analyst, he believed that altering the family structure or organization was a highly effective way to help people. In 1965, he became the director of the well-known Philadelphia Child Guidance Clinic. Under his direction, the center became a mecca for family therapy.

Minuchin discovered that there are two basic problems with dysfunctional families. Here they are. Number one, family members are enmeshed, chaotic, very closely interconnected, or number two, the other problem, family members are disengaged, unrelated, and isolated.

According to Minuchin, the family is a multi-bodied organism with **three key subsets**. The **marital spousal subsystem** that governs husband–wife interactions, the **parental subsystem** that governs parental interaction with children, and the **sibling subsystem** that deals with the interaction among siblings.

In Minuchin's structural theory, boundaries are very important. Minuchin basically believed that the job of the

therapist is to loosen or establish boundaries between the members of the family. Healthy families have clear boundaries. Clear boundaries are said to be firm, yet flexible.

Dysfunctional families sport rigid or diffuse boundaries. Rigid boundaries cause people to disengage. "Handle it yourself, son. I've got my own problems," is an example of rigid boundaries. A child in a disengaged family may need support from outside the family system.

Dysfunctional relationships are also spawned via diffused boundaries. Diffused boundaries are basically the opposite of rigid ones. Everyone is in everybody else's business even when it isn't necessary. This is the parent who is totally consumed with parenting their child. The child will have trouble leaving home and becoming their own person.

According to Minuchin, a generation gap between kids and parents is a good thing. The parents should be seen as the top of the hierarchy in the family, not as an equal, not as a friend to the children.

What does a structural family therapist do? First, the therapist relies on several critical steps. **First, in the initial session, the counselor engages in the first step, known as joining.** The therapist attempts to be on the same wavelength as the clients. The helper meets and greets everyone in the family and has a social exchange with every member.

To help with the joining process, the helper will often use what is known as tracking. Tracking really boils down to using a lot of person-centered techniques such as reflecting, attending, and relying on open-ended questions.

When the therapist engages in tracking, they will use metaphors to reveal patterns of family communication. A family that is very interested in electronics or perhaps computers might be told, "You guys are wired together." A mechanic might be told, "Your family really needs an overhaul," or "Your family is like an eight-cylinder engine running on four cylinders."

The therapist might even join the family by imitating certain body postures or nonverbal behaviors of a given family member, thus aligning themselves with that person. **Mimicking is known as mimesis.**

Another therapeutic technique in structural therapy is known as **reframing**. Reframing is used to change the perception that a client has about themselves. I'm sure you have heard the old adage that a glass of water could be described as half empty or half full. The glass of water statement is the quintessential example of reframing. A client could be described as anorexic, or just a child who doesn't like to eat. Reframing implies that you redefine or relabel the problem.

Structural family therapists also use a technique called intensity. Intensity is achieved when you repeat a message again and again or you change the distance between family members. Intensity can also occur if the counselor encourages a family interaction to go beyond the time that the discussion would normally occur.

Sometimes intensity has been referred to as "putting pressure on the family." The extra time can create nurturing or produce a higher level of conflict to help the family get to a new level of functioning.

Minuchin focuses on parent–child relationships rather than on the three-generational model proposed by Bowen. Social worker **Harry Aponte (1935–)**, a marriage and family therapist in Philadelphia, Pennsylvania, is also associated with the structural model.

Moving right along, I'm going to discuss Jay Haley's strategic marriage and family therapy. It is also called the MRI approach since Haley came to the Mental Research Institute in Palo Alto, California, in 1962. This approach is also known as the problem-solving model.

Initially, Haley was not trained in counseling, psychology, psychiatry, or social work. His degree was in arts and communication. In 1967, he became the director of the prominent Philadelphia Child Guidance Clinic. In 1976, he created the Family Therapy Institute with Cloé Madanes in Philadelphia.

Jay Haley (1923–2007) coined the term strategic therapy in 1973. He used the term to describe the way the late, great Milton H. Erickson performed therapy and hypnosis. In addition to Haley and Cloé Madanes, people like Paul Watzlawick (1921–2007), John Weakland (1919–1995), social worker Lynn Hoffman (1924–2017), and psychiatrist Richard Rabkin (1932–) – who often focused on family therapy and physical illness – were major players in the strategic movement.

Haley's paradigm has several interesting caveats. Here they are. Number one, you should always see the entire family if possible. Number two, use a second therapist if you can, or a team of therapists behind a one-way mirror as consultants.

Number three, assume that the first session must be successful to perform successful therapy.

Number four, during that crucial first session, try to engage every family member. Number five, during that first session, redefine the problem as that of the family, not the identified patient. Initially, let the family discuss the problem. Don't you get involved as the counselor. Number six, give a directive at the end of the session.

In other words, give the family an assignment or a prescription that focuses on a single goal. Paradox is used a lot in this model. Hence, a client who has panic attacks is instructed not to try to stop them but rather to hold on to them and even intensify them.

Yes, you heard me correctly. The therapist prescribes the problem to the client as a homework assignment, often without an explanation.

A school of thought that is similar to Haley's is solution-focused therapy or brief strategic therapy. This model has made its way into self-help literature recently. Names associated with this approach include Steve de Shazer, Bill O'Hanlon – both of whom studied under Milton H. Erickson – Michelle Weiner Davis, Paul Watzlawick, Bob Bertolino, and Insoo Kim Berg.

This approach is used with families and individuals, and it is often unbelievably brief. Some therapists have even dubbed it "one-session therapy." Solution-focused therapists do not focus on what caused the problem. In fact, they intentionally avoid problem talk. In this approach, the therapist focuses on what has worked in the past, exceptions to the problem, if you will.

The therapist might ask, "Was there ever a time in your marriage when you did get along with your wife?" **This is known as the exception question**. Then, the therapist might ask, "How were you behaving at that time?" The therapy dialogue has shifted from problem talk to solution talk.

The solution-focused therapist wants the client to outline specific goals. Hence, counselors of this ilk will also use **the famous miracle question. The therapist would ask, "Suppose you went to sleep, and your problem was solved; how would you know it? What would be different?"**

O'Hanlon, who received training from Erickson in exchange for being his gardener, now calls *this modality* *possibility therapy*. This model clearly does not promote catharsis, abreaction, or ventilation.

Your exam might also ask you about the **Milan model**. Originally, the Milan model relied on co-therapists, a male and a female therapist, who were observed by members of a treatment team. Sessions were approximately once a month and limited to ten sessions. The team approach, also used by strategic family therapists, initially used a one-way mirror.

Then, in 1980, social worker **Peggy Papp (1923–2021) brought the team directly into the therapy session room and termed it the Greek chorus. The team might even disagree with the therapist and would interact with the therapist as well as the family**.

Research on the Milan approach revealed that clients often felt therapists were not warm and that the team wasn't very personal. In fact, they were impersonal. Finally, **none of the original pioneers of this model still adheres 100% to its principles. That's not a good sign**.

Before I round them up and move them out in this section, I'd like to mention another topic that counselors have asked me for information on, and that is **consultation**.

Consultation is the act of working with individuals or groups who are working with clients. The person that the consultant is attempting to help is known as the consultee. The consultant and the consultee work together in a joint problem-solving venture. This is known as collaboration or a collaborative effort.

A training workshop is often a form of consultation. For example, you might work with a group of teachers for a day or so to help them deal with difficult students. One-way mirror exercises could even be used.

Another type of consultation is called mental health consultation. This method is based on the work of crisis intervention pioneer Gerald Caplan (1917–2008), a British born psychiatrist who even worked with Anna Freud.

Caplan asserted that consultation can be focused on the client. It can also be focused on the consultee's own dilemma. Consultation can even be focused on the actual program at the agency or practice. Finally, it can be focused on the consultee's administrative duties.

Caplan emphasized that the consultee must not be plagued via lapses of objectivity. For example, the consultee who is in love with a client cannot truly help this client. Thus, a consultee who has unresolved personal issues may not be effective.

If this sounds a bit like Freudian countertransference, you should know that this model is sometimes called the psychodynamic model of consultation.

Your exam will probably also mention the work of Edgar Schein, a former professor of management at MIT (1928–), who created the so-called doctor patient model, in which the consultant is brought in to diagnose the problem, and then, just like a doctor, prescribes something to fix it. Schein feels that in this model, diagnosis is a good thing. Something or someone in the organization is sick.

Schein also delineated a purchase of expertise model, in which the consultee knows what is wrong, and a consultant is hired to come in and fix it or rectify the problem. In addition, Schein is known for his process consultation model in which seven steps are used to enhance decision making and interaction in an organization.

When consultations are focused on information and knowledge, they are called content consultations. When they focus on the actual communication process nevertheless, they are generally called process consultations.

Your exam may also mention behavioral consultation. Just like behavioral procedures for individuals, families, and groups, this approach uses behavior modification or applied behavior analysis strategies and social learning theory. In other words, change the environment. This approach is very popular with teachers, who can be taught by the consultant to apply behavioral strategies.

Now we've finished up consultation and family therapy, so let's forge on to professional orientation and ethical practice.

10

Master Lecture 9: Professional Orientation and Ethical Practice

I'd like to begin a new section. Professional orientation and ethics. Now, amazingly enough, unless you graduated recently, it's possible that this area was not adequately covered in your program. In fact, when I first started teaching and creating exam preparation materials, many textbooks didn't have a chapter on ethics and in some instances did not even list the word in the index. Seriously, you can't make this stuff up!

Nowadays, however, each professional organization wants their members to know their own ethical guidelines. For example, psychologists abide by ethics set by the APA. Social workers adhere to ethics created by NASW, or the National Association for Social Workers.

In this program, I shall focus on ethical guidelines set forth via the ACA and NBCC. **Ethics are guidelines, conduct codes, if you will. Ethics are not laws, although laws are generally supportive of ethics**.

Just to use an outlandish example to make certain you get the point, if you said to a new client, "Gosh, you really seem like a great person, I'd like to take you out to dinner and movie after this session," that's highly unethical. Nevertheless, if the client decides to call the police SWAT team, I don't think they'll be taking you off in handcuffs.

DOI: 10.4324/9781003149712-10

This short scenario illustrates the point that codes of ethics generally have higher, more stringent standards than the law.

Now, listen: here's an exception, some states have adopted ACA's code of ethics, or they post a code of their own ethics for licensed counselors. **In this situation because the code has state guidelines, a violation of the ethical code would, I repeat, would be a violation of a state law. Also keep in mind a popular principal in the helping professions that "laws supersede ethics."**

Let's look at some **ethical standards of practice**. The first important point is that counselors must **respect diversity and should never discriminate against clients due to age, race, sexual orientation, religion, gender, marital status, or socioeconomic status. In addition, helpers should never engage in sexual harassment**.

Counselors should inform clients, preferably in writing, about the counseling process before it begins, and they should continue to inform them throughout the duration of counseling. This is known as informed consent.

A simple question to ask yourself to help uphold informed consent is: Have I given the client the information necessary to consent to the process or procedures (for example, the cost of the sessions; who is responsible if the insurance company refuses payment; when and how long will the counseling sessions be; what standardized tests will and used, if any; why they are being implemented; etc.)? **Services to your clients should not begin until verbal and written consent has been provided to you as the counselor! If you are working with a minor, then consent would need to be obtained from a legal guardian**.

It is vital that during the counseling process you should never impose your values on a client.

In general counselors should steer clear of dual/nonprofessional relationships or so-called multiple relationships. This occurs when you have a relationship with the client or supervisee that has nothing to do with counseling. For example, you could be a relative of the client. You could be dating the client. You could be using the client to build a new bedroom on your house.

Dual relationships impair professional judgment, and they get in the way of objectivity. If a dual relationship cannot be avoided, say, for example, the nearest counselor is 175 miles away and the construction worker who's putting that new room on for you needs counseling, then you should engage in the counseling process, but **you must ensure that no exploitation occurs**.

At one time this would be the end of the story, but that is no longer the case, and I promise I will have a lot more to say regarding this topic later in the book, so stay tuned and don't tune me out!

Ethics also stipulate that you should never have sexual intimacies with a current client or supervisee. **According to NBCC and ACA you must wait a bare minimum of five years after the counseling is terminated before you are sexually intimate or romantically involved with a former client. Listen closely, even after the five years are up, the counselor must be certain that the relationship is not exploiting the client**.

Also keep in mind that a counselor should not accept an individual they have had a former romantic or sexual relationship with as a client; nor should they accept friends or family members of this person.

If you run a group, you should screen members to see if the group will be appropriate. Another issue is safety in group work: you must protect clients physically and emotionally. Again, group leaders are responsible for the safety of the clients.

Just to make certain my students really understand this concept, I share a simple example from the trust walk team-building ice breaker assignment, which is very popular in business as well as counseling groups. In this assignment participants are blindfolded and paired with another group member who leads them around. The idea is that you are supposed to learn to trust the person leading you. If, however, the trusting blindfolded participant is led to walk out of a 14-story window, you, as the group leader, will be responsible.

The principle also applies to research, meaning that counselors must avoid physical or psychological harm to subjects in a research study or a project.

Everybody involved in a research project needs to be able to behave in an ethical manner. If you're running a study, you need to be ethical. **The ultimate responsibility for ethical research lies with the principal researcher**.

Also, remember that in our field, multiple submissions are not ethical. In other words, never submit your article to more than one journal at a time. In plain everyday English, your article must be rejected by one professional journal before you can send your research or your journal article to another journal.

Fees are also an ethical issue. Be sure that you discuss financial arrangements with clients before the treatment begins. The counselor should also help the clients secure services if they are necessary after the termination of counseling.

Counselors need to avoid entering a relationship with a client that they cannot help or assist. If a counselor does accidentally secure a client that they cannot help, the counselor should immediately terminate the client and make an appropriate referral.

Everything discussed in your session should be confidential, or secret, if you will, unless something needs to be disclosed by law such as abuse, sexual abuse, neglect, and exploitation of children, disabled, or the elderly.

In the case of a client who is seriously suicidal or homicidal – in other words there is clear and imminent danger to the client and/or somebody else – then the counselor may need to break confidentiality and take reasonable action to inform potential victims or authorities.

Counselors need to take steps to ensure that administrative personnel, secretaries, or other counselors in the office or the agency respect the client's confidentiality. Ethical guidelines for research stipulate that information about the research subjects should stay confidential.

Moreover, researchers must report any variables that may have affected the research data or outcomes, and the researcher should take precautions not to distort or intentionally fabricate their findings.

Last, researchers must give appropriate credit to everyone who contributed to the research.

If you are running a group, you should clearly state that as the counselor you really prize confidentiality, but you cannot guarantee confidentiality.

Along these same lines, **if you are performing marriage and family therapy, you cannot disclose what one family member said in counseling to another family member without the first family member giving you consent**. So, to use an example, a husband says something about his wife when his wife is not in the session. You cannot tell his wife without the husband's permission.

Also, if you are going to transfer information to somebody else, say, another person or agency, you must get the client's permission unless it is abuse or neglect, as previously mentioned, or someone's welfare is in danger.

When you are doing training, teaching, research, or publishing, you need to disguise your client's true identity.

Counselors must know the boundaries of their competence and must not practice in an area where they lack the necessary qualifications. The same thing goes for testing and assessment devices. For example, if you've had no training giving IQ tests, then you should not be giving Wechsler's to your clients.

It is also unethical to use a test for a purpose other than what the test was created for. Ethics suggests that counselors should never base decisions on outdated tests. You need to explain to clients why you are giving the test and the uses of the results. Again, that's informed consent, and you do that upfront.

Ethics dictate that counselors should attend **continuing education sessions** (often called CEUs, or continuing education units) to maintain their professional competence. Ethics also addresses the issue of the **impaired professional**. An impaired professional is a counselor who has personal problems that could harm clients.

A counselor who comes to the sessions intoxicated or high on drugs would be an impaired professional. A counselor attempting to perform therapy when this helper is suffering from severe brain damage that, say, caused memory loss and disorientation would also be considered an impaired professional.

Here's an important issue. **A counselor should never ever use their job or affiliation with an agency, educational institution, or hospital to recruit clients for private practice**.

Counselors must also be certain they never misrepresent their credentials. A counselor with a PhD in art history should not be showcasing the degree on business cards on their website about their counseling practice. If a practitioner has an honorary degree, this must be stipulated as well.

If a client is seeing other providers, the counselor should get the client's permission to inform the other providers that a counseling relationship exists. If there is a disagreement between a counselor and their employer, the counselor should explain to the employer why the policy is not in the client's best interest.

However, if the counselor cannot rectify the situation, termination from the employer, such as the agency, practice, educational institution, or hospital, should be seriously considered. In other words, you should consider leaving. **Your primary responsibility is to the client**.

Moreover, if you are working for an agency doing counseling or consultation, you should not accept fees or remuneration when the agency is already paying you for the service. **Just to make myself crystal clear, do not accept personal fees for agency clients. Unlike some other professions, counselors cannot accept referral fees**.

A few ethical guideline hints for counselors who teach, train, or supervise others. First, again, **sexual relationships with a supervisee or a student is a no-no. Zero exceptions to this rule. Next, give students and supervisees credit for their scholarly contributions to research. Counselors doing supervision should be trained to do supervision**.

Counselors should tell supervisees what appraisal and evaluation measures will be used and when the assessments will occur. **Feedback should be given to the supervisee throughout the supervision period, not merely at the end of supervision**.

When teachers, professors, and supervisors provide self-growth experiences, they must be careful **not to grade participants on nonacademic issues** that may come up as a result of the growth experience. Students and supervisees who are engaged in counselor education preparation programs are expected to adhere to ethical guidelines and standards of practice, just like any other counselor.

NBCC stipulates counselors should be aware of unethical behavior by colleagues, whether the colleague is certified or not . . . it doesn't matter. Counselors need to take action through agency channels first, and then through NBCC, or the violator's profession (e.g., counseling, psychology, psychiatry etc.), if you know there is some ethical violation going on with that particular helper.

NBCC also stipulates that when setting a client's fee, you must take the client's financial situation into consideration. If a client says they cannot afford your fees, help the client find comparable services elsewhere. Since certified counselors can consult with other professionals about their clients, this fact should be mentioned to the client.

You should keep clients' records for a period of five years after the final contact with the client, even in cases where the client has died. Another point to remember is that **if you are in private practice, you should not allow your name to be used in conjunction with practice, unless you are engaged in the practice of counseling.** If you are in a leadership role, then you need to be upfront about it, but be crystal clear that you're doing leadership or administration, not counseling.

I will now switch gears and talk about ethics pertaining to counseling clients using technology-assisted distance counseling.

Internet counseling is also called Web counseling, virtual counseling, or the slang term cyber counseling. Other labels include online counseling, e-counseling, virtual counseling, and tele-counseling. I urge all readers to read what the various ethical codes say about this practice as well as telephone counseling.

Internet and telephone counseling may be referred to as technology-assisted distance counseling on your exam. Similarities and differences to face-to-face counseling are illuminated within ethical codes.

NBCC has a special certification in this area: the Board Certified TeleMental Health Provider (BC-TMH), which replaced the DCC, or Distance Credentialed Counselor.

Just as an aside, NBCC, once released this statement as the official definition of counseling:

> Counseling is the application of mental health, psychological, or human development principles, through cognitive, affective, behavioral, or systematic intervention strategies that address wellness, personal growth, or career development, as well as pathology.

Counseling can be administered via a single counselor, two counselors who work together, or a single counselor who is assisted by another counselor with specialized expertise. **The counseling process can be synchronous**. This means that the interaction between the client and the counselor occurs instantaneously. **Counseling can also be asynchronous**, such as when a client might email a counselor and the counselor responds later.

This means there's a gap or a delay between the client and the counselor. Distance counseling supplements face-to-face services by necessity or convenience. It may be used when a client is disabled and not physically able to come to the counselor's office. During the COVID-19 pandemic, the need for virtual services of this nature grew at an unprecedented rate. It could also be useful in situations where geographical separation could necessitate the service.

Technology-assisted counseling includes telephone counseling for individuals, couples, and groups. It also includes Internet counseling using email or chat-based counseling, again, with individuals, couples, families, or groups.

Finally, the practice of video-based counseling using programs like Zoom or Microsoft's Teams with the aforementioned groups is under the auspices of technology-assisted distance TeleMental health counseling model once more. **For exam purposes, and this is important, telephone, video, and chat-based interventions are classified as synchronous counseling. Email is considered asynchronous, meaning you don't get immediate feedback**.

Internet counseling ethics change on a regular basis. One thing I want to remind you is that you need to make sure your liability or malpractice insurance covers web counseling.

Check with your licensing board and local organizations before you begin doing this type of counseling. Specifics for age of consent and child abuse reporting may vary according to the client's location. Be sure you investigate these factors.

Encryption technology should be used whenever it is feasible. If you cannot employ encryption methods, you must inform the client of the hazards regarding unsecure communication, including the fact that third parties might have access to the transmissions or records of the session. Also, tell the client how long data will be kept.

Take steps to identify the identity of the web client and counselor. You might want to use code words, numbers, or graphics to ward off imposters. Certainly, you don't want to discover that your nine-year old was using your computer and counseling your clients, do you? If you need the permission of a parent or guardian to counsel the client who's a minor, verify the identity of the consenting adult.

Follow appropriate procedures for the release of information with electronic sources. Web clients deserve the same information about their counselor as face-to-face clients would receive.

Minimal self-disclosure on the part of the web counselor is appropriate. In some instances, the web counselor may indeed limit self-disclosure to ward off potential harm to themselves and their family.

Provide links to appropriate certification organizations and licensure boards to the client. This will facilitate consumer protection. Use the NBCC/CCE website or the licensing board in the state the client is residing in to **secure the name of at least one counselor who would be on call should you need them in the client's geographical area**.

The web counselor should then call, email, or visit the counselor on call in that area. Next, the web client should have local helpline numbers, 911, 988, and any other emergency numbers in case the counselor on call is not available, and that is why you need it.

Web counselors must give clients procedures for contacting the web counselor when offline. Specifically, this means **telling your client precisely how often you check your email for client messages**.

The web counselor should list problems on their website that are not recommended for web counseling, such as sexual abuse as the primary problem, eating disorders, violent relationships, or severe psychiatric disorders where the client is out of touch with reality. Discuss what can be done in the case of a technological failure. A difference in time zones or problems recovering email could cause issues.

Finally, if you are not utilizing a virtual platform such as Zoom, explain to the client how the lack of visual nonverbal cues is going to impact the client. For example, since you can't see nonverbals when you're doing telephone counseling, you might want to say something like, "I can't see your face. I can't hear the tone of your voice. I'm not sure whether you were serious or just joking about that last message."

All right, I know I really picked up on the pace in this section. Let me tell you, you can take it, you're tough. Now, listen, here's what I want you to do from here.

We've covered all the basic sections, but I have a special chapter of this book packed with hundreds of questions and answers. Some will introduce you to material not yet covered. All the questions are tutorial to boost your knowledge. This book also contains a hot off the presses section with tiny test hints that can raise your score in a big way. Most are just a sentence or two. There's also a super review that you can use a few days prior to the exam, or even on the day of the exam.

So, I guess what I am trying to say is even though I have presented on all the major areas of the exam, we aren't done yet. In fact, we are just getting warmed up!

Let's get started on those oh-so-important tutorial questions and answers.

Yours for better counseling,

Dr. Howard Rosenthal.

11

Tutorial Questions With Answers

All right, get up and stretch. Take a break. Come on, do it right now. You know you need one big time. You've been studying long enough. You need some rest and relaxation, or I'll be seeing you for counseling. Go do something you love to do, and then come back. When you're ready, we'll get started.

OK, now you are refreshed. I know you are feeling 100% more confident about taking your comprehensive exam. By golly, you should, since you are learning a lot! Nevertheless, I want to boost your confidence to even higher levels. Thus, I am now going to share literally hundreds of tutorial questions. That's right, questions that teach you the material to expand your knowledge even further.

Some of my questions and answers will help you remember key material from my lectures. Others will explain the material in a new, different, or novel manner, so you won't be thrown off course if your examination presents the concept in an innovative manner. I'll also include some new, advanced, and updated material.

As a counselor, you might wonder, "Are these questions really identical to what I will see on the real exam?" Not entirely.

First, if you are taking oral or written boards, sometimes dubbed comps, for your doctorate, these questions might be very similar to

DOI: 10.4324/9781003149712-11

what you will come face to face with on an exam. However, most students who are reading this text will be wrestling with the NCE, the CPCE, and the CECE. These exams will use an ABCD multiple choice or so-called multipoint answer stem format. Keep in mind that this text was initially an audio program. Now imagine trying to keep up with a multiple-choice format while driving down the highway with the speedometer hovering around the 70-mph mark while passing a semi; it would be nearly impossible. Try it sometime during your rush hour drive home. Hence, I shall merely state the question and then go on to give you the answer. There is no wasted time here flipping to the back of the book or the end of the chapter to find the answer. This is education at its finest with learning at warp speed.

Since listeners as well as our book reviewers loved this format, I have kept it unchanged herein. If you want the real deal . . . you know, questions with A-B-C-D answer stems, like the real thing, my *Encyclopedia of Counseling* includes over 1100 of them, which should be enough for any sane person! Simply put, I have you covered either way.

The other thing that is so awesome about this novel format is it allows you to learn a wealth of information in an exceedingly short period of time. I think you will agree this is ideal when time is of the essence as it is in our fast-paced society.

Another huge difference is that I will use the questions to impart information. I might say something like, "Ellis is the father of REBT. Who is the father of Gestalt therapy?" I can virtually guarantee you that your exam won't be using the questions to teach you that Albert Ellis is the father of REBT. (If they do, buy a lottery ticket. It is your lucky day!)

Also, when it makes sense, my questions are often purposely worded and answered in a manner that could literally help you answer more than one question on the actual exam. Here again, don't count on this occurring when you take your real exam.

Finally, the ultimate question, "Is the material identical to what will be on my test?" Folks, I have no idea precisely what questions you will see on your exam. Any licensing prep program that tells you differently is just trying to get into your purse or wallet or take a hefty chunk out of your PayPal debit card.

In fact, if you do take the exam and you do see a few questions that are identical to my questions, then my advice – yet once again – get off your duff and purchase a lottery ticket because it is truly your lucky day.

What I'm about to say is mega-important, so listen closely. There are very few things I'm willing to guarantee in life, but this is one of them. Every counselor who adequately prepares for oral and written boards, counseling exit exams, or licensing and certification exams studies a ton – I said a ton – of material that will *not* be on the exam. I guarantee it.

It would be rare, very, very rare, for a counselor to walk out of an exam and not think, "Gee, I studied this principle of stat, and there was nothing on it," or "I spent hours and hours on a certain career theorist. There wasn't even one question about this person," or "The exam didn't even mention Piaget's developmental stages," or whatever.

If that happens to you, congratulations. You are normal. But since you don't know which version of the exam you are taking, merely think of the extra blood, sweat, study, and tears as academic insurance that everybody purchases. It is part of the preparation process, and it will make you a more knowledgeable practitioner.

Let me put it across in a different way since I feel compelled to tell you the truth, the whole truth, and nothing but the truth. I suspect that for most of you, this will be the hardest-hitting statement in the entire text. Yet again, just to make certain everybody reading this is clear: **Most of what you study won't be on the exam. Sorry, but that is the truth, the whole truth, and nothing but the truth**.

It was tough to say, but now the secret is out. Again, there is no discrimination here. Even the folks who receive mind-blowing near-perfect scores must deal with this.

OK, take a deep breath and let us dive into this powerful learning experience. Since the days of the fabled audio program, I have added lots of new questions, beefed up and changed existing ones, and deleted outdated unnecessary information. What you are about to experience is the finest and most refined question and answer section of this ilk I have ever released.

Come on, it's not going to be that bad. Heck, you might even enjoy it. Let's do this!

Question 1. Who is the theorist associated with logotherapy?

Answer. Psychiatrist and holocaust survivor Viktor Frankl. Logotherapy – which literally means healing through meaning – is a form of existential psychotherapy. You should know that existential therapy has been criticized for being too heavy on philosophy and not heavy enough on technique. Frankl was heavily influenced by his own experience and the experiences of others in concentration camps.

You can read the riveting account of his experiences in his international bestseller *Man's Search for Meaning*, a book, incidentally, that he initially wasn't even going to put his name on. Another famous psychiatrist who's an existentialist is Rollo May. A third psychiatrist and therapist, Irvin D. Yalom, has been very influential in existentialism as well as in the group movement.

Question 2. Explain why classical Freudian analysis would <u>not</u> be considered a form of ahistoric, or ahistorical, therapy.

Answer. You first would have to know the meaning of the word "ahistoric" or "ahistorical." One of the purposes of this text is to help you learn the nomenclature or terminology, the lingo that is used in the counseling field. The word "ahistoric" is just a fancy term that means the therapy focuses on the here and now and not on the past.

Freudian theory focuses heavily on the past, so it would not be a form of ahistoric therapy. Realize that, in real life, no therapy is purely ahistorical. Some approaches, such as behavior therapy or reality therapy, come very close, because these perspectives do not emphasize the past.

Question 3. The American psychologist Carl R. Rogers originally called his theory nondirective or client-centered therapy. What is the new name for his psychotherapy?

Answer. In 1974, Rogers and his colleagues renamed his theory person-centered therapy. The new name emphasized the power of the self. In the late '40s, he called his approach nondirective counseling. In 1951, he changed it to client-centered counseling or therapy. Now it is known as person-centered counseling. Just in case you are wondering, the R in Carl R. Rogers stands for Ransom.

Test clue. Your exam may refer to Roger's concepts as self-theory.

Question 4. When a counselor speaks of the DOT, what is this helper referring to?

Answer. You need to know the lingo and the terminology. You also need to know the abbreviations and the acronyms that could appear on any comprehensive exam. The DOT is the Dictionary of Occupational Titles. It is the most comprehensive occupational listing and classification system. It gives brief definitions of about 20,000 occupations. All the occupations have a nine-digit code.

The DOT was published by the Employment Training Administration of the US Department of Labor in 1938. In 1998, it was replaced by O*NET, a new government classification system. Hundreds of folks worked to create O*NET, an online system that is intended to replace the DOT, and because it is digital it is updated regularly (such as when an occupation is added) and much more rapidly than a book.

O*NET can be accessed online at www.onetonline.org.

Question 5. What type of test is the Rorschach inkblot test?

Answer. The Rorschach is an example of what we call a projective test. Sometimes a projective test might be called a projective expressive test if it's the type of projective test where you are required to have to write something or draw something, which really is not the case in the Rorschach. It's pretty much a straightforward projective test.

The Rorschach, named after the Swiss psychiatrist Hermann Rorschach, who created it, uses ten inkblot cards. The TAT, or Thematic Apperception Test, is another example of a famous projective test. Incomplete sentence tests and word association tests, where you would say the first thing that comes to mind, are also projective tests.

The theory is that the client projects their own unique personality onto a neutral or innocuous stimulus, such as an inkblot card. Some accounts of his life indicate that Hermann Rorschach's nickname in high school up was Inkblot. As of late, the validity of some projective tests, the backbone of clinical psychology for years, is being challenged.

That said, Dr. John Exner developed the Exner Scoring System to score and interpret the Rorschach, which seems valid and has good inter-rater reliability. (Thus, two different clinicians scoring the same client would come up with similar conclusions about the client.)

Exner's approach might be called the Rorschach Comprehensive System (RCS) on your exam.

Question 6. Describe a bimodal statistical curve.

Answer. OK, I saw it, too – a statistics question. Pick yourself up off the floor. You can handle it. First, you must know what the word mode means. The mode is the most frequently occurring score or category. Bi simply means two (e.g., a bicycle has two wheels in most instances), so a bimodal distribution has two frequently occurring scores. The mode is the maximum point of concentration. If you graph a bimodal curve, it looks like a camel's back. You'll see two high points. A distribution with more than one mode is referred to as multi-modal. Hmm makes sense, doesn't it?

Question 7. Name the three most common measures of central tendency.

Answer. The mean, the median, and the mode. I just told you that the mode was the most common score. The mode is also the least important measure of central tendency.

The mean: if you stretch your mind and think all the way back to your third- or fourth-grade classes, you were taught how to compute the arithmetic average, where you take the sum of the scores, and you divide by the number of scores. If your home electric bill was $144 for the entire year, and you divided it by 12 months, your average monthly electric bill would be just $12 a month. $12 is the mean. I know, the example is way too low, but we can still dream!

The mean is the most useful type of average, but it is also misleading because it's affected by extreme scores, often referred to as outliers. The median is the middle value of the data when it is ranked from highest to lowest, OK?

You can remember this quite easily because the median is the center of the highway when you're driving, and a median is the center of the distribution that cuts it into two equal parts.

Now, the median is better for variables like income, family size, and biological data because it's not affected by extreme scores. Although the median is not as useful as the mean, statisticians often prefer to use it when analyzing skewed distributions.

Question 8. What was the name of Freud's theory of therapy?

Answer. Sigmund Freud was born in 1856, and he died in 1939. His claim to fame was psychoanalysis, which is a theory of therapy, but it's also a comprehensive theory of personality.

Freud believed in catharsis, free association, and dream analysis. Most scholars believe that his 1900 work entitled *The Interpretation of Dreams*, which is loosely referred to as the "bible of psychoanalysis," was his most profound work.

In the book, Freud talks about the manifest and latent content of a dream. The manifest is what you dream about, while the latent is the hidden meaning. Freud also talked a lot about instincts, which are unlearned inborn drives. For instance, Eros is the life preservation instincts, such as sex, and Thanatos is the death or self-destructive instinct.

Question 9. Who created individual psychology?

Answer. Alfred Adler, who in 1911 founded the Society for Individual Psychology. Adler rejected Freud's theory of neurosis and talked a lot about inferiority complex and organ inferiority.

Adler was convinced that we often compensate for perceived inferiority complexes. Inferiority complexes can be conscious or unconscious and are related to physical as well as psychological and social issues.

Question 10. What is the TAT?

Answer. TAT stands for Thematic Apperception Test.

This projective test was co-created by the noted Harvard psychologist Henry Alexander Murray and Christiana D. Moran, an artist and lay psychoanalyst, in 1935. The measure is used to reveal an individual's perception of interpersonal relationships. There are 31 cards in the test, but usually the person administering the test would pick a subset of 8 to 12 cards. Murray recommended using 20 cards – 1 blank card and 19 cards with pictures on them.

The person taking the test would be asked to tell a story about the ambiguous picture. Since the test is untimed, if more than ten cards are used, you would use more than one testing session on two different days. Remember that I mentioned previously that the most widely used projective test is the Rorschach inkblot test.

Reminder: In assessing responses gender, ethnicity, and culture can have a major impact. In some instances, a state licensing bureau may prohibit counselors from administering and interpreting projective tests.

Question 11. Which APA created the DSM? By the way, what does DSM stand for?

Answer. There are two APAs, the American Psychological Association, often called the big APA because of its high membership, and the American Psychiatric Association. The DSM was created by the psychiatry organization, the American Psychiatric Association.

DSM stands for Diagnostic and Statistical Manual of Mental Disorders, created and published by the American Psychiatric Association. It is a book of nosology that is used to classify different mental disorders.

If you run a private practice or agency and you want to get paid for your services, and yes, this includes things like Medicaid and Medicare, you must have a DSM diagnosis and then send in what we call an ICD, International Classification of Disease diagnosis code.

Now, if someone is paying for treatment out of their pocket, that's different. They do not necessarily need a diagnosis, but you can take it to the bank that if an insurance company or a managed care firm or an HMO is paying for it, you're going to need an ICD diagnosis code.

Question 12. In the behavioral sciences, the researcher often uses a control group. Explain this concept.

Answer. A control group does not get the experimental manipulation. In the social sciences and in counseling, we call experimental manipulation the IV, or the independent variable. Next, we have the DV, which is the thing we are measuring. An easy way to recall that the DV is the entity that we are measuring is to remember the D stands for data. Hence, DV is the outcome data.

Now, remember, the control group does not receive the experimental variable; the experimental group does. That's how you can distinguish the two. Often when conducting counseling research, people included in a control group are simply told they are being put on a waiting list.

Question 13. A group of counseling experts are given a very easy introductory test regarding counseling information. In what way would the results be positively or negatively skewed?

Answer. A skewed distribution is a distribution that, when you graph it, does not look like a mirror image. It's not symmetrical like a normal bell-shaped curve. It leans to one side.

If you get a question like this on your exam, the best thing to do is graph it, and if that is not possible, try to visualize it in your mind. Here's this group of experts, and they're taking this easy test, so their scores are going to be very high. That means that most of the scores will be on the right side of the distribution, and so if we graph the curve, it will appear to be leaning to the right.

But listen closely, the direction of the tail of the distribution tells you which way it's skewed, and the tail is going to be facing left. Thus, we would say that we have a negative skew when the test is too easy for test takers.

When the test is too hard, and the scores are low, the tail will point to the right, and this is indicative of a positive skew. My wonderful Purple Book, the *Encyclopedia of Counseling*, includes pictures of several skewed distributions.

Question 14. Explain type I and type II errors in statistics. Your exam may also call type I errors alpha errors, and type II errors beta errors.

Answer. All right, let me keep this as simple as possible. The theory is that when you do an experiment, you have at least two hypotheses.

There is a null hypothesis, which means that there's not a significant difference between the group that receives the experimental treatment and the group that does not. Then there is an alternative or experimental hypothesis that states that there will be a significant difference between the groups.

An alpha error occurs when you reject null when it is true. A beta error occurs when you accept the null hypothesis when it's false. A good way to remember this is to use what I call the RA formula. I got this idea when a residence advisor came to me and asked for a memory device. I said, "Why not remember your own title, RA?"

Reject when true. That's the first type of error, an alpha error, or type I error. Accept null when false. That's your second type of error, beta, or type II error. Maybe this memory device won't work for you, but I want you to start experimenting with these memory devices.

Incidentally, there's some research to show that even if you forget the memory device, you'll usually remember the principle if you've learned it through a memory device. Nice!

Finally, an awesome test hint. A stringent or low level of significance lowers the probability of a type I error but raises the chances of a type II error. A level of significance that is not very stringent raises type I errors but lowers type II. As one goes up, the other goes down. Just imagine two children playing on a seesaw in the playground. Yep. Now you've got it!

Question 15. According to most family therapists, who is the identified patient in a family? Is it the mother or is it the father?

Answer. Hey, trick question folks. According to most family therapists, it's the whole family. It is the family system that's the problem, not merely one person. That said, for billing purposes (translation: for you to get paid!) a family member will need to be chosen to receive a diagnosis code for the insurance company or managed care firm.

Question 16. How does a counselor know whether to classify a difficulty as a phobia or an anxiety reaction?

Answer. In a phobia, you know the situation that's causing the discord in the client.

For example, the client with a phobia will say, "I'm scared of elevators," or "I'm afraid of heights." You know the source of the situation. In anxiety, the client is vague and is unable to tell you the source of distress or discord. Still, in everyday life and even counseling we use the term loosely, such as when you say, "my client has test anxiety."

Question 17. An assertiveness trainer is most likely what type of therapist?

Answer. Well, think about it. The assertiveness trainer would most likely be a behavior or cognitive behavioral therapist. Behavior therapists, unlike psychoanalysts, do not believe in a notion of symptom substitution.

Symptom substitution postulates that if you treat the symptom, for example, nonassertive behavior, it won't really help because the problem is deeply seated in the unconscious mind. Thus, if you just treat the symptom, another behavior will pop up. The behaviorists, of course, don't believe this. Thus, behaviorists do believe in symptom removal.

Question 18. What is the Jacobson method?

Answer. The Jacobson method is a procedure for inducing relaxation. You simply have the client alternately tense and relax groups of muscles until the entire body is relaxed. Most counselors begin the relaxation session with the with the top or upper portion of the body and move toward the lower portion.

The technique is named after Edmond Jacobson, an American physician, who we know was using his strategy as early as 1908 and shared it with others in his classic work *Progressive Relaxation*, released in 1929. It's very popular with therapists who use systematic desensitization. It has been criticized because some therapists believe that if you make the client tense their muscles, this can get in the way of just relaxing the muscles. That said, for the most part, for most people, it works very well.

Question 19. Define test reliability.

Answer. A test that gives consistent, dependable results is reliable. Test reliability can be measured by a test-retest procedure, which means you give the test a second time. A split half method would be another way. Yet another way to check test reliability would be an equivalent forms method.

A correlation of 0.90 is considered quite good in terms of test reliability. Keep in mind that a test can be reliable but not valid. For example, say I had a ruler that was warped. Because it was warped, it would keep giving you inappropriate readings. It would keep giving you the same reading even if it's wrong. A scale that is two pounds off is very reliable. It's going to keep saying you are two pounds heavier than you are, but it's not valid.

Question 20. What is the definition of a parsimonious theory?

Answer. A parsimonious theory has a lot of facts and few assumptions. This is sometimes called Lloyd Morgan's canon (a.k.a. Morgan's canon) or Occam's razor. Some exams prefer the spelling Ockham.

Question 21. What are the four major stages in Piaget's model of cognitive development?

Answer. The sensorimotor stage, the preoperational stage, the concrete operational stage, and the formal operational stage. Now, it makes sense that the sensorimotor would be the first stage, since things like sucking, touching, and sensory modalities would come first.

It would also make sense that the formal operations would be last. When I think of formal, I think of somebody who is more experienced. That's the type of memory device you might want to employ. Of course, preoperational would make sense because the preoperational stage would come before concrete operational.

Question 22. What is the most important property of a test?

Answer. Validity is the most important property of a test. Here is the definition of validity, "Does the test really measure want you want it to measure?"

Now, there are different types of validity. First, experts speak of face validity, which really isn't that important. Face validity simply asks the question, "Does the test appear to test what it is supposed to test?" That doesn't mean too much. Maybe it doesn't look like it's testing a given factor but is measuring it or testing it very well.

Then, there's content validity. That is to say, "Does the test really test the content we want it to test?" Then, there's criterion validity, which answers the question of, "How does the test really compare against an outside source?"

There are two types of criterion validity. There's concurrent validity, which asks the question, "Does the test measure up to (or compare favorably) with something outside the test?" If, for example, a test purports to test how well academically somebody is doing in high school, and we have a client who is attending high school, does the test measure how well the person is doing when we examine the individual's GPA or other measures?

Here is a an easy-to-understand example for you golfers out there. If you have a golf simulator, or tracking device, and it says you hit your driver 210 yards, then when you hit the course with the same club, brand of ball, temperature, and humidity, your shots should go approximately 210 yards. If you hit the links and the ball flies just 160 yards or 335 yards (don't you wish!), then the golf tracking device does not have high concurrent validity.

The other type of criterion validity is predictive validity. Predictive validity attempts to answer the question, "Does the test predict what's going to happen in the future?" For example, the graduate record exam would try to predict how well the person is going to do in graduate school.

Then, we have construct validity. Construct validity is intended to answer the question, "How well does the test measure an attribute that is theoretical, such as IQ, or ego strength?

Question 23. How did John Krumholtz apply Albert Bandura's social learning theory to explain successful career choices?

Answer. Krumboltz, Mitchell, and Jones were behaviorists who stated that people tended to choose an occupation that included tasks that were like those that the person was successful performing in the past.

The theory predicts that individuals would avoid tasks that they are not good at. The person is seen as being reinforced for the correct job. It's very behavioristic.

This approach would say that actual visits to worksites are much more important in terms of choosing a career than, say, a paper and pencil or online test because the person could go out, look at the different jobs, experience feelings about these jobs, and then rank order the jobs.

The Krumboltz theory is basically that genetics will interact with learning, which could be classical, instrumental, or vicarious learning, and this would influence career choice. Incidentally, vicarious means that you see somebody else getting reinforced for something and so you believe that you would respond by getting a reinforcer if you behaved in that manner.

Yet another great test hint. On your exam, vicarious learning or social learning theory could be called observational learning.

Question 24. What should you do if you are sexually attracted to a client?

Answer. If it's not getting in the way of anything, you probably shouldn't do anything about it. If the feeling doesn't go away, then you should probably see a therapist yourself to see what's going on with you.

A lot of times, an exam won't give you that choice. They'll just say it's getting in the way, you are seeing a counselor, what do you do now? You should explain to the client that you're having a problem, and then refer the person out.

Get up, stretch, and then let us forge on.

Question 25. You see two research studies. One is an AB design, the other an ABAB design. Which study would be the best at keeping out extraneous confounding variables?

Answer. First, you must know what a confounding variable is. A confounding variable is a variable that might affect the experiment, but it's unwanted. We are not studying it. In a true experiment, we are only studying the impact of the IV, or the independent variable. To answer this question, you'll also have to know what an AB and an ABAB design are. Both the AB and the ABAB are research designs that examine a single person. This is also known as a case study.

Sometimes they are called $N = 1$ studies, meaning that the number of people in the study is just one person. Sometimes, an exam might call it $N = 1$ intensive design. The A stands for baseline. A baseline merely measures the occurrence of the behavior with no treatment. B simply implies that the treatment is being implemented.

Let us assume we are trying to research a client who is trying to quit smoking, and at A we tabulate just how much that person is smoking. Then let's say at B we are applying some sort of reinforcement, some sort of treatment to cut down on the smoking, something that's going to lower the level. We would examine the smoking level at B to see if the smoking lessens or improves.

Now here comes the problem. If you assume that B, the treatment, caused the smoking to go down, a lot of times you'd be wrong. Wrong because maybe the person got a raise at work that day. There's a possible confounding extraneous variable (the raise!!!), and thus, this individual is feeling wonderful and decides to cut back on smoking because of a change in mood. Maybe the person won the lottery that day. Maybe the person was too sick to smoke.

The ABAB design is what we sometimes call the withdrawal or reversal design. This approach allows the researcher or the counselor to look at the baseline twice to see if the treatment is the variable that truly caused the behavior change. It is assumed in the withdrawal design that when the treatment is not being applied at A, the behavior will move toward the baseline.

Here's the answer to the question. Because in the ABAB you're really doing the same research twice, you are better equipped to rule out a confounding variable. AB and ABAB designs are popular with proponents of behavior modification. The term behavior modification/behavior mod/behavior modifier has largely been replaced by the term ABA, which in this instance means applied behavior analysis. I purposely saved this information for last since we have enough As and Bs in this answer to capsize a cruise ship! I'd read it over at least a couple of times if I were you.

Question 26. Fritz Perls developed what brand or modality of psychotherapy?

Answer. Gestalt therapy. Gestalt is a German word that does not have an exact English equivalent. Basically, it means form, whole, figure, or configuration. It implies that the whole is greater than the sum of its parts.

Perls's Gestalt therapy is concerned primarily with the here and now. This modality of helping emphasizes nonverbal behaviors and dreams. Perls helped create the empty chair technique. Gestalt wants you to be a whole person, since Gestalt promotes the notion that there is a mind–body split causing some psychological problem.

Gestalt often focuses more on doing than talking by using experiential exercises. Gestalt has been criticized as being weak, in terms of having a weak theoretical base. It is often combined with transactional analysis to make up for this.

Critics charge that it is very confrontational, and it may be ill suited for ethnic groups and clients of any group who have difficulty showing emotion or being confronted.

Question 27. What is meant by the phrase "Little Albert versus Little Hans"?

Answer. There was a famous case study conducted in 1920 by John B. Watson and Rosalie Rayner with a young 9-month-old child they gave the name Little Albert.

Little Albert was not born with a fear of furry white animals, but every time the child would get near a white rat, Watson and Rayner would strike a bar that would make a very loud noise. This caused the child to fear the white rat. The fear began to generalize. We call this stimulus generalization. After a while, the child was even scared of Watson wearing a white Santa Claus mask.

The Little Albert experiment is supposedly indicative of the behavioristic notion that fears are learned. There's no need for a Freudian unconscious explanation of the fear.

Little Hans, on the other hand, was a five-year-old patient treated by Freud. Freud treated him by sending letters through the mail to his father. The young boy had a fear of going out into the street and being bitten by a horse. Freud resorted to the usual psychological concepts he believed in, like the unconscious mind and the Oedipus complex.

The case of Little Hans is said to be indicative of the Freudian approach, meaning that analytic depth psychology is necessary to cure the problem.

Question 28. The concept of tabula rasa was later reflected in what type of counseling?

Answer. Tabula rasa simply means blank, erased, clean, or scraped slate or tablet. The concept implies that a human is born with nothing in their mind and that the environment really serves to mold the person.

A philosopher named John Locke from the 1600s emphasized this point in a philosophy he called associationism. Experts feel that behaviorism, which also emphasizes tabula rasa, grew out of this philosophical approach.

Question 29. Who was Anne Roe?

Answer. Anne Roe was the first career researcher to define a taxonomy of occupational groups, with terms like skilled and unskilled. Her theory drew heavily on Maslow's hierarchy of needs because she felt the occupation satisfied a need.

The word taxonomy that I just used in the answer is just a big fancy word for categorization or the science of classification. Roe classified jobs in terms of fields (such as science, outdoor, or arts and entertainment) and levels (such as unskilled, skilled, and professional managerial).

Question 30. A client tells you in a confidential session that they physically abused their child. You feel you should tell no one because you feel you will be breaching confidentiality. Is this the right thing to do?

Answer. You may think it's the right thing to do, but by golly, you'd be wrong. It is unethical. Counselors are mandated child abuse reporters, and they must report this infraction of the law to the Child Abuse and Neglect Hotline. It is not only unethical but also illegal not to report it.

Question 31. Describe a statistical *z* score.

Answer. The *z* score is a standard score that expresses the number of standard deviations that a raw score is from the mean. A *z* score is simply the same thing as a standard deviation.

For example, if you have *z* equals 1.5, then that means that the client's raw score is 1.5 standard deviations above the mean. If I said *z* is –3.0, that simply signifies three standard deviations below the mean. The *z* score indicates where a score falls on a normal distribution. One memory device that you can use when you say *z* score is that it sounds like zee (the) score. Z score is like the standard deviation, the big score in statistics and research. Again, will this memory device work for you? I don't know. If it doesn't, have at it. Create your own. You can do it.

Question 32. The technique of pointing out inconsistencies in a client's behavior is known as ______________________.

Answer. Fill in the blank with confrontation. You are confronting the person on an inconsistency or a discrepancy. You are seeing something in their nonverbal behavior or actual behavior that's not agreeing with what they are saying.

Another popular technique that counselors use is paraphrasing. Paraphrasing occurs when you restate the client's message in your own words to let the client know that you, as the helper, really, truly understood what has been said.

Paraphrasing that focuses on emotion or affect lets you accomplish what we call reflecting or reflection. It lets the client become aware of feelings. The word affect could pop up on your exam and is merely an old word for emotion.

Question 33. Who is Eric Berne?

Answer. Berne is the father of TA, transactional analysis. For many years, Eric Berne tried to get into the American Psychoanalytic Association, and they kept telling him no. Finally, when he became famous and created his own theory, again, called TA or transactional analysis, they wanted to let him in. He said, "You can keep your organization."

Berne was the author of some popular books such as *Games People Play* and *What Do You Say After You Say Hello?* TA was made even more popular by a psychiatrist named Tom Harris, who wrote a book called *I'm OK – You're OK*.

Just for the record, studies show that most therapists don't really consider themselves a TA therapist, a logotherapist, a Gestalt therapist, or a practitioner of any single school of psychotherapy. They are very eclectic, meaning that they take the best from all different types of schools, even though they don't necessarily subscribe to all the theoretical positions that these schools have.

Such therapists don't believe that one single theory of therapy can fit the needs of every client.

Test hint. Recently, the term theoretical integration or psychotherapy integration is becoming popular and is replacing the practice of eclecticism. Simply put, the counselor synthesizes the strong points of two or more theoretical approaches, with the thought that the outcome will be superior to the outcome of using a single counseling theory.

Why are we going toward a model of psychotherapy integration? Expert Gerald Corey tells us that no school of therapy is comprehensive enough to take into account all forms of human behavior.

Question 34. You are a consultant to a therapist who is treating a 29-year-old client. You are helping the therapist decide on a suitable plan of intervention. Is this a program-centered consultation, a consultee-centered consultation, or a client-centered consultation?

Answer. First, you must know these three types of consultation.

Consultation, according to Kaplan, who's written extensively on mental health consultation, notes that all consultation involves three players. The relationship is said to be triadic. There is the consultant, the consultee, and the client.

Program centered is incorrect because this form of consultation deals with organizational issues. Consultee centered is also incorrect because it centers around the consultee. That is to say, the consultant helps the consultee develop concrete skills. For example, in this case, the consultant might help the therapist, who is the consultee, learn how to do hypnosis or systematic desensitization.

The correct answer is client-centered consultation. First, I need to say that client-centered consultation has *nothing* to do with Carl Rogers. In client-centered consultation, the focus is on assessing or helping the client. This is important. The consultant does not necessarily have direct contact with the client. The change in the client is usually accomplished via the information that the consultee learns from the consultant.

Some exams may also talk about administrative consultations. These are often called consultee-centered administrative consultations. With this approach, the goal is to improve the administrator's management or problem-solving abilities.

Question 35. Let's pump up the volume here, folks, and get enthused. Who utilized psychoanalytic theory to explain career choice?

Answer. A.A. Brill. Brill would be a fine answer, since he helped to translate many of Freud's works into English, and he especially emphasized the ego defense mechanism sublimation.

Sublimation is a Freudian theory that asserts that you have an unconscious urge to express an unsocial drive. Perhaps you would become a boxer if you're very angry or become involved in martial arts competitions or something similar if you are very sadistic. Obviously, surgeons who often cut on people for a living are not fond of this interpretation! Freud thought sublimation was a positive factor and a sign of maturity to help cultures function.

Another career researcher who did a lot with the Freudian approach was Edward Bordin.

Question 36. What is a positive reinforcer?

Answer. A positive reinforcer is a stimulus that follows an operant or behavior and raises the probability that that behavior will occur again, or it increases the frequency of the behavior.

Question 37. True or false? Negative reinforcement is the same thing as punishment.

Answer. This statement is false. In the popular vernacular, we use the two terms in the same manner. But on a comprehensive exam, don't ever make that mistake. This is a very common question.

A negative reinforcement or reinforcer is a stimulus or stimuli such that when it's taken away, increases the probability that a behavior will occur. Repeat after me; I'm serious about this. Right now. Repeat after me: All reinforcers, positive or negative, increase behavior. Say it. All reinforcers, positive or negative, increase behavior.

In positive reinforcement, we add something after the behavior. For example, if the child behaves in a proper manner, you might give the child a candy bar. With negative reinforcement, which is usually a little harder to use, you take something away, and that would increase the behavior.

Let's say that you had an obnoxious noise in the background at work. You took that noise away and the behavior of the workers increased. We could then assert that the noise was acting as a negative reinforcer. Again, all reinforcers increase the chance that a behavior will occur. Punishment decreases the response.

On some of the newer exams, they will hit you with the terms "positive and negative punishment." Isn't life wonderful?

With positive punishment, you add something after the behavior and the behavior lessens. For example, if you yell at your kid and the behavior goes down, it's acting as positive punishment. It has nothing to do with telling the kid how wonderful he is after you punish him. That's the stuff of TV and radio therapists, OK?

With negative punishment, you are taking something away. Maybe you take away a child's bicycle or their video games and the behavior decreases; then that is negative punishment. Reinforcers and punishment, in essence, are defined by what occurs in terms of whether the behavior goes up or down.

Question 38. Who is the father of analytic psychology?

Answer. Carl Jung, who popularized the concept of the collective unconscious. The collective unconscious mind is said to be an unconscious mind that's common to all humans. Information is collected and passed on from generation to generation, and the symbols in the unconscious mind that are passed on are what we call archetypes, which is the root word of archaeology.

Archetypes are symbols that convey universal meaning to everybody, any place on the planet.

Another concept that is popular in Jungian theory is the concept of androgyny. Jung postulated that we are all androgynous. This means that we all, males and females, have a feminine side and a masculine side. Women often deny what is known as the animus or the masculine side of the personality, while the man denies the anima, or the woman within.

Let me give you a good memory device for those terms. If you remember that anima ends with MA like ma, just like mother, then you can remember it's feminine. Animus ends in MUS like muscle, and that can stand for the masculine or the male side of the personality.

Jung also emphasized the persona, which is a facade that the individual shows the world. It resembles a psychological mask that hides our real feelings and our true personality.

Question 39. What theory of counseling and psychotherapy emphasizes the ABC theory of personality?

Answer. Albert Ellis's rational emotive therapy, RET, now called REBT, rational emotive behavior therapy. A stands for the activating event. B stands for the belief system, which is usually irrational if a client is experiencing unhappiness, and C is the emotional consequence.

Most people, including many helpers, insist A causes C. Not Ellis. He says C is caused by B, the person's belief system.

Question 40. In counseling, what does the term bibliotherapy refer to?

Answer. Bibliotherapy refers to readings, such as articles or self-help books. For example, in REBT, the book *A Guide to Rational Living* written by Robert Harper and Albert Ellis has been instrumental in helping literally thousands of people.

The idea here is that you would have the client read something pertinent to the therapy process outside of the therapy session. According to most experts Ellis was the first therapist to champion bibliotherapy.

Question 41. A symmetrical bell-shaped curve indicates what type of distribution?

Answer. It represents a normal distribution. A normal curve looks symmetrical because the left half is a mirror image of the right half. There are a lot of traits in life such as height, weight, and IQ that are normally distributed.

Now, here's how a normal distribution is defined: 68.2% of the population is within +/–1 standard deviation, 95.4% of the population is within two standard deviations, and 99.7% of the population is within +/–3 standard deviations from the mean. On an exam this might be called the 68–95–99.7 rule or even the 3-sigma rule.

Sometimes the normal curve is referred to as the Gauss curve. The name comes from the creator of the normal distribution, K.F. Gauss, who lived from 1777 to 1855. He was a Russian astronomer and mathematician.

Question 42. Name the four major features of Donald Super's career theory.

Answer. All right, here they are. One, the life stages. Two, the career patterns he delineates. Three, the vocational self-concept, and four, career or vocational maturity that he talks about. On some exams, career maturity will be called vocational maturity.

Question 43. A clinical diagnostic question on your exam uses the abbreviation MDD. This will most likely stand for ______________ ______________________?

Answer. Let us fill in those blanks with major depressive disorder. This is a mood disorder that interferes with everyday life activities and goes on for at least two weeks. It impacts women nearly twice as often as men. When the individual has comorbidity such as substance use disorder or panic disorder it raises the possibility of suicide. Like suicide, it occurs more in rural than urban settings. Ten to 15% of individuals with this diagnosis will take their own lives.

Question 44. What does the acronym WAIS stand for?

Answer. WAIS stands for what is generally cited as the most popular standardized IQ test in the world, the Wechsler Adult Intelligence Scale. The test has a mean of 100 and a standard deviation of 15. It can be administered to persons from 16 to 90 years 11 months.

There is also the Wechsler Intelligence Scale for Children, or the WISC. It is usually suitable for children from ages six to 16 years 11 months.

The WPPSI is the Wechsler Preschool and Primary Scale of intelligence for ages 2 years 6 months to 7 years 7 months.

In the very first course I ever took in college, I read an article called, "The IQ Is an Intelligence Test." Can you guess who wrote it? It was none other than David Wechsler, creator of the Wechsler IQ tests.

Exam booster: The age ranges quoted here are current as of this writing, but they often change over the years. Checking these prior to your exam could prove helpful.

Question 45. During the COVID-19 pandemic, did the number of women in the workforce increase or decrease?

Answer. According to most statistics, although the number of men and women in the workforce decreased during the COVID crisis, the number of women decreased the most. Thus, most experts agree that although the pandemic affected nearly everybody, the impact was greater on women than men.

Question 46. Which theorist is associated with psychodrama?

Answer. Jacob Moreno, who coined the term group therapy and also popularized the concept of role playing. You will recall that

Jacob Moreno created psychodrama. Some exams will mention that his wife, Zerka T. Moreno, was a co-founder of this approach.

Question 47. You are a private practice counselor.

A 13-year-old seriously threatens to take their own life using their dad's old army rifle in the basement. True or false? It is against the law and unethical for you to tell his parents.

Answer. False. You should tell his parents. You have a duty to warn the parents *and* a duty to protect the child.

In fact, according to ethical guidelines, anytime you have a client who is endangering their own life, those of others, or both, you should breach confidentiality. Some quick facts about suicide. In general, suicide is a male phenomenon since statistically, males take their own lives about three times as often as females.

Women attempt suicide about four times as often as males. Is suicide a problem in this country? You bet it is. It is generally approximately the 12th leading cause of death and the 2nd or 3rd leading cause of death in teens each year.

Question 48. Should solution-focused counseling and narrative therapy be classified as psychodynamic, behavioristic, cognitive, postmodern, or humanistic approaches?

Answer. According to scholar and noted counseling textbook author Gerald Corey, these approaches fall into the postmodern approach category.

Question 49. The Myers-Briggs Type Indicator, or MBTI test, is based on whose theory?

Answer. It's based on the work of C.G. Jung, the founder of analytic psychology who emphasized introversion and extroversion. In fact, Jung goes as far as feeling that his own break from Sigmund Freud may have occurred because he was an introvert and Freud was an extrovert.

Question 50. In terms of interventions, school counselors provide direct services and indirect services. Is consultation with a teacher a direct service or an indirect service?

Answer. Consultation is deemed an indirect service; so is coordination. Examples of coordination would include creating a job fair or administering a student orientation.

Individual counseling, on the other hand, group counseling, and any type of psychological education, which is also known as classroom guidance, are considered direct services. An interesting tidbit: some research indicates that quality school counselors spend most of their time doing direct practice and consultation.

However, in average and below-average schools, counselors spend most of their time doing clerical work. ACA recommends that school counselors spend 75% of their time doing direct practice. Several states already have direct practice time allotments for counselors.

Question 51. True or false. Classical conditioning, as developed by Ivan Pavlov, is also known as respondent conditioning.

Answer. This is true. B.F. Skinner, on the other hand, created what we call operant conditioning or instrumental conditioning. Incidentally, the B in B.F. Skinner stands for Burrhus.

Here's a great little memory device. When you think of Pavlov's experiments, you probably think of his dog studies based on reflexes such as salivating. Reflex starts with an R and so does respondent. Experiment with these memory devices and maybe you can come up with some that are even more creative.

Question 52. Explain the concept of a Likert scale.

Answer. The Likert scale, named after Rensis Likert, the social and organizational psychologist who created it, is an attitude scale that asks the individual how much they agree or disagree with something. Likert scales are extremely popular when constructing questionnaires. The Strong Interest Inventory uses a Likert format. A small glitch is that some folks mark the choice that they believe is socially acceptable. With a concept like this, you could use a memory device like, how much do you like or Likert something? Sure, it's corny, but it might just work.

Question 53. What technique did Franz Anton Mesmer help develop?

Answer. Hypnosis. Interestingly, Freud gave up on hypnosis. Freud once said that psychoanalysis is the administrator of the estate left by hypnotism. By all reports, however, Freud was a poor hypnotist, and he believed that his female patients were falling in love with him as he was hypnotizing them.

Question 54. How does psychodynamic therapy differ from classical psychoanalysis?

Answer. Classical psychoanalysis uses the couch, just like you see in the movies.

The patient – also called the analysand – lies on the couch and is analyzed about three to seven times per week for about three to five years. It is very expensive. Some estimates are that New York City, it'll cost you over $100K for a complete analysis. Psychodynamic therapy is usually only once or twice a week, unlike classical analysis. Also, it does not use the couch.

Psychodynamic therapy is face to face, and it's a little bit shorter term. It is, nevertheless, based on analytic principles such as the unconscious mind. Freud once made the statement that he could not stand to be stared at for hours and hours a day. Maybe that's why he used the couch. Hey, just saying! He felt it facilitated free association.

Question 55. Who developed projective measure known as the TAT, or Thematic Apperception Test?

Answer. Henry Murray, who created a theory called personology. Murray talked of needs like achievement, play, understanding, and dominance, activated by the press or pressure from the environment, for example, such as other people's cultures. He called this the needs press theory.

Robert Hoppock, a career researcher, drew heavily on Murray's theory to create a theory of career choice.

Question 56. You see a lowercase *r* in a statistical study in one of your journals. What does it mean?

Answer. *r* signifies a Pearson product-moment correlation coefficient, which is a parametric correlation coefficient.

Let me save you a few points on the test here. Correlation coefficients run from –1 through 0 up to +1. A correlation simply shows a relationship, the strength or magnitude of a relationship, or the lack of a relationship between two variables.

Now, listen closely. Correlation does not imply causation. A positive correlation occurs when two factors, X and Y, change in the same direction. For example, height and weight. Generally, the taller you are, the more you weigh.

On the other hand, a negative correlation, also called an inverse correlation, occurs when one variable goes up and the other goes down. For example, when severe test anxiety goes down, National Counselor Exam scores go up.

A correlation of 0 is indicative of no relationship or association between the variables. An example is IQ and the number of shoes sold.

Squaring the correlation coefficient will show you how much variation of one factor can be accounted for by another. Hence, if we correlate study time for the National Counselor Examination with scores on the test, and we get a correlation of 0.80, then we take the 0.80 and square it, which gives us 0.64. This tells us that 64% of the NCE grade is accounted for by study time.

Question 57. Name the ego states in TA, a.k.a. transactional analysis, created by psychiatrist Eric Berne.

Answer. Very simple. The ego states are the PAC, the parent, the adult, and the child.

Question 58. Name the ego states in Freud's theory.

Answer. Freud's ego states roughly correlate with Berne's theory because Berne's theory was a popular way of expressing Freud's theory. Freud starts with the id, which is the primitive unconscious component of the personality. It's often called the pleasure principle. It's chaotic and has no sense of time.

Then there's the ego, sometimes called the reality principle. The ego is like a balance beam that keeps the id and the superego in check. Then we have the superego, which includes the "shoulds" the "oughts" and is sometimes called the ego ideal. The ego ideal contains the perfect person.

Freud's superego is like the parent in TA. The ego in Freud's theory is like the adult in TA, and the id is similar to the child in TA. In Freudian theory, questions on the exam might include the word libido. This means instinctual or id energy. A lot of therapists use the word libido to mean sex drive, but today it has a broader meaning.

Question 59. Provide an example of displacement, which is an ego defense mechanism.

Answer. The typical or prototype example is the person who is mad at the boss but can't express it because of fear of retaliation. Hint, hint, the boss might fire this employee. So, the individual comes home and yells at their kids or kicks the family dog. I humorously like to add: Hopefully, the family dog will kick back.

Question 60. What ego defense mechanism is the main target (most important) for psychoanalysis?

Answer. Repression is not technically the same as suppression, although we might use it that way in everyday life, but don't confuse this on your exam.

Repression means that something happens to you that is so painful that you automatically forget it. It occurs involuntarily. For example, a traumatic childhood sexual abuse incident. Suppression is when you say to yourself, "Gee, I don't want to think about taking the National Counselor Exam. So, I'm just not going to think about it." It's a conscious or voluntary decision.

Some books will call suppression denial. Other defense mechanisms include reaction formation, regression, rationalization, undoing, projection, sublimation, displacement, and identification.

Question 61. What famous theorist postulated a series of eight psychosocial stages from birth to old age?

Answer. Erik Erikson. Remember for your test that Erikson's stages are psychosocial and not psychosexual, like Freud's.

Question 62. What is a paradoxical technique?

Answer. Well, the word paradox can roughly be defined as something that seems one way, but it's really another. With a paradoxical technique, you tell the client to exaggerate the inappropriate symptom or behavior, sometimes in a different setting or changing it slightly.

For example, you have somebody who shakes when they get up in front of a graduate class to give a speech. You would advise that person to try to shake as hard as possible, or to really do it up right, as they often say.

I remember one time I had an inpatient client in the hospital who told me she hadn't slept a full night in six months. When I asked her why she couldn't sleep, she said, "Well, I have an anxiety attack every night that wakes me up." I told her that she was to practice having the greatest anxiety attack of her life, and the nurses would be right there to monitor it. Basically, she told me I was crazier than her.

The next morning, she came to the hospital group and told me that she slept like a baby for the first time in six months. Unfortunately, the strategy doesn't *always* work that effectively!

A lot of therapists have used paradoxical techniques. Viktor Frankl used it because he believed in humor in the therapy process. Jay Haley, who studied under Milton Erickson, used a lot in family therapy. It's not a new technique.

Knight Dunlap, who founded the *Journal of Comparative Psychology* (studying animals to learn about them and relate findings to humans) spent most of his entire life studying the making and unmaking of habits. He created a technique called the beta hypothesis, which really is like paradox. To implement the beta hypothesis, you simply would tell the client to practice the inappropriate dysfunctional behavior, such as blushing or nail biting, when it would not normally occur.

By doing this, it would cause the behavior to go away because you acquire some sort of conscious control over the behavior.

Remember, do not make paradox mystical. Explain it to your clients if they ask you what you're doing. Based on the principle of informed consent, this is the ethical thing to do.

Question 63. A physician refers a client to you for biofeedback. Briefly describe your technique.

Answer. Biofeedback consists of hooking the client to a sensitive electronic device that will give a person some sort of biological feedback about their bodily functioning. Now this sounds hopelessly complex, but I assure you it is not.

A bathroom scale is a biofeedback device. So is a mirror. Try putting on your makeup or shaving without a mirror. Try it and you will discover what I mean in record time! First, let me say that I should get my money back from taking Psychology

101 because in that course they told us that it was not possible to control the autonomic nervous system processes, such as your hand temperature, your pulse rate, the temperature of your baby toe, whatever. It turns out that with biofeedback, you can control all those things if you learn how.

A funny story is that Neal Miller was teaching rats to control their autonomic nervous system processes when he heard that humans could be taught to do the same thing using biofeedback meters. After hearing this he quipped, "I believe that in this respect men are as smart as rats."

The Menninger Clinic, when they were in Topeka, Kansas (now located in Houston, Texas), is rather famous because they found out, quite by accident, that when people would learn to raise their hand temperature, their migraine headaches would often go away.

When a researcher looks for something and then finds something more important, like this study at Menninger Clinic related to migraines, we call it a serendipitous discovery, after the "Three Princes of Serendip" fairy tale.

Also, to get very technical here, when the feedback is based on the brain, the term neurofeedback is more appropriate. Thus, if your exam wanted to split hairs, it might stipulate that neurofeedback is a specific type of biofeedback.

Question 64. Lawrence Kohlberg is best known for his work in what area?

Answer. Moral development. He postulates three levels of moral development, preconventional, conventional, and the postconventional or self-accepted moral level.

Question 65. Briefly define the DSC movement.

Answer. To tackle this question, you'll need to know that DSC stands for developmental school counseling. This approach to intervention has been embraced by nearly every state. According to proponents of DSC, school counselors traditionally waited for students with difficulties to seek them out. On the other hand, a DSC counselor is proactive, is wellness oriented, and has a focus on prevention.

The DSC counselor teaches life skills to every student via the curriculum or through programs. This is the key. The counselor's role is to match their work to the developmental growth stages of the children.

Question 66. What is the difference between a ratio scale of reinforcement and an interval schedule or scale of reinforcement?

Answer. In a ratio schedule a certain number of behaviors would be emitted before the behavior is reinforced. In other words, you don't give the reward until the person does something, say, five times. In the interval schedule, a certain amount of time passes by before the behavior is reinforced. Your monthly paycheck from your agency or school where you work is a fine example.

There's a real easy memory device for this one. You can remember that interval reinforcement occurs via time, and ratio is something else, because in everyday life, we talk about time intervals. In interval reinforcement, time must go by. We don't care how many behaviors are emitted.

Question 67. A token is a secondary reinforcer. True or false?

Answer. This is true. What is a token? You've probably even heard the phrase token economy, because it was the title for a famous book by Nathan Azrin (1930–2013) and Theodoro Ayllon (1929–), two behaviorists, called *The Token Economy* written in 1968.

A token is nothing more than a little plastic chip. It looks like a coin, except that it's usually made from rubber or plastic. These little chips or coins can be turned in at the end of the day or the end of the hour, whatever, for primary reinforcers, things that the client really wants. The token is said to be a secondary reinforcer or a backup reinforcer because it symbolizes a primary reinforcer, something the client really wants. The smell of cherries or talking while feeding a baby would be other examples of secondary reinforcers.

Question 68. Joseph Wolpe's systematic desensitization, which can be used in an individual or a group setting to treat phobias, uses a hierarchy. Explain this concept.

Answer. First, let's explain the process of systematic desensitization. First, there is relaxation training from four to six sessions. That's step one. Then, we construct the anxiety hierarchy.

A hierarchy is just a series of grades or rank-ordering situations that produce anxiety. You assist the client in creating a hierarchy from situations that are not very threatening, up to the real situation that the person is working on that's the most threatening.

Let's take an example. Let's say that we have a client who is afraid to ride an airplane. The hierarchy might begin with something like thinking about riding an airplane. The second step on a hierarchy might be having the client image driving past an airport. The third step might be to imagine going into the airport. Finally, the client would get to the point where this individual could imagine riding an airplane.

We go from relaxation, step one, to the construction of the anxiety hierarchy, that's step two, to the desensitization in imagination, to in vivo desensitization. In vivo means that you attempt to experience the steps in the hierarchy in real life, such as the client driving to the airport, entering the terminal, and taking a flight on a plane.

Question 69. You decide to do a research study with a normal population. You will have three groups: a control group, a group that receives three sessions of reality therapy, and a group that receives six sessions of reality therapy. You want to find out the effect that reality therapy has on depression. What type of statistical test will you use?

Answer. You will use the ANOVA, which stands for analysis of variance. This parametric test is used when you have two or more groups you want to compare. Generally, the t-test is used for two groups because it works better, so the analysis of variance is recommended usually for three or more groups.

This study would be classified as a one-way analysis of variance because we have one IV, one independent variable, and we have two levels of that IV, but it's still one IV. If the study were a little different, say, we had a control group, a reality therapy group, and a narrative therapy group, then we would use what is known as a two-way analysis of variance.

Some exams will use the term factorial analysis of variance to describe a situation with two or more IVs. The number of "ways" (i.e., a two-way, three-way ANOVA) refers to the number of independent variables. Again, the independent variable is the experimental variable.

Question 70. A child is taught to relax using a biofeedback meter. Every time the child relaxes to a desirable level, it activates a model car, which speeds the car around a toy racetrack. In this case, the model car is acting as a ___________.

Answer. Let's fill it in with the fact that the toy race car is acting as a positive reinforcer. We're trying to do something to increase the probability that relaxation will occur. One thing you will discover on comprehensive exams is that they often present the material in indirect ways. For example, this question appears to be a biofeedback or neurofeedback question, but when you investigate it, the question has nothing to do with biofeedback and everything to do with reinforcement theory. Read the questions carefully.

Question 71. Your supervisor tells you to do a study utilizing the concept of random sampling. What does this entail?

Answer. This is like putting your hand in a fishbowl and picking out a name. In random sampling, every member in the population has an equal probability of being selected. The selection of one member of the population has no effect on the selection of another member.

The reason that we rely on random sampling in a true experiment is so you can't kind of accidentally on purpose . . . if you get my drift (!!!!) pick people that will make your hypothesis come true. Also, remember that to have a true experiment, you *also* need randomization of groups. You must pick the people for the control groups and the experimental groups using random sampling.

There are usually random sample tables in the back of statistics books. You probably have noticed that there are computer programs and a host of internet sites that will generate random numbers for studies.

Question 72. In a classical conditioning experiment, a CS, a bell, caused a dog to salivate. Now, a researcher pairs the bell with a green light. Eventually, the green light alone causes the dog to salivate. What has occurred?

Answer. We call this higher-order conditioning. When you pair another stimulus or stimuli with the CS, and it takes on the power of the CS, then higher-order conditioning is evident.

Question 73. Name the four scales of measurement. This is a very common question, incidentally, on all kinds of exams.

Answer. The memory device that I use to remember the order of the four scales of measurement from lowest to highest is the word for black in French. That's spelled NOIR. I use this to remember the order, which is nominal, ordinal, interval, and ratio.

The nominal scale is unordered, mutually exclusive categories, things like Republican/Democrat, religion, or nationality. Nominal describes in a qualitative rather than a quantitative manner.

Next, we have the ordinal scale, which describes ordered categories like first place, second place, or runner-up.

Then, there is the interval scale. This is quantitative with no absolute zero: things like Fahrenheit temperatures, centigrade temperatures, and IQ scores. Think about it. You could have an IQ score of zero, but that doesn't mean you have no intelligence; at least, hopefully it doesn't mean that.

Then, there's the highest scale, the ratio scale. The ratio scale has an absolute zero point, such as the price of an item, the Kelvin scale (where zero is indeed absolute zero it is truly the coldest possible temperature), height, weight, or the distance of a golf hole.

Remember this, parametric statistics rely on interval and ratio data. My memory device for this is I and R, such as information and referral. Information and referral services are popular processes. Parametric tests are generally more popular than nonparametric, and they are more powerful in most cases than nonparametric.

Question 74. Here's a behavior therapy question. Giving Antabuse to an alcoholic client is what type of conditioning?

Answer. To answer this question, you really need to know what Antabuse is. It's really a trade name for the drug disulfiram. You probably won't have to know the disulfiram name for the test, but you might need to know what Antabuse is.

Antabuse is a nausea-inducing drug causing persons to be nauseous when they ingest alcohol. This is what we call an aversive or noxious stimulus because it reduces the attractiveness of a dysfunctional behavior, in this case drinking alcohol. Mild electric shock would be another example of a noxious or aversive stimulus. In ABA, or applied behavior analysis, noxious or aversive modalities are avoided.

Question 75. Piaget mentions four stages, sensorimotor, preoperational, concrete operations, and formal operations. Describe the major characteristic of the preoperational or second stage.

Answer. The child experiences symbolic schema or representational thought ages two to seven. In other words, the child starts using symbols (e.g., pretending a chalk eraser is a cell phone) to describe things.

Question 76. Describe positive and negative transference.

Answer. Transference occurs when the client acts toward the counselor in the manner that they reacted to a significant other in the past. When a client treats the counselor unknowingly, or maybe even knowingly, like a parent or a caretaker, then the client is experiencing transference at that point.

When positive feelings are expressed, it's known as positive transference. When negative feelings are expressed, we refer to it as negative transference. Another term that you'll come across that is used in some multicultural literature when working with clients from other cultures is what we call ambivalent transference.

Ambivalent transference theory says that the client will treat the counselor just like they would anybody in an authority position, with ambivalence.

Question 77. All right, time for some old standbys in the field. What is the Rosenthal effect?

Answer. First, it's no relation to me. Here, we're referring to the psychologist Robert Rosenthal. On your test, the Rosenthal effect could be called the experimenter effect or the Pygmalion effect. The Rosenthal effect is a self-fulfilling prophecy, if you will.

The researcher falls in love with their hypothesis and makes it happen unconsciously. Let me give you a few great examples. Did you know that rats can be genetically bred to be maze bright or maze dull? Maze bright really means the rats are smart and can run through a maze rapidly and efficiently. Maze dull implies that the rats are not nearly as smart and are not adept at navigating a maze.

Rosenthal gave rats to researchers and experimenters, and he lied to them. He told them that certain ones were maze bright when they weren't and maze dull when they weren't.

What happened at the end of the study? The rats that the researchers thought were smarter, even if they weren't, got faster. The ones the researchers thought were dull became slower. Now, this brought up the most important question of all: What was going on here?

The best explanation seems to be that the researchers treated the rats a little differently based on their thoughts. Next Rosenthal asked an even more important question: Does this apply to humans?

In the 1960s, Rosenthal took a group of elementary school teachers. He lied to the teachers. He told him that certain students were tested psychologically, and they were going to be late bloomers. Moreover, by the end of the year, they were going to show some great academic gains. Rosenthal just made this up. He picked the kids at random.

Keep this in mind. The kids were <u>not</u> told that they were bloomers. The children didn't know anything, so this has nothing to do with their internal position or thoughts about themselves. The teachers didn't tell the kids whether they were bloomers or not, but somehow by the end of the year, especially in the earlier grades, like the first and second grade, the students' IQs and academic performance really did go up.

Now before we go any further, I want to share a major misconception counselors have about the "Social and Cultural Diversity" section or questions on your exam. This misconception is that it is composed *only* of questions related to multicultural diversity. Wrong! Many exams have a healthy dose of social psychology, and by not studying this area (such as the Rosenthal expectancy effect), the test taker is at a HUGE disadvantage. Questions of this ilk might also appear on the research portion of the exam, so it is often up to the test makers. Again, I wouldn't waste time worrying about the section or domain: just learn the material.

Do you want to know what is usually in shouting distance of the Rosenthal effect question? Well, I can tell you . . .

Question 78. Explain the Hawthorne effect and its implication for research scientists.

Answer. A test without the Hawthorne effect? I doubt it. The Hawthorne effect is so famous that you might think it occurred at the dawn of civilization; however, it refers to some research conducted by a team that included Elton Mayo 1927 to 1932 at the Hawthorne Works at the Western Electric plant in Illinois.

Mayo, an American psychologist born in Australia who was interested in industrial issues, and his colleagues were researching lighting to see if improving the lighting would improve work output, and of course, it did. Then they tried something else. They started dimming the lights, and lo and behold, the work still improved. In fact, the work didn't go down until the lights were so dim that it was the equivalent of trying to thread a needle by candlelight, and they just couldn't see the work anymore.

Researchers wanted to know what was going on. The phenomenon has been billed as the Hawthorne effect. What's going on here is that the novelty or newness of the study produced positive results, such as improved work output. The attention that the workers were receiving likely probably improved the output as well.

Anytime you look at a study, you must ask yourself, is it the experimental variable that's causing the changes, or is it a Hawthorne effect? The Hawthorne effect is what we call a threat to internal validity. That is to say, the methodology, and not the IV, is causing the changes.

Mega test hint. When a study has good internal validity, extraneous or confounding variables have been properly controlled and are not impacting the experiment.

Question 79. Who is the "father of guidance"?

Answer. Don't miss this one, folks. It is none other than Frank Parsons, who set up community centers to help people who were looking for work in the early 1900s.

Question 80. John Holland's psychological/personality theory of career development is probably the most popular theory in career and vocational counseling. Explain the basic assumption of this so-called typology approach.

Answer. Holland delineated six personality types and six corresponding or matching work environment types. The notion is that you should try to match the personality style to the work setting that has the characteristics for that personality style. In other words, the client needs employment that allows the person to express their personality. This approach *does* rely on stereotyping.

The six personality types/work environment types are realistic, investigative, artistic, social, enterprising, and conventional, sometimes referred to as RIASEC. A large body of research verifies that Holland's concepts are accurate.

Question 81. Who were the first developmental career theorists to view a career as a longitudinal process rather than a single decision?

Answer. Ginzberg and his associates, Ginsburg, Axelrad, and Herma. In 1951, they made the statement that career process is not a single decision but rather a series of decisions made over a period of years. This is what we call a developmental approach to career. These same researchers thought that career decision choice was irreversible early in their own career, but they did change their minds.

Question 82. A therapist using systematic desensitization uses the acronym SUDS; what does it mean?

Answer. The acronym SUDS, created by Joseph Wolpe in 1969, stands for subjective units of distress or disturbance. Zero means no anxiety, 100 is the maximum level of anxiety. You have the client utilize the subjective units so that you can create the hierarchy for performing systematic desensitization that we talked about earlier.

Question 83. What do the letters HIPAA stand for?

Answer. HIPAA stands for the Health Insurance Portability and Accountability Act of 1996. The act stipulates guidelines for client privacy. For example, since a fax machine in your counseling office could reveal information about the clients, the machine must be physically positioned so that only those who have permission to view client information can see it.

The regulations also specify that electronically transmitted client information must be encrypted. The full text of HIPAA can be accessed at www.aspe.hhs.gov.

Question 84. Who is the famous behaviorist who created job clubs?

Answer. Nathan Azrin. If you recall, just a few questions ago I mentioned Azrin's work related to token economies.

Mini test hint. Remember that job tenure is often related to job satisfaction.

Question 85. At one time, psychometricians who gave the Stanford Binet intelligence test had to compute an intelligence quotient, or so-called IQ. How was this mathematically accomplished?

Answer. Notice the words "at one time" because in 1986, the actual IQ, or intelligence quotient, bit the dust, and the tests started using the SAS, Standard Age Score.

The word quotient means the answer when you divide one number into another. The formula used for the Stanford Binet before '86 was MA, the mental age, that's the numerator in the equation, over CA, that's the chronological age, or actual age. Then you would take MA/CA × 100 and that would equal the IQ.

A great memory device here would be to remember that MA is a high degree, so you're going to put it on the top of the equation. See how easy these memory devices can really be? They can really work for you.

Question 86. What popular personality test had over 500 true/false self-report questions?

Answer. The Minnesota Multiphasic Personality Inventory, or MMPI-2, that sported 567 true/false statements. The test has a lot of computer programs out there to score it. It also had scales to prevent people from faking the test, and it even has psychiatric classifications. In 2022 a new MMPI-3 was created to update the test and provide new relevant scales. The MMPI-3 also took race, ethnicity, education, and age into consideration based on the newest census data. The measure sported 335 questions.

Question 87. When would a licensed professional counselor request a Bender Gestalt test of motor integration, often called the Bender for short?

Answer. The LPC would probably opt for this test when this clinician suspects that the client might have a neurological difficulty. Based on the results of the test, a referral might even be made to a psychiatrist, or perhaps a neurologist. The Bender Gestalt is what we call a test of organicity, meaning that a neurological problem might be present.

Question 88. Define the acronyms NCC, CCMHC, NCSC, AAMFT, CRC, CACREP, MAC, and NCGC.

Answer. NCC is a National Certified Counselor by NBCC, it is a *generic certification*. CCMHC is a Certified Clinical Mental Health Counselor. NCSC is National Certified School Counselor. AAMFT is the American Association for Marriage and Family Therapy.

CRC is Certified Rehabilitation Counselor. CACREP is the Council for Accreditation of Counseling and Related Programs established by AACD in 1981. Just because you go to an accredited school doesn't mean that you don't have to have a license to practice.

MAC is Master Addictions Counselor. NCGC is National Certified Gerontology Counselor (credential retired in 1999). VERY IMPORTANT FOR YOUR CAREER: To hold the CCMHC, the MAC, and the NCSC, the professional must hold the NCC credential as a prerequisite.

Just for the record, counselors are not psychologists. After graduating from an approved APA graduate program, psychologists must take the EPPP exam, the examination for professional practice in psychology.

Question 89. What analytic theory emphasizes birth order very heavily?

Answer. Alfred Adler's individual psychology postulates that the firstborn child is usually a leader and conservative. The second child is usually extroverted and seeks outside attention.

Adler felt that sibling interaction was stronger at times than parent–child interaction. When siblings fight a lot or strive for power between themselves, this is called sibling rivalry. Not everybody believes in birth order theories, although they are popular right now.

Question 90. A counselor who tells a client to recount a dream in the present tense or talk to their hand is most likely a __________ type of therapist.

Answer. Let's fill in the blank with the word Gestalt. At one time, Gestalt was the most popular theory in the whole world.

Question 91. True or false? There are instances when a licensed professional counselor should not explain the purpose of testing or paradoxical homework assignments to a client.

Answer. This statement is false. You should explain it; do not be mystical. The explanation is what we call informed consent. You're giving the client the information to consent to the procedure.

Question 92. You see a graph of a normal curve. Which will have the highest value, the mean, the median, or the mode?

Answer. Well, folks, the answer is I tried to trick you. All these statistical entities will be the highest value. Remember that the curve will look like a bell: it will be symmetrical, and the mean, the median, and the mode will all converge in the middle at the high point.

Question 93. A researcher gives a group of students Omega-3 fish oil capsules to see if this nutritional supplement helps fight depression. What is the IV and what is the DV in this experiment?

Answer. Remember that IV stands for independent variable, a.k.a. the experimental variable. In this case, that would be the fish oil capsules, and the DV, remember, D as in data, would be the score on some test or inventory that measures depression.

Question 94. Who wrote the famous 1969 book *Schools without Failure*?

Answer. William Glasser, the father of reality therapy. He also wrote *Choice Theory* and *Positive Addiction*.

Glasser was not a fan of psychiatric drugs. He believed that the DSM does describe symptoms; however, he disagreed with the DSM that these symptoms are a manifestation of mental disorders. He stated that when clients make better and more satisfying choices, symptoms disappear.

According to Glasser, brain scans show that even brain chemistry changes without drugs. Today's major contributor to reality therapy is Robert Wubbolding.

Criticisms of reality therapy? It ignores the impact of the past such as traumatic experiences, it puts no stock in dreams, and it does not deal with unconscious material.

Question 95. List Freud's psychosexual stages in their proper order.

Answer. Freud's stages are the oral, the anal, the phallic, the latency, and the genital. Some exams could leave out the latency phase.

Question 96. You are reading a statistical study which shows a lowercase p and says $p = .05$. What does this convey?

Answer. P = the probability that the differences in a study are real and not caused by chance. For example, .05 means that 95 times out of 100, the results are not an accident in the study. If $p = 0.01$, this means that 99 times out of 100, the results are not an accident.

P at the .05 level and p at the .01 level are the two most common levels used in social science research. Some exams will refer to .05 as the 95% confidence level or .01 as the 99% confidence level. Statisticians are not overly fond of this terminology, but you could see it on the exam.

Question 97. What is a stanine score?

Answer. First, you should know that stanine stands for standard nine. A stanine score divides a distribution into nine equal parts, with 1 being the lowest 9th and 9 being the highest 9th, and 5 is in the mean range.

This scale was developed by the Air Force in World War II to use with punch cards. The military thought it would be an easy score to use because it dealt with single-digit numbers. You might contrast stanine scores with T-scores, where there's a mean of 50 with 1 standard deviation for every 10 points.

For example, in a T-score, 1 standard deviation is 60. This is a positive deviation. One negative standard deviation would be 40 in a T-score. If you've been away from statistics for a while, I'd recommend reading this question a second time.

Incidentally, for all you visual learners out there, in my book, *The Encyclopedia Counseling*, you'll find a chart of *all* the standard scores in the graphical representations section.

Question 98. A t-test is used to test a null hypothesis between two normal samples. What type of statistical test can be used to compare more than two groups?

Answer. I know this is repetition, but it's not going to hurt you. The ANOVA or analysis of variance can be used when there are more than two groups. Also, if a researcher is interested in an analysis of variance that is looking at two or more dependent variables or DVs, we call it a MANOVA, which stands for multivariate analysis of variance.

Question 99. True or false? Research indicates that computer-assisted guidance systems such as SIGI 3, the System of Interactive Guidance and Information, are very effective.

Answer. True. However, a major caution when using computers in the process of career counseling is confidentiality.

Question 100. As a counselor, you find it very difficult to see a certain client. You vehemently dislike this client, and you find yourself becoming very sarcastic toward the client during sessions. What is the technical name for this phenomenon?

Answer. This phenomenon is what counselors have labelled countertransference.

Remember, transference is where the client relates to the counselor as if the counselor is somebody significant from the past, usually a parent or a caretaker. Transference refers to behavior on the part of the client; however, in countertransference, it is the counselor's behavior we are concerned about. Exaggerated countertransference can interfere with efficacious treatment.

Positive feelings can also be indicative of countertransference. For example, if you have a client that you're constantly obsessing about, and you're really upset because the client didn't make it to a session, or you can't wait for that client to show up, or you're sexually attracted to the client, these are likely indicative of countertransference.

Question 101. What is a distribution called when the mean, the median, and the mode all fall at the same point?

Answer. This is a normal bell-shaped symmetrical distribution. A normal distribution can be utilized for parametric statistics.

When a distribution is not normal, we use nonparametric statistics. Your test might refer to nonparametric tests as distribution-free tests. Be aware that basic curves in statistics are called frequency polygons. Another way to display information in addition to graphing data with a curve or a line is to use a bar graph, also known as a histogram. Histograms are helpful when you compare two groups.

For example, you have a control group and next to it you have an experimental group. You can place each one of the groups in a bar graph and they can easily be compared. When you display two different groups, the graph becomes a double bar histogram.

Question 102. You see a correlation coefficient of –.50 between variables *X* and *Y*. This indicates that if *X* goes up, variable *Y* goes ________.

Answer. If variable *X* goes up and the correlation is negative, then variable *Y* will go down. For example, good grades and test anxiety. Most likely when severe test anxiety goes down, grades go up. Or try this one. How about brushing your teeth and dental caries? Presumably, the more you brush your teeth, the fewer cavities you're going to have. Negative correlations of this nature can also be called inverse correlations.

Question 103. What is it called when the same group of subjects are used in a research study under two or more different conditions?

Answer. A repeated measures comparison is often contrasted with the independent group comparison design in which we use different groups of people and the performance of one group does not influence the other group being studied.

Question 104. Agree or disagree with this statement: In terms of group stages, the working stage generally occurs prior to the transition stage.

Answer. False, strongly disagree. Yes, I would commit the order of the stages in a group to memory. OK, sports fans, here they are. The first stage, or stage one, is known as orientation or the forming stage. The second stage is the transition stage, sometimes called storming. The third stage is the norming cohesive stage. Many exams will not acknowledge this stage.

Then, moving along, the next stage is the working or performing stage, and the final group stage is termed adjourning or the termination stage.

Question 105. After a particularly emotional session in which you feel you are making a lot of progress with the client, you feel close to the client emotionally. You decide to hug your client, which certainly goes along with the way your client feels. Your client hugs you willingly. Is this ethical?

Answer. I'm not sure if you're going to like my answer to this or if I can give you an answer regarding this scenario. Ethics are not always cut and dried and codes are not always the same. At one time under the ethics set forth by the National Board for Certified Counselors, non-erotic touching was not considered an ethics violation.

The current 2016 NBCC ethics under "NCCs take appropriate action to prevent harm" does not address the issue directly; however, number 7 states: "NCCs shall not engage in sexual harassment, which is defined as a single act or multiple occurrences of verbal, nonverbal or physical actions that are known to be unwelcome or that are of the severity to be perceived as harassment by a reasonable person."

Since your client willingly hugged you, this would seem ethical.

Some authors in the field feel that hugging can be therapeutic. Nevertheless, hugging is clearly delineated as an ethics violation in the state where I currently reside since they do not use NBCC ethics. A member of a state licensing board once told me that in some states hugging is no different than having sex with a client. My advice is to get in touch with your licensing bureau and see what its position is on hugging and related ethics before you take your state licensing exam.

Moreover – listen to this, this is very important. NBCC or any other body could change their position. Promise me right here, right now, come on, that you're going to make it *your responsibility* to check out the newest ethical guidelines before you take your exam. Do not, I repeat, do not count on my study materials or those authored by others to be 100% accurate in this respect.

Question 106. Why would a counselor working with a 17-year-old teen who is a headbanger be reluctant to use behavior modification or the applied behavior analysis (ABA) technique of extinction?

Answer. Well, to answer this, first, let's define extinction. Extinction is often described as a lack of reinforcement. In other words, you generally ignore the behavior. The theory being that if you ignore the behavior, it will start to dissipate, abate, and it will go away.

However, there is a fly in the oatmeal. Research shows what we call a response burst or an extinction burst. This means that when you first begin to ignore (i.e., provide no response) the behavior gets worse/increases before it gets better. This would imply that a behavior such as head banging could severely harm the client. Thus, certain behaviors are not appropriate to use with the extinction model.

Another thing you need to keep in mind is when parents and caretakers use extinction since they are not trained counselors. Hence when you talk with parents about discipline and parenting their children, a lot of times they don't understand response bursting. What happens is that if you have a child that is engaging in a behavior that's not harmful to the child, and the parent ignores the behavior, it gets worse before it gets better.

The parent starts thinking, "Gee, this technique isn't working," and guess what? The parent stops ignoring the behavior at that point. Sometimes the dysfunctional behavior stays at an all-time new, higher level. What do you do? You tell parents that they must stick with the process, even *though things get worse before they get better*.

Extinction can also occur in classical conditioning. In fact, do you know what happens if you produce a CS, a bell, and do not show the dog meat after it? In other words, you keep ringing the bell, but you don't produce any meat. What will happen is that the salivation response, the salivating that you've conditioned, will temporarily go away.

Question 107. Studying for a long time without a break is called massed practice. Studying for shorter sessions with breaks is known as spaced practice. Which type of practice would be the most effective when studying for a state counselor licensure exam?

Answer. Okay, listen up. Your answer would be the same for any type of exam. Given the same amount of time, spaced practice, also called distributed practice, wins over massed practice. In other words, if you split your study time up, rather than pulling those marathon study sessions, you'll usually do better on your exam.

Question 108. Who coined the term "group therapy"?

Answer. In 1932, psychiatrist Jacob Levy Moreno coined the term group therapy and created the first journal to focus primarily on groups, today published under the name *Group Psychotherapy, Psychodrama, and Sociometry*.

In 1941, Moreno founded the American Society of Group Psychotherapy and Psychodrama.

Question 109. Here's an easy one. What does the T in T-groups stand for?

Answer. The T stands for training.

T can mean several things in counseling and psychotherapy. It can mean training, as in T-groups. It can mean *T* score, which is a type of score that has a mean of 50 and each standard deviation is 10, always using positive integers. We also have a statistical *t*-test to determine whether differences in research groups or populations differ.

Question 110. What is the advantage of a variable schedule of reinforcement over a fixed schedule of reinforcement?

Answer. The variable schedule is more difficult to extinguish. In a fixed schedule, a certain length of time or a certain number of behaviors occurs before the reinforcement is given.

In a variable schedule, just like the name sounds, you vary the number of behaviors necessary, or you vary the time interval before the reinforcement is given.

Question 111. In group dynamics, the rules of conduct are called ________.

Answer. Let's fill in the blank with the word norms. Norms define the acceptable parameters of behavior. They are generally unwritten.

Question 112. A counselor reinforces a child as the child gets closer and closer to approximating the target behavior. What is this procedure called?

Answer. It is called shaping.

Some exams will call it shaping using successive approximations.

Question 113. Here's an analogy question. Sensorimotor is to Piaget as oral is to Freud as __________ is to Erik Erikson.

Answer. Let's answer this one together. Again, this is a prime example of an analogy question.

Questions of this ilk are common on comprehensive exams. An analogy is a way of relating two things that are in one sense similar, but in a lot of other ways, they're different. Let's look at the question. The first part says, "Sensorimotor is to Piaget." You ask yourself: what do we know about the sensorimotor stage?

Well, simply put, it is Piaget's first cognitive stage. The second part of the question says, "As oral is to Freud." Bingo, the oral stage is Freud's first psychosexual developmental stage. The last part of the question says, "As blank is to Erik Erikson." The question is really asking, "What is Erik Erikson's first psychosocial stage?"

The answer is trust versus mistrust. Your exam may also toss out what we call the best answer questions. Best answer questions mean that A, B, C, and D could all be correct, but only one of the answers is the best answer. Another type of question you might see is called a reverse type or negative exception question.

This is the question that will say something like, "All of the following are behavioral counseling techniques, except . . . " It's a negative question. Another example of a negative question might be, "All of these statements are indicative of countertransference, except . . . " Moving right along.

Question 114. Do you agree or disagree with this statement: Most tests constructed by high school teachers are normative based.

Answer. Agree. It's true. The actual information the student knows is less important than how much the student knows compared to the norm group, which is usually the classroom.

The other type of assessment or test is what we call a criterion referenced test. This occurs when one compares individuals to predetermined standards.

Question 115. An Asian American counselor wants to learn more about Native American culture. The counselor thus decides to live on a reservation for a year.

Is this counselor relying on an emic are an etic approach to multiculturalism?

Answer. This is an emic approach. The emic approach champions the idea that you can learn more about a culture from being a part of the culture's system. The etic approach would assert that the culture is best studied from outside the system.

Question 116. Here's an easy one. Who coined the term behaviorism?

Answer. John B. Watson in 1913. Watson said he could turn a baby into almost anything he wanted. His exact comment was, "Men are built, not born." Obviously, this approach relies heavily on environmental changes to mold the person.

Question 117. A 16-year-old client tells you during an individual counseling session that they are using crack, an extremely dangerous form of cocaine. After the session, the client's father demands to know if the client is using any type of illicit drugs.

Should you tell the client's father?

Answer. This is a tough one. I think a lot of people would miss it. There are exceptions to confidentiality. One of the exceptions applies to clients who are under 18 years old. If we go back to an oldie but goodie, from an AACD publication (now ACA), a 1991 issue of *Guidepost*, (the publication's name was changed to *Counseling Today* in 1994), there's an excellent landmark article on confidentiality.

In the article, Ted Remley, an expert on confidentiality and privileged communication issues, is quoted, and he lists nine exceptions to confidentiality. Here they are. Number one, the client is a danger to themselves or somebody else. Number two, the client will request a release of information.

Number three, a court order stipulating the release of information. Four, when there is clinical supervision of a counselor. Five, when clerical assistance processes information and papers about the client. Six, legal and clinical consultation. Seven, when clients raise the issue of their mental health in a lawsuit.

Eight, a third party is present in the room. Get this, folks, number nine. Here's the clincher. When clients are younger than 18 years of age.

In the article, Remley, a counselor and lawyer, says, and I quote, "If a client is a minor, their parents or their guardian can demand information about the session." You would do well to try to talk the parent or caretaker out of it, but I want you to know that there are exceptions to confidentiality. Sometimes it is ethical to breach confidentiality.

Another hint that this question should really give you is that there are a lot of wonderful ideas that you can find in journals and in professional newsletters and newspapers before you take your exam.

Question 118. Define the term cultural encapsulation.

Answer. This is a term dating back to 1962 coined by Gilbert Wrenn, who penned the classic *Counselor in a Changing World*. This term basically means the same as ethnocentrism. It occurs when you think that your culture is kind of a yardstick, and you are encapsulated in the sense that you can only see your point of view of your culture, not the practices from other cultures. You find those difficult to assimilate.

Study reminder. The popular or dominant culture in a society is often referred to as macroculture, national culture, or majority culture.

Question 119. Name Lawrence Kohlberg's three levels of morality.

Answer. Level one is the preconventional level, which is approximately ages nine and under. At this level you live by rules that are outside of the self. Level two is the conventional level that most adolescents live by, and that's where you conform to authorities. Then there's level three, which is the postconventional level that is reached by only a minority of people after age 20.

At this level you make decisions based on principles, not rules. This is sometimes called a prior to society perspective or viewpoint.

Question 120. Explain the law of effect.

Answer. Edward Thorndike's law of effect purports that behavioral responses that are accompanied or immediately followed by satisfaction are repeated. The notion also postulates that behaviors followed by dissatisfaction are less likely to occur. Of course, B.F. Skinner elaborated on this concept; hence, the law of effect was a forerunner to behaviorism. In 1898, Thorndike wrote a monograph titled "Animal Intelligence" that marked the beginning of serious animal research in the behavioral sciences. Thorndike has been called the modern father of educational psychology.

Thorndike, like Joseph Wolpe, who created systematic desensitization, worked with cats.

Question 121. What is conservation and what Piagetian stage does it occur in?

Answer. Here's a great memory device. First, the only Piagetian stage that begins with the letter C is concrete operations. You can remember that conservation occurs in a concrete operation stage because they both start with a C. Nice! Right?

No behavioral science or developmental book seems to be complete without a picture of a young child where the child is looking at a tall skinny glass of water and then the water is being poured into a small squatty glass, and seemingly, the child is not able to understand that the two glasses hold the same amount of water.

Very often the child thinks that the tall skinny glass has more than the small squatty glass. When a child cannot tell the difference, we call it a lack of conservation. When a child masters this distinction, we say the child has mastered conservation.

If you take, for example, a child that is in the preoperational stage and that child has not mastered conservation, and you show that child a cake that is cut into two pieces, and then you have another cake that is exactly the same size but is cut into five pieces, the child in the preoperational stage will believe that the cake that has five pieces is larger than the cake with only two pieces.

Question 122. A child says, "The sun is following me." This is known as ego centration or centration. That is to say, the child sees only one outstanding feature of an object. What Piagetian stage does this occur in?

Answer. The second or preoperational stage, ages two to seven of Piaget's model. This is the stage that comes before the concrete operational stage listed in the previous question. The child in the preoperational stage is incapable of reversible mental operations and can't really distinguish an internal state from external reality.

Question 123. In Freud's theory, is it the id, the ego, or the superego which houses the basic biological drives?

Answer. The id. The child ego state in transactional analysis, also known as TA, is very similar to Freud's id.

Question 124. A 19-year-old client you are having an individual counseling session with cusses you out. He then demands to read the record. Are you obligated to comply with this belligerent request?

Answer. The fact that the child cursed you has nothing to do with the answer. According to ethical standards, a 19-year-old has a right to read their own record. In fact, anybody over the age of 18 has a right to read their own record, and anybody over the age 18 has a right to read their child's record. Again, just for review purposes, from a legal standpoint, an individual under the age of 18 does not possess a right to confidentiality in counseling and therapy, despite what most people believe.

Question 125. During Piaget's first stage, the sensorimotor stage, the child develops object permanence. This is an important developmental milestone. Define this concept.

Answer. Object permanence is the ability to recognize that an object continues to exist even when the object is out of the child's presence. The child achieves what we call representational thought. The child can think of an object that is out of sight, such as an adult holding an object behind their back. Piaget felt this ability took place around eight months; however, newer research suggests it might take place as early as four to seven months.

Question 126. A Native American counselor tells an Asian client that she must change the unfair policies toward Asians at her place of employment if she wishes to improve her situation. Is this counselor using an alloplastic or autoplastic approach to multicultural counseling?

Answer. Alloplastic. Here's why. The word alloplastic was originally used in psychoanalysis to refer to the fact that the libido energy was turned toward the environment. In multicultural counseling, the term is often used to suggest that the counselor tells the client that the client needs to change something in the environment.

Autoplastic, on the other hand, means changes in the self, so autoplastic interventions occur when you tell the client to *change something in themselves*. If this counselor said "Look, you need to change your thinking to cope better," that would be an autoplastic approach.

A great memory device: just remember that when we talk about things like autosuggestion and autohypnosis, we're trying to change the person, and of course, alloplastic would be the opposite of that.

So, in multicultural counseling, the autoplastic/alloplastic dilemma is: Should the counselor change the client's self: autoplastic?

Or should the counselor have the client work to change the environment? Alloplastic.

Question 127. In what stage does Piaget feel that abstract thought emerges?

Answer. This takes place in the final stage, formal operations, approximately age 12 and on. An individual at this point goes beyond what is to what could be.

Question 128. In the famous Little Albert experiment by Watson and Rayner, a loud noise was paired with a harmless white rat. The white rat was the CS, or conditioned stimulus. What is the loud noise?

Answer. The loud noise was the UCS or US. It's an unconditioned stimulus, the thing that causes a reflex. If you remember that unconditioned is something you need not learn, and conditioned is learned, it'll make it a lot easier.

For example, if somebody strikes an iron bar like Watson and Rayner did behind your head, you don't have to learn to jump. You don't need to take a three-credit hour graduate course in jumping . . . you are usually going to be startled and jump! It's automatic.

Question 129. Instrumental learning is also called _________.

Answer. Fill in the blank with operant learning or operant conditioning. This is the paradigm researched by B.F. Skinner. And just in case your exam asks, Skinner made it very clear he was not a cognitive psychologist.

Question 130. What type of therapy has been called too mechanistic, and too simplistic, because it focuses too heavily on overt behavior?

Answer. That's an easy one, folks. The answer, behavior therapy.

Question 131. Two techniques of behavior therapy are flooding and implosive, or implosion, therapy. Differentiate one from another.

Answer. I admit, this is one tough question, but I've got a little memory device to help you out. Flooding – or in vivo exposure therapy – takes place when you *expose* the client to a fearful situation. In implosion or implosive therapy, you have the client fantasize about the fear. It's done in the imagination. One way to remember or distinguish the two approaches is to remember that implosion starts with an I, and so does imagination. Now, here's another test hint. Some exams might not distinguish reality from imagination in the question. Thus, the other difference is that in implosive therapy, psychodynamic symbolism is used in fantasy. Of course, to use psychodynamic symbolism, the approach would pretty much have to be done in the imagination.

Question 132. We're moving along. Primal scream therapy – the name of a popular 1970 book – a.k.a. primal therapy, takes advantage of catharsis and abreaction, which are old word meaning to express or experience emotions. Primal merely suggests clients relive painful early traumas and express repressed feelings and emotions not liberated during the original incident. Who is the founder of this type of therapy?

Answer. Arthur Janov. The APA does not endorse this form of treatment.

Another therapy that is highly cathartic is Canadian therapist Al Mahler's experiential therapy.

Question 133. A career counselor who believes in John L. Holland's theory gives a client a self-administered, self-scored test. What career assessment instrument is the counselor using?

Answer. The counselor is most likely utilizing a career assessment tool that has been used with over nine million people. It is called the SDS or Self-Directed Search, and it reveals a three-letter personality work type. SDS literature in 2022 suggests the instrument is now the most widely used career inventory in the world. It has been translated into 25 languages. The whole test takes about 35–45 minutes to complete.

Time for another mega test hint. The SDS has been attacked on the basis that it is gender biased and that it limits the career considerations for females. Finally, that was a tough question because some of you might have accidentally said the Strong Interest Inventory, or SII for short.

The Strong is intended to be used with the counselor and a computer grading the test. It's not self-administered and scored. Remember that the Strong is also based on Holland's theory. Holland's theory is very popular.

Question 134. A *T*-score is also known as a transformed score. Describe the nature of *T*-scores.

Answer. A *T*-score has a mean of 50 and a standard deviation of 10. *T*-scores are used for convenience and comparability purposes.

A *T*-score of 30, for example, would be minus two standard deviations or a negative two Z-score. A *T*-score of 80 would be a positive 3 SD or, to put it a different way, three standard deviations above the mean or plus three in a Z-score. Read that back at least twice if you've been out of statistics for a while. Come on, don't say you're going to do it, do it.

Exam booster. *T*-scores are often desirable because they are never negative integers. If you are a bit rusty on some of these terms that I'm using, I highly recommend you walk, no make that run, to your nearest local or Internet bookstore or check out my website at www.howardrosenthal.com and secure a copy of my excellent text, the *Human Services Dictionary*.

It's an awesome reference for bringing your vocabulary up to licensing and certification exam speed.

Question 135. You are a middle school counselor who wishes to investigate the progress that students have made in their studies. Will you utilize an achievement test or an aptitude test to determine this?

Answer. You will use an achievement test. Achievement tests measure what has been achieved. An aptitude test implies what could be accomplished, or what your client's potential is. It's measuring something a little bit different.

Question 136. What historical counseling practitioner was associated with the so-called Minnesota point of view?

Answer. E.G. Williamson, Edmund Griffith Williamson, who was associated with the University of Minnesota for over 40 years. The Minnesota viewpoint is the only school of counseling developed from a base that focused on vocational and educational development. This type of intervention utilized an actuarial approach, which means that the practitioner uses tests and statistics and probability to help a person make lifestyle and career choices.

The idea of the Minnesota approach was to match the characteristics of the person to jobs that required those characteristics. Sometimes loosely in the field, we refer to the Minnesota point of view as the matching approach or know the client, know the job approach.

Williamson's famous 1939 book *How to Counsel Students* is viewed as a historical landmark publication in counseling.

Question 137. Carl R. Rogers's technique was termed nondirective, as opposed to Albert Ellis's REBT, which is considered a _______ approach.

Answer. Well, your answer is Albert Ellis's approach is very directive, or what we sometimes call active directive, and is very didactic, which means that we teach the clients something.

In didactic approaches or teaching approaches, the counselor may talk as much if not more than the client.

Question 138. A counselor educator lectures on sour grapes and sweet lemon. What ego defense mechanism is this professional focusing on?

Answer. Rationalization. The story goes that the fox couldn't reach the grapes, rationalized them as sour, and said, "Well I probably don't want them anyway."

The human version might go something like, "I really didn't want to be accepted to a top graduate school anyway. Only eggheads attend such schools."

Sweet lemon is another variety of rationalization and takes place when the client says they like an undesirable situation. Somebody who works in an extremely hot unairconditioned factory says, "Oh, gosh, I really love it. I'm sweating a lot, and I'm getting rid of all this water weight I needed to shed." Yeah, right. Sure.

So, to recap: sour grapes, underrate the reward or circumstances. Sweet lemon, overrate the reward or situation.

Question 139. What therapist is associated with the term individuation, which refers to the process throughout the client's life of becoming an individual who is separate and unique from others?

Answer. Carl Jung, the Swiss psychiatrist who created analytic psychology.

Question 140. Here is a true/false question. According to ACA ethical guidelines, all counselors must provide at least 85% of their clients with pro bono services.

Answer. This statement is false. To answer the question, you would have to know that pro bono refers to providing free services.

Now, if you peruse the ACA ethics, you will discover the code indicates that counselors should "devote a portion of their professional activity for which there is little or no financial return (pro bono services)." It does **not specify precisely what the portion would be, such as 50% or over 85%.** The NBCC Code of Ethics states, "NCCs shall provide referrals if the client cannot afford services, at the client's request or as appropriate at the conclusion of a professional counseling service relationship." Note the absence of the terms "free" or "pro bono."

Exam cautionary hint, ethical guidelines and terminology do indeed change with every update. Check the current NBCC ethical guidelines prior to your exam at www.nbcc.org.

If your university or professors will use a comprehensive or exit exam based on ACA ethics, go to www.counseling.org for information. Psychologists taking the EPPP or other comprehensive exams should check out APA ethics at www.apa.org.

Question 141. You are teaching a client who is training to be a counselor to relax using EMG biofeedback. The purpose of this relaxation is to help the client reduce anxiety so this grad student can do well on the CPCE. You notice that although this counselor has learned to relax quite well, there is still a touch of anxiety when this client thinks about taking the exam. According to the Yerkes Dodson law, this is not an undesirable thing and should *not* be treated by the counselor. Explain this strange position.

Answer. First, let's go over what the question is really asking. You've got this client who's trying to reduce anxiety, so the client, who is a counselor in training, can do better on the CPCE. You're putting the client through EMG or electromyography, which is just a very big term for muscle relaxation.

To answer the question, though, you do have to know what is meant by the Yerkes Dodson law. The Yerkes Dodson law states that when you have a complex task, a minimal level of anxiety is necessary. And, my dear reader, that is precisely what's going on here in this question.

You've reduced the anxiety quite a bit, but there's still a minimal level there. Your hypothesis, at least according to the Yerkes Dodson law, is that the counselor will do a tad better on the exam if a little bit of anxiety is present. Now, remember that when you personally take the exam. So, I ask, "Is life beautiful or what?" I mean, really. A tad of anxiety could *help* your score.

Question 142. According to Leon Festinger's principle of cognitive dissonance, a conscientious objector (i.e., somebody who is against war, serving in the military, and bearing arms) who was drafted to fight in a war and began shooting at others might say ________________ about their shooting behavior during a post-traumatic stress disorder (PTSD) group.

Answer. First, keep in mind that PTSD is a DSM diagnosis. Dissonance means an inconsistency. Cognitive dissonance theory says that people do not like inconsistencies between their thoughts and behaviors, so they will try to rid themselves of this dissonance.

To do this, this conscientious objector who is now attending group counseling will probably begin to change their attitude in favor of this behavior and tell you why it was a positive thing and why a soldier must shoot people. (Keep in mind I am not suggesting that you personally would agree or disagree with this; however, this is a common or typical scenario that might show up on questions related to cognitive dissonance.)

Question 143. A counselee is given a math test and scores a 95 on it. The literature on the test indicates that the test has a standard error of measurement (SEM) of 3 points. How must the counselor interpret these results?

Answer. The counselor must realize that if the client took the test again, the client is going to score between 92 and 98 approximately 68% of the time because the test has an error factor of +/-3. The standard error of measurement is really like a distribution of one person who keeps taking the same test again, again, and again. A smaller SEM in an instrument such as a psychoeducational test is desirable.

This is a very important concept for counselors to know. Say a client comes to you and they have two children. One has an IQ of 101, and the other child sports an IQ of 103, and the standard error of the test is 3. Then the one with the higher IQ is not necessarily more intelligent due to the error factor of the IQ test.

Question 144. A counselor snares a new position at a counseling agency. The counselor is given a questionnaire they will read to each client during the initial interview. The purpose of this initial interview will be to determine what services and what practitioner will be best for the client. Is this a structured or an unstructured interview?

Answer. Interviews that are based on questionnaires are considered structured.

Question 145. Research on career maturity is usually associated with what expert? ________.

Answer. Fill in the blank with J.O. Crites, who created the Career Maturity Inventory (CMI) based on Super's theory. Donald Super believed very heavily in the importance of the self-concept in job selection.

Question 146. A psychiatrist requests your records on a counselee you've been seeing for the past six months. This is not an emergency. Under what two conditions, according to the NBCC Ethics, are you allowed to turn these records over?

Answer. Number one, if the client gives you permission and signs a release of information. Do not use a copy of the client's signature. Number two, if the record is subpoenaed by a court of law.

Question 147. You become a licensed professional counselor in one state, but in a year, you decide to move to another state. The new state informs you that they will grant you reciprocity. Do you need to take another comprehensive exam?

Answer. Good news on this one, folks. The answer is no, you will not have to take a new exam. The definition of reciprocity is that one state accepts your license from another state. Of course, it's not true in every state, so if you do move, check. It's very possible you would have to take courses, or a different internship, a different number of graduate hours, or even a different exam.

Question 148. Here's a true/false question. Federal laws under Title VII of the Civil Rights Act and Title IX of the Educational Amendment prohibit discrimination on the basis of gender regarding payment received for work. Because of this, women now make the same salary basically as men.

Answer. False. In 2022 women earned on average 17% less than men. We refer to this as the gender pay gap.

When we have a situation where women make less than men for doing the *same work*, we call it sex-based wage discrimination. It is not uncommon for women to hold jobs that are low paying and lack status. Crites found that even though girls score higher on career maturity than boys, their aspirations are still below their potential, and some counselors feel this is a major factor regarding salaries.

Question 149. Here is a historical question. Always expect a few questions of this ilk on a comprehensive exam. True or false? ACA, which was once the AACD or the American Association for Counseling and Development, used to be called the APGA or the American Personnel and Guidance Association. How's that for some serious alphabet soup?

Answer. True. The American Personnel and Guidance Association was founded in July of 1952 and became the AACD in 1983. The current ACA name was adopted in 1992. I'll tell you something even sadder. Some of us, yeah, me included, are old enough to remember when ACA was APGA since we had APGA memberships.

Question 150. Musterbation, you heard me correctly, means using too many shoulds, oughts, and musts, which are called absolutist thinking. What theorist came up with the term "musterbation"?

Answer. Albert Ellis, who founded REBT. Ellis humorously tells us that musterbation is a lot more pernicious than masturbation. Some of you may recall that Benjamin Rush, who is the father of American psychiatry, once held the position that masturbation was related to insanity.

Incidentally, Albert Ellis should not be confused with another well-known sexologist, Havelock Ellis, a British physician who that came before Albert Ellis.

Question 151. The Oedipus complex is to males as the __________ complex is to females. All right, another simple analogy question.

Answer. Freud suggested that a man who wants to marry his mother and kill his father is a victim of the Oedipus complex. In females, Freud believed that the girl wants to marry her father and hurt her mother.

This is what we call the Electra complex, which is the answer to the question. Hence, the blank would be filled in with Electra. According to Freud, the Electra complex is resolved when the child identifies with the parent of the same sex and realizes that the child can't have the parent of the opposite sex. It's been said that the Oedipus/Electra complexes constitute the most controversial part of Freud's theory.

You can remember that the Oedipus complex occurs in the phallic stage of Freud's theory because they both have a P . . . good memory device. Supposedly, the complex is resolved in the latency stage.

Question 152. What type of therapy parallels the scientific research approach?

Answer. Behavior therapy. Now, I've seen variations of this question on a lot of advanced exams. This is likely because proponents of behavior therapy, and even applied behavior analysis, quip that treatment is somewhat analogous to conducting an experiment or research on a single client.

Question 153. A child sees another child receive a reward for a behavior and now begins acting the same way as the other child. What theory is operating here?

Answer. Albert Bandura's social learning theory, also called cognitive symbolic mediational process. The child is not reinforced directly; it's just symbolic.

This is sometimes called vicarious learning, or, more recently, observational learning. (Wouldn't it be wonderful if exams only used a single term to describe each key concept? My answer. You bet, but it's merely wishful thinking and seemingly as time goes by more and more terms can apply to the same principle.)

Surprising exam booster: I have seen study guides and YouTube programs claim B.F. Skinner is the primary pioneer of this concept. Not true! The principle can be traced back to Albert Bandura. Bandura's 1961 Bobo doll experiment is often cited as the quintessential example of this style of learning. Seriously people: be careful when you find free websites and videos not authored by trained counselors in the field.

Question 154. During a counseling session, you notice that a client seems to be rating everyone else's behavior against their own ethnic group. What is the clinical name for this phenomenon?

Answer. We call it ethnocentrism.

Question 155. Name the counseling theory which views games as exchanges of strokes, also known as recognition, that end in a bad feeling for at least one player.

Answer. TA, or transactional analysis, created by Eric Berne. The unpleasant feelings that one feels after a game are called rackets, and they are part of one's life script.

Question 156. True or false? A therapist who hires a client to paint the family home has entered into a dual relationship with the client. Ethical guidelines frown on dual relationships, as they often impair professional judgment and objectivity.

Answer. True.

What if you don't like the paint job? Think about how you're going to react to this client during the next counseling session. It's hardly going to be an objective. Exam reminder: don't be surprised if your exam refers to dual relationships as multiple relationships, or even nonprofessional relationships.

Question 157. True or false. An ethical counselor should screen clients before they enter group therapy.

Answer. True. This does not happen as often as we would like in the real world. But like it or not, according to ethics, you should screen your clients.

Question 158. According to Freud, dreams are ______.

Answer. According to Freud, dreams are wish fulfillments. Freud called dreams the royal road to the unconscious mind. Most analysts feel that his 1899 work entitled *The Interpretation of Dreams* was his most important work. Analysts often call it the bible of psychoanalysis.

An analysis of psychoanalytic questions and your exam: Freud's theory has had a huge impact on our field over the years. That said, on an actual comprehensive exam there might be only two or three questions pertaining to his analytic concepts. Truth be told, there might *not* be any!!!! This could be said of *any* of the theories, theorists, or concepts covered in all the areas on your exam. This is a great example of my contention that **most of what you study won't be on the exam. Everybody who does well on**

their exam studies a lot of extra stuff. Sorry, but that's the cold hard truth. A lot depends on who is writing the exam questions and which version of the exam you are taking. Also keep in mind that with the exception of the CECE, most counseling exams have pilot or field-tested experimental questions that do not figure into your final score, although you will not be told which questions fall into this category.

Question 159. The terms anima and animus refer to ____ and ____.

Answer. These terms were proposed by the Swiss psychiatrist C.G. Jung, who believed that all people are androgynous. In other words, males have female qualities (blank one, anima) and females have male qualities (blank two, animus).

The anima is the feminine side of the person. You can remember that because it ends in ma like your ma, your mother. Ma is female. The animus, that's the masculine archetype, is easy to remember since mus could stand for muscles such as in males. (Not 100% accurate since any gender can have stellar muscular development, but nevertheless, a valid memory device counselors can use when preparing for exams.)

Question 160. A group of criminals receives reality therapy with choice theory. The criminals are then observed over a five-year period. Is this a cross-sectional study or a longitudinal study?

Answer. This is a longitudinal study because the same subjects are used over a time interval. It is not cross-sectional because cross-sectional uses different subjects in a short period of time.

Question 161. A professional wrestler enters boxing tournaments during weekends. This can be explained by the _______ theory of leisure.

Answer. Let's fill in that blank with the spillover theory, which asserts that you do the same activities (or at least similar activities) outside your work during your leisure time as you do during work.

Question 162. A librarian also works as an NFL cheerleader. What theory of leisure would explain this phenomenon?

Answer. This is what we call the compensatory theory of leisure. It says that you compensate for things you cannot do on the job, so you do them during your leisure time.

Question 163. Which statistic is impacted the most in a distribution with extreme scores? The mean, the median, or the mode?

Answer. The mean is also known as the most useful average since the statistic considers all the scores.

However, if you have a situation where a certain score is extreme, it can have a major impact on the mean. For example, say you took a graduate class in counseling, and there was one multi-millionaire in the class. That would throw off the average class member's salary by a landslide. In a case like this, you would want to use the median as the average instead of the mean.

Question 164. True or false? According to Carl Jung, the shadow archetype represents unconscious drives.

Answer. True. Sometimes, the shadow is called the person's dark side. The shadow is often revealed by the individual's projections, a common defense mechanism. Something you don't like about others is really a part of your own self. Accepting the shadow can lead to self-forgiveness and improved mental health.

Question 165. According to Carl R. Rogers, the structure of the personality is based on the _____ and the ______ constructs.

Answer. Rogers based his theory of personality on the organism and the self. The organism is the way the person really is when this individual is accepted. The self is the person that you become to meet environmental needs.

Question 166. True or false? Lawrence Kohlberg felt that morality is a decision and not a fixed trait.

Answer. True.

Question 167. A 16-year-old client is sent to you for treatment. The client displays a lot of aggression, even toward pets. In addition, this client repeatedly lies and breaks rules. The day before the client came for counseling this individual purportedly smashed a neighbor's fence with an axe. This behavior has been evident in the client for several years. Could this client be diagnosed as having a conduct disorder?

Answer. True. This sounds like a textbook case of a client with a conduct disorder. Although the DSM diagnosis of conduct disorder can occur in adulthood, the diagnosis usually applies to children and peaks in adolescence. Bullies often fall into this category.

Question 168. What theorist postulated that neurotic needs fall into three categories, movement toward people, movement away from people, and movement against people?

Answer. Karen Horney. The movement toward people is seen as the love present in the personality. The movement away from people is seen as the need for independence, and the movement against people is seen as the need for power.

Here's a helpful test hint. The neoanalysts like Karen Horney, Alfred Adler, and Erik Erikson felt that Freud minimized social features and factors in the environment. He was too obsessed about what went on in the mind and not the environment.

The neoanalysts, also called ego psychologists, are more worried about the ego, whereas Freud stressed the importance of the id rather than the ego.

Question 169. You are seeing a client who has never worked outside the home. This person is taking care of seven children and just went through a divorce. You will be counseling this person to help them snare a job. What would the literature refer to this type of client as?

Answer. Well, there is an excellent chance that the literature would call this client a displaced homemaker.

Question 170. An elementary school child's score lands on the 55th percentile. What does this mean?

Answer. It means that 55% of the examinees scored at or below this level.

Now, what I'm about to say is mega important. Percentile is not the same as percentage. Just because this child scored at the 55th percentile doesn't mean the child scored 55% on the test. The child could have scored 20% on the test or scored 90%. We just don't know.

Question 171. Sam and Bill both take the state counseling test. Sam scored the lowest score ever posted on the test. Ugh, poor guy. Bill scores the highest score ever received on the exam.

What would most likely happen if both counselors took the exam again?

Answer. According to the concept of regression toward the mean, Sam, who made the lowest score ever, will likely discover his score is probably going to go up if he takes it again. On the other hand, Bill, who made the highest score ever, will most likely see his score plummet.

Extreme scores move toward the mean when they are compared to initial scores on a measure. Now, will Sam beat Bill if he takes the exam again? Probably no chance, even according to this theory.

Question 172. What career theorist based career intervention strategies on a psychological need's theory with six occupational orientations or relationship patterns between the individual and their job?

Answer. John Holland, of course. Here are the six personality and work environment types.

Number one, the realistic, where the person likes to deal with concrete things like farming, factory work, or bookkeeping.

Number two, the investigative, where you use your intelligence, such as an astronomer, but you avoid interpersonal relationships.

Number three, the artistic, where you dislike structure, but you enjoy expressing yourself. Nonconformist jobs such as acting or music really cater to the artistic personality.

Then we have number four, the social. This is the person who likes jobs dealing with others such as teachers, counselors, therapists, personnel workers.

Number five, the enterprising. This person likes to dominate, like the mayor of a city, an accounts representative who sells to others, or a business owner.

Number six, the conventional. The person who likes rules and regulations. Clerical workers are often cited as falling into this category. Holland does believe in stereotypes and that they can influence career choice.

Remember, the Strong is based on Holland's work, as is the SDS or Self-Directed Search. A good memory device to recall the categories – not recommended in most textbooks – is AS RICE. Remember AS RICE, and that will give you the first letter of the six categories.

Question 173. Name the book that most scholars would say was the most influential in the entire history of counseling.

Answer. Carl R. Rogers's 1942 classic, *Counseling and Psychotherapy*, which went against the trait factor model and the psychoanalytic and directive models that were emphasized by Williamson and Parsons.

During the post–World War II years, Rogers gained popularity. By the 1950s, counseling replaced testing as the key strategy for guidance workers. For the record, Glasser's 1965 text *Reality Therapy* is considered the second most influential work, with Rogers taking the number three spot with his 1961 classic, *On Becoming a Person*.

In 1993 counselors picked Rogers as the most influential theorist. He got three times as many votes as Ellis, Glasser, and Minuchin, who all tied for second place. Freud, by the way, snared the third place slot by himself.

Question 174. What was the role of Jesse B. Davis in the history of the guidance movement?

Answer. Jesse B. Davis was a Michigan high school principal. Davis is cited as the first person to systematize guidance in the school system in 1907 and give vocational guidance to young people who were entering into the industrial age. Today Davis is considered the first school counselor in the United States.

Davis utilized a high school English comp course and taught vocational and moral guidance one session per week. Here's a small hint for you. Frank Parsons, although he was the father of guidance, did not work in the school system.

Question 175. True or false? Prior to the 1930s, the word counseling was rarely used.

Answer. True. Prior to 1931, you'll probably find the word guidance in the literature, which referred to advice related to educational, job, or vocational areas. Earlier in 1908, guidance was institutionalized by Frank Parsons, who set up the Vocational Bureau in the Civil Service House in Boston.

Question 176. A psychiatrist refers a couple to you and suggests that you use the behavioral process of sensate focus, developed by sex therapists William Masters and Virginia Johnson, to help the couple deal with their sexual anxiety. Briefly explain this strategy.

Answer. You will instruct the couple to avoid intercourse initially, but you will encourage non-erotic touching. As the couple becomes more comfortable and less anxious, you will slowly introduce more sex play until intercourse is achieved. This progressive model of intervention is very well known in the field of counseling.

Question 177. Although there is no such thing as the perfect group member, the success of a counseling group in terms of achieving its goals depends on the composition of the group. What strategy helps ensure an acceptable mixture of people?

Answer. A pre-group screening interview. You try to find people who can trust others. The ability to trust is the most important factor. You want members who will not be overwhelmed by anxiety since that seems to be the number one reason people drop out of groups rapidly.

Question178. True or false? An accurate statement might be that most of the research shows that group therapy is effective, but we are not 100% sure why.

Answer. True. I guess it's the old adage that says that science is what works. We're not sure why groups can be so helpful, though experts like Irvin Yalom have come up with a dozen plausible factors.

Question 179. What is the most outstanding aspect of Donald Super's lifespan developmental approach to career theory?

Answer. According to most experts, it would be his life stages. There are five of them, and somebody who purchased my materials said Super has five letters, and there are five life stages, and that makes a good memory device. Hmm, agree! Here are the life stages.

Number one, growth, from birth to age 14. Two, exploration, from 14 to 25 years. Three, establishment, ages 25 to 45. Four, maintenance, 45 to 65 years old, and the fifth stage, decline, age 65 and beyond.

Again, Super emphasized that you choose a job that is consistent with your self-concept. A memory device you might use here to remember the stages is: GEEMD; since you have two Es, it would make sense that exploration would come before establishment.

Test hint. Super's model is often dubbed the CDAC model, which literally means career, development, assessment, and counseling model.

Question 180. During a confidential counseling session, a woman seriously threatens to shoot her husband. According to the Tarasoff decision, what step should you as the counselor take?

Answer. You should breach confidentiality and inform the husband about this imminent danger. Anyone else who might be in danger should also be informed.

Question 181. An educational psychologist feels computerized teaching machines will raise students' scores on the new history exam. A true experiment is set up. Identify the IV and the DV. The results will be plotted on a chart to show the schoolboard. Which variable, the IV or the DV, will be plotted on the ordinate?

Answer. OK. I know. That's a long question, but a lot of comprehensive exams include these monsters. Believe me, I hear this complaint very often after counselors finish their exams. Here goes, the IV, the experimental variable, is going to be your computerized teaching machine. The DV will be your data, your measurement; thus this is going to be the score on the new history exam.

Will the IV or the DV be plotted on the ordinate? When we plot experiments on a graph, we have what is called the x-axis and the y-axis.

The x-axis is horizontal. It goes from left to right. The y-axis goes up and down. Here is a nice little memory device based on a mental image. The letter Y goes up and down, so this axis is vertical. Now, the x-axis is called the abscissa. The abscissa plots the IV. Ready for your final answer. The ordinate, a.k.a., the y-axis that goes up and down – yes, it's vertical – plots the DV.

You're probably going to need to read this answer once again. So why not do it right now?

Question 182. You are the clinical director for a large metropolitan counseling agency. The executive director, who is your supervisor, states that the board of directors wants the agency to utilize more standardized tests. What online resource could you secure that would give you a review of nearly all the available standardized tests?

Answer. Just like the last question, on long questions, forget all the fluff, all the irrelevant stuff. The fact that the agency is metropolitan rather than rural, and the fact that you are the clinical director rather than a program coordinator, has about as much to do with answering the question as the price of tea in Columbia, Missouri.

The issue is, what website provides (or can link you) to a comprehensive review of most standardized tests? The answer is the Buros Center for Testing, named after Oscar K. Buros, who authored the now-famous *Mental Measurement Yearbook* first published in 1938. Check out the answer for yourself at https://boros.org.

Question 183. True or false. You have NCC status. Your first cousin needs to be supervised to secure NBCC's NCC credential. It is perfectly ethical to supervise this relative.

Answer. This is the kind of question and answer that you can figure out simply by reading the NBCC's Code of Ethics. In the first section "NCC take appropriate action to prevent harm," the final sentence in directive #14 reads, "Supervisors shall not supervise relatives." It doesn't get much more direct than that folk! Answer: False.

Question 184. A power test has no real-time limit, while a speed test, for example, a keyboarding test, is _______ and assesses accuracy.

Answer. Timed.

Question 185. What type of therapy states that healthy communication and transactions between individuals will not be crossed?

Answer. Eric Berne's TA or transactional analysis.

Remember for test purposes that TA is associated with the so-called Karpman's Drama Triangle, which suggests a person who engages in dysfunctional TA games will go from a victim to a persecutor to a rescuer role. Exam reminder. TA is often combined with Gestalt therapy.

Question 186. During a group counseling session, the therapist says, "Mary laughs every time Jennifer talks." Is this a product statement or a process statement?

Answer. This is a process statement. A process statement illuminates the dynamics or exchange between two people. It focuses on what's going on between two people or more than two people in the group.

A product statement focuses on content, so behavioral groups would probably be more interested or more slanted toward content. Psychoanalytic groups mainly focus on content. Transactional analysis groups, obviously, are very process oriented.

Question 187. Some group counselors believe that a group has four stages. One, orientation. Two, transition. Three, the action or working stage. Four, the completion stage. In what stage would the most conflict between group members and rebellion probably take place?

Answer. Please expect to see a question like this on the test. Honestly, I would be surprised if you didn't. That's why I have quite a bit of repetition on this concept. The answer is the transition stage. There would not only be conflict between the group members but also struggling for power in terms of whether the therapist takes over as a leader. This stage is billed as "storming" on some exams.

Question 188. True or false? You receive your NCC designation. Several weeks later, you're giving a standardized test to a client. There is a penalty for guessing. Should you convey this information to the client before the exam begins?

Answer. Absolutely true. According to ethics, you should share with the client the conditions which produce the most favorable test results. These conditions must be known to the client.

Question 189. What would an older adult client need to accomplish to reach Erik Erikson's final eighth stage, integrity versus despair, in which the individual must accept life's finality and the feeling that one has led in meaningful and productive life?

Answer. Erikson's stages follow the epigenetic model, a term he borrowed from biology and embryology that assumes that growth has an orderly sequence from birth to death. Each stage must be resolved to move the person on to the next stage.

Therefore, for the person to reach the final stage, this individual must have resolved all the crises presented in previous stages.

Question 190. A client who is alcoholic and abuses cocaine calls your counseling practice for assistance. This client wishes to use insurance to pay for counseling. Is this a realistic possibility? If so, why?

Answer. First, let me state forthrightly that more alcoholics should be coming in for counseling. Expert David L. Ohlms suggests that only 1 in 36 alcoholics receives treatment and gets well.

Back to the real question. The insurance company will pay for counseling because alcoholism and drug abuse are classified as disorders or diseases, and thus, insurance companies should pay for this service.

Clients with substance use disorders are often referred to support groups without a fee and therefore there is no charge to the client or the insurance company such as AA, Alcoholics Anonymous; CA, Cocaine Anonymous; or OA, Overeaters Anonymous, to name a few. These groups really supplement the counseling process. These self-help groups are also dubbed mutual aid, 12-step, or support groups.

In a self-help group a professional therapist does not necessarily lead the group since the leader is a peer. In fact, the group is made up of all people who have the same type of problem, and some self-help groups have a rule against using professional therapists as leaders.

Question 191. In a new study, you have a control group, a group that receives motivational interviewing, another group which receives narrative therapy, and a group that receives TM, or transcendental meditation. At the end of the experiment, you will give all the subjects the Beck Depression Inventory (BDI). Groups are randomly assigned.

You suspect, however, that IQ is an extraneous variable that correlates with depression, the DV. The population is normal.

What statistical technique could you use to control the extraneous variable?

Answer. Since the study has extraneous variables or what we call a covariance, you could use the analysis of covariance or ANCOVA. Some sources describe it as a blend of the ANOVA and regression.

Question 192. Define internal and external validity as these factors relate to experimentation.

Answer. Internal validity refers to whether the experimental treatment (the IV) caused the effects. External validity answers the question: Can the experimental results or research be generalized to other individuals or circumstances?

It is almost a sure bet that you will see a question on these concepts on your exam. Must know hint: an experiment must have good internal validity to have good external validity, although having good internal validity will not guarantee this.

Question 193. Name the therapist who created multimodal therapy and the acronym BASIC ID.

Answer. Arnold Lazarus, and this is a holistic approach. BASIC ID means behavior, affective responses, sensations, imagery, cognitions, interpersonal relations, and drugs.

Lazarus was very creative and individualistic in his approach to therapy. At one time, he worked very closely with psychiatrist Joseph Wolpe, who created systematic desensitization.

Exams often classify multimodal therapy, although it is behavioristic and holistic as a therapy, that encourages technical eclecticism.

Hey, come on. The exam studying process wouldn't be any fun without a few big terms, like technical eclecticism. The term means that you scientifically, not haphazardly, introduce techniques from different models.

Question 194. What therapist wrote *Schools Without Failure*, believes in choice theory, and speaks of the three Rs of therapy: **r**ealism, **r**ight and wrong, and **r**esponsibility?

Answer. Psychiatrist William Glasser, the father of reality therapy. Interestingly, reality therapy is sometimes classified as a type of behavior therapy, although Glasser rejects operant and classical conditioning because he feels change comes from within, not from the environment. Several important principles about reality therapy. Number one, you don't give up on your clients. Number two, you never use punishment. Number three, when you do talk about the past, you talk about successes and not failures.

This type of therapy does not concentrate on childhood issues very heavily since this is not seen as something that's pertinent. Robert Wubbolding is another big name in reality therapy.

Question 195. Explain the Premack principle.

Answer. Simple enough. David Premack says that the choice of a positive reinforcer is what your client likes to do. Eating a candy bar, for example, is not a positive reinforcer for somebody who dislikes candy bars; however, if your client is fond of candy bars, it could be an excellent choice.

In any event, the Premack principle says that you can reinforce a lower probability behavior, or LPB, with a higher probability behavior, or HPB. For example, if you read a section of a counseling code of ethics, probably an LPB for many of us, then you can go watch your favorite TV show or slam down your favorite candy bar, an HPB. This scenario would be a perfect example of the Premack principle.

Question 196. A counselor runs a psychoeducational group for 11-year-olds with the hope that this group will curb teen pregnancy. Is this group A, a primary group; B, a secondary group; C, a tertiary group; or D, a self-help group.

Answer. Choice A, this is a primary group. Why? Well, primary groups work with a normal population in trying to ward off a problem before it occurs. That's easy enough to remember since primary starts with a P, and so does preventive.

With a secondary group, there is some stress involved but not necessarily any major problem.

With a tertiary group, the problem is usually longstanding, such as a group for hospital schizophrenics. A severe problem is evident when somebody joins a tertiary group.

Question 197. Here's a true or false question. Two major risks of group work are breach of confidentiality and ganging up on a group member.

Answer. True.

The act of ganging up on a group member is a dynamic known as scapegoating. The person they gang up on, logically enough, is labeled the scapegoat.

Super test hint regarding group counseling. Ethics stipulate that you should emphasize to group members the importance of confidentiality; however, you should inform the group that you cannot guarantee that members will keep everything confidential. You cannot control everybody's behavior.

Question 198. Nonparametric tests have lower statistical power than parametric tests, or, in simple everyday English, they are not as sensitive in terms of detecting differences between groups. What nonparametric test can be used to determine whether an obtained distribution is significantly different than an expected or theoretical distribution?

Answer. An example of a nonparametric test is the chi-square test, or chi-square test of association of categorical variables. For example, the chi-square test can be used to determine if there is an association between gender and education. If the chi-square indicates a significant difference between expected and observed data, then indeed an association between gender and education exists.

A chi-square test can determine if there is a difference between the expected frequencies and the observed frequencies of groups. The IV and DV are both categorical variables (measured at the nominal or ordinal level).

Question 199. A researcher rates the effectiveness of female middle school counselors. He tends to rate those whom he finds physically attractive as the best counselors regardless of their intervention styles. What is this called?

Answer. Many experts would rightly call it sexist, but strictly speaking, it's known in the literature as the halo effect. The halo effect results when you are rating an individual on one characteristic, but you're really influenced by another characteristic, such as attractiveness, that you should not be rating at all.

We're finally up to question 200, and you, my dear reader, have already learned a ton of information. Don't look so surprised. I told you in the beginning, I was going to make you feel so superior to your exam that you wouldn't believe it.

Question 200. A *t*-test is a parametric test that can be used to test a hypothesis about the means of two samples when the sample distributions are normal. If the test reveals that the two samples are different at a statistically significant level, will you accept or reject the null hypothesis?

Answer. Null means no difference. In this question, nevertheless, I have just told you that there is a difference. In this case, you will reject null and accept the alternative, or what we often call the experimental hypothesis. Listen closely, if your distribution was not normal, then you would need to run a nonparametric test instead of a *t*-test. You could use the Mann Whitney U test if you have two uncorrelated or unmatched means, instead of a *t*-test, used for uncorrelated, independent, or unmatched means. If the two groups are correlated, you could use the Wilcoxon. Basically, my point is that researchers have nonparametric tests that parallel the parametric measures.

Question 201. One of the most popular vocational interest inventories for career assessment is the Strong Interest Inventory, or SII. It was originally created by Edward K. Strong in 1927. It consists of 291 items and takes approximately 30 to 45 minutes to complete, although it's not a timed test. It must be computer scored. It can be given to anybody who can comprehend the test. Usually, this would be somebody 14 and over who can read at the eighth-grade level. What does the Strong tell us about the person?

Answer. The Strong does not tell us how successful a person will be in an occupation, but it does predict whether the person will remain in a particular occupation. After all, the Strong score expresses how much an individual resembles others who are in the field.

Although the correlation between the Strong score and self-related job satisfaction may not be all that high, people who score high in a specific interest area still like their jobs better on the whole than those who score points toward a different occupation. Career counseling test hint. The Strong is based on the work of John Holland's RIASEC work personality theory.

Overall, the Strong is useful for career education, and yes, even leisure planning.

Question 202. Define a dual-career family and describe whether a dual-career family has more leisure time or less leisure time.

Answer. The dual-career family is a family in which both partners work and they're both committed to their careers.

In dual-career families, the tendency is to wait a little longer to have children. In other words, in single-career families where perhaps just the male works, very often the mother will have children at an early age. In the dual-career family, usually the couple waits until the wife is established in her career.

To answer the question directly, dual-career families have less leisure time than the average family.

Question 203. According to the ethics developed by NBCC for NCCs, if there is a discrepancy between the counselor's job and the client's needs, the counselor must rectify the situation by A, referring the client to another professional agency, or B, terminating their affiliation with the agency.

Answer. Well, strictly speaking, it is not A or B. The answer is true for both. NBCC ethics stipulate your primary responsibility is to your client, regardless of what your well-meaning supervisor tells you.

A helpful exam hint. According to NBCC, private practitioners must adhere to the same ethical guidelines as counselors working for not-for-profit agencies.

Question 204. In 1900, the average life span was 49 years. Today it is 77.8. Gerontological counseling is the process of counseling older adults and is a growing specialty. Agree or disagree with this statement. Most older adults who need counseling are mature enough to seek out this assistance.

Answer. Unfortunately, disagree. This is false. Only a small portion of older adults seek out counseling services.

Question 205. You have just completed a journal article which you feel is so powerful that it will change the entire field of counseling and psychotherapy. In essence, it is so important, it must be published at any cost. You adhere to the literary principle of multiple submissions, and you send the manuscript to nine different professional journals simultaneously. Is your behavior ethical?

Answer. You may feel it's the humane thing to do, and that your article is the greatest article since sliced bread and your theory is better than Ellis's, Maltby's, Beck's, De Shazer's, Rogers's, or anybody else.

However, according to NBCC ethics and ACA guidelines, your behavior is *unethical*. You should never submit an article to a second journal until the first rejects you. Also, if your paper has joint authorship, you must give the other person or persons – and, yes, students – credit and acknowledgment.

Now, just to clarify this again, multiple submissions means that you are sending the same manuscript out to several journals at one time. Although this is ethical in other fields of writing, like, say, magazine articles or books, it is not ethical in terms of scientific journal writing.

Question 206. The so-called sociometric approach of appraisal often relies on a sociogram. Define and describe the sociogram.

Answer. The sociogram, created by Jacob Moreno, is used very often in conjunction with group counseling and psychotherapy.

It's a graphic display or picture, if you will, so you can see at a glance, who the leaders and followers of the group are, as well as who is isolated or a member of a subgroup.

Experts tell us that the sociogram, which really charts person-to-person relationships, is most valuable for elementary school children and older adults, as they openly express differences as well as dislikes and likes, a little bit better than other groups.

Question 207. Who is Arthur Jensen, and what is the BITCH test?

Answer. Arthur Jensen is a must-know name. In 1969, Jensen reported in the prestigious *Harvard Educational Review* that

Black students scored 10 to 15 points lower on standardized IQ tests than white students.

The BITCH test, and no, I'm not cursing at you, stands for Black Intelligence Test for Cultural Homogeneity. It was created by the African American psychologist Dr. Robert Williams.

The BITCH test attempted to show that IQ tests were culturally biased. The BITCH was basically written in Black English, and white children really struggled with the test.

Question 208. Briefly describe how humanistic psychology differs from classical psychoanalysis and behavior therapy.

Answer. Humanistic psychology does not view people as an organism driven by instincts and drives, such as in psychoanalysis, or simply an animal shaped by stimulus response, such as behaviorism.

Instead, humanists feel that an individual can make choices to master the challenges of living. The emphasis is on potential and self-actualization, not merely eliminating mental health and emotional difficulties.

Question 209. Which model of decision-making asserts that "Information is the fuel of the decision maker"? And the types of information required will depend on which of three systems is operating. Name the systems?

Answer. The Gelatt decision model was proposed by the late H.B. Gelatt, a well-known teacher, school counselor, and director of guidance for the Palo Alto school system.

The three systems are the predictive system, which deals with information outcomes and alternative actions. Two, the valuing system, which has to do with information about the individual's preferences. Three, the decision system, which considers the person's wishes and priorities.

When using this theory and working with a client, we would say that you're using a decision approach to lifestyle that has its roots in probability and in economics rather than trait factor theory or matching.

Question 210. You are running an experiment with a pretest and a posttest. You are worried that the pretest may affect your results. What research paradigm could help eliminate this problem?

Answer. The Solomon four group design. Here's how it works. You have two experimental groups and two control groups. One control group gets the pretest, and the other doesn't. One experimental group gets the pretest, and the other doesn't. That way you can ferret out the effects of the pretest and determine whether the pretest had anything to do with the results.

Question 211. A client vehemently campaigns against pornography because this individual unconsciously wishes to view the material. What defense mechanism is in action here?

Answer. There are two correct answers, but I want you to have mega-confidence, so give yourself credit if you came up with either answer.

Sublimation is one answer. It occurs when you take an unacceptable urge and you put it across in a socially acceptable manner (e.g., a campaign against pornography). The other correct answer could be reaction formation. Shakespeare's quote in *Hamlet*, "the lady doth protest too much," certainly rings true here. That's the essence of reaction formation.

Somebody is trying to cover up an opposite impulse. In other words, the person's true feelings are the opposite of what they are showing the world.

Question 212. A graduate counseling student has just learned the technique of paraphrasing and reflection. To be certain this helper in training does not use the techniques inappropriately, they keep repeating verbatim the client's statements. What is this called?

Answer. We have a name for it; we call it parroting. Parroting is not a good thing to do because a lot of times the client will respond with something like, "Gee, I just said that." Research tends to indicate that parroting can make some clients frustrated and angry.

Question 213. Which scale of measurement suggested by psychologist Stanley Smith Stevens, the nominal, the ordinal, the interval, or the ratio, best describes the numbering of baseball players' uniforms?

Answer. The nominal scale is often called the weakest scale of measurement since it provides you with the least information.

Performing arithmetic using nominal data is useless since the data are qualitative. Measurement scale questions of this ilk are common on social service and mental health exams.

Question 214. You were a consultant doing program-centered consultation with a donut shop. They have a problem with employees secretly eating lots of donuts. Thus, they must hire only honest employees who will not eat the donuts. Could you legitimately recommend a polygraph test?

Answer. You could not. A polygraph is a lie detector test. In 1988, the government passed legislation saying that most private firms could not use polygraphs for screening. The only exceptions are for drug companies, private security companies, and those people dealing with public health and national safety. I don't think that the person's sneaking a donut is threatening our national safety.

Incidentally, some studies have shown that the polygraph method is not very effective. In fact, it's a very poor predictor of job success and honesty.

Question 215. Albert Bandura, who pioneered social learning theory, discovered that when a child sees an adult performing antisocial behavior in a movie or a film, the child may repeat the behavior. What is the name of this process?

Answer. The name of the process is modeling, and it's a form of imitation. Therefore TV, movies, videos, and even video games can lead to violent behavior in children.

Question 216. In Schein's process consultation, which is also known as organizational development, the counselor works as a consultant to improve communication between employees, administration, and so on. True or false? When using this model, the counselor is not usually an expert in the field they are consulting for.

Answer. True. For example, the counselor who is consulting a firm that builds aircraft doesn't necessarily need to have great knowledge about building planes. However, the consultant does need a lot of knowledge about human interaction and counseling theory.

Question 217. You work for a counseling practice. You will be out of the country for one year. Can you ethically use your name in a private practice telephone book or Internet ad?

Answer. Ethically, you cannot. Maybe your colleagues think that using your name is going to bring in a lot of business, but ethically you should not do it. The only exception would be that your name could be listed *if and only if* you stipulate that you are not doing counseling or therapy at the present time.

Question 218. True or false? When conducting person-centered therapy, the client assumes the responsibility for the direction of the therapy.

Answer. True. This explains why the Rogerian model was once called nondirective therapy.

Question 219. Which therapy, REBT, or Gestalt, recognizes nonverbal behavior as the primary factor in treatment?

Answer. Gestalt.

Question 220. True or false? When you go to the DSM and find a diagnosis that fits your client, the DSM will offer a treatment program.

Answer. False.

Question 221. True or false? Career counselors must help clients to make a good first impression when they go to a job interview since career decisions in interviews are often made in the first few minutes of the interview.

Answer. You betcha. This is true whether you like it or not.

Research shows that the person conducting the interview often comes to a decision about the person applying for the job in the first four or five minutes. In other words, first impressions are very important.

Also, unfavorable information has more impact when the personnel officer hears it than positive information about the candidate. It's been shown that personnel officers look for negative information or try to verify it.

Question 222. What is the significance of PL 94–142 passed in the 1970s?

Answer. It relates to special education. It says that all handicapped children (an early phrase for children with a disability) have a right to free appropriate public education in the least restrictive environment. This includes ages 3 to 21. Least restrictive environment means an environment that closely resembles a regular school program.

Question 223. Does the DSM-5-TR rely on a multi-axial system?

Answer. It does not.

Question 224. What theorists argue that <u>all</u> aggressive acts are caused by frustration, and what famous therapist has criticized this notion?

Answer. John Dollard and Neal Miller believed that all aggressive acts are caused by frustration. Albert Ellis, on the other hand, the father of rational emotive behavior therapy, felt this principle was downright incorrect and that it is not frustration but rather the client's own internal verbalizations – often dubbed self-talk – and cognitions, irrational ideas, if you will, that cause the problem.

In fact, Ellis felt the Dollard Miller hypothesis, which has been stressed by psychologists, has caused problems for clients and that they don't need to believe it.

Question 225. True or false? A researcher who performs correlational research has conducted a true experiment.

Answer. False. Correlational research is not a true experiment. Since the experimenter has not used randomization and the experiment does not manipulate and control all the variables, it could not be considered a true experiment.

Question 226. A correlation of 0.00 indicates what type of relationship between variables X and Y?

Answer. It signifies that there is *no systematic relationship* and that the change of variable X has almost nothing to do with variable Y.

Correlations that are either –1 or +1 are perfect correlations and they are very rare in the social sciences, although you will find them when you look at physical measurements (for example, weight in pounds and weight in ounces). Some books logically describe it in this manner: In a perfect correlation you can predict one variable if you know the other.

Question 227. Buros's Center's *Mental Measurement Yearbook* and its companion *Tests in Print* contain valuable information on standardized tests. Name another recommended source of test data.

Answer. I'll give you a bonus. I'll give you three of them. You can go to professional journals; textbooks on measurements would be another one, and number three, test materials such as a test manual or specimen set for a given test.

Question 228. You are a program consultant for a firm that manufactures plastic eating utensils. The mean rating for workers on their yearly assessment is 50. A score of 100 would be perfect. You note that a certain supervisor who has rated 206 employees had a range of ratings from 56 to 64.

As a consultant, you will explain to the consultee that this supervisor is a victim of _____ bias. What type of bias is really being illuminated by this question?

Answer. All right, this is a tough one. Fill in the blank with central tendency rater bias.

If you look at the range, it's only eight points. The average is 50. Here's this guy who's rated everybody, all 206 employees, between 46 and 54. The central tendency bias asserts that the rater stays near the middle of the rating scale. If you ever had a teacher boast, "I give almost everybody a C," now, LOL, you can label that teacher's rating bias.

Question 229. During a case conference, a behavior therapist mentioned successfully treating a 41-year-old client with a fear of elevators using systematic desensitization. Unfortunately, two days later, the client developed a facial tic. How would a psychoanalyst present this at a conference to explain the phenomenon?

Answer. The psychoanalyst would most likely say that the facial tic occurred because of what the analysts refer to as *symptom* *substitution*. In psychoanalysis, the analyst has the belief that the unconscious is causing the problem.

Thus, if you cure the elevator phobia using systematic desensitization, you'll just get another symptom, say a facial tic, because you have not really dealt with the unconscious conflict. Of course, the behaviorists do not believe in symptom substitution.

Question 230. A colleague has practiced transactional analysis group therapy for over nine years. What type of therapy would this practitioner most likely combine with TA?

Answer. Gestalt. This is a very common combination. Some say it's a good combination because Gestalt is very nonverbal oriented and TA is very cognitive oriented. Hence, the two modalities complement each other.

The argument against the combination: Despite the popularity years ago of this dynamic duo of treatment, many counselors say it is akin to mixing water and oil and because they're so different, they don't really mix.

Question 231. You are teaching a counselor education class in which the students are graded on videos of their counseling sessions during the semester. Jenna receives an F for the first five sessions, a grade of D for the next five sessions, and an A for her last two sessions. You give Jenna an A for the course. What type of rater bias is operating in this instance?

Answer. This is what we call the recency effect. The rater is swayed by the recent behavior of the person but has ignored the other ten sessions of Jenna's performance. A rater who is not biased looks at the entire rating period.

Question 232. 500 college students take two different versions of a personality test. Both forms of the test yield almost identical scores. In fact, the correlation between the two sets of scores is 0.93. What term best explains this concept?

Answer. It's what is known as high parallel forms, test reliability, or high alternate form reliability. Just for the record, most comprehensive counseling exams have parallel forms so if you take the test again all the questions would NOT be identical.

Question 233. You are in blatant violation of ACA ethics. This necessarily implies that you are also in violation of a state law. True or false?

Answer. False. Try this one on for size. Say I decided to run a therapy group and I don't screen the members. That's probably unethical, but I'll tell you. You're going to have one heck of a time if you call 911 and try to get me carted off to jail for this. Laws are usually neutral or supportive of ethics, but they're not always identical.

Key exception exam hint. Ethics written via the state rather than organizations are generally laws. If your test includes a state exam, then the ethics set forth by your state could indeed be laws. Finally, many states use ACA ethics as state ethics, and therefore in these states a violation of such ethics would constitute breaking the law.

Question 234. A group counseling class takes their final exam. The lowest score on the exam is 100. The highest score is 150, and the mean 125. Compute the range.

Answer. When you get a question like this, throw out the irrelevant data. The mean is totally irrelevant, so pitch it. You don't need it. All you need to know is the two extreme scores. You take 100, the lowest score, and you subtract it from 150, the highest score. That gives you 50, which is your answer.

Remember, the range is a measurement of variability or dispersion. Dispersion means the spread of scores. Of course, it has limited usage because it's only based on the two most extreme scores.

Advanced exam hint. Some tests will define the range in precisely the manner I computed as the exclusive range. However, once in a blue moon an exam will ask you what the inclusive range is. To get this figure you merely add one to your answer. In this case, the answer would be 51. Truthfully, I doubt whether you'll have to deal with that on most comprehensive counseling exams.

Uplifting exam thought. Most counseling exams have few if any computation questions. If a computational question appears, it should be like this question where the math is extremely simple.

Question 235. A distribution of scores includes the numbers 1, 2, 3, 4, and 5. What is the median?

Answer. The median is three because there are two scores below three, 1 and 2, and two scores above three, 4 and 5.

Question 236. A distribution of scores includes the values 1, 2 3, 4, 5, and 6. What is the median?

Answer. When the number of scores is even rather than odd as in the previous question, you take the two middle scores and average them.

For example, the two middle scores in this question would be 3 and 4. You add them together, and you get 7 and now divide by 2. That gives you a median of 3.5. If your last stat course was in the 80s or 90s, I'd probably read this answer a couple of times if I were you.

The median is either a score or a hypothetical score that cuts the distribution in half. Just like the median of a highway cuts a highway in half.

Question 237. Provide a simple definition of neuroplasticity.

Answer. This popular neurocounseling term relates to the fact that the brain can change, adapt, or mold itself throughout life based on life experiences. Therefore, counseling and therapy can truly have a physical impact on the brain of the client . . . and, yes, on the counselor!

Question 238. True or false. When a client is very depressed, an ethical counselor will forthrightly ask if the client is suicidal.

Answer. Absolutely true. Ask the client if they are suicidal. This is not going to put the idea in the client's head. In fact, it will give the client a chance to discuss this critical issue. If you're personally interested in suicide prevention, or you have clients who are suicidal and might benefit from bibliotherapy, I highly recommend an oldie but goodie book that I wrote, *Not with My Life I Don't, Preventing Your Suicide and That of Others*. The text is suitable for clients in the 8th grade through adulthood.

Question 239. An 11-year-old boy suffers from enuresis, also known as bedwetting. You decide to use reality therapy as an approach.

What would be the first step you would take in terms of treating this young man?

Answer. Surprisingly, the problem is irrelevant because step number one in reality therapy is always the same. You create a supportive, accepting relationship with the client, and you want to become the client's friend.

Other steps in reality therapy are step two, focus on current or present behavior; step three, allow the client to evaluate their behavior; step four, help the client develop a plan of action; step five, get a commitment to carry out the plan; step six, refuse to accept excuses; step seven, refuse to use punishment; and step eight, refuse to give up. Don't assume that the client is hopeless or cannot change.

Question 240. You are running a group in which the group must make an urgent decision. Which leadership style would be the best for you to use? The autocratic style, the democratic, or the laissez-faire?

Answer. First let me define laissez-faire since you need to know the terminology to answer the question. It means hands off. You let the group run itself. With this approach there is minimal interaction between the group and the leader. When employing the laissez-faire style, the group, rather than the leader, is making group decisions. According to a famous 1939 study by Kurt Lewin, Ronald Lippitt, and Ralph White using ten-year-old boys and their reaction to three different leadership styles (and this experiment has been quoted extensively), the democratic style is the best overall style. For the purposes of this question, however, since a decision must be made in an urgent manner, then the autocratic style, in which the leader dictates decisions, is often superior.

Your exam might refer to this as the "Kurt Lewin Leadership Experiment."

Question 241. True or false? You are running a men's group and a structured exercise is obviously not working. You should keep insisting that the group focus on this exercise for their own good.

Answer. False.

Question 242. True or false? Regarding group work, the working stage will occur after the transition stage but before the final stage, also known as the termination stage, adjournment, or the closure stage.

Answer. A one-word answer will suffice here: true.

Question 243. You are running a closed group composed of shoplifters. After the fifth session, you discover that a client you are seeing for individual therapy has been stealing tennis shoes from department stores. True or false: You would generally allow this client to join the group intended to help shoplifters?

Answer. False, but maybe ***not*** for the reason you thought it was false. The reason is, by definition, closed groups do not allow new members to join after the group is up and running. The first session or two of a closed group would be the only time you would allow new members. After that, you're not going to let anybody in.

A drawback, of course, of the closed group is that everybody can quit and basically, folks, you are left with no group. A plus is that cohesion occurs more rapidly in closed groups than in open groups where they do let people in at any time.

Question 244. A female counselor educator is offered $45,000 a year to take a given job. She then discovers that her friend, Bob, was offered $50,000 for the same job. This is a case of sex wage discrimination. Assuming that the female counselor had been offered the same salary as Bob, one could assume that ________existed. What term would best fill the blank?

Answer. Fill in the blank with the words "pay equity," which is really the converse or opposite of wage discrimination.

Question 245. True or false? Although the popular press seems obsessed with divorce, statistics show that only 12% of all marriages end in divorce. What do you think? Is this accurate?

Answer. Absolutely false. The divorce rate in this country currently hovers right near the 42–50% mark. Married people under the age of 24 generally sport a rate of over 50%.

Exam hint. Second marriages fare even worse than first marriages, with about 60% of all second marriages ending in divorce. The third time is not a charm, with approximately 73% ending in divorce. The good news is overall the divorce rate between 1990 and 2022 has been falling. Also, in case your test should ask, the marriage rate in 2022 was approximately half of what it was in 1990.

Question 246. You are a consultant for an addiction treatment program. The program wishes to cut down on the relapse rate of clients. You should suggest total abstinence for clients who've completed the program.

Answer. True. From what we know, clients who are abstinent in terms of using drugs have a lower relapse rate than those who try to take the drugs on a limited basis. The harm-reduction model views abstinence as desirable but nevertheless not achievable in every client.

Question 247. It is said that the United States is falling behind other nations in terms of science education. In the United States, there's only one ethnic group that has a high percentage of individuals working in science careers. Name this group.

Answer. Asian Americans.

Question 248. You are a middle school counselor. The mother of a student comes to you because she is concerned that the child is getting poor grades. You suggest an IQ test. The mother shakes her head and shows you an IQ test that this child took as an infant and remarks that the score is extremely low.

What could you tell this parent about the relationship of the infant IQ test to the client's current level of intelligence?

Answer. Well, I told you that the child was in middle school, so she's probably in what, seventh or eighth grade? The answer is that infant IQ tests are not good predictors of future IQ scores. Hence, your best bet is to give this child a current IQ test, and you should explain to the mom that giving the IQ test would not be a waste of time.

Question 249. A professor of counselor education has instructed practicum students to give batterers and perpetrators of domestic violence a 240-volt electric shock each time they look at a picture of a perpetrator hitting a partner. The counselor educator will view the procedure to evaluate the students on this aversive conditioning technique.

Based on your knowledge of the famous Milgram studies, what do you think the practicum students will do in this situation?

Answer. In a famous series of experiments by Stanley Milgram, people were asked to shock learners who were strapped to a chair if they gave incorrect answers to questions.

The people were told that they could give the learner electric shocks of more than 435 volts. Now, here's what's amazing: 26 out of 40 subjects gave the learners who answered incorrectly the highest level of shock. Luckily, unbeknownst to the individual giving the shock, the shocks weren't real.

Now it gets even more interesting. In some of the experiments, Milgram gave the people administering the shocks a real 45-volt shock, so they could experience the pain themselves; so much for empathy here.

Just in case you missed the point, the obedience to authority experiments would suggest that since this counselor educator is standing there watching his students – and don't forget this educator is an authority figure – these practicum students would probably shock the daylights out of these batterers and perpetrators.

Incidentally, this experiment has been controversial because even though it's world-famous, in today's world it would be unethical to perform such an experiment.

Question 250. A TA therapist mentions that a client is very creative. According to TA theory, is this client operating out of the parent, adult or child ego state?

Answer. The person would be operating out of the child ego state in what is known as the little professor part of the child ego state. The little professor is creative, manipulative, and intuitive. TA believes that the expression of creativity occurs when the little professor teams up with the adult ego state.

Question 251. What percentage of the US population is African American?

Answer. About 13.6%. Nearly 19% of the population is Hispanic/Latinx. I have included this since many students I have worked with erroneously believe the percentage of African Americans is higher than the Hispanic/Latinx population.

Question 252. Name one advantage of co-leadership when running a group.

Answer. Once again, I'm going to give you a bonus. Here are four advantages of coleadership or co-facilitation in which more than one person shares the leadership duties.

One, when one leader is ill and must miss a group, the other leader can run the group.

Two, discussions between group sessions can help both leaders curb burnout and deal with their own feelings.

Three, if one leader is plagued with countertransference, the other leader can handle the group member who is sparking the countertransference.

Four, it's easier for two leaders to see everything that is going on in a circle.

Question 253. The late great Carl Rogers, unlike many psychoanalytic practitioners, did not believe in differential diagnosis and psychological testing. What did he mean when he used the term congruence?

Answer. Rogers, who called group work the basic encounter, said that congruence is a state of behavior in which the person's experiences are consistent with their self-concept. Congruence is a state of unification, if you will, in which awareness and experience are very closely aligned.

You'll recall that Rogers's person-centered therapy also popularized the notion that to promote change, you must give the client unconditional positive regard, empathy, and congruence.

Quick exam hint. When a counselor is congruent, your exam may refer to this state as genuine.

Question 254. Define the term young old.

Answer. The term young old applies to individuals 65 to 74. Middle old depicts those that are 75 to 84. Oldest old refers to people who are 85 and older.

Currently, those in the oldest old category constitute the fastest-growing segment of the population over 65. In fact, the number of people aged 65 and over has tripled since 1900.

Question 255. Zipping right along. What does the term ceiling mean in psychological testing?

Answer. It has nothing to do with an issue that you might be concerned about if you're going to paint the interior of your house!

In this context, ceiling refers to the highest score or level of ability that a test will measure. A so-called ceiling effect occurs when a test is too easy and many people score too high or make a perfect score on the test.

Question 256. A counselor educator gave the students an essay test for their Human Growth and Development Class. The professor gave Ginger, a student in the class, a C+.

Unfortunately, when midterms grades were due, the professor discovered Ginger's essay was lost. Ginger, however, had saved the paper on her computer drive and therefore was able to turn in an ungraded, unaltered copy. The professor graded the essay and gave it a grade of A. Was this counselor educator plagued by intra-rater reliability or inter-rater reliability?

Answer. Low intra-rater reliability can be evident when the same rater does not agree with themselves when assessing the same phenomenon. Please do not confuse intra-rater reliability with inter-rater reliability, which measures how well different persons assess or score the same phenomenon. So, let us assume another professor in the department graded Ginger's essay and gave it a D. This would be indicative of lackluster inter-rater reliability.

Question 257. Name the theorist associated with intergenerational family therapy.

Answer. Murray Bowen, who popularized the genogram.

Question 258. Name the theorist associated with strategic family therapy.

Answer. I would say that would be Jay Haley, who uses paradox to destroy negative communication patterns that exist in the family.

Haley often used the paradox called restraining in which he, get this, told the family that they should not try to change.

Question 259. Name the major theorist associated with structural family therapy.

Answer. That's Salvador Minuchin, who uses a here-and-now active directive approach. Minuchin is known for his technique of joining in which he blends with a family by using their verbiage and behaviors.

Question 260. Who is the major theorist behind the learned helplessness theory of depression?

Answer. Martin E.P. Seligman, a past president of the American Psychological Association, who says that one of the cures for a learned helplessness syndrome would be optimism or an optimistic viewpoint. This is a cognitive rather than a biochemical viewpoint. Seligman is also famous for championing positive psychology, a term first coined in 1954 by Abraham Maslow. A number of books consider positive psychotherapy (PPT) a valid modality of treatment.

Question 261. According to brief strategic therapists like Don Jackson, Paul Watzlawick, and Steve de Shazer, first-order change occurs when the family makes a change, but the rules do not change. What term would an expert use to describe a family in which the rules change?

Answer. Second-order change.

Question 262. A husband and wife are having frequent arguments. The husband begins telling a secretary at work, who agrees with the husband's position about the arguments, and the secretary becomes the husband's ally.

What does intergenerational therapy expert Murray Bowen call this dynamic? This is a term you will hear family therapists throw around a lot.

Answer. This is a term you will hear family therapists throw around a lot, and that the term is called triangulation. It occurs when a dyad, two people who are having problems, begin to involve a third party, which could even be a child. It seems like a good move at the time, but usually it creates additional problems.

Important exam hint. Bowen and followers of his approach generally meet with just two family members at a time rather than the entire family. Moreover, followers of Bowen often have family members talk to each other rather than the therapist to ward off stressful interactions.

Question 263. True or false. Family therapists who believe in psychodynamic approaches, REBT, or behavior therapy primarily use strategies and theories that are like what an individual or group therapist would use who champions one of these approaches?

Answer. Absolutely true.

So, a behavior therapist who is doing individual therapy, group therapy, family therapy, or even consultation might use contracting, modeling, social learning theory, extinction, and reinforcement, while an analytic therapist might analyze transference relationships. A therapist using REBT in a family session would focus on irrational beliefs, and so on.

Family therapy exam hint. A lot of counselors I speak with are not familiar with the name Richard Stuart. Stuart's name can easily pop up on exams since he has done extensive work with behavioral family and couples therapy.

Question 264. During a family counseling session, a husband complains that his wife never washes the dishes. With the help of the therapist, the decision is made that the wife will wash the dishes if her husband agrees to take out the trash. What is the name of this brief solution-focused family therapy strategy?

Answer. It's a tongue twister, folks. It's quid pro quo.

Question 265. In a college counseling experiment, the researcher secures a list of all the college students in the school. The researcher then picks every ninth student to participate in the study. Is the researcher using random sampling or relying on systematic sampling?

Answer. When you pick every ninth person from a list, or every nth person, it doesn't matter whether it's the sixth, the seventh, the ninth, and so on, then the procedure is called systematic sampling. This procedure is often contrasted with random sampling. Most researchers still prefer traditional random sampling, indicating they feel it is the more accurate of the two.

Question 266. You are seeing a family for counseling. During a session in which the husband is absent, the wife tells you she would like to have an affair with their next-door neighbor.

Should you tell the husband during the next session?

Answer. According to ACA, you have violated the ethic of confidentiality if you do tell the husband. According to ACA ethics, you must not disclose to one family member in counseling anything another family member told you unless you have prior consent.

Question 267. Who wrote the 1978 book *Seasons of a Man's Life* and postulated that a midlife crisis would occur roughly between ages 40 and 45? The book was the result of interviewing 40 American men during a series of six to ten interviews, each lasting one to two hours.

Answer. Daniel Levinson, who postulated several major transition stages, is also well known for coining the term BOOM, or becoming your own man.

Note that Levinson felt there was some overlapping between his stages. First is the early transition stage, which is about ages 17 to 22. Typically, adolescents display discontinuity or a tendency to create a life different from their parents. This phase emphasizes the change from dependence to independence. Ages 22–40 have been called the "novice adult phase." The second is the middle adult transition stage from 40 to 65. In this stage the individual decides they are satisfied with their life, or they will make major dramatic changes to reinvent their life such as going back to college or getting a divorce. The third is the late adult transition stage from ages 60 to 65.

Just as an aside: Folks over 85 are the fastest-growing segment of people over 65 in terms of their population growth. Except for the fact that older individuals have a tougher time with perceptual spatial activities, their intelligence does not seem to decline.

Question 268. True or false? Holmes and Rahe, who created the Holmes-Rahe Stress Scale, have suggested that even a seemingly positive event could be stressful.

Answer. This is a common question on exams. It's true because things like getting married or even going on vacation have been deemed stressful.

Question 269. What theorist created a model that applies to ethical and intellectual development of college students?

Answer. William Perry, who postulates nine positions or schemes in four categories. The first category is called dualism, in which the individual views the world in terms of absolute right or wrong.

The second category is termed multiplicity, and it illuminates that there can be multiple viewpoints. The third category is relativism, where knowledge is viewed as relative and contextual rather than right or wrong.

The fourth and final category is called commitment, in which relativism occurs, and the person takes responsibility for their identity and commitments, and identity is confirmed via one's lifestyle.

Question 270. True or false? A client mentions abusing her four-year daughter. You need not make a child abuse report.

Answer. Absolutely, positively false. PL 93–247, also known as the 1974 National Child Abuse Prevention and Treatment Act, stipulates that physical or mental abuse, neglect, exploitation, sexual abuse, and maltreatment must be reported to your state abuse hotline in a timely manner.

Remember that the counselor's job is not to prove that the abuse or neglect occurred, just to report it. Counselors are mandated reporters. Not reporting the abuse would put you in violation of the law as well as being an ethical violation.

Question 271. True or false. You are the leader of a Gestalt therapy group. During the initial session, you should guarantee members that what they say in a group will remain confidential.

Answer. Absolutely false. A counselor in any group counseling or therapy session should indeed stress the importance of confidentiality, but according to ACA ethics, and I quote, "The fact that confidentiality cannot be guaranteed is clearly communicated to group members."

Question 272. During an individual therapy session, a woman tells you that she has a communicable disease that is fatal.

She is angry at her husband for having an affair and has thus decided not to tell him about her disease and the fact that he could catch it. Should you as the counselor inform the husband?

Answer. Whether you like it or not, ACA ethics clearly stipulate that if the client is not going to disclose a fatal communicable disease to an identified party who is at high risk for the disease, you are justified in disclosing this information.

Question 273. You are counseling a family using Stephen deShazer's one-way mirror therapy that makes use of a family treatment team behind a mirror who will give you feedback. Should you keep the treatment team a secret from the family you are counseling?

Answer. ACA ethics say, "No way." Clients must be informed that there is a treatment team, and they must know who is on the team. By the way, Steve de Shazer, who studied under John Weakland at MRI, teamed up with his wife Insoo Kim Berg to create brief strategic solution-focused therapy (BSFT).

Question 274. You are teaching in a graduate counselor education program at a top-rated university. Can you use a textbook that you personally authored to teach the course?

Answer. Unless it violates a school or university rule at the educational institution where you are teaching at, the answer is feel free to use the book you authored, since as of this date counseling ethics do not prohibit this practice.

Question 275. You have a master's degree in counseling and a doctorate in economics. You open a private counseling practice. Should you call yourself doctor and use doctorate in your announcements pertaining to your practice?

Answer. According to ACA ethics, you should not use the title since it is not from a closely related field and therefore it could be misleading to clients.

Oh yes, when you open that wonderful private practice of yours, remember that in our field, it is decidedly not ethical to give out payments to others who might be capable of making referrals to you. Nor can you accept fees for referrals you make to other counselors.

Question 276. Three years ago, you terminated a client you were seeing. Now, you just ran into her at a party, and you begin dating her. You would like to have a romantic relationship with her. Will this relationship be in violation of the ACA Code of Ethics? And will your behavior violate NBCC ethics?

Answer. At this point in time NBCC stipulates that you must wait five years after terminating the client before you engage in this behavior. ACA raised the bar from two years to five years way back in 2005 when they updated their Ethical Code; thus a romantic relationship with the client would violate the ethical code.

Question 277. What does the term enmeshment mean in family therapy?

Answer. It implies that the members of a family are overinvolved in each other's lives; hence the persons cannot be autonomous.

Question 278. A family says to a counselor, "No matter how we handle this situation with our daughter, it always ends up in a screaming match, and our daughter runs out of the house crying." Is this equifinality or equipotentiality?

Answer. It's equifinality, a concept that literally means equal ending. The concept asserts that a system can reach the same final state under different conditions. Equipotentiality means that different final states can be reached via the same initial condition.

Noted family therapists Ray and Dorothy Becvar suggest that these concepts shift the emphasis in family therapy from why to what and from the past to the here and now.

Question 279. A client cannot secure a desirable job. This individual constantly blames the economy for this situation. According to Julian B. Rotter, is this client acting on an internal locus of control?

Answer. No. The person is acting from an external locus of control. The external person sees life events as outside of their own control and believes, "My behavior is the result of chance factors."

The healthy individual, on the other hand, takes responsibility for their own behavior, which would be called an internal locus of control, according to Rotter. Unfortunately, most people embrace the unhealthy external locus of control.

Question 280. The process consultation model that draws heavily from social psychology is associated with what theorist: ________?

Answer. Fill in that blank with the name Edgar Schein. Schein feels that the process consultant need not be an expert regarding the nature of a certain industry or organization they are working with. Nevertheless, the consultant should have a knowledge of interpersonal communication patterns and organizations.

Schein also suggested the so-called doctor–patient consultation model in which the consultant diagnoses a problem and then prescribes a course of action to ameliorate the problem just like a doctor would. He also proposes a purchase of expertise model where the organization buys a consultant's knowledge or services.

Bonus test hint. Gerald Kaplan is associated with mental health consultation based on psychodynamic theory.

Question 281. Historically speaking, what major event caused the group movement to become popular in the United States?

Answer. A shortage of individual therapists after World War II was evident, and groups allowed mental health personnel to see more clients during the same amount of time. The answer: World War II.

Question 282. A researcher switches the order in which stimuli are presented to a subject. What is the name of this procedure?

Answer. This procedure is known as counterbalancing. It ensures that the order that the stimuli would be presented is not impacting the experiment.

Question 283. A fellow counselor is coming to work intoxicated and seeing clients. What is this phenomenon called in counseling literature?

Answer. Ethics call this an impaired professional.

Question 284. If your state has privileged communication, then you have the privilege of deciding whether you want to reveal confidential information about your client in court. How about it? Is that statement true or false?

Answer. A lot of people miss this. The answer is absolutely, positively false. Privileged communication is a legal term suggesting that the client, not the counselor, has the privilege to make the decision whether the counselor should or should not reveal confidential information in court.

Legal and ethical exam reminder. Privileged communication does not apply to child abuse and neglect cases, criminal intentions, malpractice suits, homicide, suicidal threats, or clients who must be hospitalized.

Question 285. In group therapy, the ______ stage is characterized by power struggles, control issues, and resistance of group members.

Answer. This is the transition stage, which occurs after the first or initial stage of the group. The stage has also been called storming, for obvious reasons.

Question 286. A question on your exam uses the term optimization when referring to Ginzberg's theory of career development. What is the meaning of this term?

Answer. Optimization reflects the individual's attempts to balance their career with the rest of their life.

Question 287. You are viewing a graph. A linear regression slope goes down as you go from left to right; in other words, the left side is higher than the right side of the line. Is this a positive or a negative correlation?

Answer. Pictures of scattergrams, also called scatter plots, can be found in my book, *The Encyclopedia of Counseling*. This would be a negative correlation.

Question 288. What experiential family therapy expert identified four dysfunctional communication roles that are evident when a family is under stress?

Answer. I fully expect you to see some sort of question related to this issue. The answer is Virginia Satir, who wrote the classic book *Conjoint Family Therapy*.

The roles are: the placater, who tries to please everybody; the blamer, who invariably finds fault; the responsible analyzer, who really can't deal with emotions and thus resorts to intellectualization; and the distractor, who can't deal with the issues and thus interrupts or changes the subject.

Another famous experiential family therapist is psychiatrist is Carl Whitaker, who helped popularize the idea of using cotherapists in family counseling. Whitaker liked to refer to his research as experiential, symbolic family therapy.

Whitaker believed that experience, not education, changed families. Whitaker has been called radical or even wild. He often espoused the paradox that the therapist needed act crazy so the family could become sane.

Question 289. Is a suicide prevention/crisis hotline a source of primary, secondary, or tertiary prevention?

Answer. Most counselors I have talked to miss this one and will say the answer is primary prevention!!!! Experts classify these centers as secondary prevention since they are generally intended for use by folks who already have an issue (say the person calling is suicidal or depressed). A mammogram is another example of secondary prevention. In everyday life we say mammograms are a prevention strategy, but technically since the test detects something that is already there it qualifies as a form of secondary prevention.

Question 290. True or false? More counselors are working with preschool children than in the past.

Answer. Absolutely true.

Question 291. True or false? Measures of central tendency are used to find the center of a distribution of scores.

Answer: True. Typical examples include the mean (a.k.a. the arithmetic average), the median, and the mode. In a normal curve the mean, the median, and the mode are all identical (since they have the same value). The mean, the median, and the mode are classified as descriptive statistics. The normal curve is symmetrical since the right and left sides are mirror images.

Question 292. You are looking at a graph with a distribution of scores. If one tail is longer than the other tail, then the distribution is ________.

Answer. Skewed. I would also accept "not a normal curve," as an acceptable answer.

Question 293. The most common age for sexual abuse is 8 to 12 years old. Who is more likely to abuse their daughter? A natural father or a stepfather?

Answer. Stepfathers. Also, remember that women are generally sexually abused by other family members, but men are generally abused by perpetrators outside the family.

Question 294. True or false? A career counselor gives you an interest inventory. This test will predict how well you will do in each job.

Answer. False. You may be extremely interested in golf, but that doesn't mean you'll be a terrific golfer.

Question 295. Agree or disagree. Career is often defined as work plus leisure in one's lifetime.

Answer. This is true.

Question 296. Agree or disagree. The term avocation is sometimes used in place of the term leisure on exams.

Answer. True.

Question 297. The term vocation is often used as a synonym for the term occupation. Is that true or false?

Answer. We have another true. Occupation or vocation describes similar jobs in a variety of work settings. For example, different jobs in counseling.

Question 298. Most multicultural experts would agree that the melting pot analogy/metaphor is misleading. Thus, experts now recommend the _____ bowl analogy.

Answer. Fill in the blank with salad. The salad bowl analogy suggests that different cultures exist, but they retain their uniqueness. They don't just melt into the rest of the culture never to be seen again. Some counselors, especially trained in Canada, believe the term cultural mosaic, or even tossed salad, is preferable.

Question 299. Anne Roe proposed a personality career theory, while Ginzberg proposed a ______ career theory.

Answer. Developmental. In Ginzberg's theory, occupational choice is influenced by one's stage of life. Most experts agree that Ginzberg's theory is considered the most comprehensive developmental theory.

Question 300. You want to recommend a job-hunting career life planning book to a client; what is the bestselling book ever published for this purpose?

Answer. Richard Nelson Bolles's book titled *What Color Is Your Parachute?* The book includes information on establishing goals, résumé writing, and how to handle interviews. Although he died in 2017, new versions are still available.

Question 301. A journal article found that the correlation between academic success and FSIQ on the WAIS measured 0.64 or positive 0.64. FSIQ stands for Full Scale IQ. Is this a good example of an inverse correlation?

Answer. Hello. I don't think so. Inverse correlation is a fancy term often substituted for the term negative correlation. In a negative correlation, one entity goes up while the other entity, or variable, if you will, goes down. As an example, let's say that you jog a lot, and the more you jog, the lower your pulse rate gets. That would be a negative correlation.

In the journal article example, a true example, I might add, since 0.64 is a positive correlation, it does not fit the definition of an inverse correlation. If the journal article had stated that the correlation was –0.64, then, yes, the correlation would be an inverse correlation.

Question 302. Who was Lev S. Vygotsky? This is a tough one.

Answer. Vygotsky's name might be uttered in the same breath as Piaget, Erikson, and Havinghurst, since he, too, was interested in development.

Vygotsky, who was a Soviet psychologist born in 1896, stressed that what separates us from other animals is our ability to use tools and symbols to create a culture. Because of our culture, we develop language.

Vygotsky proposed three stages in the development of speech. The first stage is called social or external speech. In this stage, Vygotsky tells us that speech is not related to one's intellect. Instead, it expresses simple thoughts and emotions. Crying and laughing would be examples. "I want a cookie" would be an example of speech during this first stage.

The second stage is known as egocentric speech and is characteristic of three- to seven-year-olds. A child may talk to themself or out loud even if nobody is around. An example might be a child playing soccer by themself saying, "One goal, two goals, three goals," as the child kicks the ball.

The final stage is dubbed inner speech and is preferred by older children and adults. This is the stage of soundless speech such as doing a math problem in one's head. In this stage, higher mental operations come into play.

Question 303. What is the double bind theory of schizophrenia created by anthropologist Gregory Bateson?

Answer. The theory, which had a tremendous impact on the family therapy movement, was delineated in a 1956 landmark paper titled "Toward a Theory of Schizophrenia." The hypothesis asserted that schizophrenia is caused by paradoxical or double-bind family communication. This is sometimes called contradictory communication.

Here is a commonly cited example. A mother would visit a psychotic son in an inpatient facility. He would begin to approach the mom for a hug, but would notice mom's arms were folded and thus would not do so. Mom would then scold the child, saying that the child needed to be more affectionate. This would then create a psychotic episode.

The paradoxical story behind the theory is that Bateson came up with the double-bind hypothesis in 1954, yet he never saw a family until 1956 or 1957. The paper was written in June of '56 and published in September, or what some humorously call the fastest published article of all time.

Question 304. A narrative therapist says to a client, "How do high-fat, sugary desserts make you overeat?" What is the name for this type of intervention?

Answer. We call this "externalizing the problem." In narrative therapy, the therapist talks about the problem as if it's outside or something apart from the client. Narrative therapy was created in the 1980s by Michael White and David Epston who were attempting to apply MRI and Milan family therapy to their practices in Australia.

White and Epston also believe in discussing the larger issue of historical oppression, including economic inequities and historical persecution, with the client. Some experts have suggested that perhaps Caucasian American therapists working with African American or Native American clients should adopt this procedure.

Narrative therapy is very closely related to Bill O'Hanlon's possibility therapy, in which the therapist talks with the client about political, cultural, and social concerns while focusing on the positive aspects of the client's life or relationships.

Question 305. Your exam uses the term career lattice. Give an example of this term.

Answer. This term describes a job that allows you to make lateral transfers as well as going up and down on the career ladder. For example, say you had a job counseling perpetrators of domestic violence and transferred to a job in your same organization where you did grief counseling.

If the jobs paid the same and required the same level of training, we would say that the change in jobs was a lateral transfer as opposed to the term career ladder. The term career ladder generally refers to job moves that go up and down on the pay scale or up and down in prestige and responsibility.

Question 306. The PEF approach to career counseling is most closely associated with which well-known career theory?

Answer. PEF, which stands for person environment fit, is considered a modern offshoot of Williamson's trait factor theory.

It goes beyond the original theory by emphasizing emotional issues, clinical data, and the counselor's role is less directive. In its infancy, PEF was termed PEC, person environment correspondence.

Question 307. You are writing a journal article. Should you use the term sexual orientation, or should you use the term sexual preference?

Answer. The term sexual orientation is currently the correct choice. Preference implies that the individual had a choice, and this is not documented in the counseling literature. The question really focuses on a movement to avoid heterosexual bias in language.

The term gay, incidentally, is preferred over the term homosexuality in the literature since the term homosexuality is associated with mental illness, pathology, and criminal behavior in the mind of some individuals.

Question 308. True or false? Members of the LGBT+ community constitute about 20% of the US population.

Answer: False. In 2022 a Gallup poll determined that 7.1% of the US population falls into the LGBT category. Bisexual is the largest segment at 3.1%, and .6% are transgender. Out of all the generations (X, Baby Boomers, etc.) Generation Z (born 1997–2002) has the highest numbers in the LGBT statistics.

Question 309. True or false? American culture is more accepting of same-sex orientation than traditional Asian culture.

Answer. True. The mere discussion of sexual orientation in many Asian cultures is considered taboo.

Question 310. The DCC, or Distance Credentialed Counselor, was replaced with ___________.

Answer. BC-TMH or TeleMental Health Provider.

Question 311. What famous therapist worked as Milton H. Erickson's gardener to secure training?

Answer. Bill O'Hanlon, a pioneer in brief strategic therapy, has now created possibility therapy. He has humorously been dubbed Erickson's only work-study student.

Question 312. You wish to counsel a family who has insurance. Unfortunately, their plan will not pay for couples or marriage and family therapy. Their plan will, however, pay for individual therapy. Therefore, you list a family member as the patient and bill it with an individual treatment CPT code as if you are doing individual therapy. You do this for insurance purposes.

Is this practice recommended by most experts?

Answer. Once again, hello, I don't think so. Agencies and counselors do it all the time, but it's not permissible, and constitutes insurance fraud.

Question 313. Your exam uses the abbreviation SFBT; what does it mean?

Answer. Solution-focused brief therapy. The focus, as the name implies, is on solutions, not on analyzing the problem. Focusing on the problem is seen as detrimental rather than a therapeutic plus.

Question 314. What does FFST stand for when using SFBT?

Answer. Whoa, it's quite a mouthful. FFST means formula first session task. It refers to a type of homework assignment that solution-focused brief therapists often give to clients to complete between the first and second sessions.

Question 315. Which form of psychotherapy, REBT, Rogerian, Gestalt, or narrative therapy, would emphasize that we live our lives by the stories we tell about ourselves and the stories others tell about us?

Answer. Narrative therapy, usually classified as a postmodern or social constructivist viewpoint.

Question 316. You are a school counselor who is asked to run a small group counseling session. By definition, how many students will be in this small group?

Answer. Typically, a small group in a school is defined as four to six students. Due to the nature of the school environment, the group will meet for a set number of sessions.

Question 317. True or false? K through 12 counselors do more group counseling than individual counseling.

Answer. False. Most school counselors do more individual than group counseling.

Question 318. True or false? In the 1970s, it was noted the children were maturing at an earlier age, and thus, seventh through ninth grade junior high schools were replaced with sixth through eighth grade middle schools.

Answer. True. Middle schools began to replace junior high schools.

Question 319. You are planning on conducting a research study. How could the Hatch Amendment impact your research?

Answer. The Hatch Amendment stipulates programs that receive federal funding cannot make children participate in experiments that involve psychological exams or research without permission from a parent or a guardian.

Question 320. Which minority group in the United States is growing the fastest? Asian Americans, Native Americans, African Americans, or Hispanic Americans?

Answer. Hispanic Americans. On an exam you could also expect the alternative terms Latino (for boys or men), Latina (for girls or women), or Latinx. Latinx is the non-binary or gender-neutral term.

Question 321. Agree or disagree with this statement. Researchers should use universal informed consent forms.

Answer. Strongly disagree. At this point in time, none exists. Each researcher must create their own informed consent document, and the researcher must keep a copy as well as the person participating in the research.

Question 322. You refer a client you are counseling to a psychiatrist who prescribes lithium. Your client most likely suffers from a feeding or eating disorder, an anxiety disorder, pica, ADHD, crack addiction, or bipolar disorder?

Answer. Bipolar disorder, or what we once referred to as manic depressive illness.

Question 323. True or false. Appropriate body language and good eye contact are examples of good attending behavior.

Answer. True.

Question 324. A counselor suspects that a client is suicidal. The counselor should: A. give the client a personality test like the MMPI-3, B. give the client a projective test such as the Rorschach, C. conduct a lethality assessment on the client, or D. counsel her client using positive psychotherapy.

Answer. Don't miss this important one, folks. The answer is C, conduct a lethality assessment.

Question 325. A client is struggling with feelings that the world is a dangerous place, and it was their own inadequate behavioral response that caused them to be raped and experience trauma.

The ideal form of cognitive therapy would be A. REBT as set forth by Ellis; B. cognitive therapy as practiced by Aaron T. Beck; or C. cognitive processing therapy (CPT) created by American psychologists Patricia Resick, Candice Monson, and Kathleen Chard?

Answer. Yes, all three approaches are cognitive; however, only choice C, CPT, was originally created to assist with rape, sexual trauma, and then PTSD. CPT can be used in individual and group settings and generally consists of 12 sessions. Each of the 12 therapeutic sessions is outlined in a manual and popular in treating veterans. Your exam could label this approach a manualized form of treatment.

A popular concept in CPT is the so-called impact statement: This is a written explanation depicting how the patient's traumatic situation has affected their life, including an account of the patient's beliefs about the cause of the event and of each of the following five primary themes that are be addressed in CPT: safety, trust, power/control, esteem, and intimacy. The impact statement is used as a practice assignment in sessions 1 and 11.

Question 326. Some social justice advocates are moving from an equality framework to an equity framework. What's the difference?

Answer. Equality means that everyone gets the same treatment. However, is that always ideal? For example, everyone gets 3 hours and 45 minutes to take a comprehensive counseling exam. However, would this be enough time for someone using an interpreter? Maybe not. That's why some counselors have moved to an equity lens.

Equity is based on the different needs of different people. Equity recognizes and celebrates differences among people. It also recognizes that historical disadvantages lead people to have different needs for true justice. Moreover, equity accounts for intersectionality or the connections and overlap of social identities that may impact privilege and disadvantage. Equity helps to eliminate imbalances in the social justice system. According to this principle, treating everybody equally is *not* the answer.

Question 327. True or false? A culturally encapsulated counselor is a counselor who could be considered culturally competent.

Answer. False. Based on the definition of a culturally encapsulated counselor, the exact opposite would be true. A counselor who is culturally encapsulated often has little knowledge of other cultures and may be intolerant or insensitive to cultures different than their own.

Contrarily, cultural competence includes knowledge and respect of one's own culture as well as other cultures. It would be important to note that cultural competence is an ethical issue.

Question 328. Often used as an umbrella term for different social movements, what is meant by the term social justice?

Answer. Though you may not be able to quote the definition word for word, you should know that social justice is focused on ensuring *all members* of a society have access to similar (but not necessarily equal) opportunities and resources.

Question 329. True or false? Both the NBCC and ACA's Codes of Ethics include statements about multicultural competence.

Answer. Absolutely true. Under the NBCC's Code of Ethics, NCCs are expected to show efforts towards growth in multicultural competence. Similarly, the ACA Code of Ethics discusses the importance of multicultural competence throughout. This includes working with culturally diverse families, provision of referrals, assessment, intervention, diagnosis, and even supervision.

Question 330. What is considered the fifth force in counseling and psychology?

Answer. The five forces model groups counseling approaches and theories. The so-called "fifth force" is social justice and represents a broader understanding of a movement towards equity and cultural competence. Since we are on the topic of the five forces, the other four are psychoanalytic, cognitive-behavioral, existential-humanistic, and multicultural. In some books, you might see different terms such as "behaviorism" instead of cognitive-behavioral. If you're feeling inclined, take a moment now to consider the forces in the context of their respective zeitgeists (i.e., the spirit or that which is symbolic of the historical period).

And what if my exam doesn't list social justice as an answer for the fifth force? Great question. Then look for CAM, or complementary and alternative medicine, or complementary and alternative methods (such as neurofeedback, massage, hypnosis, herbs, aromatherapy, etc.)

Question 331. Let's start with the basics of gender, sex, and sexuality. What do these terms mean?

Answer. Sex is easy. Sex is a classifier based on sexual reproductive function. Internal and external features, primary and secondary sexual characteristics, hormones, and chromosomes are used to classify people as male, female, or intersex.

Gender, or gender identity, is a bit different. This is often defined as a person's internal sense of their gender. Generally, people who have a gender which is the same as the sex they were assigned are called cisgender. People who do not experience this alignment sometimes use the term transgender, though there are many other terms that people may use, such as gender nonconforming, nonbinary, agender. . . . People may also use pronouns which they feel express their gender identity.

Finally, sexuality, or sexual orientation, describes whom someone is sexually or romantically attracted to. Someone who is attracted only to people with the gender opposite their own are often called heterosexual. Many terms describe people who are not heterosexual, including bisexual, gay, lesbian, asexual, or queer. Note: queer is usually described as a reclaimed term and may be used or viewed by people differently. Reclaiming occurs when a group takes a word used against them (with a negative meaning) and changes it to mean something positive within that group. Often this reclaimed term becomes something that is only acceptable to say within the group.

Question 332. Was homosexuality ever classified as a disorder in the DSM? If so, how is it viewed now?

Answer. Absolutely. The pathologizing of homosexuality in the DSM occurred until the APA voted to remove the diagnosis in 1973, though related disorders, including sexual orientation disturbance and ego-dystonic homosexuality, remained after this. Pathologizing sexuality also existed in the ICD. Some groups continue to work to depathologize (stop treating something as a disorder or disease needing treatment) other identities such as gender identity because this can be a form of discrimination.

In fact, the newest version of the DSM, DSM-5-TR, specifically aimed to be more intentional about culture, racism, and discrimination. For example, the DSM-5-TR uses the word "racialized" to acknowledge that race is a socially constructed concept. The use of the gender-neutral "Latinx" and avoidance of the term "minority" are also intentional changes in language. Additionally, the DSM-5-TR includes some prevalence data based on ethnoracial groups as well as information variations in symptomology based on demographics. The hope is that misdiagnosis for oppressed groups will decrease.

Question 333. What is the name of the movement that is focused on ending sex-based discrimination and helping women advance based on the equality of sexes?

Answer. Feminism.

You may hear about the waves of feminism, which are based on the focus of the movement at a given time. There are arguments about whether there are three, four, or even five waves, though some argue that this conceptualization isn't helpful.

Question 334. Which researcher is well-known for research on sexuality and the heterosexual–homosexual rating scale?

Answer. Dr. Alfred Charles Kinsey researched sexual behavior in the 1940s and 1950s. Revolutionary at the time, the documents that came from Kinsey's research, the Kinsey Reports, led to the development of the so-called Kinsey scale, which is a 7-point scale that ranges from 0 (exclusively heterosexual) to 6 (exclusively homosexual) with an added X classifier which describes no socio-sexual contacts or reactions. In summary, Kinsey suggested a continuum when classifying homosexual–heterosexual behavior. In recent times, the generalizability of the research has been questioned.

I have included extra questions and answers in this area for two key reasons. First, I have heard from numerous counselors who attended grad school many years ago and share that the topic of sexuality was not covered in their program. Second, the terminology has changed markedly at a very rapid pace.

Question 335. What does the acronym LGBTQ stand for?

Answer. The letters in LGBTQ correspond to terms related to sexual orientation and gender identity. Specifically, the letters stand for lesbian, gay, bisexual, transgender, and queer. There are other versions of the acronym such as GLB, LGB+, LGBTQIA, LGBTQ+, and so on. The plus stands for the multitude of terms people use to describe their gender identity or sexual orientation. A comprehensive counseling exam might use one or several different acronyms.

Question 336. True or false? LGBTQ+ youth and adults have a higher risk of experiencing mental health conditions, including mood disorders, substance use disorders, suicidal ideation, and suicide attempts.

Answer. True. Research is growing on disparity in both rates and outcomes of mental illness among the LGBTQ population. Some studies suggest rates of 2–4× more than the non-LGBTQ population. It is important to note the disparities may not come from internal factors but the social experiences of LGBTQ folks. For example, the discrimination, rejection, housing insecurity, lack of adequately trained mental health practitioners, and more are likely connected to the disparities in mental health among LGBTQ people.

Question 337. The DSM-5 boasted the addition of several new diagnoses. One of these is the sole non–substance related behavioral addiction. Which diagnosis am I talking about? Bonus: how many new diagnoses were added in DSM-5-TR?

Answer. This would be gambling disorder. Were you thinking about internet gaming addiction? While not included in the behavioral addition categories, internet gaming addiction is included in Section III of both the DSM-5 and DSM-5-TR as a condition for further study. We'll have to wait and see whether it is classified as a full diagnosis in future editions of the DSM.

Just one new diagnosis, prolonged grief disorder, was added to DSM-5-TR, though it included revisions to more than 70 diagnoses. These changes included additions of categories and specifiers, clarification of language, and information specific to the nuances of diagnosing young children, as well as the return of features from previous editions.

Prolonged grief disorder is said to be the continuation of distress related to grief that continues for at least 12 months after the loss of the person close to the bereaved. Symptoms include intense longing, preoccupation, emotional numbness, intense emotional pain, and avoidance of reminders of the death of the person. The DSM-5-TR also makes note that these symptoms exist beyond what would be expected in the context of one's culture. Interestingly, this diagnosis specifically relates to the death of a person and does not incorporate a more expansive definition of grief and loss.

Question 338. Not only did the DSM-5 add new diagnoses, but it also changed in structure. What structure used in the DSM-IV-TR was replaced in the DSM-5 and continued in the DSM-5-TR?

Answer. The Diagnostic and Statistical Manual of Mental Disorders, fourth edition, text revision (or DSM-IV-TR) used a multi-axial diagnosis system. Specifically, it used five domains or axes. This system was eliminated in DSM-5 and did not return for the most recent edition, the DSM-5-TR. Again, just to be crystal clear: the DSM-5-TR does NOT use the multiaxial diagnosis system.

Question 339. Addictive disorders were revised in many ways in DSM-5. For one, the previous categories of substance abuse and substance dependence became a single "use disorder" measured based on severity. Additionally, cravings were added as a criteria and problems with law enforcement were removed. Of the substances listed in the DSM-5-TR, one is included, but not as a substance use disorder. Which substance is that?

Answer. Caffeine. Caffeine use disorder is included in Section III of the DSM-5. Caffeine intoxication and withdrawal, however, are both included as diagnoses in DSM-5 and DSM-5-TR.

Question 340. One diagnosis that gained pushback for its exclusion from DSM-5 was Asperger's disorder. How would someone who may have been previously diagnosed with Asperger's disorder be classified now?

Answer. The DSM-5's autism spectrum disorder consolidates several diagnoses from the DSM-IV: autistic disorder, Asperger's disorder, childhood disintegrative disorder, and pervasive developmental disorder not otherwise specified. Individuals with a prior diagnosis of Asperger's disorder would be considered for an autism spectrum disorder diagnosis under the DSM-5.

Controversy about the autism spectrum disorder diagnosis in the DSM-5 and DSM-5TR stems from two main tenets. First, the removal of Asperger's disorder was viewed by many as a change that took away a label many individuals with the diagnosis found a shared community with. Second, DSM-5 and DSM-5TR's autism spectrum disorder criteria are more narrow and restrictive when compared to Asperger's disorder in the DSM-IV. Several studies showed that a significant percentage of individuals diagnosed with Asperger's disorder would not qualify for an autism spectrum disorder diagnosis under the DSM-5.

Question 341. You might be surprised to know that body dysmorphic disorder is listed in the Obsessive-Compulsive and Related Disorders section of the DSM-5-TR. However, when you look at the criteria, this makes a bit more sense. Which symptom of body dysmorphic disorder helps clarify why it is in this section?

Answer. The DSM-5 included the addition of "repetitive behaviors or mental acts in response to preoccupations with perceived defects or flaws in physical appearance" as a criterion for body dysmorphic disorder. In plain terms, these are the compulsions that can exist with the obsessions about physical appearance.

Question 342. A client who witnessed a violent mugging at a store two weeks prior presents with recurrent memories of the event, nightmares, insomnia, and increased anxiety that manifest as dizziness. Their performance at work has decreased and they have avoided returning to the store. Would post-traumatic stress disorder, or PTSD, be an appropriate diagnosis for this person?

Answer. No, well at least not yet. Although the person has symptoms consistent with PTSD (re-experiencing, avoidance, negative mood, and hyperarousal), the timeframe is off. PTSD is diagnosed after at least one month post-exposure to the traumatic experience. DSM-5-TR also removed a redundancy in the criterion for PTSD for children six years old and younger that specified that witnessing the event had to be in person. This means that someone would not be diagnosed with PTSD if they had witnessed violence through media, TV, or movies.

Question 343. The DSM has had a fair share of criticism over its many versions. One ongoing criticism is its tendency to pathologize sexual and gender identity. Which diagnosis replaced gender identity disorder in DSM-5 and how did it address the criticisms?

Answer. Gender dysphoria is considered a less pathological term by taking out the term "disorder." The criteria for gender dysphoria were also changed. DSM-5-TR included additional changes in language as an effort to be more culturally sensitive. For example, "desired gender" was changed to "experienced gender." Current treatment recommendations include helping people experiencing gender dysphoria to access gender-affirming care.

Question 344. Personality disorders are typically classified into three clusters. Cluster A, odd, eccentric cluster. Cluster B, dramatic, emotional, erratic cluster. And cluster C, anxious, fearful cluster. Which cluster does borderline personality disorder fall into?

Answer. That would be cluster B, the dramatic, emotional, erratic cluster. Borderline personality disorder is characterized by intense and unstable emotions and relationships, impulsive or self-harm behavior, polarized thinking, avoidance of perceived abandonment, and inconsistent sense of self. Interestingly, there is an additional model of personality disorders included in Section III of both DSM-5 and DSM-5-TR.

Question 345. A male client, 35 years old, middle-class, white comes to his first session well dressed. During the assessment, the client describes periods of eating a significantly large amount of food in a short amount of time. He states that he feels his ability to stop eating during these episodes is out of his control. These episodes often happen at night when his partner and child are sleeping. He often feels guilty afterwards but denies engaging in compensatory behaviors such as overexercising. He shares that this happens about twice a week and has been occurring since his late 20s. What is the most likely diagnosis?

Answer. Binge eating disorder (BED) was a newly classified diagnosis in DSM-5, which is interesting as BED is considered the most common eating disorder in the United States. This disorder is marked by episodes of rapidly eating large amounts of food in a short amount of time (binges). This differs from bulimia nervosa, which also includes episodes of binge eating, because of the lack of compensatory behaviors. The severity is classified by the number of binge-eating episodes per week with one to three being considered "mild."

Question 346. What is the difference between a sexual dysfunction and paraphilic disorders in the DSM?

Answer. Sexual dysfunctions describe disturbances in sexual functioning, whereas paraphilic disorders describe disturbances in sexual behavior that cause distress or impairment. It is important to note that human sexuality includes a wide range of behaviors that would not be considered a disorder such as a sexual fantasy or fascination with nonhuman objects such as clothes. While all behaviors are not socially sanctioned, it doesn't mean that the person is distressed by the behavior. To simplify the paraphilic distinction, some experts have suggested that virtually anything other than sexual behavior between two consenting adults could be included in this category. (Note: When the behavior has been or can be of harm to others, it *is* labeled as a disorder.)

Question 347. A GAF score may still be used in some professions. However, the GAF, or Global Assessment of Functioning scale, was replaced by what in the DSM-5 (also used in the DSM-5-TR)?

Answer. The World Health Organization Disability Assessment Schedule 2 (WHODAS 2.0) replaced the GAF. DSM-5-TR added additional instructions for calculating summary scores. Considering the attention to culture, racism, and discrimination in the DSM-5-TR, the binary (male/female) checkboxes were removed from measures listed in section III.

Question 348. The DSM is the main diagnostic manual in North America. What is the global counterpart that is often used in North America for billing purposes?

Answer. At the time this question has been created, the International Classification of Diseases is in its 11th edition (ICD-11) and serves as a global categorization system for both mental and physical illnesses. It has both similarities and differences from the DSM. Note: ICD-11 is still being adopted, and the transition from ICD-10 will take time.

Question 349. Personality disorders were originally viewed as untreatable and incurable. Which treatment for borderline personality disorder (or BPD) helped challenge this view? Bonus question, who is credited with creating this treatment?

Answer. DBT, or dialectical behavior therapy. This approach was founded by the American psychologist Marsha Linehan in the 1970s. Dialectical simply means using discussion, dialogue, or discourse to investigate and combine opposing ideas.

Question 350. During assessment, your client exhibits perfectionistic behaviors, inhibited emotion, and low social signaling. Their assessment leads you to believe they have an overcontrolled personality style. Is traditional DBT or RO-DBT (Radically Open DBT) likely to be more effective in treating this client?

Answer. RO-DBT is a more appropriate treatment for an overcontrolled client. Whereas DBT helps people gain emotion regulation skills, people who are overcontrolled may struggle with overly inhibited emotional expression. RO-DBT is like DBT in many ways; however, there are some important differences. In RO-DBT, the therapist may be less directive and more focused on external skills like building connections and engaging openly with others.

Question 351. What is the fundamental dialectic of DBT?

Answer. Once again, let's first define dialectical in DBT. *Dialectical means a combining of opposing ideas*. The foundational dialectic in DBT is between acceptance and change. DBT asks both the therapist and the client to accept the client wherever they are and to understand that change may need to happen. This is mirrored in the DBT skills. Mindfulness and distress tolerance are acceptance focused, while interpersonal effectiveness and emotion regulation focus on change.

Question 352. Let's do an easy one. What do the letters in ACT stand for as they relate to the therapy model developed by Steven Hayes?

Answer. On the surface ACT stands for acceptance and commitment therapy. Okay, a bit of a trick question because, interestingly, ACT also stands for the focus areas of the treatment. A is for "accept," as in accepting your thoughts and feelings by being present. C is for "choose," as in choosing a valued direction. And T is for "take," as in taking action.

Question 353. Defusion is a core aspect of ACT. What does defusion mean?

ACT posits that we can become fused (attached, stuck) to our thoughts. This becomes problematic when our fused thoughts direct our behaviors. Defusion is the process of becoming detached, getting distance from, or separating from our thoughts. A basic example is to label thoughts as such. Let's say you are currently thinking "there's no way I'm going to pass this exam." You could think "I'm having the thought that there's no way I'm going to pass this exam." Becoming defused from these thoughts may not change the outcome, but it could help you choose actions that are more value- and goal-oriented, like continuing to study.

Question 354. Which treatment is grounded in Steven Hayes's relational frame theory (RFT)?

Answer. This should not come as too much of a surprise, as the treatment was also founded by Steven Hayes. The answer is ACT, or acceptance and commitment therapy. Let's delve just a little bit deeper into RFT since it is one of the unique aspects of ACT. RFT is a psychological theory of human language. It proposes that human language is developed from relating concepts to each other. The language we use and connect with to describe our experience can impact our reality and increase suffering. Take a moment to think about the language of mental illness.

Question 355. Once viewed as pseudoscience, this increasingly popular therapy developed by Francine Shapiro is well known for using bilateral stimulation. What therapy am I describing?

Answer. Although being widely questioned as a valuable treatment in the past, EMDR (eye movement desensitization and reprocessing) has been well studied at this point and is accepted as an efficacious treatment.

Question 356. What is EMDR most well-known for treating?

Answer. Trauma. You could also say the clinical diagnosis of PTSD (post-traumatic stress disorder). In particular, the short duration of treatment along with the lack of talking about trauma in detail are some of the noted benefits of EMDR for the treatment of trauma. There has been a push to study the effectiveness of EMDR with other disorders including panic disorder, obsessive-compulsive disorder, and even eating disorders.

Question 357. One of the eight phases of EMDR is the body scan. This is viewed as a type of somatic intervention. What does this mean?

Answer. Somatic is simply defined as relating to the body in a way that is distinct from the mind. Therefore, somatic interventions put particular focus on *body awareness*. This is distinct from therapies which are particularly or specifically focused on mind awareness. Somatic interventions like EMDR represent a push for increasing awareness about the connection between the body and the mind.

Question 358. Historically, psychotherapy has been stereotyped as a patient reclining on a couch speaking with a psychotherapist taking notes. Will the stereotype of the future be an avatar patient on a virtual coach with an avatar psychotherapist and a virtual notepad? Or even text messages between the patient and the psychotherapist? Does the latter describe synchronous or asynchronous care?

Answer. This would be asynchronous, also sometimes referred to as "store-and-forward." Any counseling that is not in person or on video falls into the asynchronous care category since there is lag, though it may indeed be very brief, in communication.

Question 359. What are some potential benefits for clients using telehealth?

Answer. Convenience, accessibility, saving time, saving money. These are only a few of the potential benefits. If you've named one I haven't and it seems reasonable (elimination of symptoms after the first visit is not what we're talking about), then you are probably spot on. The important thing to know is how to take a balanced view of the pros and cons of telehealth.

Question 360. Telebehavioral health has led to many questions about licensing and practicing across states. This gave rise to the Interstate Compact for Licensure Portability. What does the initiative address?

Answer. The challenges of transferring licenses across jurisdictions due to differences in requirements for licenses and rules have clinical impact. For example, a client who moves to another state may have to end care with a counselor due solely to the counselor's license. The Interstate Compact tries to address this by providing a process by which counselors could practice throughout various states based on an agreement about license reciprocity.

Question 361. A counselor is meeting with their client for the first time. The client and counselor had a brief conversation over the phone and decided that telebehavioral health, or distance counseling, would be appropriate. They have never met in person. The counselor joins the video session, and the client joins shortly after. The counselor is excited to begin working, briefly introduces themself, and jumps into a conversation about informed consent. Is there anything the counselor should have done to engage in ethical practice according to the ACA Code of Ethics?

Answer. Yes; the scenario never mentions that the counselor verifies the client's identity. According to the ACA Code of Ethics (H.3, Client Verification), counselors should verify the client's identity at the beginning and throughout therapy. An example would be using a code word with the client and obtaining a copy of their ID card.

Question 362. True or false? Telebehavioral health and technology-assisted services are appropriate for all clients.

Answer. False. Guidelines in the ACA Code of Ethics state that counselors must attempt to "determine that clients are intellectually, emotionally, physically, linguistically, and functionally capable" of engaging in these methods of therapy.

Question 363 What are some of the potential challenges for clients when using telehealth? Do counselors have a responsibility to educate clients about these?

Answer. There are many potential challenges for clients when using telehealth. Some examples would be lack of ability to guarantee privacy on the client's end, difficulties with the technology, disruptions in connection, and misunderstandings due to communication differences (such as delays and verbal or nonverbal cues). According to the ACA Code of Ethics, counselors should outline these as part of informed consent and provide ongoing education and prevention to overcome communication differences.

Question 364. A counselor can share client information through popular social media platforms. True or false?

Answer. False. The ACA Code of Ethics and NBCC Policy on Distance Professional Services both address security of client data and confidentiality. Social media platforms *do not* rise to the required level of security. It would also be a HIPAA nightmare. Hopefully this easy question boosted your confidence.

Question 365. Name some additional ethical considerations for counselors providing distance counseling?

Answer. There are plenty. Competency, social media policies, additional information for informed consent, platform security, client preference, and safety are just a few. If you couldn't name one, take this as a reminder to study the ACA and NBCC codes of ethics before your exam. Even if you could name some or all of them, a review of ethics codes would be beneficial.

Question 366. The so-called "therapeutic factors" in group therapy were identified by which psychiatrist?

Answer. Dr. Irvin Yalom. Let's take a second to review these therapeutic factors or primary change agents. They are instillation of hope, universality, information giving, altruism, corrective recapitulation of the primary family, development of social skills, imitative behavior, interpersonal learning, cohesiveness, catharsis, and existential factors. Interestingly, Yalom changed the name to "therapeutic factors" from "curative factors." Additionally, the original 11 factors were increased to 12. Although slightly different language may be used in other sources, if any of these didn't sound familiar, now might be a good time to pick up your second-edition *Human Services Dictionary* and review these (look in the "Y" section).

Question 367. You are hosting a closed psychotherapy group that has been meeting for a few weeks. You notice that one member has taken the lead in preparing the room for the group and volunteers regularly for leadership responsibilities in the group. Another member has also taken notice. Although silent about this shift in the past couple of weeks, the second member begins to express frustration about the first member being "bossy." You, being the well-studied clinician that you are, recognize this as which of Tuckman and Jensen's five stages of group development model?

Answer. This would be the storming stage (sometimes called the transition stage), which is characterized by disagreements and power struggles. As a bonus brain jog, the other four stages are forming (sometimes initial), performing (sometimes working), norming, and adjourning (sometimes termination or mourning).

Question 368. Alcoholics Anonymous (or AA) meetings are sometimes called closed or open. This describes the type of people who can participate. A "closed meeting" is only for people who identify as someone who may struggle with alcohol use and has a desire to stop drinking. An "open meeting" is for anyone, including observers. This is different from the terms "open" and "closed" as they relate to groups. What do open and closed mean in terms of groups?

Answer. A closed group does not allow entry of new members after the first meeting or first few sessions. This can help with group cohesion but may lead to a lack of new views and unstable membership because members who leave aren't replaced. Open groups, on the other hand, allow members to join at any time. This helps keep group numbers stable but can cause tension because of the different places group members may be in the process.

Question 369. If I were to ask you to tell me about RIASEC, you might stare at me as if I'd just given you a random assortment of letters. If I then tell you RIASEC is related to John Holland and career development, you might recognize it. What is RIASEC?

Answer. These letters stand for the six personality types (and corresponding work environments) that make up the Holland Codes. The letters stand for realistic, investigative, artistic, social, enterprising, and conventional. Holland's theory of career choice suggests that a good match between personality and work environment leads to higher levels of success and satisfaction.

Question 370. According to Ginzberg and associates, in the first developmental model of vocational choice, people pass through three stages. Name or describe these three stages.

Answer. The three stages are fantasy, tentative, and finally the realistic stage. According to this model, childhood, up to about age 11, is characterized by *fantasy* related to career choice. The next stage, *tentative*, occurring in early adolescents, is marked by exploration of interest and abilities as it relates to career choice. Finally, in young adulthood, people are said to gain a more *realistic* view of their career choice. The realistic stage is broken down into three sub-stages: exploration, crystallization, and specification.

Question 371. Anne Roe developed a theory of career choice and development that is based on the idea that early life experiences guide people into particular career choices. For example, a child who experienced emotional neglect would develop an orientation away from people. In turn, in adulthood this person might choose a non–people-oriented career such as a park ranger. This seems to have roots in what other developmental theory?

Answer. That would be Freud's psychoanalytic theory.

Question 372. Anne Roe developed a two-dimensional system to classify occupations. "Service" is an example of which of the dimensions?

Answer. Service is one of the eight fields of Roe's theory. The other dimension is made up of the six levels of occupational skill.

Question 373. The trait-and-factor-matching theory would be most likely used by a counselor practicing in what specialty area?

Answer. This counselor would likely be engaging in career counseling. This theory suggests that people can be successful in their careers when they have a good understanding of the match between aspects of their own traits and the factors of certain vocations.

Question 374. You have been going to class, writing papers, going to practicum or internship, and are now studying for this exam all to enter the counseling vocation. When (yes, when) you pass this exam and are a counselor, I hope you will also be engaging in enjoyable activities that you choose outside of work. What would this time be called in career counseling terms?

Answer. This is leisure, of course. Leisure activity can also be called an avocation.

Question 375. Many career development theories have garnered criticism for being limited in their ability to capture the experiences of diverse groups. Why do you think this is?

Answer. Many of the theories that gained popularity in career counseling were based on the narrow experience of a limited group of people. Specifically, they are often based on the experience of white, heterosexual, abled, cis men with class privilege.

Question 376. Are you feeling like you are going to ACE this exam, yet? I hope so. The exam might ask about a different type of ace. What does ACE stand for in terms of trauma?

Answer. ACEs stand for adverse childhood experiences. A study conducted in the mid- to late 1990s surveyed people about their childhood experiences and their health. Perhaps not shocking to us today, as well-trained counselors, it was revolutionary to see a correlation between experiences of childhood abuse and neglect and poor health outcomes. It showed evidence that early life experiences can have lifelong consequences.

Question 377. The field has become increasingly aware of the impact of trauma on functioning. This led to increasing awareness of trauma-informed care. What does trauma-informed care mean?

Answer. Trauma-informed care can be defined as an approach that recognizes the impact of trauma leading to efforts to recognize and respond to trauma without increasing harm through re-traumatization. In essence, it is a response that leads to better recognition and response for people who have experienced trauma (a significant portion of the population).

Question 378. Trauma-informed care actively works against re-traumatization. What does "re-traumatization" mean?

Answer. Re-traumatization can occur when a person encounters a reminder of a past traumatic experience that can lead that person to re-experience thoughts, feelings, and behaviors related to the initial trauma. As an example, a person who has a history of childhood sexual abuse may be re-traumatized by body cavity searches conducted in the criminal justice system.

Question 379. The six core principles of trauma-informed approach are safety, trustworthiness/transparency, peer support, collaboration, empowerment/choice, and awareness of cultural/historical/gender issues. When a trauma-informed counselor encourages a client to develop treatment goals with them, what principle or principles does this serve?

Answer. The counselor is using a collaborative choice that empowers the client to have a choice in their treatment. It can also be a transparent practice that allows the counselor to be responsive to any cultural or other issues.

Question 380. What level of an organization does a trauma-informed approach impact?

Answer. True trauma-informed care happens on all levels of care and is integrated within different interventions. This includes policies among governance and leadership, how the physical environment is set up, with both clinical and non-clinical staff, and throughout the stages of treatment (from pre-encounter to termination). For example, trauma-informed care in leadership might look like encouraging space for all voices to be heard in a meeting.

Question 381. What is defined as "having conscious awareness of the present" and is a concept that has become well known in the counseling field?

Answer. This would describe mindfulness.

Question 382. Mindfulness-based interventions have become increasingly popular. Many of the well-known interventions incorporate mindfulness. Where did mindfulness practices originate?

Answer. Mindfulness has origins in the spiritual practices of the Eastern world. It is commonly traced back to Buddhism. However, mindfulness in counseling is often secularized and thus not associated with religious or spiritual concerns.

Question 383. Dialectical behavior therapy (DBT) incorporates mindfulness as a core module. DBT further describes the three states of the mind. Two of these are reasonable mind and emotional mind. What is the third state of the mind according to DBT?

Answer. Wise mind is considered the integration of logic, or reasoning, and emotion. This integration of these two states of mind is said to lead to the centered state of wise mind.

Question 384. True or false? Acceptance and commitment therapy (ACT) is another type of therapy that incorporates mindfulness.

Answer. True. ACT incorporates mindfulness in the service of not avoiding painful or challenging emotions. According to ACT, this allows people to make space for challenging thoughts and emotions to allow eventual acceptance and value-based action.

Question 385. Is it true that mindfulness and meditation the same thing?

Answer. You might have heard the phrase mindfulness meditation. In some ways, mindfulness and meditation are similar and can have similar positive effects. However, there are some key differences. Meditation is usually a focused practice with set-aside time. For example, in breathing meditation, you might focus on the inhale and exhale for ten minutes. Mindfulness is a practice that focuses on awareness of the present moment without judgment. Meditation is one way to develop mindfulness, but mindfulness can also be practiced in exercise, eating, and throughout daily activities. Mindfulness can also be a form of meditation.

Question 386. We often talk about crisis such as the global warming crisis or an economic crisis. In terms of counseling, what is a crisis?

Answer. A counseling definition of crisis has a few important elements. First, a crisis has a large impact. Typically, this impact is at least emotional. Second, crisis disrupts typical functioning. This can be called disequilibrium. Third, crises don't respond to traditional coping skills. All together, crisis can be defined as an emotionally impactful event that leads to disequilibrium and doesn't respond to traditional coping.

Question 387. The goals of crisis counseling differ from other types of counseling. What is the primary goal of crisis counseling?

Answer. Through crisis intervention, a counselor and client will work to relieve systems, identify what led to the crisis, and take action to resolve the crisis. Ultimately, the counselor will be working to help the client to return to their previous level of functioning. This differs from other counseling approaches that may work to improve functioning past baseline.

Question 388. A counselor is asked to visit the site of a deadly flood. Many people have been displaced from their homes and are being temporarily housed at the local elementary school. The counselor greets a woman in the temporary shelter. The woman explains that she hasn't been able to locate her husband. She's worried about him because he requires daily medication for his heart condition. She is feeling guilty because they were arguing the last time they spoke. The counselor begins to ask questions about the history of their relationship and the lack of boundaries in the relationship. The counselor then teaches the woman about healthy boundary setting. Is this appropriate in terms of crisis intervention?

Answer. Although it is appropriate to assess for contributing factors in a crisis, the counselor should not be working on educating this client on a skill like healthy boundary setting. The client is likely more concerned about locating her husband and figuring out how to access basic needs like her husband's medication. Learning about healthy boundary setting, in this situation, would be more appropriate for longer-term interventions, perhaps couples counseling.

Question 389. A counselor begins working with a client who was recently terminated from his job. The termination was unexpected. The client was so surprised that he was unable to look for another job. He reports feeling disoriented and stuck. He can't sleep and has a hard time focusing while looking at job postings. He doesn't know what to do and is starting to worry about losing his home. The counselor believes that the client is in the vulnerable or pre-crisis stage of crisis. Is this accurate?

Answer. No, the client is in the active, or acute, phase of crisis. Some clues are the likely precipitating event (job loss), additional impacts (worry about housing loss), and symptoms of disequilibrium (disorientation, sleep disturbance, and lack of ability to act). Starting in pre-crisis, a precipitating event along with other vulnerabilities may lead to active crisis. Eventually, people may naturally move into a state of chronic crisis or restoration of equilibrium.

Question 390. What are some of the main differences between crisis intervention and other types of intervention?

Answer. A few have been pointed out in other questions, but I'm banking on the fact that a little repetition and review will prove helpful. One difference is the focus of the intervention. Crisis intervention focuses on returning people to their original level of functioning, whereas other interventions may try to help increase functioning at or above baseline. Crisis intervention is focused on resolution of the immediate situation. Other interventions may focus on resolving past or future challenges. Crisis intervention is specifically short term. Other interventions may be brief or longer term. A counselor may have a more active or directive approach in crisis intervention. Despite the differences, however, crisis intervention has additional similarities to other interventions.

Question 391. Within the framework of Erikson's stages of psychosocial development, explain the stage that older adults would be in.

Answer. Erikson's eighth stage, integrity versus despair, encompasses the experiences of older adults. In this stage, people are often reflecting on their lives and exploring any regrets they may have. The ideal outcome would be for older adults to feel an overall sense of fulfillment and satisfaction with their lives. However, another possible outcome is feeling regret, leading to bitterness and resentment.

Question 392. You have been working with a 72-year-old man and his family. When the family comes to session, the man's daughter explains that the man has been making odd statements and not responding to questions appropriately. She reports that he seems confused. He has been unable to focus on reading, a daily enjoyable activity, for three days. Should you diagnose the man with delirium?

Answer. It is important to do a thorough assessment before diagnosing. In the case of this man, with his presentation of acute disturbance in consciousness, you might ask about illness, changes in medication, and substance use. You may refer the client for a physical exam and a neurological workup if the physical exam turns up empty-handed, before choosing a diagnosis. Assessment is always important and can be even more so when working with older adults since delirium may be impacted by medications, physical ailments, and substance use.

Question 393. True or false? Older adults generally have a low risk of suicide when compared to other age brackets.

Answer. False. Historically, suicide rates generally increase with age, and older adults often post some of the highest rates of suicide. There are many factors that experts believe could impact this risk. Some factors believed to be involved include the loss of support systems, undiagnosed and untreated mental health conditions, isolation, and the impact of physical ailments. Reminder: Just like all your clients, assess your older patients for suicide risk!

Question 394. What types of maltreatment should counselors who work with older adults be looking for?

Answer. When we talk about mandated reports of maltreatment, we are often thinking of abuse and neglect of children and minors. In many states, however, mandated reporting refers to any vulnerable person, including older adults (a.k.a. adult protective service). Moreover, counseling ethical codes stipulate that we should ethically report cases of abuse, neglect, and exploitation of older adults.

Older adults can be subjected to the same types of maltreatment as youth, including sexual abuse, physical abuse, emotional abuse, and neglect. When working with older adults, counselors should also look for signs of financial abuse and self-neglect. Signs of maltreatment among older adults can be obvious or non-apparent. For example, medical conditions or medications that lead to easy bruising may hide signs of physical abuse.

Question 395. Is the number of persons in the adult generation, those over 65 years of age, increasing, decreasing, or staying about the same?

Answer. With a little knowledge of generational birth patterns, one would notice that a good portion of the baby boomer generation is 65 or older or approaching that age. It is true that the population of older adults is increasing. In fact, by 2050 it is estimated to the number of older adults will double from 2010. This likely means that the need for counseling skills specific to older adults will also increase.

Question 396. What is cultural competence, anyway?

Answer. Although there isn't an agreement on the exact definition, cultural competence includes a counselor being mindful of their own culture as well as the client's. Hence, the culturally competent counselor considers culture when choosing interventions and interacting with others.

Question 397. Many theories of development failed to consider culture. However, one theory which does consider culture was developed by Lev Vygotsky. What is Vygotsky's theory called?

Answer. Vygotsky's sociocultural theory of development brought to light the importance of considering the role of society in a person's development. Moreover, Vygotsky's theory contains a concept called the "zone of proximal development." This explains the difference between what a person can learn on their own and the skills, knowledge, and learning that are gained with help from others.

Question 398. You are in diversity training being hosted by your organization. A colleague raises their hand and asks, "Wouldn't it be better to see everyone as the same rather than stereotyping people based on the groups they belong to?" As a culturally competent counselor, you recognize this ignorance of difference based on culture as an example of what multicultural concept?

Answer. This is an example of cultural blindness. Although your colleague is right that we shouldn't stereotype people, it isn't beneficial to overlook the importance of history and culture in peoples' lives. If we view everyone as the same, we may be ignoring histories of oppression and discrimination as well as histories of privilege. This can be harmful and lead to inappropriate and unethical behavior.

Question 399. A white, cisgender male, heterosexual, middle-aged, Jewish counselor is working with a Latinx, gay, male client who recently immigrated from Peru. The client speaks English and Spanish. How would the counselor approach work with this client in a culturally competent way?

Answer. Hopefully the counselor would have done some work to build self-awareness as it relates to his own culture, including his beliefs and biases. He would also want to examine any beliefs he has about the identities his client holds. What does he believe about gay men and immigrants? The counselor would also educate himself about the client's culture. However, he would not use any understanding gained to generalize regarding this client. He would allow the client to speak about his beliefs and experiences as an individual without expecting the client to educate the counselor on the client's beliefs. He would use this information to pick interventions that are appropriate for the client in the context of his culture.

Question 400. What does "worldview" mean and why is it important in counseling?

Answer. Worldview is a person's personal understanding of life within the context of a variety of internal and external factors. Simply put, worldview is one's view of the world. This encompasses personal beliefs, identity, hopes, cultural upbringing, traditions, family, language, and so much more. It is important for counselors to understand clients within the context of their worldview to better understand and support the client while avoiding harm.

12

Tiny Test Hints for Big Exam Scores

Is it possible to learn a lot of concepts in a few short minutes to raise your comprehensive exam score? You bet it is. Here's proof! Just study a few hints at odd moments in the day to get the most out of this section. Short study sessions outperform long ones every time. Your micro exam prep sessions could take place while you are waiting for your child's soccer game to begin, waiting (translation, possibly wasting time!) for the microwave oven to let you know your food is ready, relaxing on the beach, or when you have a few minutes before your next counseling class begins.

If you review just five questions daily – a reasonable number – you will have mastered 150 valuable hints in approximately a month. That's huge. Without any further ado, let's get this show on the road.

1. In research and evaluation: A biased sample is any sample that does not represent the population being investigated.
2. A double-blind study occurs when neither the experimenter nor the subjects know who is receiving the experimental variable.

DOI: 10.4324/9781003149712-12

3. Equine therapy uses horses to facilitate the treatment process. It has also been dubbed horse therapy or equine-assisted therapy.
4. Formative evaluation takes place while a program/treatment is occurring or ongoing. Some exams may use the term process evaluation. Summative evaluation takes place after a program/treatment has ended.
5. In statistics: Cohen's *d*. Statistician/psychologist Stanley Cohen's statistical technique for computing the effect size (ES). Goes beyond significance to reveal the magnitude of the effect. When comparing the means of, say, two groups: .2 or less is small, .5 is medium, .8 or more is large, 1.2 is very large, and 2.0 and over is huge. When comparing correlations XY .10 or less is small, .30 or less is medium, and .50 or more is large.
6. Cis, also known as cisgender. This is the child's gender assigned at the time of birth. Not related to romantic or sexual attraction.
7. Non-binary. Occurs when an individual does not identify with male or female genders or feels like a mix of genders.
8. Gender binary, the notion that only two genders, male and female, exist.
9. Ableism/ablism. Discrimination against an individual with a disability.
10. Bamboo ceiling. Career discrimination against Asians preventing them from entering management and leadership jobs.
11. Sticky floor barrier. Suggests Asians can land excellent jobs, but often there is no room to advance or move up the career line.
12. Outliers. In statistics, extremely high or low scores. Outliers can impact the mean even though it is the most useful average. (Imagine computing the average salary in your counseling class and then Bill Gates joins the class as your new student! The average salary would go through the roof.)
13. Congenital conditions are present at birth, though they are not necessarily inherited.
14. Confabulation occurs when memory gaps are filled in with events that never happened, although there is no intent to deceive.
15. Absolute confidentiality: The notion that confidentiality is never broken. Contrasted with relative confidentiality, suggesting that there are times confidentiality must be broken such as when a client is going to hurt themselves or others.
16. Asch situation. Named after social psychologist Solomon Asch. Takes place when an individual agrees with others in a group

situation even when it is very clear people in the group are obviously wrong!

17. Claims malpractice liability insurance *only* covers incidents occurring while you are paying for your insurance. Thus, if you had claims insurance in 2021 and a client takes legal action against you in 2023 (and you have another brand of insurance in 2023) for something you did in 2021, the insurance will *not* pay for it. Occurrence insurance *does cover* you into the future; however, it is generally costlier.
18. Aspirational ethics, also known as best practices, takes place when you go beyond ethical requirements to provide the finest service. Providing a free session when ethics do not stipulate this practice would be an example, as would providing bibliotherapy works for the client.
19. Pro bono services occur when the counselor receives no payment. Often applies to counseling clients with a low income.
20. Cultural incompetence takes place when a counselor does not possess the skills to help clients from other cultures.
21. A culturally encapsulated counselor (or cocoon) is a practitioner who has little or no knowledge of other cultures.
22. Gilbert Wren coined the term culturally encapsulated counselor in 1962 while writing an article for the *Harvard Education Review*.
23. CPT codes, also known as current procedural terminology, specify the service (e.g., individual or group psychotherapy) provided by the counselor, physician, dentist, and so on. A CPT code and International Classification of Disease Diagnosis will be required for third-party insurance and managed care payments.
24. A behavior typical in a culture is often termed culture specific.
25. Cultural blindness takes place when all clients are treated the same and differences in culture are ignored.
26. Neuroplasticity conveys the notion that the brain can change after a stroke, damage, or other injury. At one time it was thought that only children had this ability; however, this has been proven false. Your exam may use the term brain plasticity. Plasticity in this case means malleability.
27. A single nerve cell is a neuron.
28. A neurotransmitter is a chemical that allows transmission between nerves or nerves and muscles.

29. Neurofeedback is another name for biofeedback, often teamed up with behavioristic procedures.
30. Intensity takes place in family therapy when a therapist puts pressure on the family (often for an extended period of time) to change.
31. LPCS. Usually refers to a licensed professional counselor supervisor.
32. LPC-I or LPCI typically stands for licensed professional counselor intern.
33. Marijuana and alcohol are often called gateway drugs, meaning their usage can lead to more addictive and dangerous substances such as heroin or cocaine.
34. Gender fluidity suggests a person is not limited to a single gender. Could feel like a male at one time and a female at another. When the individual feels like a mix of genders, this is known as multi-gender. Changes can take place with or without a conscious decision.
35. In career counseling the concept of the glass ceiling suggests organizations often discriminate and therefore women and minorities cannot secure the highest positions.
36. EMDR stands for eye movement desensitization and reprocessing. This is a therapeutic approach created by Francine Shapiro intended to help clients overcome traumatic events. It is considered a valid evidence-based treatment for post-traumatic stress disorder or PTSD.
37. Bilateral stimulation is a term often associated with EMDR interventions. Lateral eye movements and tapping back and forth on shoulders would be examples. Nobody is certain why these actions can be therapeutic. One new hypothesis: These may impact the amygdala of the brain.
38. Face validity refers to whether an educational or psychological test appears to measure what it is purported to measure. Most experts agree it is of minimal importance.
39. The facial feedback hypothesis asserts that a given facial expression such as a smile will result in an emotion. For example, a person smiling would be more positive than someone who is frowning. Research does not generally support this view, pointing out that a depressed person can remain depressed though smiling.

40. Co-facilitation/co-therapy occurs when more than one person runs a counseling session, group, or workshop.
41. In legal matters: A fact witness, unlike an expert witness, can only provide observations and not opinions.
42. In behavior modification and applied behavior analysis (ABA), fading occurs when a stimulus (say, a positive reinforcing stimulus) is gradually added or removed.
43. Using several tests – rather than a single measure – to come up with a diagnosis, assessment, or prognosis is called a battery of tests.
44. Prognosis refers to a prediction of the outcome. For example: "After six sessions of career counseling this client will secure gainful employment."
45. The term prognosis guarded suggests that the client or patient may not recover from whatever is being treated.
46. In research: wash-out period. Having a subject discontinue a medication or treatment (say, an anti-depressant) before a trial begins to wash it out of the system. This ensures the current treatment (the independent variable) is responsible for the changes. Ethically, the risks of a wash-out must be taken into consideration.
47. Warm-up refers to get-acquainted exercises performed in a group setting.
48. In an individual setting, warm-up refers to conversation unrelated to counseling such as the weather or poor road conditions.
49. In group work, we-ness refers to the cohesiveness or unity in the group.
50. Exogenous. Any emotional or physical problem caused by factors outside the body. For example, anxiety caused by life events rather than a chemical imbalance.
51. Ice breaker. Any technique or activity to help group members get to know each other better and feel more comfortable. These experiences should not be threatening.
52. In Freudian psychoanalytic doctrine, hysteria occurs when a patient has symptoms which cannot be traced to physical difficulties. Many exams call this a conversion reaction.
53. A geriatrician is a medical doctor who is trained in health issues prevalent in older adults.
54. Gig economy refers to the practice of using temporary workers or contractors in place of traditional employees. Although beneficial

for some companies, the practice can undermine opportunities for persons seeking a long-term career.

55. Trait-factor vocational guidance is the oldest and longest-lasting theory of career choice. Championed by Frank Parsons, the so-called father of vocational guidance. Exams can use the terms matching, actuarial, or trait and factor approach to refer to this method, which relies heavily on tests and assessments.
56. *N* = 1 is a study with a single individual. Sometimes called a case study, this paradigm was popularized by Sigmund Freud, who worked extensively with psychoanalysis. For many years, the case study was not used extensively, but as of late it is becoming more popular, or, as some authors put it, the case study model is making a comeback.
57. Consider employing nontraditional counseling strategies such as using pictures and photographs, watching movies, telling stories, using a running or walking session with the client, or cooking a recipe that depicts their situation.
58. CAM stands for complementary and alternative medicine or complementary and alternative modalities.
59. Popular CAM interventions include music, movement, and dance therapy (DT); acupuncture; massage therapy; aromatherapy; biofeedback/neurofeedback; hypnosis; nutritional supplements or herbs such as St. John's Wort, which alter neurotransmitters for depression; ginkgo biloba or pregnenolone, a prohormone for enhancing memory; meditation; and chiropractic.
60. Carl Jung was an analyst who broke away from Freud and started his own school called analytic psychology. A major difference was Jung emphasized sex less than Freud.
61. Sexual addiction is *not* a legitimate DSM diagnosis.
62. The term nice counselor syndrome or NCS – first used to describe school counselors – coined by Fred Bemak and Rita Chi-Ying Chung in 2009, describes a counselor who values harmony over conflict and avoids dealing with social justice issues. This is not a good thing.
63. Pro-ana (meaning pro anorexia) websites often glorify anorexia and bulimia, praising extreme weight loss while discouraging a normal body image. Sometimes dubbed "thinspiration" sites. On occasion sites promoting bulimia are called pro-mia sites.

64. Charles Spearman in 1904 postulated the statistical technique for factor analysis summarizing lots of variables using the most important underlying factors. For example, a statistical analysis of excellent counselors might show that five common elements are evident in all the helpers out of 150 elements analyzed.
65. Central tendency bias occurs when a supervisor, boss, or evaluator rate most, and on some occasions all, supervisees/employees as average.
66. Central tendency bias can also refer to the tendency for persons completing an evaluation or survey to shy away from picking choices on the fringe of a scale (such as "the counseling session was the best ever" or the "worst counseling session I have ever attended.")
67. The GAF, or Global Assessment of Functioning, is *not* used in the DSM-5-TR.
68. DSM-5-TR should *not* be written with a Roman numeral such as DSM V.
69. In a quasi-experiment ex post facto design (literally meaning "after the fact"), there is no random assignment to the control and treatment groups. Thus, the researcher is unable to say that the IV caused the DV. Quasi means the paradigm resembles a true experiment; however, in the true experiment the subjects *are* randomly assigned to control and treatment groups.
70. Tabula rasa (meaning blank tablet, sometimes called blank slate in the literature or on exams) signifies that the mind is empty at birth. The concept was espoused by John Locke – and originally known as Lockean empiricism – and is emphasized in behaviorism.
71. Empiricism suggests all knowledge comes from experience.
72. Law of effect refers to Edward Thorndike's research demonstrating that a behavior followed by a pleasant consequence is strengthened or repeated. This later became popularized via B.F. Skinner's behaviorism.
73. The term conditioning simply means learning. Often applies to the work of Ivan Pavlov (i.e., Pavlovian a.k.a. classical conditioning), or B.F. Skinner (a.k.a. operant, instrumental, or Skinnerian conditioning).
74. Interval schedules of reinforcement in operant conditioning are based on time.

75. Fixed interval (FI) schedule example: The client receives one dollar for every five minutes for working on math homework. (It does NOT matter how many problems are completed or attempted!) This is the weakest schedule of reinforcement.
76. Ratio schedules of reinforcement in operant conditioning are based on performance or work completed. Fixed ratio (FR) schedule example: The client receives one dollar for every five problems completed from the math homework. (It does NOT matter how much time has passed.) A variable ratio (VR) schedule is considered the strongest schedule of reinforcement.
77. In variable schedules of reinforcement, the timing or number of responses necessary to receive the reinforcement changes or varies. (Example: A child is given a dollar after completing six math problems and then, say, after completing four more.)
78. In continuous reinforcement, a reinforcement is provided each time the target/desirable behavior is reached. Often the preferred method for shaping a new behavior at first.
79. Coming out: A person who openly discloses their sexual orientation or gender identity. Some exams use the term "coming out of the closet."
80. Four-phase treatment model for individuals, families, groups, and even organizations: 1) Engagement (using rapport to secure the client's trust). 2) Assessment (what are the client's needs?). 3) Intervention (plans for reaching the client's goals also recognizing possible barriers). 4) Evaluation/termination (if the goals have been achieved).
81. Four steps used in motivational interviewing (MI): 1) Engaging (creating a working relationship). 2) Focusing (i.e., on change). 3) Evoking (elicit ideas about change). 4) Planning . . . or a so-called plan of action.
82. Motivational interviewing, an evidence-based humanistic modality, was created by William R. Miller and Stephen Rollnick. It was originally intended to help clients with substance use disorders.
83. RFL. In suicide prevention, stands for reason for living. A higher level of reason for living generally indicates a lower chance of suicide.
84. Hope squads. A peer-to-peer suicide prevention program utilizing squad members nominated by peers and trained by advisors to stop suicide via peer intervention.

85. Operational definition. A set of instructions so detailed another individual can replicate them for research or treatment. Thus, not operational: The client took medicine for her depression. Operational: The client took 20 mg of XYZ medicine upon waking up at 6:30 AM each morning.
86. Preconscious (Pcs). In classical Freudian psychoanalytic theory: Feelings, impulses and thoughts which are not conscious but can be called into awareness such as recognition of a person or event. In Freud's topographical notion the preconscious is sandwiched between the conscious (Cs) and the unconscious mind (Ucs).
87. High-stakes tests/testing. Tests like the NCE, CPCE, counselor's license, comps, or even your driver's license, which can have a huge impact or consequences on your life or career. Or, to put it another way: passing or failing (i.e., the outcome) has a major influence on your future. There are positives (test takers take exams of this nature more seriously) and negatives (test takers often experience high levels of stress and professors are apt to ignore important material not likely covered on the exam).
88. The Tarasoff Decision: 1974, a duty to warn, and 1976, a duty to protect a client, refers to legislation from the California court system.
89. An independent organization known as the Master's in Psychology and Counseling Accreditation Council (MPCAC) exists as an alternative to CACREP since this organization will certify master's programs in psychology or counseling and psychology, while CACREP will not. However, currently, ACA only recognizes CACREP as the official institution accrediting body in counseling. I would check with your licensing board before enrolling in an MPCAC institution to ensure attendance would allow you to take the state counselor licensing exam.
90. Donald Meichenbaum is famous for his contributions to CBT such as CBM, or cognitive behavior modification, focusing on self-talk. In the 1980s, he pioneered stress inoculation training (the title of one of his books) to help curb anxiety.
91. Collateral information is any information obtained from a source other than the client, such as the client's attorney, a previous counselor, or test results obtained by from a different clinician or agency.

92. Hospice care is compassionate comfort care *without* treatment for terminally ill patients. Again, there is no curative intent. The patient cannot be cured, has a limited lifespan, or the treatment side effects outweigh the benefits. Palliative care is comfort care, with or without curative intent, and can be instituted at any point in treatment, ideally begun at the point of diagnosis. Palliative care often relies on life-prolonging medications or procedures.
93. The term encore career was popularized by Marc Freedman in his book *Encore, Finding Work That Matters in the Second Half of Life*. It refers to paid employment in a nonprofit, educational setting, social service agency, and so on as a substitute or alternative to traditional retirement. It provides a sense of fulfillment, generally doing something to benefit society or the community.
94. The phantom: A disruptive group member who arrives late and leaves early. The person could have too many outside commitments or might be using the behavior to secure attention.
95. ACT stands for acceptance and commitment therapy and is pronounced like the word "act." Created by the American psychologist Steven C. Hayes in 1982.
96. ACT fuses behavior therapy, mindfulness, cognitive behavior therapy, counterconditioning, and positive reinforcement.
97. ACT has six core principles: 1) Cognitive fusion. Step back. Detach. Your own thoughts and images are not always true. 2) Contact the person in the present moment. Use mindfulness, also known as "be here now." 3) Acceptance. Allow thoughts to come and go. Do not fight them. 4) Self-as-context. Some exams call this "the observing self." The you observing changes stays the same. 5) Values. What really matters and is important in your life? What is the big picture? 6) Committed action. What will it take to live your values?
98. Critics of ACT believe this modality is not truly different from other models.
99. ACT can be used with and without neurofeedback.
100. Telebehavioral health is covered in Section H, *Distance Counseling, Technology, and Social Media*, of the 2014 ACA ethics. Counseling is not limited to face-to-face interactions. Knowledge and competency in distance counseling, social media, and technical and legal considerations such as special certification or course work are important.

101. In telebehavioral services and (also called telemental health services) counselors are subject to laws in both the counselor's practice location and that of the client.
102. Clients have freedom of choice to use distance counseling, social media, or other technology as part of the counseling procedure. Always emphasize strengths and limitations and maintain a professional website with links to relevant licensing and certification sites.
103. Informed consent issues that go beyond the traditional face-to-face counseling process and must be delineated when using telebehavioral health distance counseling, technology, and social media include the specific location where the counselor's practice is located, contact information, distance counseling credentials, risks and benefits versus face-to-face counseling, what to do when the technology fails including alternative methods of service delivery, typical response time, emergency procedures when the counselor is not available, time zone differences, cultural/language differences/barriers and how these impact the sessions, the fact that insurance benefits could be denied, and finally your social media policy.
104. When using telebehavioral counseling, the counselor shares the limitations of confidentiality when relying on electronic records and transmissions including authorized and unauthorized transmissions to colleagues, supervisors, employees, and IT workers. This is known as acknowledgment of limitations in the ethics.
105. ACA's section H of the ethical code stipulates counselors use encrypted websites to meet legal standards and take reasonable precautions to ensure confidentiality when using any electronic means. The client should be informed regarding how electronic records are maintained and how long archival storage lasts.
106. ACA's Section H stipulates counselors create websites to provide access to persons with disabilities.
107. ACA's Section H stipulates counselors maintain separate professional versus personal social media web pages, making it easy to discern which sites are for which purpose.
108. ACA's Section H notes that counselors should take steps to avoid disclosing confidential information via social media sites.
109. Counselors performing distance counseling verify the client's identity using code words, numbers, graphics, and other nondescript means of identification.

110. Ideally, a lethality or so-called danger evaluation component should be included as part of the biopsychosocial assessment interview. Such an assessment will help determine how likely it is that the client will hurt themselves, often labeled as suicidality; somebody else; or both.
111. A biopsychosocial interview is conducted at the beginning of treatment as a valuable holistic assessment. It yields biological, psychological, and social information to form a more complete picture of the client's situation.
112. The biopsychosocial interview covers biological/physical issues such as ADHD, visual issues, dementia, alcoholism and drug abuse, hearing difficulties, medical procedures, and so on; psychological issues such as feelings, emotions, and family patterns including abuse, neglect, exploitation, and sexual abuse inflicted on the client; and finally, social issues such as problems making friends or bullying.
113. Systematic desensitization for phobias and anxiety, created by the South African psychiatrist Joseph Wolpe (pronounced volpay), is based on classical conditioning.
114. The two most important properties of a psychoeducational test are validity and reliability.
115. Validity is the most important property of a test, and reliability is the second most important property.
116. Validity addresses the issue of whether the psychoeducational test really tests what it purports to test accurately. High validity is better than low validity.
117. Reliability addresses the issue of whether a test gives consistent results. Here again, high reliability is better than low reliability. If you step on a scale one time and it says 150 pounds, and you step on it again moments later and it says 142 pounds, it is not reliable.
118. A valid test is always reliable. If you weigh 150 pounds, the scale will consistently/always say you weigh 150 pounds.
119. A reliable test, however, is not always valid. A reliable scale might always register your weight as 142 pounds. It is consistent, but if you weigh 150, it is consistently wrong! Think about it.
120. A correlation coefficient is often abbreviated using a lowercase *r*.
121. A correlation coefficient shows an association or relationship between variables rather than causation.

122. A correlation of .22 is smaller and shows a smaller association than, say, a correlation of .92.
123. In a positive correlation both variables go in the same direction, such as height and weight.
124. In a negative correlation (also called an inverse correlation on some exams) one variable goes up while the other goes down. Brushing teeth more should lead to fewer cavities.
125. A correlation of –.95 is stronger than a correlation of .94 even though it is a negative correlation. A negative correlation is still illuminating the strength of the relationship of the variables.
126. A statistic of zero in terms of correlation indicates a total lack of association between the variables.
127. There are only two perfect correlations: 1 (a.k.a. positive 1) and –1. A perfect correlation is virtually never seen in the real world except in the realm of mathematics, such as the length of an object measured in inches versus centimeters (a metric reading) as you would see on a tape measure or a ruler.
128. Neo-Freudians. Theorists who derived their theories from Sigmund Freud's psychoanalytic theory.
129. Neo-Freudian theories emphasize social, cultural, and interpersonal factors more than Freud.
130. Neo-Freudians de-emphasize sex and biology when compared to Freudians.
131. Notable neo-Freudians include Alfred Adler, Erik Erikson, Erich Fromm, Karen Horney, Harry Stack Sullivan, and Carl Jung. (Note: On rare occasions an exam will exclude Adler and Jung based on the fact these theorists broke away from Freud in the early stages of their careers.)
132. The American psychiatrist Harry Stack Sullivan applied psychoanalysis to treat schizophrenics and others with severe mental disorders. He also popularized interpersonal psychoanalysis, which emphasized interpersonal/interactional relations more than Freud's classical psychoanalysis.
133. Harry Stack Sullivan illuminated the good me, bad me, and not me concepts.
134. The good me is composed of things you like about yourself: things your parents would approve of. The bad me is composed of things you don't like about yourself. These behaviors are often disguised or hidden from others and even yourself. The not me

is made up of unconscious things that provoke so much anxiety they can result in horror, dread, nightmares, and even schizophrenic behaviors.

135. The concept of parataxic distortion, devised by Harry Stack Sullivan, refers to the fact that people often use projected distortions or fantasy when viewing others. A person in love might see the other person (erroneously or in a skewed fashion) as a nearly perfect soulmate. Some exams refer to this concept as transference distortion and categorize it as a defense mechanism.
136. Cultural humility: As a counselor, be humble, do not feel superior, and respect the other person's culture. Demonstrates the limits of cultural competence (i.e., realizing you can never totally understand the life-long experience of living in another culture). The concept was first created by Melanie Tervalon and Jann Mary Garcia in 1998 for health care settings.
137. Prejudice – ideas and opinions based on stereotypes/opinions and not facts – can be positive or negative. Positive: All persons of a certain culture are good at science and technology. Negative: All persons of a certain culture are not good at endeavors in science and technology.
138. Implicit prejudice is said to occur when prejudice is outside of the counselor's awareness.
139. Heteronormative society. A society accepting heterosexual behavior as the normal, preferred, or so-called default sexual orientation.
140. If another colleague is behaving in an unethical manner, your first step is to approach the colleague to discuss the behavior.
141. If you know the correct answer on the real exam, chose it as your answer stem. Duh. But, statistically, if you absolutely, positively do not know the answer to a question . . . you have no clue . . . on the real exam, your best guess is choice "B." "C," contrary to popular belief, is the worst choice!
142. If you absolutely, positively have no clue what the answer is on the real exam and perhaps "B" seems flat out wrong, choose the longest answer even if you must count the words!!!
143. If you absolutely, positively do not know an answer on the real exam and a stem has "all of these" or "none of these," there is a high percentage chance on your exam that one of them is correct!!! Note: For a full discussion of this topic, watch my popular

YouTube video *Dr. Rosenthal Swears These Tips For Guessing NCE, CPCE and Other Counseling Exam Answers Are Ethical.* Packed with over 30 minutes of information you have likely never heard before!

144. One popular theory is that low serotonin in the brain leads to depression.
145. Anti-depressants often keep serotonin in the brain or raise serotonin levels produced by the body.
146. A person's mood is often based on serotonin. Although too little is bad, too much is detrimental and has been referred to as serotonin syndrome.
147. Serotonin syndrome (again, higher than desirable levels of serotonin) can be brought on by adding – also called stacking – a natural antidepressant (say St. John's Wort or 5 HTP) to a prescription medicine such as Prozac. On some occasions just the prescription medicines alone can bring on the condition, especially when more than one antidepressant is prescribed.
148. Symptoms of serotonin syndrome include elevated body temperature, headache, shivering, sweating, confusion, nausea, diarrhea, and tremors. In extreme instances the condition can be life-threatening.
149. Cultural mosaic describes the cultures and ethnicities in the United States better than the old melting pot analogy.
150. Bicultural refers to flexibility between the dominant culture and the individual's culture of origin. More common in third-generation immigrants.
151. Traditional, when referring to acculturation, means adhering to the person's culture of origin while rejecting the mainstream culture. More common in first-generation immigrants.
152. Acculturated describes an individual who has moved away from their culture of origin and has now incorporated key components in the mainstream or in the past called dominant culture. Like the bicultural status, more common with third-generation immigrants.
153. Marginal or trapped, when referring to acculturation, describes an individual who is unable to incorporate the mainstream or the culture of origin. More common in first-generation immigrants.
154. In general, the more acculturated a client is, the less important it is to have a counselor who is matched in terms of ethnicity

and similar cultural background. However, a client who is in the beginning of the enculturation process may view a culturally matched counselor as more trustworthy. Assessing the level of acculturation is an important step in counseling.

155. Big five model. Also called the five-factor model, or even the big five factors of personality. Exams may also refer to it as OCEAN.
156. The acronym OCEAN stands for **O**penness to experience, **C**onscientiousness, **E**xtraversion, **A**greeableness, and **N**euroticism. Some exams use the acronym CONOE. These acronyms can also serve as memory devices.
157. NEO-PI-3 is a personality inventory – hence the PI in the name – used to assess an adolescent or adult's big five personality domains, mentioned in the OCEAN/CONOE acronyms.
158. The NEO-PI-3 is a clinical tool but is not considered a diagnostic assessment.
159. BDI stands for Beck Depression Inventory, a self-report questionnaire.
160. BAI stands for Beck Anxiety Inventory, also a self-report measure.
161. The Beck Inventories were created by the American psychiatrist Aaron T. Beck, sometimes cited as the father of cognitive therapy and the father of cognitive behavior therapy in the 1960s. This is debatable since Albert Ellis was using this approach prior to Beck, but exams often list Beck as the only choice.
162. One disadvantage of group work is that there is a lack of flexibility when compared to individual therapy. For example, most groups have a set date and time. If a client misses the group, there is not generally a way to make up the unique session.
163. In virtually every instance, a client receives less therapeutic time in a group session when compared to an individual session of the same duration.
164. Another disadvantage of groups is that since there are other members privy to client information, maintaining confidentiality is more difficult.
165. A disadvantage of group work is evident when a leader cannot block an emotionally harmful behavior from impacting another group member.
166. The Cattell-Horn theory postulates two types of intelligence: fluid and crystallized.

167. Fluid intelligence does not rely on the past, or previous knowledge. It allows the individual to solve abstract, novel problems. It seems to decline with age.
168. Crystallized intelligence relies on the past and prior learning. Examples include recalling historical events, key dates, and vocabulary. It has been defined as the sum of knowledge. Does not necessarily decline with age.
169. Jacob Levy Moreno and his wife Zerka T. Moreno co-founded psychodrama.
170. Psychodrama has often been dubbed the original form of group psychotherapy.
171. Jacob Moreno coined the terms "group therapy" and "group psychotherapy."
172. Triage: Sorting out the people in a crisis/disaster who can benefit the most from immediate intervention.
173. On exam questions dealing with triage, medical concerns (such as a cardiac emergency) should be addressed before tackling emotional difficulties such as a fear of public speaking. Remember that suicidal, homicidal, or self-harm would be the exception since although these are emotional difficulties, each constitutes a medical emergency as well.
174. Triad model: Another name for Freud's id, ego, super-ego theory of the mind. (Triad literally means three people or a group of three. Thus, in Freud's theory, three key points.)
175. Triad training model for improved multicultural counseling. A counselor works with a client from a different culture. An anti-counselor points out the differences in expectations and values. A third member (hence the term triad) is the pro-counselor and points out similarities.
176. Suicide is generally one of the dozen leading causes of death in the United States. More suicides occur in the United States than homicides . . . generally, over twice as many suicides!
177. Unlike counseling/therapy, crisis intervention is provided in close proximity to the event. Crisis intervention also relies on immediacy or providing treatment as soon as possible after the event.
178. In crisis intervention the focus is the current crisis, and the goal is to reinstate the client's functioning to that which was evident prior to the event. Counseling and therapy differ in the sense

that they often focus on events that are not current (say, the client's childhood) and the goal is to improve the client's functioning to go beyond pre-treatment levels.

179. If you believe a client might have suicidal tendencies, you should ask the client if they are suicidal. It will not put the idea in their head. In some settings all clients are asked this question as part of the initial assessment/evaluation.
180. An example of ageism (discrimination based on age) is evident when professional counselors report they perceive older adults as more difficult to work with.
181. Ageism is also evident when an individual is denied a job strictly because of their age. Often, when this is the situation, an older person does not get the job and the position is given to a younger person.
182. Alexander Wolf is often mentioned in the history of the group movement as helping to popularize psychoanalytic group therapy.
183. In immigrants, mental health wellness is associated with the perception that there is less distance (i.e., not a huge difference) between the mainstream culture and the person's immigrant culture.
184. DBT stands for dialectical behavior therapy, created by Marsha Linehan. It was initially created to help people diagnosed with borderline personality disorder (BPD).
185. DBT emphasizes mindfulness; a state of awareness of the present moment related to one's thoughts, feelings, experiences, emotions, and bodily sensations.
186. A state of mindfulness is a nonjudgmental state.
187. A longitudinal study follows the same group of people over time. It could be a short time or a prolonged period. An example would be following children who received advanced educational training in elementary school and tracking them through high school. Your exam might use the term cohort design. The researcher does not interfere or manipulate the subjects.
188. A longitudinal design is often contrasted with a cross sectional study where different populations are analyzed at a single point in time. A cross-sectional study is more like a photograph or a snapshot in time.
189. Dr. John E. Exner, an American psychologist, created the Exner scoring system for the Rorschach test.

190. The Rorschach, a projective ten-card inkblot test – created by the Swiss psychiatrist Herman Rorschach – is administered primarily by psychologists. The instrument is used much less by school psychologists than clinicians working in other settings.
191. Your exam could refer to the Exner scoring method as the Rorschach Comprehensive System (RCS).
192. Psychologist Dr. David A. Jobes created the Collaborative Assessment and Management of Suicidality, which might be referred to as CAMS on the exam.
193. When using CAMS, the client becomes the co-author of their own treatment plan, hence the concept that this approach is collaborative.
194. CAMS is a clinical philosophy of care. CAMS never uses shame or blames suicidal individuals.
195. CAMS is an evidence-based form of intervention targeted at suicidal risk.
196. Another evidence-based approach when working with suicidal clients is dialectical behavior therapy, or DBT.
197. CT-SP, or cognitive therapy for suicidal patients, based on Aaron T. Beck's work, also falls into this category.
198. CT-SP utilizes a ten-session, 50-minute approach with a manual.
199. Reaction formation is a defense mechanism.
200. In reaction formation the individual substitutes a diametrically opposed behavior that is the opposite of an unconscious impulse. For example: A person who fears gay impulses criticizes the gay lifestyle or engages in multiple heterosexual encounters.
201. Psychiatrist William Glasser coined the term positive addiction – also the title of one of his books – to refer to activities like jogging or meditation that enhance mental health by making life more satisfying.
202. In research, the hypothesis is an educated guess of the outcome (e.g., in an experiment).
203. Some experts are calling neuroscience the fifth force in counseling (first force psychoanalysis, second force behaviorism, third force humanistic approaches, and fourth force multiculturalism). Note: Some exams will list CAM, or complementary and alternative modalities, as the fifth force or include it in this category.)

204. Compassion fatigue (CF). Mental and physical exhaustion, stress, and burnout, experienced by police, firefighters, nurses, caregivers, and, yes, counselors/helpers of all kinds working with traumatized individuals.
205. Self-help groups can also be called mutual help groups (MHGs) or mutual aid groups. Alcoholics Anonymous (AA) and 12-step recovery programs would fall into this category.
206. In an experiment, the DV or dependent variable is the outcome variable or data. If you wish to research whether eating carrots raises IQ scores, then IQ scores are the DV. Carrots would be the IV, or independent variable, manipulated by the researcher.
207. Commit to memory: In a normal distribution, approximately 68% of the scores fall between plus/minus one SD (standard deviation); 95% two SDs, and 99.7 three SDs from the mean. This phenomenon is often called the 68–95–99.7 rule or the empirical rule.
208. According to the ACA Code of Ethics, counselors may provide a diagnosis if they have the knowledge, skill, and legal authority to render a proper diagnosis.
209. Counselors can be sued or have licensure complaints made against them if a misdiagnosis is made.
210. Lawsuits pertaining to failure to recognize suicidal or homicidal issues – from making a misdiagnosis – often yield very large legal settlements or verdicts if negligence is an issue. (Negligence is evident when the counselor did not provide reasonable or proper care and a harmful situation occurred.)
211. Since states vary widely in their regulations and statutes, counselors should contact their state licensing boards to be certain they have the necessary prerequisites to render a diagnosis. Some states will not specifically address this issue.
212. Although school counselors are often held to the same standards as LPCs outside of the school system in a crisis or emergency, a school counselor would typically not need to render a diagnosis for a student.
213. From a legal and ethical standpoint, counselors are expected to conduct a complete client history before providing a diagnosis.
214. An accurate client history should include prior therapy, symptoms, relevant medical history, medications, and a medical history related to the family of origin.

215. Upcoding – a form of insurance fraud – occurs when submitting a diagnosis or CPT code for services beyond what is necessary or performed to an insurance company, Medicare, managed care, and so on to raise the bill.
216. Downcoding constitutes another form of fraud, also called undercoding, and is often caused by insufficient documentation. The opposite of upcoding. Here the counselor provides a less serious diagnosis and/or CPT which brings in less money. (For example: A counselor might appear unqualified if the real diagnosis is used. Or the counselor appears to be a cost-effective helper in the eyes of the insurance company or managed care firm. Undercoding ensures a serious or strong diagnosis/label is not associated with the client.)
217. Never post information on the web which can lead to the identification of a client. When this occurs, it is known as "compromising confidentiality." This is true even when you have the best intentions and are trying to find a referral for a client using social media, listservs, or email groups. ONLY REVEAL FACTS THAT ARE ABSOLUTELY NECESSARY FOR OBTAINING THE NAMES OF QUALIFIED PRACTITIONERS! Merely changing the client's name or a small detail may not be sufficient to preserve the client/family confidentiality.
218. October 11th is Indigenous Peoples' Day, which celebrates, honors, and reminds us of losses endured by Native American people. Since it falls on the same day as Columbus Day (a federal holiday), some states celebrate this holiday, others don't, and a few celebrate both holidays.
219. Do not rapidly diagnose a client based on the diagnosis of the previous helper. Ask yourself if the symptoms and behaviors support the past diagnosis. Perform a complete assessment yourself.
220. Try to ascertain how a previous diagnosis was made and how the client identifies (or still identifies) with the diagnosis.
221. In recent literature, gambling, sex, pornography, and gaming addictions are often dubbed "behavioral addictions." Dopamine spikes in the brain resulting from engaging in these activities may fuel these addictions very much like drugs. This is sometimes called "stimulating the reward system."
222. Counselors should be familiar with 12-step programs in their catchment area for behavioral addictions (e.g., Gamblers Anonymous,

Sexaholics Anonymous, Food Addicts in Recovery Anonymous, Workaholics Anonymous, or Technology Addicts Anonymous).

223. In some instances, several groups may exist to help the same problem and it is best if the counselor has knowledge of the differences to make an appropriate referral.
224. The United States is generally seen as an individualistic culture. However, in collectivist cultures, self-identity is de-emphasized, and the group or family identity is at a premium. As an example, choosing whom to marry is often a family decision in a collectivist culture.
225. EBT, or evidence-based treatment, refers to approaches validated by using the scientific method with empirical data.
226. The symptom checklist 90-R – the R stands for revised – also called the SCL-90-R, is a short self-report instrument to evaluate psychological symptoms and psychopathology.
227. The SCL90-R gets its name from the fact that the questionnaire has 90 items and takes roughly 12 to15 minutes to complete. Can be used for clients 13 years of age and older.
228. The SCL-90-R is also valuable for research or measuring progress or lack of it after treatment.
229. Persons taking the SCL-90-R rate themselves for the last ten days on nine symptom dimensions: somatization, obsessive-compulsive, interpersonal sensitivity, depression, phobic anxiety, hostility, paranoid ideation, and psychoticism.
230. ESTs stands for empirically supported treatments listed by the American Psychological Association's Division 12 Society of Clinical Psychology, recommended treatments for specific psychological disorders. A resource for the public, practitioners, researchers, students, and clients. https://div12.org/psychological-treatments/.
231. Monoracial means having a single race or ethnicity. A person who does not have a mixed-race identity.
232. Multiracial individuals/persons. People who possess more than a single race or ethnicity. On exams biracial, multiracial, and multiethnic clients fall into this category. This includes over 7 million people in the United States.
233. Retired NCC status can apply to persons with NCC and NCC specialty status (e.g., CCMHC, MAC, NCSC) who are *not* practicing counseling or working in the field as a volunteer.

234. Persons with retired NCC status must adhere to NBCC ethics. A person with retired NCC status receives a reduced annual fee for the certification.
235. A retired NCC is not required to complete continuing education hours.
236. A retired NCC may use the designation NCC. There is no time limit on the retired status.
237. NCCs who apply for NCC reduced practice status may use the NCC designation; however, they must practice counseling for less than ten hours per week and thus can see a few clients and do volunteer work. Ten hours of continuing education is required every five years. Once again, they must adhere to NBCC ethics and there is no time limit on this status.
238. Temporary inactive NCC status can be used for health, family, or military service circumstances. Documentation is required and lack of employment or maternity/paternity leave are not acceptable reasons. This status may be retained for two years, and no fee is required. After this period the counselor returns to regular NCC status or relinquishes NCC certification.
239. NCC temporary inactive status does not allow the person to use the NCC designation. They must adhere to NBCC ethics and no continuing education hour requirement is mandated.
240. NCCs with retired, reduced practice, or temporary inactive status will receive *NBCC's Visions* and newsletter publications.
241. RCT stands for random controlled trials, sometimes dubbed "the gold standard in research"; however, this concept is currently under some scrutiny.
242. To rule out a pretest as a confounding variable in research, use the Solomon four-group design created by experimental psychologist Richard Solomon. Two of the groups will not receive the pretest, while two other groups will receive the pretest.
243. In the trait-factor theory of career counseling, the word "factor" refers to interests, values, abilities, and personality of the client related to job success and satisfaction generally ascertained from aptitude, personality, inventories, and other standardized tests.
244. When administering tests, counselors do not use outdated versions and only change portions of the test if this has been approved by the publisher of the instrument.

245. The APOE4 gene is often cited as the biggest genetic risk factor for the progressive neurogenetic condition Alzheimer's disease (AD). This form of dementia is named after the German psychiatrist and neuropathologist Alois Alzheimer (1864–1915).
246. A very common early symptom of AD is an inability to recall recent events.
247. AD is the most common type of dementia.
248. Bouts of clinical depression, high blood pressure, and head trauma appear to be risk factors in developing AD.
249. Trauma-focused therapy, or trauma-focused cognitive behavior therapy (TF-CBT), was originally used to help sexually or physically abused children. Today the scope of the modality is much broader, and it is common to use it with people experiencing PTSD.
250. Prolonged exposure therapy (PE) is often used in trauma focused therapy. PE consists of helping clients talk about (or imagine) and experience situations (in vivo) they have avoided since the initial trauma.
251. Piaget is often cited as the first major pioneer in the constructivism philosophy of education, as his cognitive theory of development emphasized that knowledge is attained by interaction with the environment. Or, to put it another way: Learners construct knowledge; they are not merely passive learners.
252. In Piaget's four-stage model all humans go through the same stages in the same order. This is a biological maturation model in the sense that interactions with the environment are emphasized. Intelligence undergoes changes as the child matures.
253. The term animism is often used in conjunction with Piaget's model. It is said to occur in the preoperational stage when a child gives an inanimate, a.k.a. not living, object human lifelike characteristics. For example, "My puppet feels cold outside and needs a coat."
254. Information processing theory views the human mind like a computer. Something transpires, your mind processes/encodes it in your memory, and then there is output including actions and behaviors.
255. Information processing theory (often included in the developmental portion of the exam) has several recommendations for teaching, including the use of mnemonic or memory devices (a favorite of mine as you know from my materials!), pairing

students to learn and review material, breaking down material into small parts, and putting both negative and positive comments on student's papers.

256. The information processing model is cognitive and focuses on how information is received (i.e., input or stimulus), processed, stored, and retrieved.
257. Names associated with information processing theory include George Armitage Miller, one of the founding fathers of cognitive psychology; John William Atkinson (a.k.a. Jack Atkinson); Richard Schiffrin; Alan Baddeley; and Graham Hitch.
258. In social psychology, attribution refers to what a person believes caused an event or behavior. For example, a friend's relationship with a significant other did not last because the individual was too co-dependent.
259. Austrian American Gestalt psychologist Fritz Heider is labeled as the father of attribution theory.
260. The fundamental attribution error asserts we emphasize internal sources, also called dispositional attribution sources (lack of people skills), more than external sources (poverty) when describing another person's behavior. In our own behavior we emphasize external sources, also known as situational attribution.
261. In social psychology, negativity bias suggests that negative traits and events have more of an impact on us than positive ones. A common example: In a job interview one negative thing you say when the interview committee asks about your limitations could easily outweigh numerous things when you verbalized about your strengths.
262. Some experts insist motivational interviewing (MI) is not a separate modality/school of counseling but rather a humanistic client-centered orientation to counseling.
263. MI – although based on client-centered/person-centered modality – stresses clear-cut goals more than traditional Rogerian counseling.
264. Correspondence bias is another name for the fundamental attribution error that could appear on your exam!
265. Confirmation bias is the tendency to believe, interpret, memorize, and even seek out information to confirm existing beliefs. A counselor who is convinced that Rogerian counseling is the best approach might ignore information that is critical of the approach or champions other schools of counseling as being superior.

266. Cherry picking is a specific type of confirmation bias in research where data are presented (or omitted) to support a theory, viewpoint, position, or procedure. A helper who is critical of career counseling might ignore 100 favorable studies but cite a single critical one, making it look like the scientific literature is not supportive of career counseling.
267. EMDR has been successfully used with children as young as four years old who are struggling with PTSD and is also a viable treatment for teens.
268. Systematic Training for Effective Parenting (STEP) began as a book in 1976 authored by Don Dinkmeyer Jr. and Gary D. McKay. The book has sold over four million copies and is based on the work of Alfred Adler.
269. Jane Nelson's positive discipline – also the name of her 1981 book – is also grounded in Adler's work and that of Rudolph Driekhurs.
270. On your exam, Latine can be used as an adjective or noun in place of the term Latinx. Like Latinx, this newer term is gender neutral and not gender binary. No consensus on which one is currently preferable; however, Latine is easier to use in Spanish than Latinx. Often pronounced LATEENA (just like the letter A in the alphabet). Along these same lines, the term Chicanx sporting a gender-neutral suffix might appear on the exam in place of the terms Chicano (masculine) and Chicana (feminine) Mexican Americans.
271. According to the American Psychiatric Association in a post made in 2019, about 75% of clients show some benefit from psychotherapy. Fewer sick days and improved work satisfaction were evident. Historically a less positive position was taken by the psychologist Hans Eysenck.
272. In 1952 psychologist Hans Eysenck concluded in a landmark study, "The Effects of Psychotherapy, An Evaluation," that psychotherapy was not effective and that the majority of the clients got better within two to three years (a.k.a. spontaneous remission) whether or not they were in therapy.
273. Eysenck's criticisms were aimed primarily at Freud's psychoanalysis and eclectic psychodynamic treatments. He was a huge proponent of behavior therapy but had serious reservations about cognitive behavior therapy, or CBT.

274. The Zeigarnik effect postulates you will remember unfinished tasks, or situations that are interrupted, better than those you completed. Cliffhangers in a television program (continued next week) or even a therapy session will be easier to remember. ("Next week when the group meets, we will talk about how students snared extremely high paying jobs.")

13

Final Overview and Last-Minute Super Review Bootcamp Version 4.0

Review this material *after* you have completed the entire *Vital Information and Review Questions, Master Lecture Series* text. **Do not skim over this review: it is a very powerful learning device and goes a long way to eliminate test anxiety**. I've even added a few last-minute concepts that can be explained in a sentence or two as exam insurance! You should begin scanning this chapter at least a week or so before the exam and even peruse it the night before or the morning of the exam. Here is your mini review on a little more than the head of a pin! Best wishes!

HISTORIC NBCC ANNOUNCEMENT

On November 17, 2014, NBCC president and CEO Dr. Thomas W. Clawson sent a communication revealing that NCC applications received after **January 1, 2022,** would only be accepted if the applicant possessed a master's degree or higher from a program accredited by the Council for Accreditation of Counseling and Related Programs. The date was subsequently changed to **January 1, 2024**. This will reduce the difficulty of securing a license when a counselor moves.

DOI: 10.4324/9781003149712-13

This will ***not*** affect anybody who currently has NCC status. The ACA is backing this position. Also, many states do not – repeat, do not – require licensed counselors to secure a degree from a CACREP-accredited institution.

NONPROFIT COUNSELING ORGANIZATIONS

Nonprofits must adhere to the **IRS 501(c)(3)** guidelines and will be exempt from paying federal income taxes. The organization will have a **board of directors**, and this board will be legally responsible for the agency's actions. In most states you must have at least three founding board members. The board sets policies and is not paid, and the staff will implement the policies.

ROSENTHAL'S 44 KEY RULES FOR AVOIDING LAWSUITS, ETHICAL VIOLATIONS, AND MALPRACTICE DIFFICULTIES

1. Get a medical diagnosis on clients to rule out physical and organic problems. You never want to treat a problem as a purely psychological (functional) disorder when it is organic.
2. Don't break confidentiality unless legal and ethical guidelines stipulate you should do so. Confidentiality lives on after the client is deceased.
3. Inform the client upfront that there are times when you need to break confidentiality, for example, you are subpoenaed and asked to provide information about a client. This is known as "relative confidentiality" or the "limitations of confidentiality." Your informed consent information statement should also delineate freedom of choice issues, fees, techniques you utilize, and your qualifications.
4. If you haven't been properly trained to treat a problem, don't treat it.
5. If you haven't been properly trained to use an approach, don't use it.
6. Never promise or guarantee that you will cure the client.
7. Never have sex or become romantically involved with a current client, client's partner, family member, or supervisee or use the relationship for monetary gains. According to the ACA,

you may have a romantic or sexual relationship with a former client if you wait five years after the last contact. NBCC states five years after termination as well. The relationship cannot be exploitative.

8. If you don't know how to handle a case, get supervision or seek out a consultation. The "standard of practice or care" concept refers to the fact that competent peers would have handled the situation in the same usual or customary manner as you.
9. Document your work by keeping good accurate records. Computerized or so-called electronic records require restricted access so only appropriate staff can view them.
10. Breach confidentiality if a client threatens to hurt themself or someone else relying on the principle of "minimal disclosure."
11. Always contact a hotline regarding child abuse and abuse of the elderly or adult with a disability. Counselors are mandated reporters.
12. Counselors and counselors-in-training should peruse the current NBCC Code of Ethics related to face-to-face counseling and technology-assisted distance counseling (i.e., Internet counseling, telephone counseling) and read ACA's Code of Ethics.
13. Practice fidelity by keeping promises and being loyal to clients. Lying, not keeping appointments, and breaking confidentiality for no good reason are examples of behavior that violates fidelity.
14. Always ask a client before you audiotape or videotape the session and explain how the recording will be utilized. Clients are not obligated to agree to this practice. Allowing supervisees and students to take recordings home could be detrimental to confidentiality.
15. Always secure malpractice (liability) insurance.
16. Initially provide the client with a written informed consent/disclosure statement with a transfer plan (in case you become ill, incapacitated, retire, die, or leave the practice) for the record and treatment.
17. Do not perform conversion or reparative therapy to convert members of the LBGTQ+ community to heterosexuals since LBGTQ+ lifestyles are not considered abnormal.
18. If you are running a group, let the group know that confidentiality is crucial, but you cannot guarantee it.
19. Refrain from giving the client a diagnosis in cases where the diagnosis might harm the client.

20. Steer clear of dual/multiple relationships with current or former clients unless the relationship is beneficial to the client (e.g., attending a graduation or visiting the client in the hospital). Document the reason you feel the interaction is beneficial in advance whenever possible. If a nonprofessional situation or relationship is targeted at meeting your needs and not the client's, then you should avoid it!
21. If you are a counselor educator, you must infuse multicultural and diversity material into all courses and workshops.
22. Never use a test, inventory, or assessment tool on a population unless that instrument has been normed on that population.
23. Never use a test or inventory that is obsolete or make client decisions based on obsolete test scores.
24. Use the title Dr. only if your doctorate is in counseling or a closely related field. If a degree is an honorary degree (versus a degree which is earned), this must be disclosed.
25. Do not use your regular counseling job to recruit clients for your private practice.
26. Do not use the label counseling psychologist unless you are licensed as a psychologist.
27. Do not make multiple or so-called duplicate submissions to professional journals.
28. If you are working with a terminally ill client who wishes to hasten their death, you have a right to break or not break confidentiality after you consult with appropriate professional and legal sources.
29. Work with your clients to jointly devise a counseling plan and review the plan on a regular basis.
30. If you are using a treatment team, you must inform the client. In addition, you should reveal the composition of the team.
31. If a client gives you a small gift based on the client's cultural norms, you could accept the gift if you feel the monetary value of the gift is appropriate ($20 or less, according to most experts) and the motivation for giving the gift is acceptable. It should not be a recurrent event and should promote, not endanger, the client's welfare.
32. Counselor educators who are book authors are permitted to use their books for classes and workshops.
33. A wealth of new technology-related ethical imperatives now exist. If you provide technology-assisted services (e.g., telephone

counseling, software, online counseling, websites, online assessments etc.), use encrypted websites and e-mail communications. If this is not possible, only use communications that are not client specific. Check legal regulations and the licensing bureau of the state where the client resides to determine if you must be licensed in that particular state. Provide language translation services for clients who communicate in a different language. Also, establish a password or set up a webcam system at the beginning of each session to verify the identity of the client. Consider taking NBCC's training to become a Board Certified TeleMental Health Counselor (BC TMH).

34. If you provide technology-assisted services, give the client emergency procedures in case technology fails and let the client know what services are covered under insurance. Moreover, ensure that technological accessibility meets the Americans with Disabilities Act (ADA).
35. If you are using a technique or treatment modality that is not proven via empirical evidence or a proven scientific foundation, always inform the client that the intervention is "unproven" or "developing." Discuss the possibility of harm with the client. If you are unsure whether a treatment modality is unscientific, consult with a former professor, colleagues, or other expert. Keep up with the latest research by reading textbooks and journals and attending professional workshops. Moreover, if you do harm a client unintentionally, you need to show that you attempted to remedy such harm.
36. Counselor supervisors should not counsel their supervisees.
37. Counselor supervisors should provide an on-call supervisor to assist supervisees in their absence.
38. A supervisor can legitimately recommend that a supervisee be dismissed from a training program or a professional setting.
39. Either a supervisor or a supervisee can legitimately terminate a supervisory relationship. A referral should be given to the supervisee.
40. Whenever possible, do not use deception with subjects in research studies. If you cannot find an alternative, then debrief the subjects as soon as possible.
41. Avoid fee-splitting and never accept a referral fee for a client.
42. Beware: Ignorance of ethical guidelines is not considered a valid excuse to violate them!

43. NBCC says you should not solicit testimonials from current clients. Wait five years. ACA also agrees you should not solicit testimonials from current clients or from others who might be "vulnerable to undue influence." ACA does not mention any waiting period.
44. Excessive self-disclosure pertaining to your own problems that will not help the client could be an ethics violation.

Ethical codes protect counselors, their clients, and the community. Moreover, such codes provide an outline for professional accountability and acceptable practice. These codes are not static and therefore do change over time.

HUMAN GROWTH AND DEVELOPMENT

The application of human growth and development theories to the practice of counseling became popular in the 1980s. In 1981 CACREP included this as a core content area. In 1983 APGA (now ACA) changed its name to the American Association for Counseling and Development to help emphasize the developmental aspects of our profession. Development is ongoing, systematic, orderly, and sequential and is said to build upon itself. The term *continual* implies that development occurs throughout the life span.

There is speculation as to whether individuals are active or passive in terms of influencing their development. Another issue centers on the nature or nurture debate. Is behavior the result of inborn tendencies/heredity (i.e., nature) or the environment (i.e., upbringing, nurture, and learning)? Current theorists insist it is both but disagree on the amount of impact exerted. The third arm may be **fetal origins**, referring to what happens to the fetus during gestation.

Changes can be **quantitative** (measured) or **qualitative** (change in organization or structure).

Many theorists stress the notion of **critical periods (also called sensitive periods or all or nothing periods)** where a behavior or developmental process, for example, language or types of visual acuity, can be acquired; otherwise, it is nearly impossible to develop at a later time of life.

Ironically, young children have **more neural connections than adults**.

If **genetics** play such a strong role in development, why are children from the same family often so much different? The current notion is that **shared experiences/influences** (all family members attended the same family functions, went on identical vacations, etc.) have less impact than **nonshared individual experiences/influences** (siblings may have different teachers, friends, etc.). Also, individuals may perceive the same event in totally different ways.

MAJOR THEORIES AND THEORISTS

G. Stanley Hall

Founder of psychology in the United States and the first president of the American Psychological Association. He popularized the study of the child and child guidance. Wrote seminal works on adolescence.

Behaviorism

Behaviorism was outlined by John B. Watson, Ivan Pavlov, Joseph Wolpe, and B.F. Skinner. Initially the mind is a blank slate, and the child learns to behave in a certain manner. This is basically a passive theory. The mind can be compared to a computer being fed information. This model relies on empiricism – John Locke's view that knowledge is acquired by experience. All behavior is the result of learning.

Erik Erikson's Eight Psychosocial Stages

Erikson's stages are delineated in his classic 1963 work *Childhood and Society*. The stages are based on ego psychology and the epigenetic principle that states that growth is orderly, universal, and systematic. The stages are: **trust versus mistrust** (birth to age 1½ years), **autonomy versus shame and doubt** (1½ to 3 years), **initiative versus guilt** (3 to 6 years), **industry versus inferiority** (6 to 11 years): **identity versus role confusion** (12 to 18 years), **intimacy versus isolation** (18 to 35 years), **generativity versus stagnation** (35 to 60 years), and **integrity versus despair** (age 65 and beyond).

Jean Piaget's Qualitative Four Stages of Cognitive Development (Genetic Epistemology)

Theory: Sensorimotor (birth to 2 years), **Preoperational** (2 to 7 years), **Concrete Operations** (7 to 12 years), and **Formal Operations** (11/12 to 16).

- Patterns of thought and behavior are called **schema** or the plural, schemata.
- **Adaptation** occurs *qualitatively* when the individual fits information into existing ideas (also known as assimilation) and modifies cognitive schemata to incorporate new information (this is called accommodation).
- **Assimilation** and **accommodation** are said to be complementary processes. The ages in the Piagetian stages can vary; the order is static.
- **Object permanence** occurs in the sensorimotor stage (an object the child can't see still exists).
- **Centration** is the act of focusing on *one* aspect of something. It is a key factor in the preoperational stage. Typical example: child looks at the number of pieces of a sliced cake but not the size of pieces.
- **Conservation** takes place in the concrete operations stage. The child knows that volume and quantity do not change just because the appearance of an object changes (e.g., pouring a short glass of water into a tall skinny glass does not alter the amount of the liquid). The child comprehends that a change in shape does not mean a change in volume.
- **Abstract scientific thinking** takes place in the formal operations stage.

Robert Kegan's Five Stage Adult Constructive Developmental Framework Model

Keagan's model emphasizes the impact of interpersonal interaction and our perception of reality relying on five stages of development. The self-concept is influenced by two major motivations, wanting to be autonomous yet also wanting to be part of a group.

Lawrence Kohlberg's Three Levels of Moral Development

Each level has two stages: **preconventional level** – behavior governed by consequences, **conventional level** – a desire to conform to socially acceptable rules, **postconventional level** – self-accepted moral principles guide behavior.

Carol Gilligan's Theory of Moral Development for Women

Gilligan's 1982 book *In a Different Voice* illuminated the fact that Kohlberg's research was conducted on males. Women have a sense of caring and compassion.

Daniel Levinson Four Major Eras/Transitions Theory

In a 1978 classic book titled *The Seasons of a Man's Life*, Levinson depicted the changes in men's lives throughout the lifespan. The four key eras include: childhood and adolescence, early adulthood, middle adulthood, and later adulthood.

Lev Vygotsky (1896–1934)

Vygotsky proposed that cognitive development is not the result of innate factors but is produced by activities that take place in one's culture. His **zone of proximal development (ZDP)** refers to the difference in the child's ability to solve problems on their own and the capacity to solve them with help from others.

Freud's Psychoanalytic/Psychodynamic Five Psychosexual Stages

Freud's stages are **oral** (birth to one year), **anal** (1 to 3 years), **phallic/Oedipal Electra complex** (3 to 7 years), **latency** (3 to 5 until age 12), and **genital** (adolescence and adulthood).

Libido is the drive to live and the sexual instinct that is present even at birth. It is said to be sublimated in the latency stage, as the individual has little interest in sex. This ends when puberty begins.

- **Regression** is the return to an earlier stage caused by stress.
- **Fixation** implies that the person is unable to move to the next stage.
- Freud is criticized for focusing on sex and not including the entire lifespan in his theory.

Abraham Maslow's 1943 Hierarchy of Needs

Maslow interviewed self-actualized people. His work is commonly represented as a pyramid (the pyramid itself was not created by Maslow but by others who prized his work) with lower-order physiological and safety needs at the bottom that must be fulfilled before self-actualization can occur near the top of the pyramid.

William Perry's Three Stage Theory of Intellectual and Ethical Development in Adults/College Students

Dualism, in which students view the truth as either right or wrong. **Relativism** is the notion that a perfect answer may not exist. There is a desire to know various opinions. **Commitment to relativism** – in this final stage the individual is willing to change his or her opinion based on novel facts and new points of view.

James W. Fowler's Pre-Stage Plus Six-Stage Theory of Faith and Spiritual Development

Fowler conducted 350 structured interviews and drew on the work of Piaget, Kohlberg, and Erikson. **Stage 0 undifferentiated (primal) faith** (infancy, birth to 4 years); **Stage 1 intuitive-projective faith** (2 to 7 years, early childhood); **Stage 2 mythic-literal faith** (childhood and beyond); **Stage 3 synthetic-conventional faith** (adolescence and beyond), a stage of conformity); **Stage 4 individuative-reflective faith** (young adulthood and beyond); **Stage**

5 conjunctive faith (mid-thirties and beyond), openness to other points of view, paradox, and appreciation of symbols and metaphors; and **Stage 6 universalizing faith** (midlife and beyond) – few reach this stage of enlightenment.

- According to Fowler, faith is not identical to one's belief in religion. "Faith can be religious faith, but it can also be centered on a career, a country, an institution, a family, money, success, or even oneself." Faith grows and changes throughout the lifespan.

Diana Baumrind's Typology of Parenting Styles

Authoritative: High expectations for the child but is warm and nurturing. The child is **given an explanation of the rules.** Generally, produces a child who is happy, does well in school, and has good emotional regulation and fine social skills

Authoritarian: Characterized by bossy parenting that **champions "follow my orders" with no explanation**. Punishment and verbal insults are used liberally. Can produce anxious, withdrawn children who are likely to engage in antisocial behavior, including alcohol and drug abuse, stealing, and gang activities.

Permissive Passive Indulgent: Parent has a low level of control and is easily manipulated. Rarely says "no" to a child and is nonpunitive. **Very affectionate and wishes to please the child like a friend**. Child can display a lack of social skills and boundaries and can be extremely demanding. Children often use drugs and alcohol.

Teen Pregnancy

Yes, often included on this area of the exam; although the number of teen pregnancies is declining, the United States still sports the third highest rate of any industrialized nation. Both moms and kids have more difficulties such as preeclampsia (very high blood pressure during pregnancy), prenatal addiction, children with low birth rates, and children who are delinquent and have mental health and addiction issues. Children born to teen moms are statistically more likely to become teen moms themselves.

SOCIAL AND CULTURAL FOUNDATIONS

Culture is defined as habits, customs, art, religion, science, and the political behavior of a given group of people during a given period of time. Cultures are said to be **dynamic:** each culture changing or evolving at its own rate. The dominant or major culture in a country is the **macroculture**, often contrasted with the smaller **microculture**. Learning the behaviors and expectations of a culture is known as **acculturation. Cultural humility** is a way to view **cultural competency** as an ongoing process and not an end product. The construct suggests you need a lifelong commitment to perform self-evaluation, fix power imbalances where they should not exist, and develop partnerships to advocate for others.

The goal of understanding diversity is to become a **culturally competent counselor** who will treat the client with respect regardless of their race, culture, ethnicity, traditions, religious beliefs, sexual orientation, and anything else that makes them unique. The goal is improved counseling outcomes. The United States continues to become more diverse, and the population is getting older. The most vulnerable populations (children under 17 and adults over 65) are growing, signifying a need for adept counselors.

Universal culture implies that we are all genetically and biologically similar: **"biological sameness"** (i.e., we all need air, food, and water); **national culture** can determine our language, political views, and our laws; **regional culture** gives us the behavior for a certain region; and **ecological culture** where factors such as earthquakes, floods, and food supply may influence our behavior.

- **Racism** occurs when one race views itself as superior to others. A given race has a set of genetically transmitted characteristics such as Caucasian, African American, or Asian. **Institutional racism** occurs when policies, laws, or institutions provide different access to goods, services, resources, or opportunities based on race. Racial profiling is cited as a common example.
- **Ethnocentrism** means that a given group sees itself as the standard by which other ethnic groups are measured.
- **Emic versus etic** distinctions. In the emic approach, the counselor helps the client understand their own culture. In the etic

approach, the counselor focuses on the similarities in people, treating people as being the same.

- **The autoplastic–alloplastic dilemma**. Autoplastic implies that the counselor helps the client change to cope with their environment. Alloplastic occurs when the counselor has the client try to change the environment (e.g., advocate for a wheelchair ramp).
- **Tests** and nosological systems such as the DSM can have a Eurocentric or Euro-American bias.
- **Paralanguage** implies that the client's tone of voice, loudness, vocal inflections, speed of delivery, silence, and hesitation must be taken into consideration. It is part of the study of nonverbal communication and is usually considered more accurate than verbal communication.
- **Low-context communication versus high-context communication** was postulated by anthropologist **Edward T. Hall.** Low context implies that there will be a precise *explicit* verbal explanation and possibly repetition, such as summarizing at the end of a class, meeting, or a group counseling session. Popular in the United States, United Kingdom, Canada, and Germany. High-context communication is *implicit*. It is common in the Middle East, Italy, Spain, and Asian countries. It relies on nonverbal over verbal, respect for tradition and the past, and is readily understood by others in the culture with a shared frame of reference.
- **Stereotyping** is the act of thinking that all people of a group are alike. Stereotypes can be good or bad.
- **Prejudice** occurs when we have an opinion based on insufficient evidence.
- **Androgynous/androgyny** the notion that psychologically healthy people possess both masculine and feminine characteristics.
- **Proxemics** addresses the issue of personal space, also known as **spatial relations**. A counselor who sits too close to a client, for example, may make the client uncomfortable. Communication and social relations are impacted by proxemics.
- **Means tests** determine whether a client is eligible for a social program or benefit such as temporary assistance for needy families (TANF) or food stamps/Supplemental Insurance Nutrition Program (SNAP). Income and assets such as bank accounts are often used to make this determination. Often contrasted with **social insurance programs** such as social security for which an extremely wealthy person could still be qualified.

- **Social comparison theory,** popularized by early research conducted by **Leon Festinger**, simply postulates that we evaluate our behaviors and accomplishments by comparing ourselves to others. Festinger is also well known for his **cognitive dissonance theory** asserting that individuals will change their beliefs to match their behavior when there is a mismatch. This reduces the tension created by the initial inconsistency.
- **Confirmation bias.** Acknowledge information that supports your point of view and ignore that which does not.
- Counselors strive to understand a client's **worldview** (the way the client sees the world due to attitudes, value systems, and beliefs).
- **Socioeconomic factors** must be considered when counseling clients. Over 11% of the US population lives below the poverty threshold set by the US government.
- **Social comparison theory.** We compare ourselves with others to evaluate ourselves. **High self-monitoring individuals** care about their self-image and what others think of them.
- The affiliation statement **misery loves company (or literally miserable company!)** is often true, according to **Stanley Schachter**.
- Women are more apt to talk to others (especially other women) in a social situation.

Anglo-conformity theory asserts that people from other cultures would do well to forget about their heritage and try to become like those in the dominant macroculture.

- **The five-stage Atkinson, Morten, and Sue racial/cultural identity development model (R/CID)** a.k.a. the minority identity model: 1) Conformity (lean toward dominant culture and prefer a counselor from the dominant culture); 2) Dissonance (question and confusion, prefer a counselor from a minority group); 3) Resistance and Immersion (reject the dominant culture while accepting one's own culture); 4) Introspection (mixed feelings related to the previous stage, prefer a counselor from one's own racial/ethnic group); and 5) Synergetic Articulation and Awareness (stop racial and cultural oppression, prefer a counselor with a similar attitude or worldview over merely a counselor who is the same race/ethnicity but has different beliefs). Not everyone goes through all stages, and some individuals never progress beyond the second or third stage. An individual can also go backward.

- **Gay and lesbian couples** raise children who are as happy as children raised by heterosexual couples and possess good cognitive and social skills. In every area, including mental health, these children fare as well as children raised by heterosexual couples.
- **Sexual orientation, identity, and terminology related to sexual questions on your exam. LGBTQ+** is the acronym for lesbian, gay, bisexual, transgender, and questioning (unsure regarding source of attraction/identity). The "Q" can also stand for queer. The + at the end refers to other gender identities or sexual orientations. **Transgender:** Term describes individuals where gender expression or identity does not match gender assigned at birth. Transgender persons can be gay, asexual, bisexual, lesbian, or heterosexual. **Pansexual:** Attracted to people regardless of gender. **Cisgender/Cissexual:** Identification with gender assigned at birth. **Homophobia/Biphobia/Transphobia:** An exaggerated irrational fear or discrimination against homosexual, bisexual, and transgender persons and behavior. **Internalized Homophobia/ Biphobia/Transphobia:** Self-hatred and/or shame over homosexual, bisexual, or transgender identity and/or attraction. **Transgender, MTF:** Gender assigned at birth was male, but person identifies as a female. **Transgender, FTM:** Person was assigned a female gender at birth, but currently identifies as male. **Cross-dresser:** Wearing or dressing up in clothes worn by a different gender.

Machismo may be used to describe the belief that women are subservient to men, or dominated by them, and that men are expected to provide for the family. Can also signify overly assertive or aggressive masculine behavior.

Colorism is discrimination predicated on skin tone or skin color. Colorism is often perpetrated by persons of the same racial or ethnic group. Light skin is often favored over dark skin.

Person-first language, a.k.a. people-first language. The person should be designated first and then their condition. Example: Do not say "a visually impaired client" but rather "a client with a visual impairment." A disability should not be the defining feature or the primary characteristic, and therefore it should not come first in written or oral communication. Person-first language shows respect for the individual. The terms handicapped, invalid, birth defect, and cripple should be avoided.

Isms are suffixes added after a term to show prejudice or discrimination toward a person or a group. Common examples include racism, religionism (other religions are inferior to yours), classism (blue collar, white collar, middle-class etc.), ableism (persons with a physical, intellectual, neurological disability), or sexism (belief that one sex is better than another), and ageism. In terms of **ageism** (also spelled agism), not hiring a qualified individual because they are "too young" or "too old" would be an example.

Five Famous Experiments in Social Psychology:

1. **Phillip Zimbardo (1971 Stanford Prison Experiment)** A situation can control behavior as well as assigned roles, such as telling subjects to be a guard or a prisoner. Would not be ethical today.
2. **Muzafer Sherif and Carolyn Wood Sherif (1954 Robbers' Cave Experiment)** Two opposing groups of boys ended up working together because they were both attempting to solve the same problem (called a superordinate goal).
3. **Solomon Asch/Asch Situation (1950s studies regarding conformity based on the length of a line)** In a social or group situation people would sell out and agree with the opinions of others about the length of the line even when they knew the individuals were clearly wrong!
4. **Bystander Effect/Apathy** The greater the number of people in a group, the *less* likely they are to assist a person in need (and will be slower if they do intervene)! The 1964 case of Kitty Genovese is seen as the quintessential example. Also billed as "group inhibition for helping."
5. **Stanley Milgram (1963 publication of obedience to authority experiment)** 65% of subjects gave painful electrical shocks to innocent victims when instructed to do so by an authority figure! None stopped even when a participant said they had heart trouble! Some experts insist this could explain the Holocaust.

THE HELPING RELATIONSHIP

There are over 400 approaches to psychotherapy and counseling worldwide. Most counselors claim they use several approaches and thus would be classified as eclectic or integrative. **Very important:** Research illuminates that the therapeutic relationship contributes to 30% of the client outcome.

The Helping Myth

Research demonstrates that having a counselor and a client of the same gender and ethnicity does not necessarily produce a better therapeutic relationship. The data are not strong, and clearly more research is necessary.

Happiness

Most people overestimate the impact an event will have on their degree of happiness or unhappiness. For example, individuals believe that marriage or winning the lottery will make them happy. The happiness boost for marriage lasts roughly two years, while the increase from winning the lottery spans about six months. In general, people are poor at forecasting affective/emotional reactions.

Psychotherapy and Counseling Are Cost Effective

Cost benefit analysis (CBA) reveals that therapy reduces mental health expenditures in the community. Unfortunately, insurance and managed care firms primarily push medication as a first line of treatment for mental health issues.

Minimal encouragers and lead statements – often classified as a micro-skill – are used in most counseling sessions to encourage clients to say more and let the client know you are listening. Could be a statement like, "tell me more, "continue," or even a nonverbal such as a smile or nodding one's head.

Sigmund Freud's Psychodynamic Psychoanalysis

Psychoanalysis is a theory of personality and a form of psychotherapy. It is a long-term form of treatment often lasting three to five years or more. In classical analysis, the patient (the analysand) is seen four or five times per week. This form of therapy is said to be historic since it focuses on the past.

- Patient is asked to engage in **free association**, which is saying whatever comes to mind.
- **Dreams** are very important and generally viewed as a process for wish fulfillment. Research does not support the Freudian wish fulfillment notion.
- **Unconscious material** is examined.
- **Freud emphasized ego defense mechanisms: repression** (most important) – something that is too painful to face is totally involuntarily forgotten; **displacement** – taking your anger out on a safe target rather than the source of your anger; **projection** – you can't accept a quality about yourself, so you attribute it to others (i.e., you think that you are looking out a window but you are really looking in a mirror); **reaction formation** – you deny an unacceptable unconscious impulse by acting in the opposite manner; **sublimation** (often cited with career counseling) – you express an unacceptable impulse in a socially acceptable manner; **rationalization** – when a person overrates or underrates a reward or outcome; **identification** – joining a feared person (such as a gang) to relieve your anxiety; **suppression or denial** (not unconscious or automatic) – occurs when you purposely don't think of a situation.
- **Transference** is also a key principle. The analysand (client) behaves as if the analyst is a parent or caretaker from the past.
- The discharge of repressed emotions is called **abreaction or catharsis**.
- According to Freud's structural theory, the personality has three systems, a **superego** (the moral seat of the mind housing two entities, the **conscience and the ego ideal**); **the ego** or **reality principle** that balances the id and the superego; and **the id**, which houses biological forces, especially sex and aggression. The id operates on the **pleasure principle**, striving for immediate gratification and tension reduction.

- **Eros** is the life instinct, **thanatos** the death instinct.
- Critics charge Freud used only case studies to test analysis rather than using true scientific experiments.

Carl Jung's Analytic Psychology

Carl Jung broke away from Freud in 1914 because he felt Freud overemphasized the role of sexuality. His approach, like Freud's, is psychodynamic.

- The unconscious has two parts: a **personal unconscious** (very similar to what Freud postulated) and **the collective unconscious** (an unconscious that one inherits which is common to all individuals). The collective unconscious is composed of archetypes (original models or prototypes) passed down through the ages.
- Archetypes include the **persona**: a social mask the person wears. To explain gender Jung cites the **animus** or the masculine side of the female and the **anima** or feminine side of the male. Individuals are said to be **androgynous**, having both male and female characteristics. He also speaks of the shadow, or the so-called dark side of the personality related to animal instincts. **The self** is symbolized via a mandala (a magic circle in Sanskrit) or a balance between the personal unconscious and the collective unconscious.
- Jung created extroversion/**introversion typologies**. Jung felt that we possess both; however, one is dominant. The Myers-Briggs Type Indicator (MBTI) has its roots in his work.
- **Individuation** was Jung's term for becoming a unique human being.
- **Synchronicity** suggests that meaningful coincidences not related by any obvious causal relationship may be worth analyzing.

Alfred Adler's Individual Psychology

Alfred Adler broke away from Freud to create his own theory. Adler's individual psychology is a psychodynamic approach that focuses on the fact that behavior is one's unconscious attempt to compensate for feelings of inferiority. An individual constructs a lifestyle which is chosen.

- Adler stressed the **"will to power"** to generate feelings of superiority.
- The theory adheres to the principle of fictional finalism or the notion that behavior is motivated primarily by future opportunities rather than the past.
- Adler felt **birth order** (also called place in the family constellation) was important. First-born children are conservative leaders. Second-born kids tend to be more competitive and rebellious. Sibling interaction can have a greater impact than parent–child interaction. Since Adler felt behavior is highly influenced by future goals rather than one's past, this is a **teleological theory**.

Behaviorism, Applied Behavior Analysis, Behavior Modification, and Behavior Therapy

Key reminder: newer exams often refer to **behavior modification** as **applied behavior analysis (ABA)**. ABA looks at observable behavior rather than hypothetical constructs. **The key concept is that behavior is learned and not pathological**.

John B. Watson coined the word *behaviorism*, while Arnold Lazarus created the term *behavior therapy*. Counselors who use these approaches assume that behavior is based on learning rather than insight into the unconscious mind. The criticisms of behavior therapy are that it does not yield insight; it treats symptoms, not the root cause; and it can be manipulative and often changes behavior but not underlying feelings.

- **B.F. Skinner's radical behaviorism** purports that behavior is molded solely by its consequences. This paradigm is known as operant or instrumental conditioning.
- **A positive reinforcer** is a stimulus that raises the probability that a behavior will be repeated. The reinforcer must come after the behavior (or operant).
- **Negative reinforcers** also raise behavior. For example, a recruit in the military makes a bunk bed to avoid being yelled at by a drill instructor. All reinforcers, whether positive or negative raise behavior. All reinforcers are said to follow or come *after* a behavior (e.g., a youngster gets a prize after she completes a math problem).

- **Albert Bandura** speaks of **social learning theory**. Here the person's own behavior increases when they see somebody else getting reinforced for it, also referred to as vicarious learning, observational learning, or modeling.
- **Punishment** is intended to lower behavior by suppressing it.
- Behaviorists champion role playing (e.g., assertive behavior).
- **Extinction** (such as time-out) will lower behavior after an initial extinction burst or response burst.
- **Ratio schedules of reinforcement** rely on work output whereas **interval schedules** rely on time. **Ratio schedules are more effective than interval schedules**.
- **Continuous reinforcement** occurs when each behavior is reinforced. Good when first learning a new behavior.
- **Intermittent reinforcement or variable reinforcement** occurs when the desired behaviors are reinforced some of the time, but not all the time (e.g., a child gets a treat for every third math problem). **Variable reinforcement is more effective than a fixed schedule where you always reinforce in the same manner (e.g., after every instance of the behavior)**.
- **Shaping with successive approximations** is reinforcing small chunks of behavior that lead to the desired behavior.
- **Differential reinforcement of other behaviors (DRO)/differential reinforcement of alternative behavior (DRA)** takes place when the helper reinforces behaviors other than the dysfunctional behavior to reduce the dysfunctional **target behavior** (e.g., you want a child to quit talking in class, so you give a gold star only when the student is doing work and not talking). Procedure relies on reinforcement and extinction.
- In Skinnerian **operant conditioning**, the behavior is affected by the consequences that come after the behavior.
- **Ivan Pavlov** popularized what is now known as **classical conditioning**. **John B. Watson's** work was also significant. Behavior modification/applied behavior analysis is generally based on **Skinner**, while behavior therapy usually has its roots in **Pavlov. Interventions based on classical conditioning include sensate focus, systematic desensitization, flooding (a.k.a. in vivo exposure with response prevention or deliberate exposure with response prevention), implosive therapy, and assertiveness training**.

Classical or respondent conditioning = learning by pairing things together.

Operant conditioning based on the work of Skinner and Thorndike = learning by consequences occurring after a behavior.

- **Joseph Wolpe's systematic desensitization** can be conducted individually or in a group to curb fears and abate anxiety. Wolpe believed his technique of counter-conditioning was based on Pavlov and relied on relaxation and imagining feared stimuli. That said, newer research using dismantling (which deconstructs a procedure) revealed that relaxation is not necessary, and therefore it is extinction, and not counter conditioning, that is making the difference. Along those same lines, it has also been discovered that Dr. Francine Shapiro's **eye movement desensitization and reprocessing therapy (EMDR)** can be effective for ameliorating conditions caused by trauma or disturbing events *without the eye movement*, once again indicating that extinction is likely the curative factor.
- Behaviorists may also use **implosive therapy** where the client imagines scary or feared stimuli in the safety of the counselor's office.
- **Biofeedback/neurofeedback** devices are used to enhance the client's self-control of the autonomic nervous system. Examples include heart rate, brain waves, or warming cold hands with thermal training for migraine headaches or Raynaud's phenomenon. This is a form of operant conditioning. Biofeedback/neurofeedback is popular in **neurocounseling** in which the practitioner attempts to understand the brain's role as it relates to counseling.
- **Criticisms of behavior therapy**: It does not yield insight; it is mechanistic; it treats symptoms and not the cause; it can be manipulative; generally, ignores developmental stages; and it often changes behavior but not underlying feelings. This approach deals with behaviors rather than the whole person.
- **Hint:** A great way to determine whether a question is referring to reflexive classical conditioning or Skinner's operant conditioning is to ask yourself a simple question: Would this reflex occur with every member of the species who does not have a disability? If the answer is *yes*, then it is most likely Pavlovian conditioning (e.g., all dogs salivate . . . an unconditioned/unlearned response (UR) when they see meat . . . an unconditioned stimulus (US) . . . so it's Pavlovian).

Carl R. Rogers's Person-Centered Humanistic Therapy

This approach has also been called client centered, Rogerian, non-directive, or self-theory. The basic notion (a very positive one) is that human beings can self-actualize and reach their full natural potential in a therapeutic setting that fosters growth; it is classified as an optimistic form of therapy.

- **Three conditions for effective helping:** The therapist must show empathy, be genuine/congruent, and display unconditional positive regard (UPR).
- **Empathy is not sympathy! It is the ability to subjectively understand the client's world in the here-and-now – to walk in their shoes – and convey this to the client. Robert Carkhuff** created a five-point empathy scale to rate counseling responses, with a level five response as the best response.
- The counselor must be genuine/congruent. The counselor cannot be a phony. Words must match (i.e., be congruent) with actions.
- The counselor accepts the client regardless of their behavior. This does not imply that you necessarily agree with the client. This is called **unconditional positive regard**.
- The counselor will often use reflection or open-ended questions.
- Counselor strives to improve congruence so that the person is more like their ideal self.
- Rogerians are not big fans of traditional diagnosis and testing. Moreover, they do not believe in the unconscious. Humans can control their own behavior. Critics are concerned that this approach is too optimistic and may not be the treatment of choice for severely disturbed individuals or very young children. **Natalie Rogers,** daughter of Carl Rogers, created **person-centered expressive arts therapy (PCEA).** This method strives to generate a creative connection with feelings via such things as movement, sound, art, writing, and journaling, which are shared with the helper.

Albert Ellis's Active-Directive Rational Emotive Behavior Therapy

Previously known as RET. This is a cognitive behavioral (CB) form of therapy. Change your thinking (cognitions), and you can change your life. The essence of the treatment is captured in the saying of Epictetus, a first-century Stoic philosopher, "Men are disturbed not by things, but of the view which they take of them." Irrational beliefs (IBs) are replaced by rational beliefs (RBs) via the counseling process.

- Uses the **ABC personality theory and ABCDE model of therapy**. A is an activating event. B is the client's belief system. C is the emotional consequence. At D the counselor disputes the irrational belief at B. E is a new emotional consequence that occurs when B becomes rational.
- Humans have an innate tendency to think in an irrational, illogical, unscientific manner. Thought is referred to as self-talk or internal verbalizations.
- Shoulds, oughts, musts, terriblizing, and awfulizing causes irrational thought.
- This is an active directive form of therapy utilizing lots of homework, **bibliotherapy**, and even **rational imagery (RI)**.
- Critics charge that the approach does not emphasize feelings or the counselor–client relationship and that REBT is mechanistic or even sterile. May be too complex for those with psychosis or thought disorders.

Aaron T. Beck's Cognitive Therapy

Beck's cognitive therapy is like REBT, emphasizing that the client has **automatic thoughts which are distortions of reality** such as polarized black-or-white thinking, overgeneralizing based on a single event, personalization – wrongly attributing an event to yourself, and drawing conclusions without real evidence. Not as confrontational as Ellis. Socratic questioning is sometimes employed. Clients are urged to keep a record of dysfunctional thoughts.

Friedrich "Fritz" Perls's Gestalt Therapy

This **experiential/existential** approach focuses on the **here-and-now** to help the client become whole again. Gestalt is an experiential form of therapy and it relies on dream work, role playing, confrontation, the top dog/underdog concept, hot seat, and the empty chair technique. Modern gestalt therapists are not as abrupt with clients as Perls. The therapy is now considered a softer gentler treatment.

- **Gestalt** is a German word that basically means **"organized whole."** The view of human nature is that humans want to be self-actualized and complete (whole).
- **Dreams** are the royal road to integration. Counselor asks client to recount the dream as if it is occurring in the present moment.
- **What and how questions** are used more than why questions (e.g., "What is your foot doing now?").
- **Goal** is for the client to take responsibility and achieve *awareness* in the here-and-now. **Doing is emphasized over just talking about problems**.
- **Laura Perls** (Fritz Perls's wife) helped develop the approach and made it more popular with women in therapy.

Critics charge that this approach is "gimmicky," puts little or no stock in diagnosis and psychological testing, and at times is "antitheoretical." On occasion, the approach can abet self-centeredness.

Eric Berne's Transactional Analysis

A here-and-now approach that took Freudian terminology and made it fun and easy to understand. The theory considered transactions between individuals. It is often combined with Gestalt. Critics charge this is like mixing water and oil since TA is cognitive and Gestalt is experiential. Others say this is desirable since the two complement each other. The person unconsciously develops a life plan at an early age called a **life script**. **Script analysis** assumes the person is at least partially living the preprogrammed script. The script concept is also used in narrative therapy.

- **Ego states** are the **parent, adult, and child (PAC)**. These states roughly correspond to Freud's superego, ego, and id.
- Uses **Tom Harris's life positions**. I'm OK, You're OK, healthy; I'm OK, You're Not OK, I'm Not OK, You're OK; and I'm Not OK, You're Not OK.

- Games are played to avoid intimacy. Somebody is always hurt in a game.
- **Stephen B. Karpman's drama triangle (a.k.a. Karpman's triangle)**. A person changes their position from victim to persecutor to rescuer during the discussion.

  Critics note that TA promotes game calling.

William Glasser's New Reality Therapy With Choice Theory

This therapy focuses on present behavior. Clients are taught that they create their own personal reality with the behaviors they choose. Glasser believes that **"Behavior is the control of our perceptions"** and that a **success identity** is the result of being loved and accepted. Glasser has been criticized for downplaying the role of the environment in terms of impacting ethnic minorities. Reality therapy has also been deemed "weak" in terms of not dealing with dreams, the past, or traumatic memories. According to Glasser psychiatric medicines or "brain drugs" are not the answer. **This paradigm challenges the medical model of psychiatry**.

- **The eight steps of reality therapy**: 1) build a relationship with the client, 2) focus on present moment behavior, 3) help the client to evaluate current behavior, 4) develop a contract with an action plan, 5) have the client commit to the plan, 6) accept no excuses, 7) do not use punishment, and 8) refuse to give up on your client. The approach emphasizes short-term treatment and is very concrete.
- **Psychological needs include** belonging, power, freedom, and fun.
- When Glasser contributed to my book *Favorite Counseling and Therapy Techniques*, he said, "We are responsible for what we do, and we choose all we do."
- **Robert Wubbolding** expanded the theory of reality therapy with his introduction of **WDEP** model. **W for wants** (belonging, freedom, fun, belonging, power, and independence), **D for direction and doing** (is the client doing something to take the client in the best direction) **E for evaluation or**

self-evaluation (how is the behavior working for the client), and finally **P for plan**. Plan should be immediate, attainable, and measurable.

Critics charge that reality therapy is a bit too simplistic, does not consider developmental stages, and has changed its focus over the years.

Lynn P. Rehm Self-Control Therapy

This is a self-control behavioristic paradigm of therapy which relies on self-monitoring, evaluation, and self-reinforcement.

Hypnosis

Helpful for pain, insomnia, anxiety, and habit control such as overeating and smoking. Can also be used to elicit repressed memories; however, the memories are often dubbed "pseudo memories," meaning they are not accurate. Hypnosis is a controversial modality.

Feminist/Non-Sexist Therapy

No single theorist is the founder. Has its origins in the women's movement of the 1960s. Some similarities to multicultural counseling. A strong focus on women's rights, sex-role stereotyping and the oppression of women. Approach postulates that most therapies have an **androcentric bias** (centered on men) and are not ideal and sometimes harmful to women.

Postmodern Social Constructivist Theories

Social constructionism emphasizes that realities are socially constructed. Brief therapy and narrative therapy are constructivist approaches.

Narrative Therapy by Michael White (Australia) and David Epston (New Zealand)

Narrative therapy postulates that individuals construct their lives by stories they tell about themselves and stories others create about them. Stories create meaning and this becomes the client's identity.

- Therapy consists of the client describing life experiences and then rewriting or reauthoring the narrative in a new way.
- A narrative therapist externalizes the problem in their progress notes and sends it to the client as a letter between sessions.
- Rather than saying "You are a cocaine addict," a narrative therapist will tell the client, "Cocaine has been trying to wreck your life." Again, clients reauthor their lives with new stories and fresh language.
- The narrative therapist views their role as a consultant or collaborator with the client. Some cultures want an expert therapist, and thus (at times) this can create a problem for multicultural counseling.
- Often recommended – with or without CBT – for working with **refugees** (those forced to leave their home country to escape a natural disaster, war or persecution) and **immigrants** (persons who make a voluntary decision to leave their native country and want to reside permanently in another country) who want to tell their stories. Journaling works well with this population and more disclosure is generally possible in individual rather than group sessions. **Bilingual counselors** should allow the clients to choose the language spoken in the interview, and language switching is often appropriate.

Solution-Focused Brief Therapy (Steve DeShazer and Insoo Kim Berg)

SFBT focuses on solutions and *not* on an understanding of the problem. The focus is on exceptions to the rule – what is working.

- Using so-called exception questions: a client who is depressed is asked: "When aren't you depressed?"
- Goals are small and realistic. The client is also asked the miracle question: "If a miracle took place while you were sleeping, how would you know the problem was solved? How would things be different?"

- SBFT also uses formula first session task (FFST). This is a homework assignment prescribed after the first session.
- Recently, this approach has gained popularity in group treatment settings.

Brief therapy (BT) is becoming the norm in many instances since **managed care firms** (hellbent on cutting costs!) often **restrict the number of sessions** the client can attend. Most counselors dislike managed care, feeling that the managed care company is micromanaging their practice. In some states managed care firms cannot be sued for their actions. Insurance and managed care policies are responsible for the fact that many counselors spend as much time dealing with business issues as they do counseling their clients. On the **positive side**, managed care forces counselors to look at outcome measures.

Psychotherapy Integration by Frederick Thorne

Psychotherapy integration uses strategies from several counseling schools. Instead of merely using techniques from the approaches in eclecticism, the integrative approach assumes that using or integrating two or more theories will often produce results that are superior to a single school of therapy. Today support is mounting for this approach.

Family Counseling

Family counseling asserts that the pathology resides in the family system and not in an individual. The client is the family and *not* the identified patient. Family therapists believe in **circular** rather than **linear** causality. **First-order change** occurs when a client makes a superficial change to deal with a problem but the change does not alter the underlying structure of the family. **Second-order change** alters the underlying structure and thus makes a difference that is longer lasting.

Negative feedback loops are not necessarily bad but keep the family in homeostasis and functioning the way the family always has.

Positive feedback loops induce change in the family system.

Case Integration

Case integration takes place when several helpers from the same agency or different agencies work together without duplicating services to help an individual client.

Milieu Therapy

Milieu therapy urges helpers to change the client's entire environment (social and physical) to help the client. Hence, treatment is not limited to counseling sessions. In most instances, this takes place in inpatient treatment facilities.

Famous Family Therapists

Nathan Ackerman used the psychoanalytic or psychodynamic approach.

Experimental conjoint family therapist **Virginia Satir** popularized the notion that in times of stress, family members use four inept patterns of communication. The placator (who tries to please everybody in the family), the blamer, the reasonable analyzer (who intellectualizes), and the irrelevant distracter (who interrupts and changes the topic to something irrelevant).

Experimentalist Carl Whitaker could be very wild, radical, and creative and often utilized a co-therapist.

Murray Bowen is a key name in intergenerational therapy. His approach is often referred to as extended family systems therapy.

Family therapy appears to be the best treatment of choice for those with eating disorders.

- **Triangulation** (also referred to as triangles) occurs when two people who are stressed bring in a third party to reduce the dyad's stress level and restore equilibrium. Generally not a desirable action.
- **Genograms** are graphic diagrams of the family from a minimum of three generations.

- **Fusion** is a blurring of the psychological boundaries between the self and others. A person driven by fusion can't separate thinking and feeling well.
- **Differentiation** (the opposite of fusion) is the ability to control reason over emotion. People often secure their level of differentiation from a multigenerational transmission process.

Salvador Minuchin is the leading name behind **structural family therapy**. The technique of **joining** or blending in with the family is used. The therapist uses a popular strategy of joining known as **mimesis** to imitate or copy the family's communication and patterns. The therapy proposes that changes in the family system, subsystems, and family organization must take place in order for individual family members to resolve their systems. Structural therapy is directive and performed in the here-and-now.

Jay Haley and Cloe Madaness are powerful names in **strategic family counseling** (also called **MRI model** and the **communications model**). In this paradigm the therapist gives **directives or prescriptions**, often **paradoxical**, such as telling a client who is afraid they will shake to shake as much as possible, actually prescribing the symptom. (**Rosenthal reminder: Paradox is not appropriate when working with homicidal and suicidal clients. Moreover, symptoms may be caused by physiological issues such as essential tremor and this should be ruled out before prescribing paradoxical assignments.**) Reframing and relabeling problems are common in this modality. This approach warns us that **double-bind communication** (e.g., a parent telling a child how much you love them while beating the child) could cause serious psychopathology, even schizophrenia.

- **Other brief strategic therapists** that champion paradox or prescribing the symptom in individual or family therapy include Milton H. Erickson, Steven DeShazer, Bill O'Hanlon, Paul Watzlawick, Don Jackson, and Michelle Weiner Davis.
- **Solution-focused brief therapists (SBFT)** speak of first-order change, which is superficial, and second-order change that includes actual changes in the rules and structure of the organization.

SFBT or BT, brief therapy, is not the same as crisis intervention. Crisis intervention is used for people who are experiencing an expected *normal* reaction to stress. Therapy, on the other hand, is aimed at reducing abnormal and pathological behaviors and symptoms. Crisis intervention is intended to help the individual get back to the level of functioning prior to the crisis. Counseling is aimed at raising the person's functioning higher than it was during the first counseling session.

The Milan model uses a treatment team with a one-way mirror.

Consultation occurs when you voluntarily assist a counselor or counselors (known as consultees) who will be helping clients.

- Contact with the actual client is indirect.
- Gerald Caplan is known as the father of mental health consultation.
- Edgar Schein's purchase of expertise model (where you buy the person's information and knowledge), his doctor–patient model (here you aren't sure what the problem is, so you hire an expert to diagnose and treat it), and his process consultation model (where the consultant helps the consultee with the process).

Process consultation models focus on the process, while **content models** focus on imparting knowledge to the consultee.

Brain Chemicals and Neurotransmitters Related to Neuroscience:

- **Serotonin**. Most prescription medicines given to clients for mental health issues impact serotonin (e.g., SSRI and SNRI drugs or the old tricyclic antidepressants).
- **Dopamine** excess is thought to fuel schizophrenia, while very low levels are implicated in Parkinson's disease. Some experts believe addictive behaviors such as gambling can flood the brain with dopamine.
- **Lithium** is a trace mineral or rare earth. It helps stabilize the mood, especially in clients with bi-polar conditions. An excess caused by prescription dosages can cause liver damage or tremors.

The **left hemisphere of the brain** is logical, verbal, and analytic, but the **right hemisphere of the brain** is emotional, creative, and artistic. This notion is still controversial.

The **microbiome** or balance of good bacteria (such as probiotics) and bad bacteria in the gastrointestinal tract can affect our mood, digestion, and general health. **This is sometimes called the gut–brain connection**.

Popular Psychiatric Medicines:

Anxiety: Benzodiazepines: Xanax, Librim, Klonopin, Ativan, and Valium.

Depression: Selective Serotonin Reuptake Inhibitors (SSRIs): Prozac, Zoloft, Luvox, Celexa, Paxil, and Lexapro. **Selective and Norepinephrine Reuptake Inhibitors (SNRIs):** Cymbalta, Pristiq, and Effexor. **Tricyclics (TCAs):** Elavil, Tofranil, and Pamelor.

ADHD: Ritalin and Concerta (both classified as methylphenidate), Adderall, and Vyvanse (also used for binge eating). Note: the CDC now recommends behavior therapy for ADHD before using medication for children age six or under.

Bipolar: Risperdal, Zyprexa, Lithobid, Depakote, Tegretol, and lithium.

OCD: Prozac, Paxil, Luvox, Zoloft, Anafranil, and Effexor.

Panic Disorder: Ativan and Paxil.

Antipsychotic/Schizophrenia: Abilify, Geodon, Risperdal, Clorzaril, and Zyprexa.

GROUP COUNSELING

Existential Therapy Expert and Psychiatrist Irvin Yalom Outlines 12 Reasons Groups Work So Well

Originally called "11 curative factors," he has relabeled them "12 therapeutic factors."

1. **Altruism**. Giving help to others gives members a sense of wellbeing.
2. **Universality**. Simply the notion that you are not the only one in the world with a particular problem.

3. **Installation of hope**. In plain everyday English, the members expect the group to work.
4. **Catharsis**. Talking about your difficulties is beneficial.
5. **Group cohesiveness**, or a sense of we-ness.
6. **Imitative behavior**. As you know, behaviorist Albert Bandura's social learning theory suggests that we learn by watching others. In this situation the members copy or model the leader and the other members.
7. **Family reenactment**. The group helps abet family of origin issues and feelings and the group allows you to work through them.
8. **Imparting information**. This could be advice or even psychodynamic insights.
9. **Interpersonal learning**. Input: Members receive feedback regarding how their behavior affects others. Output: Members give feedback to others.
10. **Socialization techniques** such as feedback and instruction are helpful.
11. **Existential factors**, for example, discovering that life can have meaning even if it is seemingly unjust and unfair at times.
12. **Self-understanding**. Insight into one's emotions and behavior.

Yalom is a proponent of working in the here-and-now and emphasizes the therapeutic alliance was powerful ingredient. A client with anger management issues will express anger in therapy if he or she is in treatment long enough.

Yalom also wrote *Staring at the Sun: Overcoming the Terror of Death*. Freud noted that denial of sexual impulses can lead to symptoms. In a similar fashion, Yalom asserts denial of death leads to symptoms as well. Nightmares are often manifestations of one's fear of death.

Groups

- Group counseling occurs when one or more counselor works with several individuals simultaneously. Technically, a group is composed of two or more people with a shared purpose. **The ideal size** – although it varies based on the source – is 8 to 12 members, with 8 being preferable. Virtually all experts agree children's groups should be smaller. For example, for very young children, five members or less might be desirable. When compared to a large group, a small group has more cohesiveness and typically participants find these groups more helpful. **Duration** can refer to the length of the group sessions or how long the group will run. Kids groups should run for less time. Generally, 90 minutes is plenty for any adult group.

- **Group can be open** (new members can join after the group begins) **or closed** (no new members can join after the group begins).
- A group can have a **single leader** or be led by **coleaders/cofacilitators. Advantages of coleaders**: having two role models (perhaps two genders), more feedback, one leader can deal with the client if there is transference, and two leaders can better see what is transpiring in the group. **Disadvantages**: leaders can work at cross-purposes, may have conflicting models of therapy, could be in a power struggle, and may each decide to charge the client a different fee.
- Group work is cost effective, and the counselor can see more clients in the same period of time.
- Most experts believe in stage **models** to explain development and dynamics: **the initial stage, the forming stage, or the orientation stage**. This is the "get acquainted" stage. Next comes the **transition, conflict, or storming stage**. This stage is characterized by power struggles for control and resistance, and some members will rate their satisfaction as lower. **The working, productive, performing, or action stage**. Here the group works toward goals in a cohesive manner. **The termination, closure, completion, or mourning and adjourning stage**. Members must deal with saying goodbye. Members often experience feelings of improved insight, awareness, accomplishment, and enhanced self-esteem. Referrals for additional intervention may be prescribed.

Some group member roles are positive, such as helping others and being a stellar role model. Other roles, such as monopolizing the group, intellectualizing too much, being silent, or attacking others, are considered negative. The scapegoat is the member who is blamed for the group's problems. This term is also used in family therapy.

Group Leadership Styles

Adept group leaders model appropriate behavior to enhance participation. This is especially important with resistant clients. Leaders rely on a strategy called **pacing** to determine how rapidly the group progresses.

Autocratic or authoritarian style advocates making decisions for members. It is appropriate during a crisis or when a quick decision is in order, but in most situations, this approach will foster resentment.

Laissez faire or hands-off style Here the leader has little involvement. This approach is appropriate when all members are very committed to a group outcome or goal.

Democratic style allows input from members and permits group members to have input into their decisions. This is generally the best style.

Speculative leaders are often seen as charismatic. They rely on their personal power and charisma to move the group in a desirable direction. They are often adored, and group members look up to them, though they are not peer oriented.

Confrontive leadership style where the facilitator reveals the impact that their behavior has on themself as well as the impact that other group members have on this person as the leader.

- Research has not shown that the speculative style is superior to the confrontive style or vice versa. Whatever style the leader utilizes, they should not impose their personal values on group members.

Types of Groups

1. **Psychoeducational (old name guidance groups)** provide members with information relevant to their situation. Can enhance members' personal attributes and ward off future difficulties.
2. **Counseling group**s focus on conscious issues related to personal problems, growth, and development. Also helpful for those experiencing challenging life transitions.
3. **Group therapy** (a term coined by Jacob Moreno, who founded psychodrama) can focus on unconscious material, the past, and personality change. Should include a complete diagnostic assessment. Groups of this nature are treatment focused.
4. **T-groups** (training groups) are often intended for business or personal motivation.
5. **Structured groups** are centered around certain issues such as shyness or how to prepare for a job interview.

6. **Self-help groups/mutual aid/support groups** (such as AA) are not led by a professional. These groups have been dubbed support groups, and those that follow the AA model are often called 12-step groups.
7. **Task groups** intended to accomplish a specific time-limited goal.

The self-serving attribution bias in relation to groups: When the group is productive or successful the person takes credit for it, but when the group is unproductive or not successful, it is the fault of others.

The leader is responsible for the safety of group members. Exercises like hitting each other with Styrofoam bats, or other ways of venting anger, are not only dangerous, but research shows they often increase rather than decrease aggression! In essence, the notion that catharsis is therapeutic is largely a myth.

The risky shift phenomenon. Members make more risky decisions in a group than they would on an individual basis. **Group polarity** suggests that members of a group make more extreme decisions than they would individually.

Group work can be practiced ethically in a **telehealth model**.

Group facilitators should monitor and assess the impact of the group on members as well as the group as a whole and this should be ongoing. The goal is to balance the needs of the individual and of the needs of the group.

ASGW Best Practice Guidelines was superseded in 2021 by the **ASGW Principles for Group Work** intended to specifically help counselors apply ACA's Code of Ethics, values, and sociocultural foundations to the group setting. The guidelines stipulate a leader should have an evaluation plan to meet the requirements of organizations, regulatory bodies, and insurance companies when appropriate. The 2021 document updated the measures in the 2012 ***Multicultural and Social Justice Competence Principles for Group Workers***. The leader allows members to discuss diversity, power, privilege, and why social justice/advocacy issues are important.

Group members are not required to participate in an exercise or experiential activity and can quit during the experience. It is the leader's job to clarify this upfront, however, the leader should explore why a participant did not wish to participate or stopped in the middle of the exercise.

As group members get to know each other spontaneous touching may occur. That said, **forced touching exercises** are not recommended and could cause negative feelings in some members (e.g., those who have been sexually abused).

Lifestyle and Career Counseling Theories

Grad students and neophyte counselors often have a negative attitude toward learning about career counseling and do not want to engage in this practice. In reality, career counseling and personal counseling overlap. Nevertheless, career counseling is commonly seen as having less prestige than personal counseling and psychotherapy.

Trait-and-factor theory (matching or actuarial approach): Frank Parsons (father of guidance) was the author of the seminal work in the field, *Choosing a Vocation*. A client needs to know their personal attributes and interests or traits; appropriate occupations should be investigated; finally, match the client's traits to the occupation. E.G. Williamson expanded this theory to six steps: analysis, synthesis, diagnosis, prognosis, counseling, and follow-up. The trait-and-factor approach assumes that there is a single best career goal for everyone. Many experts disagree with this assumption.

Ann Roe created a psychodynamic needs approach. Jobs meet our needs determined by our childhood satisfactions and frustrations. Occupations are categorized by six levels and eight fields. Our orientation toward or away from other people can influence our career choices.

Ginzberg, Ginsburg, Axelrad, and Herma proposed a developmental theory in 1950s with three periods: **fantasy** (birth to 11), in which play becomes work oriented; **tentative** (ages 11 to 17); and **realistic** (17 and up).

David Tiedeman and Robert O'Hara rely on a developmental approach. In their model, career development is commensurate with psychosocial development as delineated by Erik Erikson's stages.

Donald Super is well known for emphasizing the role of the **self-concept** in career and vocation choice and his **Life Rainbow**.

John Holland's personality typology theory The six personality types are **realistic, investigative, artistic, social, enterprising, and conventional (RIASEC)**. He is also known for his assessment tools: the **Self-Directed Search, My Vocational Situation**, and the **Vocational Preference Inventory**.

Krumboltz, Mitchell, and Jones theorized career decision was based on **social learning theory**. Today Krumboltz followers lean toward behaviorism in general. Four factors impact career choice: genetic factors and special abilities, the environment and special events, learning experiences, and task approach problem-solving skills.

Linda S. Gottfredson emphasized **circumscription** (the process of narrowing the acceptable alternatives) and **compromise** (realization that the client will not be able to implement their most preferred choices). The client adjusts aspirations to accommodate such things as hiring practices, family obligations, or educational programs. People sacrifice interests rather than sex-type or prestige. Theory was created in the early 1980s.

Social cognitive career theory (SCCT) by Lent, Brown, and Hackett helps complement other theories emphasizing the role of self-efficacy and cognitive processes.

Mark Savickas uses techniques popularized by narrative therapy to create a postmodern constructivist approach.

CAREER CHOICE

To use computer-assisted career guidance (CAGC), such as SIGI the counselor should:

1. Screen the client to make certain this modality and computer program or online program is appropriate.
2. Give the client an orientation to describe the pros and cons of the system.
3. Follow up to make certain an appropriate plan of action is evident.

***Dictionary of Occupational Titles* (DOT)** listed over 20,000 job titles with nine-digit codes for the occupation. The *DOT* has been replaced by **O*NET**, also known as O*NET online. A text version of O*NET known as O*NET Dot or *O*NET Dictionary of Occupational Titles* is available; however, as of this writing, it is not published by the Department of Labor.

OOH, or *Occupational Outlook Handbook*, gives job trends for the future and salaries and can be accessed over the Internet.

Richard Bolles's book, *What Color Is Your Parachute?* is a fine tool for job hunting.

Eighty percent of all jobs are not advertised and thus job seekers need to network. This is referred to as **the Hidden Job Market.** Many experts today, although they will admit a hidden job market exists, are adamant the figure of 80% is likely much too high. Currently there is no consensus on the actual figure.

- Key trend: women moving into careers that were traditionally occupied by males. **Sex wage discrimination/earnings gap**: According to the US Department of Labor, women make approximately $0.82 for each dollar earned by men. This figure was $0.57 in 1973, so the situation has improved, but a wage pay gap is still evident. The pay gap for African American women and Latina women is much higher, often hovering in the $0.40 to $0.54 range.
- One in five workers still secures a job based on chance factors, and 60% of all workers would like more information if they had to do it all over again. However, overall **college students are avoiding career counseling services**.
- **Underemployment** occurs when a person takes a job below their level of skill, expertise, and training (e.g., a PhD working in an entry-level fast-food position).
- **Dislocated worker** is a term that describes a person who is unemployed due to downsizing, a company relocation, or the fact that the firm closed the business.
- **Displaced homemaker** describes women who enter or reenter the workforce after being at home. This often occurs after a divorce or the death of a partner or spouse.
- **Outsourcing** takes place when US companies rely on labor from another country to save money (i.e., the salaries would be lower). This can also result in fewer jobs in the United States.
- **Online career counseling** is a growing trend. While helpful, the practice is not as effective as the traditional face-to-face model.
- The **average worker** has nine jobs by age 36.

- **Networking** helps clients secure jobs and help them find **LGBT-friendly employers**.
- In two-parent families, if both parents work, this is called a **dual-career or dual-income family.** Strictly speaking: **Dual earner**, partners work in positions with no chance for advancement. **Dual-career** partners work in managerial or professional positions with the possibility for advancement.

Supervisors Who Rate Workers Often Suffer From Rater Bias

- When a supervisor erroneously rates the majority of workers as average, this is called the **central tendency bias**.
- **The recency effect** occurs when the rating reflects primarily the worker's recent performance (rather than the entire rating period) since this effect suggests we remember things the best that are presented last.
- A supervisor generalizing about an employee based on a single characteristic (e.g., giving a worker who is kind a higher rating than a worker who is just as good but isn't kind) is the **halo effect**. Positive and negative halo effects are possible.
- Supervisors often rate workers higher if the supervisor hired that particular worker.
- **Quality circles.** Employees with identical or similar jobs meet as a group to solve problems and come up with solutions to help management.

  Job interviews, personality tests, and **reference letters** are *not* excellent predictors of whether a person will do well in a job. **Structured job interviews** usually fare better than **unstructured job interviews.** The **contrast effect** suggests that if a job seeker is interviewed after a superb candidate, this individual does not or will not seem as desirable. On the other hand, if a very weak candidate is interviewed it will make the next job applicant appear more competent. **Interest inventories** do not predict job success well, but they do predict **job satisfaction**.

ASSESSMENT (TESTS AND DIAGNOSIS)

Tests are nearly old as the profession of counseling, but agreement over whether tests are useful has varied a great deal. According to expert Anne Anastasi, a test is an objective standardized measure of behavior. **Ideally, tests measure and provide valid and reliable data regarding your clients so you can pick the effective modalities of treatment, referral, or placement.** Critics note that tests can be faked, are mechanical, often measure irrelevant factors, and can invade privacy. Testing can also create prejudice in the sense that the counselor perceives the client in a different manner.

Standardized tests have uniform procedures for scoring and administration. In addition, these instruments have validity and reliability and norm data that has been investigated and analyzed. The ***Mental Measurements Yearbook*** **(MMY)** and ***Tests in Print*** **(TIP)** from the Buros Center for Testing (https://buros.org/) provide counselors with information on thousands of tests. Online versions are now available. Over 3500 of the tests have been critically analyzed by Buros.

A score is "**raw**" if it is unaltered. Raw scores can be converted to **standard scores (e.g., *t* scores, *z* scores, percentile rank, standard deviation, or stanine)** so that the scores relate to the **normal bell curve**. The **range** is the highest score minus the lowest score (some exams will add 1 to the answer.)

Percentile rank tells the counselor the percentage of scores equal to or below the score you are investigating. Hence, a client who is at the 75th percentile scored equal to or better than 75% of the people who took the exam. *It does not necessarily imply that the test taker answered 75% of the answers correctly since a score of 20% correct might be higher than 75% of the examinees!*

Three measures of central tendency: the **mean** or arithmetic average (e.g., if your gas bill for a year is $144, then your mean bill per month is $12 or 144 divided by 12); the **mode** is the most frequently occurring score or category; and the **median** or middle score when the data are ranked from highest to lowest. In a **normal mesokurtic curve**, all three measures of central tendency fall on the same point in the center of the bell shape. When a curve leans, we say it is **skewed**. If the tail points to the left, the curve is **negatively skewed**; if it points to the right, it is **positively skewed**.

Kurtosis, often described as peakedness, is a statistical indication of the size of the tails when compared to a normal distribution. If an exam shows you a curve with lots of outliers/extreme scores yet the curve resembles a tabletop, this is a **platykurtic distribution**. If the curve is tall and skinny like a steep mountain and has few extreme scores compared to a normal curve, you are looking at a **leptokurtic distribution**. Lepto means slender.

Standard deviation (SD) is a measure of **variability or dispersion of scores**. Are the scores bunched up close to the mean or are the scores spread out? A standard deviation of 1 is a *z*-score or standard score of one. A standard deviation of –2 is a *z*-score of negative 2, and so on. ***T* scores** have a mean of 50 and the standard deviation is 10. If your test asks: What is a *T* score when the standard deviation is 2, the answer is 70. If it asks: What is the *T* score for a standard deviation of –3, the answer is 20.

Areas under the normal curve you should commit to memory: 68% of the scores will fall between plus/minus one standard deviation from the mean, **95%** of all scores will fall between plus/minus two standard deviations, and **99.7%** of all scores fall between three plus/minus standard deviations. It is safe to say that virtually all scores fall between plus/minus three standard deviations of the mean. This is known as the **empirical 68–95–99.7 normal curve rule**.

Validity is the most important property of a test. Does the test truly test what it purports to test? The validity of standardized tests in our field is said to be on a par with instruments used in the medical field.

Reliability: Is the test consistent? Will it provide similar results if we administer it again and again? If an IQ test yields a score of 100 today and 130 for the same client tomorrow, it is not valid!

A **reliable test** is not always valid, but a **valid test** is **always** reliable.

Interrater reliability describes the consistency of two or more raters. If two counselors read the same test reports and come up with the same diagnosis, then **interrater reliability or agreement** is high. If they come up with different diagnoses, then it is low.

A test or instrument that is only **normed** on the majority culture is not appropriate for other cultures since it is misleading and could cause discrimination.

Tests can give a false positive or a false negative.

Aptitude tests predict **potential**. For example, a high score on an aptitude test for music doesn't imply that you are a great musician, but with the correct training and practice you could excel in this area.

Achievement tests give you the current accomplishments, what has been learned, or the level of performance achieved up to this point in time (e.g., she is reading at the sixth-grade level).

Intelligence tests or IQ tests such as the **Wechsler** or the **Binet** attempt to measure mental abilities. IQ tests are very controversial and have been a source of debate for counselors. Individual IQ tests are generally more accurate than group-administered measures.

Power tests Time (slow performance) is not a factor like it is in so-called **speed tests**. Speed tests are helpful in testing manual dexterity and neurological issues.

Projective tests There is no correct answer. The client merely looks at an inkblot, a vague picture, or an incomplete sentence. The client's answer is assumed to be a projection of their personality. Thus, two clients look at the same Rorschach inkblot card or TAT picture and see something totally different.

- Scoring projective tests is subjective. One rater could score it differently than another rater. Again, this phenomenon is called **interrater reliability**.

Regression to the mean states that if a client scores exceptionally low or exceptionally high on a test, then the client with the low score will go up on the next administration, while the client with the high score will go down toward the mean or average. Chance factors or everyday luck probably influenced the first score.

Diagnosis generally implies that a label is placed on the client using a classification system, generally the DSM as an assessment tool. Nevertheless, insurance companies virtually always require a diagnosis with an **ICD diagnosis code** before they will pay for treatment. Moreover, most other professionals (e.g., psychologists and psychiatrists) use diagnostic terminology and thus counselors need to use the same classification systems and terminology.

Assessment also helps determine admissions/selection/placement to schools (think your GRE score or perhaps an IQ score used to determine whether a child should be in a gifted class) and treatment organizations. Finally, assessment can help you determine if your client is truly making progress or not.

Computer-based tests generally reduce costs and can provide immediate scoring and cut the risk of scoring errors, when compared to traditional **paper-and-pencil tests.** However, because the web is expanding so rapidly, many measures on the web have low validity and reliability.

High-stakes assessment occurs when a test (say, the NCE if you wish to practice counseling or the CPCE if you wish to graduate!) is used to make important decisions about the future. Licensing exams fall into this category. Thus, without passing a driver's license test, you cannot drive a motor vehicle.

RESEARCH AND PROGRAM EVALUATION

Studies clearly indicate that only a small percentage of counselors conduct research or use research findings in their practice. Many counselors feel that research is virtually cold, impersonal, and irrelevant to their day-to-day practice and thus say that helping, rather than research, is their top priority. A gap between research and practice is evident. A high percentage of beginning master's level students resent having to take research and statistics courses. It is true that a lot of studies are not helpful to counselors. What's more, it has been discovered that research articles are perused primarily by other researchers and not practitioners. Research that is considered helpful is often dubbed experience-near research, applied research, or action research. When counselors *do* integrate research into practice, it is called empirically validated treatment (EVT) or empirically supported treatment (EST).

Correlation is not the same as causation. Correlation is simply an association. The correlation between people who have an open umbrella and rain is very high, but opening your umbrella does not cause it to rain.

- **Correlations go from negative 1 to 0 to positive 1**. Zero means no correlation, while positive 1 and negative 1 are perfect correlations. A positive correlation of .5 is not higher than a correlation of –.5. In fact, a correlation of –.8 is stronger than a correlation of .5.
- In **a positive correlation**, when *X* goes up, *Y* goes up. For example, when you study more, your GPA goes up.
- In **a negative or inverse correlation**, when *X* goes up, *Y* goes down. For example, the more you brush your teeth, the less you will be plagued by cavities.

Research is quantitative when one quantifies or measures things. **Quantitative research** yields numbers. When research does not use numerical data, we call it **qualitative research**. All research has flaws, sometimes referred to as **bubbles**.

True Experiment

Two or more groups are used.

- The people are picked via **random sampling** and placed in groups using **random assignment. Systematic sampling** where every *n*th person is chosen can also be used; however, researchers still prefer random sampling and random assignment.
- When the participants and the groups are not picked at random, or the researcher cannot control the IV, then it is a **quasi** rather than a true experiment. **Quasi-experimental research, also referred to as a natural experiment, does not ensure causation. When pitted against a true experiment, the quasi-experiment gains external validity and is often not as artificial but shows a loss in internal validity**.
- The experimental groups receive the **independent variable (IV)**, also known as the experimental variable. **There are levels of the IV, such as no counseling (the control group) and counseling (provided to the experimental group)**.
- **The control group** does not receive the experimental IV.
- The outcome data in the study is called the **DV, or dependent variable**. If we want to see if eating carrots raises one's IQ, then eating carrots is the IV, while the IQ scores at the end of the study would be the DV.
- Each experiment has a **null hypothesis**: there is no significant difference in people's IQs between those who eat carrots and those who don't eat carrots. **The experimental or alternative hypothesis** would be there is a significant difference between the IQs of those who do eat carrots versus those who do not.
- When a researcher rejects a null hypothesis that is true, it is a **type I alpha error**. When a researcher accepts null when it should have been rejected, we say that a **type II beta error** has occurred.

- The significance level for the social sciences is usually set at .05 or less (.01 or .001). The significance level gives you the probability of a type I error. Smaller is better!
- ***N* = 1** is known as a single-subject design or case study and thus does not rely on IV, DV, control group, and so on. Case studies are becoming more popular.
- **Demand characteristics** are evident when subjects in a study have **cues** regarding what the researcher desires or does not desire that influence their behavior. This can confound an experiment, rendering the research inaccurate.
- If subjects **know** they are being observed, we refer to the process as an **obtrusive or a reactive measure**. Observers' presence can influence subject's behavior rather than merely the experimental variable or treatment modality. When subjects are **not aware** that they are being measured, we say that it is an **unobtrusive measure**.
- **Internal validity** is high when an experimental has few flaws and thus the findings are accurate. In other words, the IV caused the changes in the DV, not some other factor (known as confounding extraneous variables or artifacts). When internal validity is low, the researcher didn't measure what they thought they measured.
- **External validity** is high when the results in a study can be generalized to other settings.
- **A *t* test is a popular parametric test for comparing two means.**
- The **ANOVA, or analysis of variance, originally developed by Ronald Fisher (also called a one-way ANOVA) is used when you have two or more means to compare**. The *t* test and the ANOVA are parametric measures for normally distributed populations. The ANOVA provides *F* values, and the ***F* test** will tell you if significant differences are present. Use the **MANOVA, or multivariate analysis of variance,** when you are investigating **more than one DV**. Use a **factorial analysis of variance** when you are investigating **more than one IV/experimental variable** (i.e., if you have two IVs, it would be called a two-way ANOVA, three IVs, a three-way ANOVA, etc.).
- If the population is not necessarily normal, then a nonparametric test such as a **chi square** (the most common nonparametric test) or **Kruskal-Wallace** (similar to the ANOVA) can be used.

- If the researcher did not manipulate the variable and you are looking at after-the-fact data, then the research is not a true experiment but rather an **ex post facto** or so-called **causal-comparative design**.

Descriptive statistics are statistics that describe central tendencies like the mean, median, mode, range, quartiles, variance, and standard deviation.

Quartiles are three data points dividing the distribution into four equal parts. **Q1** = 25th percentile or lowest 25% of scores. **Q2** = 26 to 50th percentile. Remember the 50th percentile is the median. **Q3** = 75th percentile and higher (i.e., 75% of scores below this value). **Interquartile or IQR** is 25th percentile to 75th percentile or **Q3–Q1 = IQR** or where approximately the middle 50% of the scores fall. If you divide the **IQR** by 2, it gives you the so-called **semi-quartile statistic**.

Statistical analyses include correlation coefficients, *t* tests, ANOVAs, analysis of covariance, chi square, Kruskal Wallis, and so on.

Cohort studies examine a group of people who have something in common (e.g., all soldiers who fought in Vietnam or all counselors who received their license in 2017).

Longitudinal research takes place when the same individuals are evaluated over time and can be contrasted with **cross-sectional research** that relies on observation or data from a given point in time.

Formative evaluation takes place during treatment or while a program is going on (e.g., a counselor educator is rated by students at the end of each class), while **summative or outcome evaluation** occurs at the end of a program or treatment (e.g., after the final session of counseling).

Between-groups design uses **different subjects** in the different groups (e.g., one group of subjects for the control group and another group of subjects for the experimental group).

Within-groups repeated measures within-subject design uses the **same subjects** for the control condition and then at a different time for the IV/experimental condition(s). **Or to put it a different way, the subject their own control**.

Institutional research board or IRB approval is required prior to conducting human research. The IRB will determine whether your research meets ethical, legal, and institutional guidelines so no subjects are harmed. You might need to through more than one IRB. For example, a dissertation using community college students as subjects would need the approval of your graduate institution's IRB as well as the IRB of the community college.

PROFESSIONAL ORIENTATION AND ETHICS

Licensing guidelines are set by states and not the federal government. When one state accepts another state's license without additional credentials, it is known as reciprocity or endorsement. The goal for the profession is portability, where your license would be valid wherever you decide to move to and practice.

The term *scope of practice* implies that you only practice if you are adequately trained in an area or with a given population. Hence, if you have no training running a Gestalt group, then don't run one. If you know nothing about clients with eating disorders – don't treat them.

A counselor's duty to warn Initially based on a California supreme court case, **Tarasoff**, this principle now states that if a client is going to harm themselves, somebody else, or both, you will break, a.k.a. breach, confidentiality and contact the appropriate people (e.g., the police, the target person) to ward off this tragedy. Some states currently stipulate a counselor (even in a school) must report it to the parents if a child threatens suicide.

Dual relationship/boundary issues (could also be called multiple or nonprofessional relationships, on your exam). This concept implies that you are a person's helper, but you also have another significant relationship with that person (maybe you are dating them or perhaps they are a relative or business partner.) Such relationships, whether in-person or virtual/electronic, get in the way of objectivity and should be avoided whenever possible unless the relationship is beneficial to the client.

Privileged communication is set by state law. Privileged communication asserts that you cannot reveal what a client said in a session in court unless the client allows you to do so. There are exceptions to this such as child abuse, suicide, homicide, and supervisory sessions or if a lawsuit is filed against you. You should never release information about the client outside of court (unless it is the exceptions just mentioned) unless the client signs a release of information consent form. Remember to disguise the identity of your clients when doing research, training, or in a work for publication.

- Always check the NBCC and ACA websites for the latest information on Internet Counseling and ethics before you take your comprehensive exam. These ethics and those related to social media are changing extremely rapidly.

****

I've enjoyed spending this time with you. Obviously, I can't cover every single concept that might pop up on exam, but I gave it a pretty good try, didn't I? Anyway, you're going to do great on the exam.

Remember, I want you as my next testimonial.

14

Test Anxiety Prevention Strategies That Work

I want to personally congratulate you on your decision to become licensed and/or certified as a professional counselor, psychologist, human service practitioner, therapist, or mental health professional.

The object of this chapter is to help improve your confidence and annihilate the number-one enemy that professionals must contend with on licensing and certification exams. Let me make it clear I am not talking about the material; I'm talking about test anxiety. Yes, test anxiety.

That sly insidious feeling that saps your confidence and gets you so nervous and jittery you simply cannot perform at your best. The good news is that literally hundreds and hundreds of counselors nationwide have used my test anxiety prevention programs with stellar results.

Calls, emails, and testimonial letters validated that my program worked. You are now reading the newest, updated, and most sophisticated program for this purpose I have ever created. What is this big bad wolf we call test anxiety? For starters, it is nothing new.

As a case in point, Sigmund Freud addressed it as early as 1900 when he wrote his classic, *The Interpretation of Dreams*. He called it examination anxiety. Anxiety is a feeling of worry, fear, apprehension,

DOI: 10.4324/9781003149712-14

danger, distress, and tension. It is a feeling of uneasiness often accompanied by a horrendous sense of dread.

Many researchers believe that when a person's anxiety level goes up too high, the individual becomes self-absorbed. That, my friend, interferes with your ability to solve problems. This is the last thing you need when you are trying to deal with a tough licensing or certification exam.

If the anxiety escalates there may be physiological, or so-called somatic, bodily symptoms. For example, your breathing may be impaired. You may experience cardiac awareness as you feel your pulse and your heart rate skyrocket.

You could even feel shaky, tremble, have butterflies in your stomach, or have sweaty palms due to poor circulation in your hands and extremities. This program, that's right, the one you are beginning to read this very moment, can help curb all of the aforementioned symptoms so you can concentrate on your exam.

Face it. A comprehensive exam is tough enough. The exam is a sufficient challenge by itself. You certainly do not need the extra burden of anxiety. As a mental health professional, I am certain you've heard the adage that avoiding or denying a fearful situation will simply make it worse. Ellis, for example, has included this idea as a key irrational idea in many of his books, articles, and presentations on REBT.

Repeatedly exposing yourself to a fearful situation is therapeutic. The technical name for progressively facing a feared situation is called systematic habituation therapy. It was first delineated in a textbook on medical psychology in the early 1920s.

Remember when you were a child and you fell off your bike and scraped your knee, and a well-meaning adult, who may not have seemed that well-meaning at the time, made you get back on that bike and ride it again. Although it may not have been all that systematic, you discovered that you could overcome your fear of riding that bike. You faced the dreaded situation.

The human body is seemingly programmed to respond to habituation, whether the situation is good or bad. Here is a terrific example. Have you ever taken a bite of a watermelon and said, "Mm, mm, mmm, that's good. I mean, that is really good. I think I'll have another slice"?

You take another slice and say, "Yeah. Hey, that is truly good, but it's not quite as good as the first slice. I think I will try another. I must have taken that good slice from a different side of the watermelon." You keep trying to find another slice of watermelon that tastes as good as the first, but curiously it never seems to happen.

As you continue to swallow one slice after another in the quest for that perfect-tasting slice again, the slices you are now eating can only be described as ordinary at best. After a while, you can barely taste them. You have become immune to your response to that slice of watermelon.

Unfortunately, you cannot keep exposing yourself to your comprehensive exams. We want you to pass it on a first try, honestly, but we can expose you to the situation again and again in your mind using mental imagery, or what is often called creative guided visualization or guided imagery.

In this chapter I will use a technique known as counterconditioning or desensitization in the imagination to help you use habituation to your advantage. Perhaps you remember the landmark famous experiment in 1924. Well, of course you remember it since you just might need to know it for your exam. Mary Cover Jones, often called the "mother of behavior therapy," took a three-year-old boy named Peter who was afraid of rabbits and gradually eliminated his fear by giving the child a pleasant stimulus, food, when the rabbit was present.

I don't have any candy or any watermelon to give you on this program, but I can use relaxation and positive imagery to desensitize your fears. Before I relax you, I want to give you several superb recommendations I am thoroughly convinced can help you. These are worth their weight in gold, so use them.

TEN RECOMMENDATIONS TO STOP TEST TERROR IN ITS TRACKS!

Recommendation 1. Find a picture or a photograph that depicts a relaxing scene from a confident time in your life. Come on, stop the program right now and crack open your trusty old photo album or your cell phone gallery. Why? Well, the answer is easy.

A researcher by the name of Richard Driscoll reported in the *Psychological Review* that pictures of positive scenes and physical exercise reduced test anxiety as much as desensitization. What I want you to do is take the quiet, peaceful, serene, and confident picture with you, and look at it before you take your exam. I say "before" because cell phones or pictures will virtually never be allowed in exam sites. This should be even easier if you are taking the exam from home.

This is a simple strategy, but numerous counselors have told me that it truly works. Use it.

Recommendation 2. Make sure you get to the exam test site on time. Ditto if you are taking the test at home from your computer. Don't be out in 105° heat moments before the exam cleaning your gas grill, rushing frantically to shut off the hose and dispose of the sponge so you won't be late! If you are in a rush, it will hinder your powers of reasoning and exacerbate your anxiety. Statistically speaking, most people feel more anxious when they are running late. Drive to your exam site prior to the actual exam, so you will not get lost. Moreover, you will know approximately how long the trip will take you, so you can gauge your time better. Internet driving directions and GPS systems are often terrific, but I don't have to tell you they are not always 100% accurate.

Recommendation 3. Do not drink more caffeine than you normally would on the day of the exam. Too much caffeine can speed up your circulation, increase anxiety, and make some people feel more panic stricken than they already feel. People who are anxiety prone often react to chocolate since it is a source of caffeine. Going without chocolate for a few hours until after the exam might be prudent.

Also, many diet and weight loss supplements contain natural stimulants. Check the label. If you notice that the supplement raises your anxiety level or makes you jittery, then once again, consider phasing it out a few days prior to the exam.

I say a few days since caffeine, or stimulant, withdrawal could be as pernicious if not more so than the actual anxiety. Check with your physician and a registered dietician if you feel this might be an issue.

Also, watch out for sugar. Yes, I said sugar. Years ago, a major company ran ads with lively music in which they called sugar "60 seconds of pure energy." Well, you know what? The ads were right. If you eat a ton of sugar, you might just get 60 seconds of pure energy, but what happens when you crash round about question 32 on the exam?

This phenomenon is often known as low blood sugar, or hypoglycemia, and paradoxically can be caused by eating too much sugar. Let me share a humorous little saga. It occurred when I was studying for one of my final exams for one of my last classes in my master's in counseling program.

Approximately one hour before the exam, I hit the school cafeteria armed with my textbooks and my notes. As I began to study, I purchased some chocolate cupcakes. I've got to say they tasted awesome.

I bought cupcake after cupcake until I probably should have given the Guinness Book of World Records a call to see if I was the new cupcake eating champion of the world. I charged into the exam. I was energetic. I could not wait to tackle that final.

Nevertheless, about 30 minutes or so into the exam, I crashed big time and came within a blink of falling asleep. I cannot say this strongly enough. Do not let this happen to you. I guess I do not have to tell you that habituation is a lot stronger with natural foods than artificial foods like cupcakes. Watermelon is natural. Watermelon candy or cupcakes are not natural, and hence you could eat more of them before the great taste is nowhere to be found, ergo throwing your blood sugar into turmoil.

Important corollary. Recently biohacking (experimenting with prescription drugs and nutrients to improve your life, longevity, and capabilities) has become extremely popular. The nootropic category, substances to improve memory and cognition, or so-called "smart drugs," has become the rage. Let me give you some sage advice here. Even if you are working with a licensed medical professional, these substances often work differently on different people.

Hence, a nutritional supplement (or prescription) that is said to improve memory might give *you* brain fog or put you to sleep even if 100 other people gave the product five-star reviews. Therefore, let me state the obvious: When test driving these mind boosters, I would suggest that you never do so for the first time when you have a comprehensive exam coming up or during the exam. Always experiment with the products well in advance of your exam to ascertain your personal reaction.

(Note: Dr. Rosenthal insists the reader check with a qualified health professional before implementing any of his strategies related to nutrition or diet.)

Recommendation 4. Yep, I'm going to mention Ellis yet again because he was fond of warning us of the negative mental health ramifications of awfulizing and catastrophizing. If you are currently telling yourself how terrible and dreadful the exam is going to be, start actively disputing your thinking.

Try to be more logical and rational about it.

Recommendation 5. Do you have a weak area, an area in which you feel your knowledge is a bit under par? If so, review your textbooks and study guides. Then imagine that you have been asked to give a lecture on this very area, the area you're struggling with.

Next, outline your lecture and dictate it onto a digital recorder. That is correct, you've become the teacher and the pupil. You could video yourself giving the lecture. Next, you should listen or watch your lectures several times to build your confidence and increase your knowledge.

Recommendation 6. Contact your state or local counseling organization to determine whether they have a licensing or certification study group in your area. Remember the group therapy principle of universality (also called mutuality), the one that states that you are not unique in terms of your predicament or fears?

Your study group will help you share coping skills and learning strategies. Moreover, many people who take comprehensive exams insist that the hardest part of the exam is not that they do not know or understand the material. It is the fact that the material is worded in very difficult ways on the exam.

Thus, why not use a colleague or partner in your study group and have that person make up questions and word them in novel or difficult ways and try to answer them?

Recommendation 7. If you are struggling with an area or a principle that you find difficult to comprehend, try to find four or five textbooks or scholarly websites that you have never read before.

Look the principle up in the index of each text, or push "find" to access it on a website and try to discover an explanation that makes sense to you. Older textbooks or works and websites from related fields can help. Thus, a counselor or psychologist struggling with a statistics concept might utilize a business statistics book or one written for social workers to try to understand the concept in question.

I also really love social science dictionaries and can personally recommend my own, which is called the ***Human Services Dictionary***. I intentionally worded the explanations for the terms in the dictionary to help you with tough, typical, or prototype exam questions. If you are looking for a single tip to raise your exam score, here it is: Simply thumb through my *Human Services Dictionary* and use it as a resource to look up the terms, experiments, theories, and theorists in question.

Recommendation 8. Curbing test anxiety means being prepared.

What about those questions that pop up on the exam that are conspicuously missing from all your textbooks, courses, and study guides? Where did they come from? Your best bet is to take a few days off work. Yeah, I am sure you could use one anyway. Everybody can use a mental health day, right?

Now, since you have a little extra study time, I want you to skim through the major journals and newsletters for the past year or two in your area of study. Also, remember that some tests, such as versions of the National Counselor Examination and the Counselor Preparation Comprehensive Examination, have questions that are being field/pilot tested. You will not know which questions these are; thus you must do your very best on every question.

What this means from a pragmatic standpoint is that you can theoretically miss questions and still get a perfect score on the exam. Is that great or what?

Recommendation 9. Fight negative and fearful thoughts with the behavioral principle of thought stopping. It is really very easy.

Whenever you are thinking a pernicious thought that really could raise your anxiety or reduce your confidence, imagine that you are holding a giant blow horn or megaphone and yell, "Stop," in your mind as loud as you can.

Recommendation 10. You can combine this hint with the previous recommendation. This strategy is as old as the hills, but some folks still swear that it works wonders.

You wear a bracelet or perhaps even a rubber band on your wrist. Every time you catch yourself thinking one of those negative, no-no thoughts, you snap the rubber band or the piece of jewelry against your wrist to remind you to get the mental blow horn out. (If you have very thin skin or take blood thinners you might want to forego this strategy for obvious reasons.)

ACTUAL CREATIVE VISUALIZATION GUIDED IMAGERY RELAXATION SESSION

I will now walk you through a complete effective relaxing creative visualization guided imagery exam boosting session. Therefore, right now, go to a very comfortable place. Never use the rest of this program while walking, driving, or operating a moving vehicle such as a lawn, tractor, or forklift. Somehow, I have this uncanny feeling you would have figured that out on your own!

Find a place where you will not be disturbed. Loosen your clothing; remove your glasses or contacts if that makes you feel more relaxed; and find a comfortable bed, recliner, couch, or chair.

For the finest results perform the imagery at least once a week. Remember the principle of habituation. "The more you use my relaxation training, the better it's going to work." Listen more than once a week if you need it, especially the night before the big exam and the morning of the big exam.

When you listen, you can visualize it as if you are watching yourself on a huge flat-screen TV or giant movie screen if that seems to make it easier for you. Though, to be sure, it is not mandatory you do it in in that manner. Like anything else, creative visualization or guided imagery takes practice and different people respond to the technique in different ways.

There are other ways to experience it that may work just as well for you. One is to have a trusted friend or family member read the instructions to you. If you work with counselors or counseling interns, why not have one of them read the script to this session? It will be a good learning experience for the counselor, or counselor in training, as well as it will be for you.

If you cannot find a friend, counselor, family member, or fellow student, consider reading the words into a recorder such as your cell phone. Next, find a comfortable place and listen to the program.

And if you cannot use any of the techniques, simply read the session – yes you will need to keep your eyes open – like any other chapter in this text. You will discover that merely reading the words in the creative visualization guided imagery session, even with your eyes wide open, is a valuable experience.

Keep in mind that when I was in private practice, if you had come to see me for a comprehensive exam test anxiety prevention session using imagery, this would be identical or nearly identical to the session I would use to help you.

In fact, the creative visualization guided imagery session that follows is an exact transcript of my most popular test anxiety prevention session of all time, used by thousands of counselors!

All right. Time to take some action. Are you ready to relax? Okay, let's do this!

The thing for you to do for your own health, happiness, relaxation, and success on your exam is to sit in a comfortable chair or lie down. If possible, close your eyes. When you breathe in, I want you to think of the word "relax." When you breathe out, I want you to think of the words "deep relaxation."

When you breathe in, think relax. When you breathe out, think deep relaxation. Allow your body to become very, very heavy; very tired; very relaxed. You feel as if you have exercised or worked very hard. Let go of all the tension. Your mind is slowing down. Keep your breathing and pulse rate slow and rhythmic. It feels good.

This is a relaxing session that you have wanted and needed for a long time. Let yourself feel very calm. When you breathe in, I want you to see the word "relax" in your mind as if it is written on a giant sheet of paper. When you breathe out, see the words "deep relaxation" written on an imaginary giant sheet of paper in your mind. See it vividly.

Your entire body feels good, drowsy, heavy, and relaxed. Your forehead muscle is becoming very relaxed. Let all the lines and wrinkles out of your forehead. It feels so good to do that.

Now I want you to allow your entire face and neck to let go of any tension. Become as comfortable as you can. Your mind is opening up to creative visualization and imagery that can help you score better on your exam and reduce fear and anxiety. Let the relaxing sensations begin to flow down your body.

If you feel any tension, stress, or nervousness, let it go. It is unnecessary. You do not need it, and you don't want it. Relaxation is now spreading into your shoulders and all through your upper body, in the front of your upper body and through your back. Even your arms and fingers are very relaxed. It feels good. Go with the feeling.

As I talk, your lower body is feeling just as good, just as comfortable, just as calm, peaceful, and serene. You feel tranquil. It feels healthy. The relaxation is spreading throughout your entire body, from the top of your head, right down to the bottom of your feet and toes. Your whole body is relaxed. It feels wonderful.

I want you to imagine yourself in a peaceful, relaxing setting. Think of the most comfortable setting you can. Perhaps you are in a beautiful green field on a nice warm sunny day, or maybe you're floating in a boat on a lake.

Let your mind go to the most comfortable place you can imagine. It can be a real place or a place in your fantasy. You will see it in your mind.

You feel terrific. Become as relaxed, warm, and confident as you can. Your arms are nice and warm. You feel good. I'm going to suggest some visual imagery. You will see it in your mind's eye as if it is happening to you right now. It will become real. As it becomes real, it will help you.

I want you to imagine that you are studying for your licensing or certification exam or oral and written board exams, and you are studying at home. You are preparing for the NCE, the CPCE, CECE, or another comprehensive exam. In the past, you felt a little uncomfortable about doing this, but not now. You feel great. You feel confident, sure of yourself, and powerful.

You are more motivated to do well on your exam than you have ever been. You are enjoying your studies. Most of all, you know you can do well on the exam. It feels wonderful. See yourself at home, or wherever you are preparing, enjoying the studying, looking forward to your next study session. That is great. What a wonderful feeling.

Now, go back to your relaxing setting. It feels great, doesn't it? You feel good. You are much happier, content and much less stressed out. You know that you are going to do wonderfully on your examination.

Now, I want you to imagine that it is the night before your examination. There is no tension, no stress. You feel good. You are much happier, much less stressed out. You know that you are going to do very well on your examination.

I want you now to imagine that it is the morning of your examination. Here again. There is no tension, no stress. You still feel great. You feel more powerful, smarter, and brighter than you have ever felt. You know the material. This is going to make you have confidence, lots of confidence. See the word confidence in your mind. Let the word get bigger and bigger . . . and bigger. The word confidence is getting huge. You can see the word confidence in your mind on a highway billboard. It feels good, doesn't it?

If you are not taking the exam at home, I want you to imagine that you are driving to the test site where you are going to take your exam. Perhaps, you are the driver. Perhaps, you are a passenger. You are looking forward to taking the test.

Whether you are at home or traveling to the exam, you are optimistic. You feel good. Your forehead is relaxed. Your hands are warm and secure. Your breathing is slow and rhythmic. You feel exactly the way you did when you went to your special relaxing place in your mind. Isn't it great to know that you are in control? Isn't it great to know that you are going to do well?

The material is in your mind. Your mind is like a giant magnet. Imagine that clearly in your mind. It has taken all the material and kept it there so you will be able to retrieve it when you need it. Now, you see yourself getting out of the vehicle and approaching the door of the building at the exam site or preparing to take the exam at home.

Still, you are feeling awesome. You have taken that feeling from your special place, and you have transferred it to the examination site. What a good feeling. Your muscles are not tense. In fact, they feel wonderful. They feel good. Just hold that feeling. Now I want you to walk inside the building. Again, the word confidence runs through your mind.

Nothing can stop you from doing well on that exam. In fact, your feelings of confidence are getting stronger as you go in the exam site or the room at home where you will take it. I want you to imagine that you are entering the exam room. You feel better than you ever imagined. If it is an exam site, you see the other people. Your pulse rate and heart rate are slow and rhythmic. Isn't this a great way to feel?

You are looking forward to taking the exam. Yes, you are truly looking forward to taking the exam. It is going to be enjoyable. You know the material. Your mind is like a magnet. You know what you need to know, and you are able to retrieve material.

Imagine now that you are taking the exam. See the computer screen. You are working at a steady but very efficient pace. You are not rushing. Your mind is filled with positive thoughts and affirmations. You know you can do it. You feel good. You feel a rush of confidence. Your body is not tensing up. Again, you have taken the power of relaxation from your special relaxing place, and you've transferred it to the exam setting.

In fact, if you feel the slightest bit of tension, or nervousness, you will momentarily go back to your special place and relax for several seconds and then return to mentally finish the exam. Now, I want you to imagine that you have finished your exam. You are confident. You have done well, and you feel terrific.

In a moment, you may open your eyes. You will feel refreshed. Your eyes will feel a little watery, and you will know you are prepared both in your mind and your body. I will slowly count to three and you will open your eyes.

One, you are getting ready to come back and open your eyes. Two, you know you are prepared for the exam. There is no reason for any anxiety. Three, if your eyes are still closed, feel free to open them. Finally, let me leave you with this comforting thought.

There is a well-known principle called the Yerkes-Dodson law, also called the Yerkes-Dodson law of arousal. Let me begin by pointing out that very high levels of stress can deteriorate performance. I am certain you know that already. Nevertheless, did you know that according to their law, a small or moderate level can lead to optimal performance and might just improve your exam score? Thus, my goal is not to curb 100% of your anxiety, just most of it, and I am confident we have accomplished that.

And as the late, great, uber-creative psychiatrist and hypnotist Milton H. Erickson used to say, "My voice will go with you."

Have a great day. You are going to do just fine on your exam.

15

Ask Doctor Rosenthal: Questions from Listeners and Readers

Welcome to a creative and excitingly different kind of program to enhance your knowledge and boost your exam score. Over the years I have received cards, letters, and emails from counselors who use my materials. A great deal of this correspondence was aimed at asking me questions or requesting clarification about counseling terms, theories, theorists, or concepts.

Sometimes these inquiries were about information I had not covered in my materials. Other requests focused on topics that were covered in my exam prep resources but obviously I could have done a better job, because my explanation was not very memorable to the reader or listener.

Quite frankly, if it was not memorable for that individual, it just might not be memorable for you either. Other counselors wanted a practical example of a concept.

Sit back, relax, and enjoy the journey. I have this uncanny feeling you will learn a lot as I share fascinating correspondence I have received. Here are some of those cards, letters, and emails . . . we are talking lots and lots of emails . . . in most instances I left them with all the idiosyncrasies and nuances.

DOI: 10.4324/9781003149712-15

For a few of the vintage questions I was forced to make miniscule updates to the information, terminology, or statistics but tried to portray the questions and answers as closely as possible to their original wording.

Dear Dr. Rosenthal,

I attended a clinical supervision workshop and the presenter kept using the terms direct liability and vicarious liability. I do not recall hearing about these in my graduate classes and was unable to find them in my textbooks. Martin.

Dear Martin,

Thanks for writing. Direct liability refers to a situation in which a supervisor's actions cause the client harm.

Say your supervisee was working with a suicidal client who was threatening to kill themself in two weeks. You, as the supervisor, suggested to the supervisee that some form of reverse psychology or paradoxical intervention might help, such as telling the client to carry out the act of suicide now, such as jumping form a high bridge, rather than waiting two weeks. If this client jumps, it could be argued that you, as the supervisor, caused the harm.

Direct liability is quite rare and is often contrasted with vicarious liability. Vicarious liability occurs when the supervisor is held liable for the actions taken by the supervisee that the supervisor did not suggest.

Here is the bad news. In cases of vicarious liability, the supervisor is unaware of the supervisee's actions. In instances of vicarious liability, a supervisor working within an agency or private practice is more likely to be held accountable than a university practicum supervisor.

Janine Bernard and Rodney Goodyear, in their text *Fundamentals of Clinical Supervision*, state that vicarious supervision is probably the worst nightmare for a clinical supervisor. Or to put it a different way: whether you told the supervisee to do something or did not know what the supervisee did, you, as the supervisor, could still be responsible.

Just for the record, Freud is often considered the father of psychotherapy supervision with his famous case of Little Hans, a five-year-old boy with a phobia being cited as the earliest example.

P.S. Most experts agree that whether you are providing good or bad feedback, it is best to provide it to the supervisee ASAP.

Dear Howard,

Thanks for creating your exam preparation materials. I keep seeing the name Holloway in my textbooks. We never studied about this expert. Dawn

Hello Dawn,

Elizabeth Holloway, PhD, has written extensively on the topic of counselor and clinical supervision. Some experts feel that the Holloway's systems model is the most comprehensive model of supervision.

Dear Dr. Rosenthal,

Several of my friends have signed up for a new course at our university called Action Research. It sounds exciting. What in the world is it? Leslie.

Hi Leslie,

Believe it or not, action research is not new. Kurt Lewin, pronounced as Levine in German – one of the key founders of social psychology – coined the term "action research" way back in the 1940s. Action research differs from research conducted by an outside researcher who samples variables.

Action research applies to research conducted by teachers, school counselors, or administrators who are trying to study and improve their own classroom. The term can also apply to those in private practice or agency settings. A private practice counselor, for example, might engage in research to enhance their own practice.

Your exam could refer to action research as participatory action research.

Hey Doc,

I'm confused. When I was in grad school in the late '80s, I was taught that a New York clinical psychologist named Albert Ellis created a system of psychotherapy called RET or rational emotive therapy. In your materials, you refer to the model as REBT. Was I given misinformation? Kevin.

Kevin,

Thanks for writing. In the early 1980s, a world-famous psychologist, Raymond Corsini, who resided in Hawaii, began urging Albert Ellis to change the name of his theory from RET to REBT, or rational emotive behavior therapy.

According to an interview I conducted with Ellis in 2002, he told me that he resisted the idea for nearly 20 years because the RET badge was already, in his words, "fairly famous." In 2003, nevertheless, Ellis threw in the towel and made the name change, adding the B to the name. As they say, the rest is history.

Ellis noted that he received minimal flack for changing the name. As he pointed out to me, his approach was, as Corsini, who penned some of the seminal works in our field, had suggested, indeed, "exceptionally behavioral."

P.S. If you have heard my lectures from years ago, you know that I recommended in the past that you try to hear Albert Ellis speak, since he was a fabulous presenter. Sadly, Dr. Ellis, a true pioneer in the counseling movement, passed away on July 24, 2007. He was 93 years of age. YouTube has a great selection of his presentations.

Dr. Rosenthal,

Since Freud is the father of psychoanalysis, often called one of the original talking cures, is he also considered the father of vocational guidance? Amanda.

Amanda,

In a word, no. That distinction is generally given to a multitalented individual by the name of Frank Parsons, who lived from 1854 to 1908. Parsons graduated from Cornell at the tender age of 18 with a degree in civil engineering. He later became a lawyer but was not moved by the profession.

In 1909 his landmark work titled *Choosing a Vocation* hit the streets. Since the book was published after his death, it is doubtful that Parsons ever realized the tremendous impact he had on the vocational guidance movement. There are still antiquated copies of the text floating around on the Internet and reproductions of the original work for a lot less money.

Dear Dr. R,

Please excuse this elementary question, but as you will note in a moment, I am severely math challenged. In your purple book, you point out that there are three measures of central tendency or averages in the social sciences – the mean, the median, and the mode.

Then you go on to say that the mean is the most sensitive to extreme scores. I still do not understand this. Can you share an example that even I can understand? Erika.

Erika,

Chances are there are hundreds, if not thousands, of counselors who do not understand this concept either. Let's try this rather dramatic example on for size:

Imagine you are sitting in Statistics class one day and the professor asks you to compute the mean income for the students taking the course. First, you add up everybody's income and secure a total. Next, you divide that total by the number of students in your class. Let us arbitrarily say that the mean, or so-called arithmetic average income, you computed came to $50,000.

But wait, things are getting interesting. As you are bringing the paper with the answer up to the professor's desk, Elon – yes, as in Musk – struts into the class and boldly announces that he is a new student in your class.

After you catch your breath and have the student next to you verify that you are not experiencing a psychotic delusion, you add Elon's mind-blowing income (nearly 200 billion dollars in net worth) to the total. Musk's megabucks salary would classify as an extreme score or what statisticians call an outlier.

Outliers are numbers that are much higher or much lower than the other numbers in a set of data. Since I did not specify the precise number of students in the class and since my calculator balked at the idea of holding all those zeros, I can't give you an exact figure, but I can promise you that the new salary mean will be a heck of a lot more than 50 grand a year once we add Musk's salary.

My guess, LOL, would be that the revised statistic could be breaking into Dr. Phil's income territory.

Would the same pattern be true of another measure of central tendency such as the median or the mode? Not necessarily. Let us take a simple example with the mode.

Say, you had a class of four students and their respective salaries were $25,000, $50,000, $50,000, and $68,000. Now, Musk enters the class with his mind-blowing income.

Since the mode is the most frequently occurring score or category, the mode is still $50,000 for the class.

Now, I am going to put the median, which is always the 50th percentile under the microscope. Say, the salaries were, $25,000, $35,000, $50,000, $60,000, and $68,000.

The median would check in at $50,000. Now, if we replace the $68,000 figure with Musk's larger-than-life, multibillion-dollar income, the median is still $50,000. Why? Since there are two scores under $50,000 and two scores over $50,000, the median salary remains $50,000 a year.

Presto. Musk's monster figure exerts no difference for the mode or the median in these instances but will yield a huge difference for the mean.

Hi, Dr. Rosenthal,

I'm really enjoying your materials. Anyway, a therapist in our town advertises VRT. What in the world is it? Kara.

Kara, virtual reality therapy, or VRT, uses computer-generated images to help clients with problems, especially anxiety, fears, phobias, and posttraumatic stress disorder.

Take a client who has a morbid fear of riding in a car. Instead of the person riding in a real car, the client might be exposed to riding in a car using a computer screen that simulates an actual ride in an automobile. This is an in vivo exposure technique.

Google Glasses are often utilized, and VRT has generally been shortened to VR.

Doctor R,

Is there any research on whether counselors seek help for their own personal problems? Brad.

Hey Brad,

Dynamite question. Some research shows that approximately 65% of counselors went to counseling themselves. The numbers are similar for social workers and psychologists who perform therapy.

By the way, according to gender statistics, roughly 75% of all therapists are females and 25% are males. Looking at the field from a multicultural standpoint approximately 76% of therapists are white, 10% Asian, 6% Hispanic or Latinx, and 4% Black or African American. Dr. Rosenthal, just wondering, what is the most popular theory of counseling? Lee.

Lee. The eclectic model, nowadays generally referred to as integrative approach, where the counselor borrows techniques and ideas from several theories, is leading the pack. Although different sources quote different statistics, only a small percentage of therapists strictly adhere to a single approach to helping. Keep in mind that in the 1970s it was common for counselors and therapists to rely on a single psychotherapeutic modality.

Dear *Encyclopedia of Counseling* author,

I am reading your book because I am attempting to secure a counselor's license. My best friend has an unusual situation. She is licensed as a counselor and a social worker.

If a client takes legal action against my friend, will my colleague be judged by counseling or social work ethical guidelines? According to what I have been able to find out, the two ethical guidelines for social work versus counseling are slightly different. Liz

Liz,

Let me tell you, that's a touchy issue, but great minds think alike, and I too have pondered the exact same question. Since I did not have a perfect answer, I consulted experts, including lawyers. I still do not have an ideal answer, but here is what they came up with.

First, was the helper practicing primarily as a social worker or a counselor at the time of the alleged ethical violation? If the helper was engaged in securing public assistance for the client, then her behavior would be slanted towards social work, and NASW ethics would likely apply.

If, on the other hand, this helper was conducting a reality therapy session or doing dream work with the client, then counseling ethics would likely apply. The court might also pick the ethical guidelines with the most stringent practices. Hence, assume one set of ethics said you must wait two years before having sex with a client and another said you should stave it off for five years, the latter would most likely be used as a yardstick. Keep in mind many counselors reading this are ACA members and will achieve NCC status. Since ACA and NBCC ethics are not identical, my point is: Even within our profession of counseling, ethics can differ and your question could ultimately apply to many of us.

Dr. Rosenthal,

I found an error or perhaps some typos in your materials. In one of your programs, it states that in terms of population Blacks are second to Whites in the US. However, in another you mentioned that Hispanics are second to Whites. Please respond before I must sit for the NCE. Keya.

Hi, Keya,

You are obviously very perceptive. Thus, I expect you to perform superbly on the exam. In fact, I will be looking forward to receiving your testimonial regarding my exam prep materials.

The answer to your question can easily be found in the publication dates in my materials. Several years ago, it was discovered by the US Census Bureau that the population of Hispanics/Latinx now exceeds Blacks.

According to the United States Census Bureau Quick Facts from July 2019, Whites constitute 76.3% of the population, with Hispanic/Latinos at 18.5%, and Blacks or African Americans constituting 13.4% of the population. Asians are listed as 5.9% of the population. Native American or Alaska Native make up 1.3% of the population.

Overall, experts noted that the US is diversifying quicker than expected and that the White population is declining.

Remember now, these numbers will change over time. So, now you have your answer, no typos needed.

Good morning, Dr R,

The clock is ticking. Only 72 hours until I take my CPCE exit exam. I still do not comprehend this research concept of *p* at the .05 level stuff versus *p* at the 0.01 level. I know it is called some sort of confidence level, but I can share with you that I'm confident I don't comprehend it one bit! I need help now. Brandon.

Brandon,

It is too late to tell you not to panic, because guess what? You are already panicking. First, go to a quiet area and spend some time reviewing my test anxiety prevention chapter in this text.

Now, for your answer. In a research study, a finding is labeled "a statistically significant result" if the outcome most likely did *not* occur by chance.

In counseling, the researcher sets a *p* value. P stands for probability. The smaller the *p* value, the more significant the study. To put it a different way, a .01 level of significance gives us stronger evidence than a .05 level of significance. With *p* at the .05 level, you could run the experiment 100 times and you will get the same result 95 out of 100 times. Alter *p* to .01 and run the experiment 100 times and you will get the same results 99 times out of 100. Again, in this case, smaller is better!

Thus, in a *p* at the .05 level of significance study, there are 5 chances in 100 that the result could have occurred by chance. In a *p* at the .01 level, there is 1 in 100 chance the phenomenon occurred by chance. At *p* at the .001 level, there is only 1 chance in 1000 that the results are coincidental.

The *p* value is the probability of committing a type I or alpha error, which takes place when you reject the null hypothesis when it is true. Statistical significance is sometimes billed as the confidence level one has in a result, hence the term .05 or .01 confidence level.

Finally, if the data reveal a *p* value less than the significance level, then null is rejected.

Hey, Brandon. By the way, the best way to know if you have committed a type II or beta error is if other researchers cannot replicate your data.

Dear counseling prep material author,

In your materials you mention that Carl Rogers has several conditions that must be met for effective therapy – congruence, unconditional positive regard, and empathy. Another study guide – I will call it Brand X – lists one of the conditions as realness. Which study guide should I trust? Russ.

Good afternoon Russ,

You can trust both of our study guides. Realness is merely another term experts toss around for congruence or genuineness. The concept suggests that the counselor does not present a facade or a mask of professionalism. Some exams use the term transparent to mean the exact same thing.

Just so you will know, some researchers and critics of Rogers's work charge that the three conditions for therapy are neither necessary nor sufficient. Please excuse my grammar, but the verdict: In this instance Brand X ain't all that bad of a preparation guide either.

Dr. Rosenthal,

I received my master's degree over 30 years ago. Many of the terms and abbreviations I see now were never used when I was in graduate school. When I was studying for my exam, I repeatedly came across the abbreviation PC. I looked up the term in several behavioral science dictionaries and came up empty handed. I know it does not mean personal computer in this case. Out of Touch.

Dear Out of Touch,

In the last few years, a bunch of cutesy abbreviations have been creeping into the literature that were never used in the past. Here is a quick review of most of those related to theories of counseling.

PC stands for person-centered Rogerian counseling. BT means behavior therapy. GT, no, it's not a sports car, but that's a darn good guess, but rather it stands for Gestalt therapy. ET is not an extraterrestrial being – I have a feeling you already knew that – but existential therapy. CT is cognitive therapy. RT is reality therapy created by William Glasser.

FT stands for feminist therapy. BFST is Bowen's family systems theory, SF is solution-focused therapy, EBT for evidence-based treatment or EBP for evidence-based practice, and AASBC signifies the American Association of State Counseling Boards.

Finally, NT for narrative therapy. Abbreviations: can't live with them, can't live without them. Come to think of it, maybe graduate school really was better 30 years ago. Perhaps we need a moratorium on abbreviations and acronyms. But until the moratorium begins, I will put in a shameless plug for the 2nd edition of my *Human Services Dictionary, Master Reference for the NCE, CPCE, and the HS-BCPE Exams*, packed with a wealth of abbreviations and acronyms and more terminology than you ever imagined.

Howard,

Hello and thank you for creating these materials. Years ago, I heard you give a spirited lecture on suicide prevention, and I fell in love with your presentation style. I was glad to hear you created materials to help counselors pass state licensing exams.

Here is a question I've never really seen discussed in counseling literature. Say you are leading a group and a group member has issues with your behavior as the leader of the group. Is it appropriate to recommend that the client work through these issues with you using the empty chair? One of the coworkers at my agency does this a lot. I know the empty chair technique is popular. However, it just seems like my friend who is leading the group is not dealing with some personal issues. Tara.

Tara,

Strongly agree and thanks for the kind words. Corey, Corey, Callanan, and Russell, in their book *Group Techniques*, do indeed mention this practice under the heading, "Using Techniques as Avoidance Devices," which should give you a pretty good hint of what they think of this practice. The authors go on to point out that the empty chair technique really should not be used when the client has a problem with the leader because when you use it, it implies that the client's issues are not legitimate issues with the facilitator, only neurotic transference.

A second cousin to this practice, which should also be avoided like the plague, occurs when a member is angry at the leader, and the leader says something condescending like, "I love it when you get mad like that." Best wishes on the exam.

Hello, Dr. Rosenthal,

What in the world is an open label trial? Heard a guy use the term on a radio talk show about anxiety medication. Rainna.

Hi Rainna,

Basically, the open label paradigm is the direct antithesis of double-blind research. In an open-label trial, no information is withheld from the participants and the researchers. Both groups are aware of precisely what the clients are receiving (say a medicine for anxiety) or not receiving . . . even if the client is receiving a placebo. It might also surprise you to know a placebo often works even when the client is aware they are merely getting a sugar pill or a gelatin capsule!!!

Open-label studies sometimes use randomness, while others clearly do not. An open-label trial might even be set up so everybody is receiving the treatment and there is no placebo group.

At this point in time critics charge the open-label format is often seen as biased; however, proponents often argue that blind trials are not always feasible.

Dear HR,

Our professor gave us a list of must-know terms for our comprehensive exit exam. One of them, the term stanine score, is missing from your materials. I'm assuming it is like a *T* score or a *Z* score. Abby.

Dear Abby,

Hmm, where have I heard that salutation line before? This seems like role reversal. Shouldn't I be asking you the question, Abby? Anyway, the term stanine score does appear in my materials, but my definition must not have been that memorable. Let me take another try at explaining it. The scale was created by the US Air Force in World War II.

The term stanine comes from the words standard nine. One is the lowest score, with nine being the highest score. One, two, and three are often termed below-average scores. Four, five, and six are billed as average scores, while seven, eight, and nine represent above-average scores. Five is the mean and falls in the center of the normal curve.

Stanine scores are nice since they represent the hallmark of simplicity. What is not so good about them? Well, stanine scores are not very precise. Since you mentioned *T* and *Z* scores, a T score has a mean of 50. A Z score a mean of zero. As I just stated, a stanine has a mean of five.

Thus, since the *T* score, the Z score, and stanine are all based on the normal curve, one type of score can be converted to another. Isn't that a nifty idea? For example, a *T* score of 60 would be a stanine score of 7 and a Z score of +1.

Still confused? No problem. Check out the "Graphical Representation" section of my *Encyclopedia of Counseling: The Authentic Purple Book*.

Hi Doc,

Am I correct that a correlation of –.90 is stronger than a correlation of 0.40, even though 0.40 is a positive number? Sonia.

Yes, Sonia, you are correct, and this is a very common type of exam question. Correlation is often expressed as an *r* value. As the *r* value gets closer to –1.00, or 1.00, then the association or magnitude of the correlation is stronger. Hence, a correlation of –.90 *is stronger* than a +0.40, even though .40 (a.k.a. +0.40) is a positive number. Statisticians sometimes draw a pictorial called a scattergram or a scatterplot to graphically show the degree of relationship between the two variables.

Good morning, Dr. Rosenthal,

I hope I am not out of line emailing you with a question since I know you're busy writing books.

I attended a counseling workshop yesterday and the facilitator was talking about how open-ended questions are usually superior to closed-ended questions. I learned what this meant from your prep course. However, she also said that direct and indirect leads are helpful. Since there was no time for questions, I never understood her point. Can you shed some light on these concepts? Victoria.

Victoria,

Thanks for taking the time to email me. Leads are merely statements that a counselor makes to help a client talk more about themselves or about a given issue.

An indirect lead is not very specific, such as, "Please continue," or "Can you tell me more?" A specific lead specifies a topic that you would like to have the client discuss, such as, "Tell me more about your anger toward your boss," or "How do you feel when you eat too much?"

BTW, on the humorous side of the coin, I am not always busy writing books. This morning I put an air filter and cabin filter in my car and hit the hardware store for some much-needed items. Just saying!

Dr. Rosenthal,

Can you provide me with a simple example of a counselor who has made a so called "depth error"? Randy.

Randy,

Sure. Say a client came to the interview late and says it is because the traffic was terrible. You, as the helper, assumed that the real issue was some deep dark secret from the client's past, but it really, truly was just the traffic. Depth errors occur when you read too darn much or too darn little into a client's statements.

Say, Doctor R.

What do mental health professionals mean by the term comorbidity? Cam.

Hey Cam,

On most comprehensive exams, the term simply means that the client has more than one diagnosis at a given point in time. Some clinicians and treatment facilities, especially those who work with substance use disorders and addictions, call this phenomenon dual diagnosis. Thus, a client might have a mood disorder, say depression, and is an alcoholic.

Dear counselor licensing doctor,

Are there any studies regarding work satisfaction and age? Lucinda.

Lucinda,

In general, and remember, this may not apply to you or a given client of yours – job satisfaction goes up with age, although this trend does not seem to apply to underprivileged workers, who express more dissatisfaction with their jobs.

As good old common sense might dictate, people in higher positions usually like their jobs better than those at the bottom of the organization. White-collar workers are generally more satisfied with their job than blue-collar employees.

Dear Dr. Howard,

If I set up an experiment and can't randomly assign the subjects to the groups, is this a true experiment? Lizzie.

Lizzie,

Nope. It's a quasi-experiment. Quasi means something resembles something else. In a quasi-experiment, you cannot assume that the IV caused the DV, since the original groups may not have been equal. That said, there are times when randomness may not be possible or even ethical. JD from Texas. "Dear Dr. R, now that I have my master's degree, counselor's license, and a tiny bit of experience I plan to go for several a job interviews. Will it impact me in any manner if the applicant before me before me has a PhD from a top school, is well known in the field, and has 20 years more counseling experience?

"Wouldn't his blow-away fantastic credentials impact the way that the interviewer views me as a candidate? I mean, wouldn't I look better if the mega qualified dude did not interview before me?"

Dear JD from the Lone Star State,

Yes, you would look better if the mega qualified dude, as you so eloquently put it, did not interview before you. On the other hand, if a counselor with considerably lower credentials interviewed prior to you, then the interviewer would perceive you as more qualified.

Keep in mind your exam could be even more specific, asking you if a situation constitutes a positive or a negative contrast effect. So let me outline it for you right now:

Less than desirable interviewee prior to you = positive contrast effect, since you look better than if you were the only interviewee.

A person with more impressive credentials than you is interviewed prior to you = negative contrast effect, since you appear less qualified than if you were the only interviewee.

Keep in mind this principle also applies to professors grading subjective papers, written exams, and essay assignments. So, make certain the person who submits a written assignment to your professor before you is not as good of a student as you . . . or, um, something like that!

Bottom line: When the interviewer's assessment of you as a job candidate is impacted by the previous interviewee, it is known as the contrast effect. The contrast effect is all about comparisons.

Hey there, Dr. R.,

Can you give me a real-life example of thinning? No jokes related to hair loss since I am losing what little I have rather rapidly, Vince.

Hey there, Vince.

Thinning is a behavior modification, ABA, or operant conditioning term. Remember, Pavlov and Watson are associated with classical conditioning. Operant conditioning is associated with the work of B.F. Skinner.

Let us say you want a child to do their math homework. You therefore decide to give this youngster a piece of candy after completing each problem. That is continuous reinforcement. But guess what? Continuous reinforcement works best at first; nevertheless, if you keep using it, the child will become satiated or will experience habituation. Translation, the procedure will not work as well. Hence, you decide to switch to intermittent reinforcement, where you only give the child a piece of candy every time they complete, say, five problems or what is technically called a fixed ratio or FR schedule of reinforcement.

The transition from continuous reinforcement to intermittent reinforcement constitutes thinning. If you went from reinforcing the child after each fifth problem to every tenth problem, then you are thinning once again. Or to quote myself from my own *Human Services Dictionary*, "Thinning. In operant conditioning, it is the process of decreasing the rate of reinforcement." So, that is the concept in a nutshell. No hair jokes needed.

Hello Dr. Rosenthal,

I have a couple of career counseling questions. I was reading about weighted job applications and the concept is still a little fuzzy. Could you provide me with an actual example of this? Also, is there any truth to the rumor that women are absent from jobs more than men? Thanks, Ming.

Hi Ming,

I have a terrific little example that I know will clear up the confusion because I see from your stationery that you work at a college. I too worked at a college for many years.

When I filled out the application for my full-time job at the college where I taught, I was informed that clinical experience was worth only half as much as college teaching experience. Thus, two years of full-time counseling was only worth as much as one year of teaching experience. Teaching experience, in this case, was given twice the weight of clinical work.

As far as your second question, I too have rubbed elbows with a body of research that indicates that women miss work more than men, most likely because they care for sick children or household members more.

Dear HR,

I am totally confused by the multicultural terms acculturation and cultural encapsulation. Every dictionary and web resource I turn to says something different. What in the world are the writers of these comprehensive exams looking for? Lost in Translation.

Dear Lost in Translation,

Your comment that different resources provide different definitions for these terms is right on target. My best guess is that for the exam, acculturation refers to the process in which a person is transitioning/adopting into a new culture – learning new behaviors and expectations – and attempting to assimilate new customs. I must tell you I have also seen the term enculturation as a synonym. The popular press often uses the word socialization.

In 1962, Gilbert Wrenn coined the term "cultural encapsulation." For your exam, the term implies that the helper, not the client, has an issue. What is the issue?

The term describes a counselor who views all clients based on their own culture and fails to recognize the significance of another person's culture. This is roughly the opposite of the way a good or adept counselor demonstrates cultural competence.

Hi Doc,

Can you provide me with an example of malingering?
Holly

Hello Holly,

Malingering occurs when a person intentionally "fakes," "feigns," or exaggerates a physical or psychological illness to get out of work, military duty, or legal encounters or achieve a desirable outcome such as paid leave or securing drugs. The DSM classifies malingering as a focus of concern rather than a diagnosis.

Hollywood accurately popularized this mode of behavior by showing prisoners purposely acting more disturbed so they could be transferred to better living conditions in a psychiatric facility.

There are lots of stories and folklore about folks who did not wish to serve in the military putting certain brands of soap under their arms to raise their body temperature prior to a medical examination. I have no idea how many were able to dodge the system by engaging in this practice.

The antithesis of malingering "faking bad" is labelled as "faking good" in the *APA Dictionary of Psychology*. Here an individual picks verbal answers or test responses on an evaluation, inventory, or interview to make themselves look good to secure a job or perhaps admission into a certain school.

Hello Dr. Rosenthal,

I'm a bit confused. Several times in your materials you emphasize that crisis intervention with suicidal individuals must be active directive/action oriented. I just finished reading some information about the nondirective suicide intervention model of John Sommers-Flanagan. Wouldn't his ideas be the direct opposite of what you are suggesting?
Ruth

Good afternoon, Ruth,

LOL. Your email could not have come at a more coincidental time. I was going through some old items in my house and came across a cassette tape recording of a lecture I presented to my employees right after I became the program director of a suicide prevention hotline many years ago. My entire lecture, a tick over 1 hour and 45 minutes, was focused on why helpers must be active and decidedly not nondirective when assisting clients in a suicidal crisis.

Now, that said, I always told my college students when I taught theories courses that when you have one theory (say, an all-meat carnivore diet) you will always have a theory proposing the direct opposite (say, a diet composed only of plant foods). Our field is no different. Consider: The Freudians had to contend with the behaviorists.

Yes, John Sommers-Flanagan is convinced a nondirective model of suicide prevention is superior. In defense of his work, several published studies support his position. Nevertheless, not all studies agree. Whether you agree or not, his ideas have caused us to think a lot more about the issue.

However, I think what you are really asking is: What should I do if a question asks about directive versus nondirective suicide prevention intervention? Well, we could probably come up with a hundred different sample questions for this topic alone (overkill and probably not a useful activity), but I think the short answer is if the question mentions traditional approaches, go with active-directive action-oriented strategies. On the other side of the coin, if the question mentions Dr. Sommers-Flanagan, the likely correct choice would be nondirective.

Hi Dr. Howard,

Can you tell me what the primacy effect is and how it is relevant to the topics on comprehensive exams?

Jerry

Hi Jerry,

That is a relevant question and I'll tell you why. Many counselors I have corresponded with who have taken multicultural diversity courses wrongly assume that the information learned will cover everything you need to know for the "Social and Cultural Diversity," formerly labeled "Social and Cultural Foundations," section of the exam.

The cold hard truth is that general questions about social psychology – or questions relating social psychology to multicultural studies – are seemingly quite common, and for some counselors this is a weak area.

Now if you had a teacher who covered this topic, that's awesome! If you did not, I will try to fill in the gaps by covering the most popular principles in my materials. So, to answer your question:

The social psychology principle of the **primacy effect** or **law of primacy** is relevant in counseling. This notion suggests that data presented initially are recalled better than information presented later. Thus, studies on job interviews often illuminate that the "real decision to hire," is made in the first few minutes of the interview. This **first impression bias** could override contradictory information acquired later in the meeting. Hope this helps.

Hello Dr. Rosenthal,

Since you too reside in the Midwest, I hope you are enjoying the sub-zero temperatures we are experiencing. NOT! What is a static group comparison, and is it the same thing as a true experiment with a control group and an experimental group you talk about?

Marissa

Hello Marissa,

Sub-zero chill factors are not my idea of pleasant weather so I'm counting the days until the thermometer reaches the 80s, 90s, and beyond once again. Once it hits 100 I might want a little of that winter chill back in the air.

A static group comparison is not a true experiment. Some texts refer to it as a pre-experiment or quasi-experiment. In this design you take two intact or so-called pre-existing groups. One receives an experimental treatment, and one does not, and you compare them. It sounds like an awesome idea and a very simple way to do research, but here is the problem.

Let's say I taught a counseling course and offered special lectures covering material on the CPCE. Some grad students in the course decided to participate, while others do not. Now all the students in the course take the CPCE, and presto, the students who attended my special lectures (now one group) scored much higher than those who did not (another group).

Yes, it might be because of my wonderful presentations (at least I would like to think that!); however, it could be that the students who participated in the CPCE training lectures were just better students, more knowledgeable to begin with, were more motivated, or a hundred other reasons. Since a static group design does not pick group members at random, you just don't know.

Hi Dr. R,

I am enjoying your exam prep materials. Wanted to know what methods of counseling and psychotherapy would fit into the contemporary therapies category.

Marquita

Dear Marquita,

At this point in time, I am uncertain whether I can provide an ideal answer. Indeed, many sources do not even mention contemporary therapies. To complicate the situation, when the category is listed, various sources list different modalities. Some candidates for this category would include mindfulness-based therapies created by Jon Kabat-Zinn, who was interested in Buddhist teachings. Psychologist Francine Shapiro's EMDR, or eye movement desensitization and reprocessing; Marsha Linehan's DBT, or dialectical behavior therapy; RO DBT, known as radically open dialectical behavior therapy for treating overcontrol issues such as perfectionism or over the top self-discipline, created by psychologist Thomas Lynch; ACT or acceptance and commitment therapy created by Steven C. Hayes; PPT or positive psychology therapy, based on the work of Martin E.P. Seligman; CPT, or cognitive processing therapy, for PTSD, helpful in cases of natural disasters, rape, military combat: a special version named RCPT or residential CPT is used by the Department of Veterans Affairs with its own manuals; and even though it is hardly new or contemporary, some sources include CBT, or cognitive behavior therapy, with roots in the work of Albert Ellis and Aaron T. Beck.

Yours for better counseling,

Dr. Howard Rosenthal

There you have it, real questions from real people. All I can say is keep those cards, letters, and mainly emails coming in.

Made in the USA
Middletown, DE
30 August 2024